Spatial Literary Studi

Following the spatial turn in the humanities and social sciences, *Spatial Literary Studies: Interdisciplinary Approaches to Space, Geography, and the Imagination* offers a wide range of essays that reframe or transform contemporary criticism by focusing attention, in various ways, on the dynamic relations among space, place, and literature. These essays reflect upon the representation of space and place, whether in the real world, in imaginary universes, or in those hybrid zones where fiction meets reality. Working within or alongside related approaches, such as geocriticism, literary geography, and the spatial humanities, these essays examine the relationship between literary spatiality and different genres or media, such as film or television. The contributors to *Spatial Literary Studies* draw upon diverse critical and theoretical traditions in disclosing, analyzing, and exploring the significance of space, place, and mapping in literature and in the world, thus making new textual geographies and literary cartographies possible.

Robert T. Tally Jr. is NEH Distinguished Teaching Professor in the Humanities and Professor of English at Texas State University, where he teaches American and world literature.

Routledge Interdisciplinary Perspectives on Literature

For more information about this series, please visit: www.routledge.com

Spatial Literary Studies
Interdisciplinary Approaches to Space, Geography, and the Imagination

Edited by Robert T. Tally Jr.

NEW YORK AND LONDON

First published 2021
by Routledge
52 Vanderbilt Avenue, New York, NY 10017

and by Routledge
2 Park Square, Milton Park, Abingdon, Oxon, OX14 4RN

Routledge is an imprint of the Taylor & Francis Group, an informa business

© 2021 Taylor & Francis

The right of Robert T. Tally Jr. to be identified as the author of the editorial material, and of the authors for their individual chapters, has been asserted in accordance with sections 77 and 78 of the Copyright, Designs and Patents Act 1988.

Library of Congress Cataloging-in-Publication Data
Names: Tally, Robert T., Jr., editor.
Title: Spatial literary studies : interdisciplinary approaches to
    space, geography, and the imagination / edited by Robert T
    Tally Jr.
Description: New York : Routledge, 2020. | Series: Routledge
    interdisciplinary perspectives on literature | Includes
    bibliographical references and index. | Summary: "Following
    the spatial turn in the humanities and social sciences, Spatial
    Literary Studies: Interdisciplinary Approaches to Space,
    Geography, and the Imagination offers a wide range of essays
    that reframe or to transform contemporary criticism by
    focusing attention, in various ways, on the dynamic relations
    among space, place, and literature"—Provided by publisher.
Identifiers: LCCN 2020026574 | ISBN 9780367520106
    (hardback) | ISBN 9781003056027 (ebook)
Subjects: LCSH: Space in literature. | Geographical perception in
    literature. | Space perception in literature. | Place (Philosophy)
    in literature. | Geography in literature.
Classification: LCC PN56.S667 S63 2020 | DDC
    809/.9332—dc23
LC record available at https://lccn.loc.gov/2020026574

ISBN: 978-0-367-52010-6 (hbk)
ISBN: 978-1-003-05602-7 (ebk)

Typeset in Sabon
by Apex CoVantage, LLC

For Ying Fang

Contents

Acknowledgements

I would like to thank all the contributors for their superb essays. Earlier versions of most of the chapters in this volume first appeared as part of a special issue of the online journal *Reconstruction: Studies in Contemporary Culture* devoted to "Spatial Literary Studies" in 2014; five others were published in a special section, "The Problematics of Place," of the subsequent issue of the same journal that year. Not long afterwards, unfortunately, the journal went offline, and the vagaries of the internet rendered this work "out of print," if not completely non-existent. The journal has since been relaunched on a new website, but at present, its earlier issues and all of their contents have not been posted. So, until now, the work remained unavailable to readers. All the contributors and I are grateful to Routledge, especially to Jennifer Abbott and Polly Dodson, for their enthusiastic support of this project. I also thank Marc Ouellette and Alan Clinton for their help and encouragement in putting together the original special issues. An earlier version of Chapter 19 appeared in the *Journal of English Language and Literature* in 2019, and I would like to thank editor Youngmin Kim for his great commitment to comparative literature and cultural exchange. This book is dedicated to Ying Fang, a remarkable teacher, scholar, and translator, and a tireless advocate for spatial literary studies today.

Introduction

Spaces of the Text: Literary Studies After the Spatial Turn

Robert T. Tally Jr.

Although many of its features can be found in earlier forms of literary criticism, history, and theory, spatial literary studies is relatively new. Whether it is understood as a discrete and recognizable subfield within literature and the humanities or in a more amorphous sense, as a general comportment toward the objects of study that happen to emphasize matters of space, place, mapping, and so forth, spatial literary studies is associated with the "spatial turn" in the humanities and social sciences. Identifying precise dates of origin are not possible or even desirable, but most practitioners locate the spatial turn as having occurred within the past fifty years or so, and various methods of dealing with space and literature have only emerged in the last few decades. Literary geography, which is arguably an older interdisciplinary field, has grown exponentially in recent years, and it has been joined, supplemented, or even challenged by other approaches involving both literature and geography, such as the Geographic Information Systems-oriented "spatial humanities" or "geohumanities," along with geocriticism, geopoetics, literary cartography, and others. Spatial literary studies contributes to, and partakes in, aspects of all of these fields.

As with any relatively new approach or set of approaches, there is a great deal of uncertainty and ambiguity about what constitutes its characteristic attributes or concerns. Such indeterminacy has also proven quite productive, however, insofar as a wide variety of approaches to the investigation of space and literature have been assayed, yielding fascinating results at times, which themselves are suggestive of paths for future inquiry and analysis. Scholars and critics engaged in spatial literary studies are thus refining and redefining the field and its practices through their work, which in part makes the area so dynamic. Spatial literary studies continues to develop, to make connections with other critical practices and disciplinary fields, and to influence the ways that readers and writers engage with the text and its spaces, broadly imagined.

As I discuss in Chapter 19, in initially using the phrase "spatial literary studies" I had not intended it to serve as a label for a discrete field or critical practice. Rather, I had intended the word *spatial* as a mere adjective, modifying *literary studies* only so far as to note that such studies emphasized matters of space, place, mapping, geography, architecture, spatial relations, and so on. I had thought this would include the sort of work being done under the name of literary geography, geocriticism, or what have you, but only to the extent that all of these practices dealt with literature and space, broadly conceived. Understandably, however, lines would be drawn and boundaries between various approaches established and recognized. Spatial literary studies may thus appear as one of many discourses in which these issues figure prominently, and the development of this and other related methodological, philosophical, or thematic approaches will undoubtedly lead to new connections, cross-pollination, and extensions into unforeseen areas in the years to come.

Spatial literary studies enable scholars to reflect upon the representation of space and place, whether in the real world, in imaginary universes, or in those hybrid zones where fiction meets reality. In examining spatial representation in literary works, spatially oriented criticism has also invoked interdisciplinary or transdisciplinary practices, frequently making productive connections to architecture, geography, history, politics, social theory, and urban studies, among other fields. Spatial criticism is not limited to the so-called real world, but often calls into question the facile distinction between real and imaginary places, while investigating what Edward Soja has referred to as the "real-and-imagined" spaces of the world. Similarly, such criticism is interested in the relationship between spatiality and different media or genres, as film or television, music, computer programs, and other forms supplement, compete with, and problematize literary representation. Spatial literary studies frequently draws upon diverse critical and theoretical traditions in disclosing, analysing, and exploring the significance of space, place, and mapping in literature and in the world, thus making new textual geographies and literary cartographies possible.

Spatial Literary Studies: Interdisciplinary Approaches to Space, Geography, and the Imagination is thus intended to be exploratory as well as explanatory. The essays in this volume represent some of that range and variety of work being done in spatial literary studies today. Although the book's five parts—labelled "Geocritical Theory and Practice," "Geographies of the Text," "Geographies in the Text," "The Problematics of Place," and the brief "Plus Ultra"—designate in a quite general way the different sorts of work being accomplished in the essays placed within them, such categories can really *contain* that work. These titles are tentative and heuristic—names that might helpful but are not required. That is, I do not want to suggest that these divisions somehow represent categories within spatial literary studies more generally, nor do I want to say that spatial literary studies must focus on matters of geocriticism, geography, or place in any exclusive sense. If these issues are prominently in view in the chapters that follow, that only shows some of the *topoi* and themes addressed in spatial literary studies today. The essays themselves certainly stand on their own.

Spatial Literary Studies begins with a series of essays on "Geocritical Theory and Practice." In Chapter 1, "Geocriticism at the Crossroads," Mariya Shymchyshyn offers a sweeping overview of geocriticism, broadly understood as including various examples of spatial literary studies in the twentieth and early twenty-first centuries. She surveys the writings of a number of spatially oriented critics, theorists, and scholars at the cutting edge of the spatial turn, while also examining the foundations for such work to be found in influential precursors, including geographers, urbanists, and philosophers. Drawing upon Mikhail Bakhtin's evocative concepts of the chronotope, Shymchyshyn argues that the geocritical theory and practice is presently at a "crossroad," in which multiple possibilities for future work present themselves to the scholar interested in literary spatiality.

In Chapter 2, "How to Do Narratives With Maps: Cartography as a Performative Act in *Gulliver's Travels* and *Through the Looking Glass*," Emmanuelle Peraldo and Yann Calbérac examine the distinction between literary narratives and maps in order to question the specificities of both words and images in the text. To that end, they focus on two major masterpieces of British literature, Jonathan Swift's *Gulliver's Travels* and Lewis Carroll's *Through the Looking-Glass*, works providing imaginary maps that enable readers to locate the plots in a discernible spatial framework. Peraldo and Calbérac argue that, rather than merely anchoring the narratives in a given place, the maps have a performative function; instead of stabilizing the characters and plots on in a homogenous graphic space, the maps trigger the action and redefine its place, in effect performing the functions commonly associated with narrative itself.

Jessica Maucione's "Locating the Limits and Possibilities of Place" offers a different sort of overview of theoretical debates regarding space and place. Maucione discusses the pitfalls of various symbolic and metaphoric treatments of space and place, arguing against a binary opposition of space versus place. She ultimately finds those narratives of place that cohere according to an imagined or real interdependence among the inhabitants of a recognized place most valuable, such that they are inspired or required to live in relation to one another. Drawing from literary examples, Maucione contends that because narratives of place revalue "minor" locales and their "minority" inhabitants, while also presenting alternative modes of being, they have the potential to disrupt the grand, totalizing narratives associated with nationalism and globalism.

The essays in Part II examine the ways that the texts under consideration map the worlds they represent or otherwise depict spatial relations. Thus, in Chapter 4, "Mallarmé, Poet of the Earthly World: On Spatiality in *L'Après midi d'une Faune*," Rogério de Melo Franco observes that the concept of space has frequently been understood in Mallarmé's writing as either part of a meditation on how to fill the blank of the page or a vaguely conceived poetic notion related to the poet's highest aesthetical aspirations, such as the ambitiously imagined *magnum opus* known simply as "the Book." Melo Franco believes Mallarmé's reflection upon properly spatial, earthy, and territorial matters has not received the attention it deserves. Focusing on one of Mallarmé's most famous poems, "The Afternoon of a Fawn," he investigates its spatiality in connection with narration, myth, and memory. Melo Franco uses the conception of the *après-midi* to suggest a theoretical unity of time and space in the poem.

Julia Kröger focuses on the construction of Parisian "lived space" in the work of nineteenth-century naturalist author Émile Zola in Chapter 5, "Zola's Spatial Explorations of Second Empire Paris." Following Henri Lefebvre's triadic theory of space production, she begins by retracing the physical and conceptual appropriation of space by Zola documented in his notebooks, the *dossiers préparatoires*. The seemingly non-reflexive perceptions noted in the *dossiers* testify to an emotive and affective real-life encounter which, along with cognitive materials, such as maps, are translated into the lived space of the storyworld via Zola's various strategies of narrativization. Kröger argues that Zola thus helps us to understand the ways that space is produced within the formal constraints of the novel and highlights the importance of real, material space in the understanding of lived space—a spatial facet that literary studies have often tended to ignore.

In Chapter 6, " 'Dr. Livingstone, I Presume?': The Demonic Grounds of M. NourbeSe Philip's *Looking for Livingstone: An Odyssey of Silence*," Kate Siklosi draws upon the work of feminist human geographer Katherine McKittrick in her innovative reading of the Tobagan-Canadian novelist's fascinating tale of memory and exploration. McKittrick had invoked the concept of the "demonic" in her ground-breaking critical text *Demonic Grounds: Black Women and the Cartographies of Struggle* in order to rethink "the complex linkages between history, blackness, race, and place." Siklosi argues that, by "opening a way to the interior" through her novella, M. NourbeSe Philip re-appropriates a colonial expression of geographic domination while enacting a "demonic" respatialisation of African cultural representation. The phrase, originally from Scottish missionary and explorer Dr. David Livingstone's travel diary, presents the colonial metaphor of Africa as the unknown "dark continent," with its embedded figuration of the eroticized black female body. This "opening of the interior," a central motif of Philip's text, thus announces the concomitant geographic and sexual violence of colonial imperialism, and also articulates a transgressive space of resistance. In Siklosi's view, the protagonist's nomadic odyssey across time and space, undertaken without maps or guides, displaces the linear geographic "truths" of colonial exploration with a demonic spatiality.

Michelle Dreiding, in "Rethinking the Beginning: Toni Morrison and the Dramatization of Liminality," observes that the beginnings in Morrison's novels enact an uncanny moment of disorientation. They are beginnings *in medias res*, and, more importantly, beginnings of spatial deictic uncertainties that leave a reader with the absence of a stable system of reference. They enact the predicament of a beginning that precludes the fantasy of an absolute point of origin. Morrison's beginnings self-consciously advocate an imperative to engage in a continual process of re-reading; of revisiting the initial disorientation so as to avoid a "conclusion to living" (as Nietzsche had put it). Dreiding finds that, in these liminal moments, Morrison actualizes the particularly American discourse of the frontier—the privileged locus of "perennial rebirth." Within this discursive American space of potentiality and of a compulsive return to the border, Dreiding argues, Morrison rewrites the American myth of the frontier and thereby moves a narrative that has been culturally marginalized to the centre. Reading the incipits of Morrison's novels *Jazz* (1992), *Paradise* (1997), and *Love* (2003), each of which dramatize a structural and geographical liminality, Dreiding discovers a spatial poetics necessary for the political project, which in turn opens up the dialogical possibility to "draw a map," as Morrison puts it, but "without the mandate for conquest."

Moving into the different but related media of theatre and television, Elizabeth Robertson examines the work of the notable British writer-director Stephen Poliakoff in Chapter 8, " 'You've been here before?': Space and Memory in Stephen Poliakoff's Dramas." Poliakoff's work has centred upon an examination of memory, history, and historical consciousness, and questions of space and place play important roles in the ways in which Poliakoff dramatizes his memory-narratives on stage and screen, occupying his dramas as physical and imaginative sites where past and present collide, and where memory can be recovered, reconstructed, and confronted. Through close reading of visual and written texts, focusing especially on scenes from the television dramas *Perfect Strangers* (2001) and *Capturing Mary* (2007), as well as the stage dramas *Blinded by the Sun* (1996) and *My City* (2011), Robertson examines how Poliakoff explores individual microhistories through the entrenchment of characters' memories in place and space, thus creating private sites of memory.

The distinction may not be entirely tenable, but the chapters in Part III tend to focus on representations of spaces within the texts under consideration, at least more so than the examination of the spatiality of the texts themselves. Thus, for example, in Chapter 9, "Caves as Anti-Places: Robert Penn Warren's *The Cave* and Cormac McCarthy's *Child of God*," Ralph Crane and Lisa Fletcher explore the unique type of space in order to reveal the spatial alterity of caves. They argue that analysing the literary representation of natural subterranean voids requires a careful re-theorisation of the dynamic relations of space and place. The difficult question of how meaning comes to be attached to a particular space, thus transforming it into place, is central to Robert Penn Warren's *The Cave* and Cormac McCarthy's *Child of God*, both of which depict male protagonists who retreat underground, albeit for quite different purposes. According to the standard definition, a cave is a natural cavity beneath the land large enough to admit a human body, but—as the novels selected for this chapter show—caves fascinate and terrify us because they confound human assumptions about our role in assigning meaning to the Earth's spaces.

Sarah Ager looks at another unique type of space in "A Geocritical Approach to the Role of the Desert in Penelope Lively's *Moon Tiger* and Michael Ondaatje's *The English Patient*." Although critics have focused on the role of history in these novels, Ager urges the reader to address the complex relationships between characters and the spaces they occupy. Written between the late 1980s and the early 1990s, both novels look retrospectively at events of World War Two in the Western Sahara, showing how the desert space changes over time and how it is perceived during the lifetimes of the protagonists. Following Marc Augé's concept of "non-places," Ager asks whether the physical desert is represented as a merely transitory space, in contrast to Gaston Bachelard's geocritical conception of "home" as a mental space. Ager argues that the space of the desert both forms and challenges the characters' sense of identity and belonging.

In Chapter 11, "Isolated Spaces, Fragmented Places: Caryl Phillips's Ghettoes in *The Nature of Blood* and *The European Tribe*," I. Murat Öner offers a geocritical reading of Caryl Phillips's deviant Othello character in *The Nature of Blood*, examining his transformation in, and perception of, the ghettoized space of Venice; at the same time, this chapter explores the real-and-fictional space of Venice in *The European Tribe* (a work of nonfiction). Using the interdisciplinary methods of geocriticism to analyse the continuously changing spatial relations and unseen power relations in these texts, Öner explores the space of the "ghetto" in these works, disclosing a map of Venice in the explicit and implicit references, allusions, and connotations in *The Nature of Blood* and *The European Tribe*.

Adam R. McKee, in "Eternal Return and the City/Country Dynamic in Milan Kundera's *The Unbearable Lightness of Being*," establishes an unlikely connection between the well-known Nietzschean themes present in the novel and the classic ideology-critique and historical examination urban and rural forms in Raymond Williams's *The Country and the City*. McKee argues that Kundera confronts the split between the country and the city from the standpoint of a Central European nation bound up in totalitarian, Soviet-communist rule, rather than through the standpoint of Williams's capitalist England, thus inverting or subverting the binary distinction. While many critics have responded to Kundera's somewhat flawed engagement with philosophical issues in the text, McKee notes, few have addressed the way in which the discourses contribute to the specific engagement the country/city divide in the novel that describe the ideologically saturated geographies of the Czech countryside and Soviet Prague. In the end, McKee argues, Kundera and Williams deconstruct this country/city binary by showing the inherent instability in both categories and their most common conceptualizations.

While noting the many shared concerns and overlapping territories of geocriticism and postcolonial theory, Dustin Crowley offers a critique of the ways that geocritical theory approaches postcolonial spaces in "Transgression, Boundaries, and Power: Rethinking the Space of Postcolonial Literature." Crowley looks at works by Kenyan author Ngũgĩ wa Thiong'o and Nigerian author Chris Abani, and he finds that their narratives represent a more complex understanding of boundedness and spatial freedom or transgression than that which is privileged in geocriticism. Drawing from this literature and the work of cultural geography and political ecology, Crowley argues that spatial literary studies should move away from the dichotomized categories it has adopted from its (predominantly postmodern) intellectual antecedents and move toward an understanding of borders and border-crossing as relational, dynamic, and equivocally available to the forces of power and resistance.

In Part IV, what unites the diverse examples of a spatially oriented criticism is a sustained consideration of place in connection to the authors, texts, and contexts being analysed. As becomes clear, *place* is a problem, or a set of problems, without simple solutions, yet all of the works under review are characterized by a sort of topophrenic engagement that considers the subject of place and the place of the subject. For example, in Chapter 14, " 'Oh, man, I'm nowhere': Ralph Ellison and the Psychospatial Terrain of Mid-Century Harlem," Walter Bosse explores the theoretical contours of Ellison's 1948 essay, "Harlem Is Nowhere." Bosse argues that Ellison's text theorizes space in a way that enables resistance against the geopolitical constraints of urban black modernity. As Bosse show, in exploring the underground halls of the Lafargue Psychiatric Clinic in Harlem, "the only center in the city wherein both Negroes and whites may receive extended psychiatric care," Ellison situates racial politics within a specific institutional milieu. At Lafargue, Ellison works as a kind of ethnographer, and records that the utterance "I'm nowhere" was commonly used by patients as an answer to the simple question, "How are you?" Of course, this response articulates the emotional and psychological severity of life in Harlem at the mid-century, but it does so in fascinating and complex ways. The phrase "I'm nowhere" not only acknowledges the constraints working against an individual's subjectivity, it also shows the respondent taking hermeneutical control over the terms of her or his existence. As Bosse concludes, the concept of being "nowhere" provides a new way of articulating displacement as a central moment in the history of the black Atlantic, and the function of "nowhere" as a potentially liberating signifier provides a unique opportunity to view the black vernacular through the lens of spatial theory.

Moving from "nowhere" to a "non place," Chris Margrave offers a fascinating reading of a key author's own sense of place in "Covington is 'The Non Place for Me': Walker Percy's Topophilia in the 'Desert of Theory and Consumption.'" Margrave observes that, through Percy's commitment to living an incarnational artistic life in the "non-place" of Covington, Louisiana, the novelist created a locus of being from which he explored the deranged abstractions and entertainments found in what he termed *the desert of theory and consumption.* While many articles about and interviews with Percy address his reasons for embedding himself in the Deep South, Margrave argues that few critics have explained how Percy's justification for choosing his geographical residence informs his artistic production. In his light-hearted essay, "Why I Live Where I Live," Percy explores the ideas of placement, non-placement, and misplacement, concepts which critics rightly contextualize as terms Percy inherited from Kierkegaard, Marcel, and Camus, among others. Drawing upon Gaston Bachelard's *The Poetics of Space*, Margrave reads Percy's non-fiction essays on place to illustrate how Percy's celebration of Covington reveals the generative source for his unapologetic expression of artistic and religious being.

In Chapter 16, "Alfred Hitchcock's *The Rear Window*: Cold War, Spatiality, and the Paranoid Subject," Beatrice Kohler addresses a different sort of place, one less attached to a given toponym and more situated in the multiple registers of the scopophilic subject, from the voyeuristic individual to an entire geopolitical system of surveillance and control. Kohler investigates the notion of an identifiable "Cold War culture" by discussing Hitchcock's 1954 classic *Rear Window*, focusing especially on spatiality and paranoia. The cinematic screen is seen as a site where socio-cultural conflict is negotiated and political reality is transcoded into fictional narratives. Extending beyond the body of criticism that discusses the movie as a prime example of scopophilia and cinematic self-reflexivity, Kohler attempts to combine extradiegetic politics with intradiegetic aesthetics. Emerging from a culture of McCarthyite furore, post-war anxieties regarding the millions of soldiers returning from World War II, and increasing governmental infringement on privacy, *Rear Window* investigates the politics of suspicion, surveillance, and individual agency by displacing these issues into multiple imaginary screens that are subject to a paranoid misreading symptomatic of the American 1950s.

Will Cunningham examines the liminal spaces of Toni Morrison's celebrated novel in "Locating the Clearing: Contesting Boundaries in Toni Morrison's *Beloved*." Morrison dedicates *Beloved* to the "Sixty Million and more" captured, displaced, and murdered Africans whose physical lives and cultural identity were terminated amidst the transatlantic slave trade. In Cunningham's reading, Morrison's invocation of the transatlantic slave trade frames the story of *Beloved* within the context of spatialized violence, a complex, industrial, and capitalistic endeavour that specifically targeted black identity. The hold of the slave ship could be viewed as a precursor to more familiar, albeit less violent, modern spaces that might be demarcated as placeless: international airport terminals and borders, refugee camps, and military detention prisons. As Cunningham reads them, these locations all occupy that liminal space between opposing binaries; this space is the "third-space," the borderland, the indefinable, a temporary and fluctuating zone governed by both regulatory and lawless forces. This tension between a space created by the material manifestations of power and the performances of identity within and through these movements of capital reveals an acute, revelatory convergence of spatial and racial identity formation. Cunningham argues that reading the confluence of space and race allows us to see in Morrison's work a critical mass of dispossessed humanity embroiled in constant relations of subversion and contestation.

Chapter 18, "Remapping the Present: Dave Eggers's Spatial Virtuality and the Condition of Literature," addresses the spatial turn in literary studies by way of a parallel turn in virtual theory. Surveying and synthesizing the many invaluable contributions to conceptualizing virtuality, from those of Bergson and Deleuze to those of Daniel Downes and Brian Massumi, Nathan Frank asserts that a "spatial virtuality" accounts for an increasing focus on digitization without dismissing the previous (and, at times, prescient) preoccupations with temporal virtualities. Frank also frames spatial virtuality in terms of N. Katherine Hayles's compelling work in which virtuality is a condition. Within such a framework, many things happen, not the least of which is a sustained meditation on an information-materiality dialectic, wherein two sub-dialectics are housed: that of pattern-randomness (information), and that of presence-absence (materiality). In Frank's argument, virtuality as a spatial condition comports with the classic tropes of power and literature, namely, circles and stories about circles. Looking at two novels by Dave Eggers, *A Hologram for the King* and *The Circle*, Frank interrogates how a re-appropriation of Judith Anderson's intertext, as a condition of potentiality and relationship, might provide the substance of that which is present without being local. In this way, "spatial virtuality" and "a condition of literature" suggest that language and texts are the presence around which information and material bodies congregate, offering new ways forward in exploring the discourses surrounding virtuality.

Finally, by way of an open-ended conclusion or *plus ultra*—the "further beyond" at the edge of the map—Part V contains a chapter in which I discuss the potential distinctions and affinities between what has become identified as *spatial literary studies* and the somewhat more established interdisciplinary field of *literary geography*. As noted previously, scholars have long examined the relationship between literature and space, place, or mapping, but formal methods or disciplines for such work have only recently come into being. Particularly after what has been called the "spatial turn" in the humanities and social sciences, researchers from various academic and artistic disciplines have developed work in connection to terms such as literary geography, imaginative geography, geocriticism, geopoetics, the spatial humanities, geohumanities, and spatial literary studies, to name a few. Understandably, there would be a great deal of overlapping interest among these emerging practices or subfields, even if the aims and methods of each may vary, and practitioners of one form may find it desirable to distinguish their field from other related ones. Recently, a leading proponent of literary geography has sharply criticized the conflation of that field with spatial literary studies, an ostensible rival primarily associated with my work as a critic and editor. In this concluding chapter, I respond to this criticism, first by explaining my use and understanding of the terms *spatial literary studies* and *literary geography*, then by attempting to create a working definition that would delineate the boundaries between these practices while leaving the possibilities for future collaboration and mutual influence open.

Spatial Literary Studies provides a reasonably representative sampling of some of the work being done in this emerging field or set of practices, but as I have said, the field is developing and changing rapidly. Undoubtedly this sort of work will continue to provide insights for literary criticism, literary history, and literary theory, and scholars working in spatial literary studies and related areas will continue to open up and explore new spaces for critical inquiry. I, for one, look forward to seeing what lies further beyond.

Part I

Geocritical Theory and Practice

1 Geocriticism at the Crossroads

An Overview

Mariya Shymchyshyn

In this essay I will outline some of the methodological and theoretical developments in late twentieth-century criticism that led to the spatial turn in the humanities. In particular, I will concentrate my attention on the concepts of space in the works of Henri Lefebvre, Michel Foucault, Gilles Deleuze, and Félix Guattari, and I will pursue how they influenced literary theory, causing the emergence of "geocriticism" (e.g., in the work of Robert Tally, Bertrand Westphal, Eric Prieto) or, using another term, "literary geography" (e.g., in Franco Moretti). I will argue that the postmodern condition generated an alertness to space rather than time in different fields of scholarship, as historicism has undergone decline under postmodernism. My conclusion is that incorporating geographical thought into a variety of domains of research offers a better understanding of human experience, social relations, and cultural production. Even though the concept of space, as well as a geographical framework in general, have been revised and injected into recent theoretical inquiries, they have not been fully applied to literary criticism. We can witness the beginning of the process of formation of a coherent spatial paradigm within literary theory.

Over the last few decades the spatial turn has become one of the main focuses in literary theory and cultural studies, enabling (re)conceptualizations of ways of thinking about space and place. The discourse of postmodernism disclosed a break from languages that emphasized history, and concentrated its attention on real and fictional milieu. Neil Smith, in his Foreword to Henri Lefebvre's *The Urban Revolution*, observes that "whereas space came alive in early-twentieth-century art, physics, and mathematics, in social theory and philosophy it was a quite different story. Space there was more often synonymous with rigidity, immobility, stasis; space itself had become a blind field."[1] Since the 1960s, space has begun to reassert itself in critical theory, not only as a subject of symbolic readings or as an empty or neutral container of Euclidian geometry, but as a fluid, heterogenic, and composite world, as a palimpsest (Gerard Genette), as a hyperspace that produces derivative spaces, as a referent for an experience of the real, as a product of speech, and as a construct of social forces and power discourses. As Russell West-Pavlov put it, "Far from being a neutral void in which objects are placed and events happen, space/ing becomes a medium with its own consistency and, above all, its own productive agency."[2] In his now famous 1967 speech "Of Other Spaces," Foucault explained that

> The great obsession of the nineteenth century was, as we know, history: with its themes of development and of suspension, of crisis, and cycle, themes of the ever-accumulating past, with its great preponderance of dead men and the menacing glaciations of the world. . . . The present epoch will perhaps be above all the epoch of space. We are in the epoch of simultaneity: we are in the epoch of juxtapositions, the epoch of the near and far, of the side-by-side, of the dispersed. We are at a moment, I believe, when our experience of the world is less that of a long life developing through time than that of a network that connects points and intersects with its own skein.[3]

Space and geography as major theoretical orientations bring new perspectives and open new horizons in the humanities.

The spatial turn in philosophy, sociology, cultural studies, and literary theory correlated with the redefinition of cultural geography's agenda. During 1980s and 1990s new cultural geographers brought the topics of sensibility and political interests to their studies. Linda McDowell observes: "what is published and taught under the rubric of 'cultural geography' changes in response to the political and economic climate of the times and the structures of disciplinary power."[4] The epistemological turn of the 1990s stressed understanding culture through space and as space. Culture is not perceived only as tradition handed down from generation to generation, a point that connects it with time and history, but as "a realm, medium, level, or zone." Space is relevant to the production of cultural phenomena and defines the ways they are produced. As Barney Warf and Santa Arians write in their introduction to *The Spatial Turn*: "Geography matters, not for the simplistic and overly used reason that everything happens in space, but because *where* things happen is crucial to knowing *how* and *why* they happen."[5] The new versions of culture that include everything or anything gave way to the intellectual traffic between philosophy, sociology, cultural studies, literary theories, and geography.

The exchange of ideas between scholars of geography and representatives of others sciences gave way to broad, non-stereotyped interpretations of space. For example, geographers like Derek Gregory, Doreen Massey, Steve Pile, and Edward Soja adapted theoretical ideas developed by Lefebvre, de Certeau, Foucault, Lacan, Deleuze, and Guattari. Productive connections between geography and literary postmodernism have been made by these spatial theorists. The postmodernist suspicion of total explanations, rejection of monopolies of truth, and accent on difference, heterogeneity, and particularity contribute significantly to postmodern cultural geography. At the same time, literary scholars Westphal, Tally, and Moretti drew upon the work of these new cultural geographers in their own criticism and theory. Thus, for instance, Moretti states that "geography is not an inert container, is not a box, where cultural history 'happens', but an active force, that pervades the literary field and shapes it in depth."[6] The geographical paradigm becomes more and more a constitutive part of literary scholarship. Although sporadic attention to space or, it is better to say, place, has always been present in philosophical and fictional writings, the emergence of geocriticism in the early 1990s re-accentuated literary discussions.

The history of perception of space and place in different historical periods and different cultures shows fundamental changes in the ways people have imagined the world. In the Renaissance or early modern period several crucial shifts took place and had lasting consequences. Among them was the development of linear perspective, "which not only enabled more 'accurate' pictorial representations in the visual arts but also occasioned a wholesale re-imagining of space and of human spatial relations. This is a crucial moment in the history of spaces."[7] According to the American scholar Leonard Goldstein, the emergence of linear perspective between the thirteenth and fifteenth centuries located space in three key aspects: (1) space is continuous, isotropic, and homogeneous; (2) space is quantifiable; (3) space is perceived from the point of view of a single, central observer. The shift from the two-dimensional artistic expression of the middle ages and the geometric three-dimensional drawings of the Italian Renaissance to the linear perspective of pictorial art of early capitalism can be explained by the emergence of new forms of private property and commodity production. As Tally observes, "Space could now be measured, divided, quantified, bought and sold, and above all controlled by a particular individual who, in theory, could be the sovereign ruler of all he surveyed."[8] Linear perspective, created in the modern period by Filippo Brunelleschi, reflected the new ways of seeing and enabled the development of a new image of the individual, who became the locus and source of meaning. Tally summarizes:

> But the new point of view, which includes linear perspective and mechanism as its method of investigation, is superior [to the earlier iconographic mode] since it gives people a greater control over the environment, both physical and social, than previous interpretations of the world.[9]

In the philosophical discourse from Heraclitus to Hegel and Marx, the illusion of a transparent, pure, and neutral space permeated Western culture. The dynamics of the understanding of space started with it being created by God (Descartes, Spinoza, Leibniz) or the Absolute (Schelling, Fichte, Hegel) and later, according to Lefebvre, it "appeared as a mere degradation of 'being' as it unfolded in a temporal continuum."[10] The geometric format of Euclidean space was interpreted by philosophical thought as absolute and from this it follows that space was used as a space of reference. In the late seventeenth and eighteenth centuries many ideas about space were developed. Thus, Descartes believed that space cannot be separated from bodies as bodies are part of space. Newton viewed space as an absolute, independent, infinite, three-dimensional container into which God placed the material universe. Leibniz developed the notion of space as the relation between bodies similar to distance as a relation between two points. Spinoza held the idea that space is God. Kant argued that the world is a subjective mental construction because it is perceived through human reason.

> Space is not something objective and real, nor is it a substance, nor an accident, nor a relation; it is, rather, subjective and ideal; it issues from the nature of mind in accordance with a stable law as a scheme, as it were, for co-ordinating everything sensed externally.[11]

The philosophers, in their capacity of epistemologists, envisaged spaces for the classification of knowledge.

In the nineteenth century, space was mostly understood as the location for great historical events. Therefore, temporality and history assumed a primary importance whereas space was viewed as static and empty. The view of space as a "container of things" diminished the importance of spatiality. The vista of a philosopher or a writer was directed to the things situated in space or to the individual consciousness perceiving them. The notion of historical progression, correlative with industrial and scientific revolutions, gave priority to the concept of time. Time was linearized while space was marginalized and conceived as given and static.

The radical metamorphoses caused by modernization in the second half of the nineteenth century and the beginning of the twentieth transformed the idea of space. Feelings of disorientation and disintegration started to characterize the individual consciousness. A break of the linear narrative in fiction and the linear perspective in a pictorial art correlated with a fragmented perception of space. Although issues of temporality were privileged in the critical works about modernism, it does not mean that spatiality did not matter for modernist aesthetics. In his novel *The Soul of London* (1905), Ford Maddox Ford wrote that "we live in spacious times." Neglecting space in favor of time is a practice that David Harvey explains in the following way: "Modernity is about the experience of progress through modernization, writings on that theme have tended to emphasize temporality, the process of *becoming*, rather than being in space and place."[12] In literary studies, objective space was substituted for the subjective image of space. Therefore, even today, the theoretical problem is to uncover the mediations between them. It is necessarily to separate "a false consciousness of abstract space and an objective falseness of space itself," as Lefebvre has put it.[13] But despite this, spatial metaphors such as fragmentation, location, center, margin, movement, belonging, and (im)migration became dominant in modernist discourse. That is why scholars today start to think about the spatiality of modernism, for example, in Andrew Thacker's excellent study of the subject.[14]

During the modernist period the new concept of space emerged in pictorial art. The experimental activity of avant-garde painters that neither imitated objective reality, nor was bound up with subjective emotions and feelings, witnessed the disappearance of points of reference and, as a result, pointed to the crisis of a subject. Picasso's way of painting can serve as an example: "The entire surface of the canvas was used, but there was no horizon, no background, and the surface was simply divided between the surface of painted figures and the space that surrounded them."[15] Therefore, space became at once homogeneous and broken; the sign became detached from what is designated. The notion of space is perfectly defined and "born as an already adult and mature consciousness of self."[16]

The rise of structuralism and later poststructuralism marked a key phase in the turn to space instead of time in critical inquiries. For instance, Edward Soja regarded structuralism to be "one of the twentieth century's most important avenues for the reassertion of space in critical social theory."[17] French structuralists and poststructuralists (including Kristeva, Genette, Derrida, Foucault, Deleuze, and Guattari) reversed "the tyranny of the diachronic perspective" (Genette) and acclaimed the "spatial turn" in human sciences. Their writings correlated with the comprehensive theory of space offered by Lefebvre, who viewed space as a void woven of the relationships between subjects, their actions, and their environment. Milieus are created by action, but at the same time, they are modeling the human actors who have constructed them.

It is worth mentioning that structuralist and poststructuralist approaches to space do not always coincide. West-Pavlov states:

> Structuralism conceived of space in a manner similar to the ostensibly undifferentiated pre-cultural field which culture then configures, using meaning—making binary oppositions. Instead, the spatial paradigms of poststructuralism stress that space persists in a constant re-configuring of already extant configurations.[18]

For poststructuralists there is no virginal space before configured space, while for certain structuralists (e.g., the early Kristeva) there is always a proto-space, a pre-existing milieu.

Theorists like Fredric Jameson, along with Harvey, Tally, and Soja, argue that the spatial turn in the humanities is a response to the postmodernist condition. In *Postmodernism, or the Cultural Logic of Late Capitalism*, Jameson, following Lefebvre and Foucault, has stated that "our daily life, our psychic experiences, our cultural languages, are dominated by categories of space rather than by categories of time."[19] Postmodern spatiality produced by the processes of globalization is defined, in part, through collapsed spatial barriers. Poststructuralists' ideas about the social construction of knowledge, human dependence upon institutionalized power networks, and impersonal social structures have evoked interest in the social production of space. Displacement of the priority of individual experience, subjective consciousness, and attention to the discourses of power explain the emphasis on the concept of space over that of place. Moreover, the spatial turn corresponds with the deep paradigmatic changes within the humanities that do not deal so much with the reproductive paradigm of meaning, do not ask what artefacts mean, but how they mean. In this context, West-Pavlov argues: "A deeper truth is not sought behind the statement, the text, the artefact, or the image. Rather the point of intellectual enquiry is to ask how that statement, text, artifact, or image came to be, what made it possible."[20] As far as meaning is produced in a specific time and context, space is crucial for understanding its production.

> Meaning is thus a function of space in which it emerges. Truth and falsehood are replaced by space as the matrix of meaning. An artifact no longer has "a" meaning, no longer unveils "a" truth under the stern scrutiny of the scholar, but rather, participates in myriad relations and connections which permit it to *be* in such a way that it can *subsequently* be asked to reveal its truth.[21]

The regime of spatial analysis is directed not towards the decoding of a hidden meaning of a work of art, but draws "attention to a complex of ambient connections which have simply been neglected until now."[22] Space gives rise to the artefacts and at the same time artefacts reconfigure space; they define each other reciprocally.

The critical attention of postmodernists to the concept of space has been evoked to a large extent by World War II and the anticolonial movements of the postwar years, which led to the problematizing of the myth of history as a single, unified narrative and the destruction of the Enlightenment metanarrative of progress. Processes of decolonization and neocolonialism, along with massive movements of populations (exiles, émigrés, refugees, and explorers), have caused awareness of geographical difference, of the distinctiveness of a given place, and differences among places. Therefore, the phenomenological perspective of space that emphasizes the subjective experience of place, profoundly worked out by Edmund

Husserl, Martin Heidegger, Gaston Bachelard, and Georges Poulet, then later renovated by such philosophers as Edward Casey, Jeff Malpas, Tyler Burke, Hilary Putman, Donald Davidson, and Francisco Varela, has given way to epistemological, environmental or ecocritical (Kenneth White), postcolonial (Aimè Cèsaire, Frantz Fanon, Homi Bhabha, Edouard Glissant, Edward Said), feminist (bell hooks, Lucy Lippard, Doreen Massey, Linda McDowell), and Marxist (Lefebvre, Jameson, Harvey, Soja, Raymond Williams) ideas about space. Their rejection of the priority of individual experience, of the notion of totalizing space as an absolute and inhuman construction, and of spatial uniformity opened up discussions about the heterogeneous nature of space.

> It is not, therefore, as though one had global (or conceived) space to one side and fragmented (or lived) space to the other—rather as one might have an intact glass here and a broken glass or mirror over there. For space 'is' whole and broken, global and fragmented, at one and the same time. Just as it is at once conceived, perceived and directly lived.[23]

Lefebvre argued against the traditional optical format of space. The logic of visualization, dependence on the written word, and the process of spectacularization, which corresponds to metaphoric and metonymic aspects, caused a vanishing of all impressions derived from taste, smell, touch, and hearing, and left the field to line, color and light. He criticized a purely visual passive space.

Many of the ideas about space developed in the second half of the twentieth century (e.g., those of Jameson, Harvey, Soja, and Westphal), were formulated in dialogue about the works of Lefebvre, who in *The Production of Space*, first proposed to distinguish between mental space and social space, and only then to reconnect them. For him

> the concept of space is not in space. . . . The content of the concept of space is not absolute space or space-in-itself; nor does the concept contain a space within itself. . . . Rather, the concept of space denotes and connotes all possible spaces, whether abstract or "real", mental or social. And in particular it has two aspects: representational spaces and representations of space.[24]

There should not be any reduction of content to its formal container, reduction of time to space, reduction of objects to signs, reduction of "reality" to the semiophere, or reduction of social space to a purely mental space.

Lefebvre interpreted space from different angles and worked out a broad typology of it. For him, space can be a field of action and a basis of action, it can be actual (given) and potential (locus of possibilities),

quantitative (measurable by means of units of measurement) and qualitative, a collection of materials and an ensemble of matèriel (tools). In
writings about spatial architectonics, Lefebvre proposed a capacious definition of space:

> Space—my space—is not the context of which I constitute the "tex-
> tuality": instead, it is first of all my body, and then it is my body's
> counterpart or "other", its mirror-image or shadow: it is the shift-
> ing intersection between that which touches, penetrates, threatens or
> benefits my body on the one hand, and all other bodies on the other.
> Thus we are concerned, once again, with gaps and tensions, contacts
> and separations. Yet, through and beyond these various effects of
> meaning, space is actually experienced in its depths, as duplications,
> echoes and reverberations, redundancies and doublings-up which
> engender—and are engendered by the strangest of contrast: face and
> arse, eye and flesh, viscera and excrement, lips and teeth, orifices
> and phallus, clenched fists and opened hands—as also clothed versus
> naked, open versus closed, obscenity versus familiarity, and so on.[25]

This profound notion of space as a locus of intersections, contacts, tensions, and relationships gives numerous possibilities to geocriticism. This
particular understanding of milieu advocates a polysensuous approach
that includes the sounds, smells, and tastes of places.

Lefebvre worked out three aspects of space: *experienced space* (physical space that can be measured), *representations of space* (space perceived
by planners, etc., and drawn on maps, diagrams), and *representational
space* (imagined by writers and artists). In a broader sense this differentiation can be extrapolated to literary theory and can help to disclose how
the representational spaces of fictional texts reflect, contest, or endorse
the geographical shaping of different *topoi* by various ideological representations of space.

Lefebvre also developed the notion of "third space" as the relationship between body and material/object that his follower and postmodern
political geographer Soja defines as a space where

> everything comes together . . . subjectivity and objectivity, the
> abstract and the concrete, the real and the imagined, the knowable
> and the unimaginable, the repetitive and the differential, structure
> and agency, mind and body, consciousness and the unconscious,
> the disciplined and the transdisciplinary, everyday life and unending
> history.[26]

The idea of a thirdspace as a mixture of a lived, experienced space and
a perceived space proposed by Lefebvre and later developed by Soja can
be extrapolated for use in examining an imaginary space. Discourse of a

body, which is produced by and is the production of space, can give us some notion of a thirdspace that may signify a fictional space. A body is not an object or subject represented by fragmented images or words, but a body that is "reflected and refracted in the changes that it wreaks in its 'milieu' or 'environment'—in other words, in its space."[27] A verbal, semantic, and semiological space can be enlarged by information from the body (smell, taste, sound). An interplay between verbal disembodiment and empirical re-embodiment helps to gain the meaning of lived experience and overcome spatialization in an abstract expanse.

The spatial theory present in the philosophical *oeuvre* of Foucault has become a paramount part of the recent "spatial turn" in literary and cultural studies. Whereas for Lefebvre, space is a product of social relations and at the same time their producer, for Foucault, space is power, as far as power is always located spatially. This idea is made most explicit in his work *Discipline and Punish*, which deals with the disciplinary power in modern societies. Social relations of power exist on macro and micro levels. As Thacker explains the difference, for Foucault, contrary to Lefebvre, "the history of spaces is not the history of relations of production, but of relations of power."[28] Of particular interest is Foucault's "Of Other Spaces," where he paid peculiar attention to the two main types of space that "suspect, neutralize, or invent the set of relations that they happen to designate, mirror, or reflect."[29] These types are the utopias (sites with no real place) and the heterotopias, a mix of real and unreal places that create a space of illusion or a space that is other. Privileged, sacred, or forbidden places belong to heterotopias, and until recently, such places were assigned to the individuals in a state of crisis (adolescents, menstruating women, expecting mothers, the elderly, etc.). Nowadays these heterotopias of crisis are being replaced by what Foucault called "heterotopias of deviation" (such as rest homes, psychiatric hospitals, prisons). They are designated for individuals "whose behavior is deviant in relation to the required norm."[30] Foucault differentiates the following main principles of heterotopias: every culture tends to form its own heterotopia; society can make an existing heterotopia to function differently; "the heterotopia is capable of juxtaposing in a single real place several places, several sites that are in themselves incompatible"; it begins to function when a person absolutely breaks with traditional time (this includes sites of accumulated time—museums and libraries— places of all times and simultaneously outside of time) or is linked to the transitory time (for example, the time in the mode of festival); heterotopias presuppose a system of opening and closing that both isolates them and makes them penetrable; and, at last, heterotopias have a function in relation to all the space that remains. Foucault's ideas about space as domains of power can be further developed into a notion of space as resistance to power. As only within the space of power emerges the space of resistance.

Following Lefebvre, Foucault, and Jameson, among others, Soja has significantly influenced the radical rethinking of the notion of space in the present moment. Drawing upon Martin Buber's 1957 essay "Distance and Relation," Soja connects spatiality with the beginning of human consciousness, stating:

> Human beings alone are able to objectify the world by setting themselves apart. And they do so by creating a gap, a distance, a space. This process of objectification defines the human situation and predicates it upon spatiality, on the capacity for detachment made possible by distancing, by being spatial to begin with.[31]

Spatial distancing allows a being to differentiate itself from objective reality and become conscious of its humanity. The first created space, separated from the totality, thus constitutes the ontological basis for distinguishing subject and object. Speaking about postmodernity, Soja argues that spatiality is the key to making practical, political, and theoretical sense of the contemporary era. He sets his argument about postmodern space within three paths of spatialization: posthistoricism, postfordism, and postmodernism. The first one implies the reassertion of space against the grain of an ontological historicism. "The second spatialization is directly attached to the political economy of the material world and, more specifically, to the 'fourth modernization' of capitalism."[32] The term "postfordism" is used to characterize the transformations of the regime of accumulation, mass consumerism, and sprawling suburbanization. The third path is connected with the emergence of a new, postmodern culture of space. Postmodernism overlaps with posthistoricism and "postfordism as a theoretical discourse and a periodizing concept in which geography increasingly matters as a vantage point of critical insight."[33] As a postmodern cultural geographer, Soja has concentrated his attention on the analysis of space and society, and offered new ways of understanding the unjust geographies in which we live. To his mind, spatial theorizations were distorted by short-sighted interpretations of spatiality that theorized space as a collection of things. Spatiality was "comprehended only as objectively measurable appearances grasped through some combination of sensory-based perception."[34] Accordingly, in the social origins of spatiality, its contextualization of politics, power, and ideology were neglected. Soja's understanding of space is grounded on the premise that spatiality is a substantiated and recognizable social product that is simultaneously the medium and the outcome of social actions. The duality of produced space lies in the fact that it is both a product and a producer of social activity.

Although clear connections exist between the concept of space elaborated by Foucault and those developed later by Deleuze and Guattari, there are also significant differences between their poststructuralist theories. If Foucault developed ideas about space in their relation to discourses of power, Deleuze and Guattari thought about space in terms of the architecture of the rhizome. As West-Pavlov observes:

> Deleuze's theory of space is not built like a tree, with a central hierarchical trunk from which subordinated 'branches' then spread out, themselves branching off into smaller twig-like subtopics. Rather, his theory of space seems to develop horizontally, spreading out tendrils and runner-shoots which then cross each other at some later point, forming a dense web of allusions and interconnections. The very construction of his theory of space itself evinces strong spatial (rather than linear or hierarchical) characteristics from the outset.[35]

Such an unconventional way of thinking causes difficulties in expressing Deleuze and Guattari's theorizing of space in a traditional academic mode. I will concentrate my attention on some aspects of their notions of space.

In his famous collaborations with Félix Guattari, as in much of his other writings, Deleuze has sufficiently enlarged the conceptual and terminological domain of spatial theory by introducing into it *diagram, plane, map, plateau, deterritorialization* and *reterritorialization,* and *smooth-and-striated spaces.* In *A Thousand Plateaus,* the second volume of their *Capitalism and Schizophrenia* project, Deleuze and Guattari distinguished between a smooth (heterogeneous) and a striated (homogeneous) space. The latter functions as a locus for the state apparatus and, being a sedentary space, is "striated by walls, enclosures, and roads between enclosures."[36] While a smooth space is directional rather than dimensional or metric, intensive rather than extensive, and a "Body without Organs" instead of an organism or organization. In a striated space, lines or trajectories tend to be subordinated to points, contrary to a smooth space in which points are subordinated to trajectory. Despite the dissymmetrical mixes between these two spaces, there are simple oppositions between them.

> The smooth and the striated are distinguished first of all by an inverse relation between the point and the line (in the case of the striated, the line is between two points, while in the smooth, the point is between two lines); and second, by the nature of the line (smooth-directional, open intervals; dimensional-striated, closed intervals). Finally, there is a third difference, concerning the surface or space. In striated space, one closes off a surface and "allocates" it according to determinate intervals, assigned breaks; in the smooth, one "distributes" oneself in an open space, according to frequencies and in the course of one's crossings (logos and nomos).[37]

The simple opposition between "smooth and striated" gives way to more difficult complications and alterations as far as space is open to the processes of homogeneity or heterogeneity and cannot be seen as stable and static. The aforementioned differences are not objective because it is possible to live striated on steppes or seas and live smooth in cities. Taking this into consideration, Deleuze and Guattari described the interaction between spaces through six models.

The principle of mixture and passage from one space to another is not at all symmetrical, but envisions variable modifications. Deleuze and Guattari distinguished the following models: the *technological* (for example, embroidery, which has a central theme or motif, and patchwork, with no center or definite construction; fabric with vertical and horizontal elements and felt with no intertwining and no separation of threads); the *musical* (for example, octave [a fixed distribution of breaks and intervals], which corresponds to a striated space, and non-octave-forming scales, which are produced through the continuous variation and development of form [smooth space]); and the *maritime* (although the sea is a smooth space par excellence, the astronomical system of navigation employs its strict striation). Regarding the latter, the empirical nomadic system of navigation based on the wind, noise, colors and sounds of the seas supported the smooth nature of a sea, but with the advent of astronomical and later map systems of navigation, a sea became a model of a striated space. It is an example of how a smooth space can be subjugated and occupied by diabolical powers of organization. Therefore, the sea is a smooth space open to striation. In the context of the maritime model it is appropriate to speak about the intermingling of spaces that is explicit in a voyage not being a measurable quantity of movement, but "the mode of spatialization, the manner of being in space, of being for space."[38] Deleuze and Guattari grounded the *mathematical* model on Riemann's notion of the "mathematical concept" as well as on Husserl's and Bergson's concept of "multiplicity" that presupposes *continuous multiplicities* and *discrete multiplicities*. A Riemann's space, "which presents itself as an amorphous collection of pieces that are juxtaposed but not attached to each other," is similar to heterogeneous and amorphous smooth space.[39] If all of the aforementioned models serve to exemplify differences between smooth and striated spaces (patchwork vs. weaving, rhythmic vs. harmony-melody, Riemann space vs. Euclidean space) the link between them can be expressed in terms of elementary physics. The *physical* model gives grounds for Deleuze and Guattari to differentiate between "free action" in smooth space and "work" in striated space. Writing about the *aesthetic* model and its possibility to represent the differences and overlapping between spaces, the authors distinguished between "close-range" and long-distance vision, between tactile or haptic and optical space. "The first aspect of the haptic, smooth space of close vision is that its orientations, landmarks, and linkages are in continuous variation; it operates step by step." In a smooth space, one never sees from a distance, is never "in front of" any more than is "in." Orientations change according to temporary vegetation, occupation, and precipitation. On the contrary, "striated space is defined by the requirements of long-distance vision: constancy of orientation, invariance of distance through an interchange of inertial points of reference, interlinkage by immersion in an ambient milieu, constitution of a central perspective."[40] The opposition between the striated and smooth is not simple; we see that one requires the other, that one gives rise to the other, and at last one tends to become the other.

Particular attention is warranted to Deleuze and Guattari's concept of *geophilosophy*, outlined in the collaborative work *What is Philosophy?* that contested against the reduction of philosophy to its history. Philosophy continually wrests itself from its history "in order to create new concepts that fall back into history but do not come from it." In its turn, geography unlike history stresses contingency rather than necessity, milieu rather than origin. Geography "is not confined to providing historical form with a substance and variable places. It is not merely physical and human but mental, like the landscape."[41] Deleuze and Guattari underline the necessity to locate philosophy in a territory, in particular to "reterritorialize modern philosophy on Greece as form of its past." The separation of geography and philosophy led to the situation when "we possess concepts—after so many centuries of Western thought we think we possess them—but we hardly know where to put them because we lack a genuine plane, misled as we are by Christian transcendence."[42]

Deleuze and Guattari argued for the development of geophilosophy, which was in their view founded by Nietzsche, who determined the national characteristics of French, English, and German philosophy. Those were the three countries that collectively produced philosophy in the capitalist world. As for Italy and Spain, they "lacked a 'milieu for philosophy, so that their thinkers remained 'comets.' "[43] Today, geophilosophy finds a way in reterritorializing itself in conformity with the spirit of a people of a particular place. For example, writing about the origins of Greek philosophy, Deleuze and Guattari stated that it appeared as result of milieu and geography rather that of an origin and a history.

Deleuze and Guattari's notions about nomadology and geophilosophy have provided the foundation for the geocentric approach of Westphal's geocritical literary studies. A geocritical approach revises the correlation between literary representation and geographical referent first through denying the assumption that "representation remains a slave to reality."[44] Rather than studying how a fictional depiction conforms to a "real" place, geocritical theorists take the spatial referent as the basis for their analysis, which allows them "to inscribe space in a mobile perspective."[45] Similar to Deleuze's idea that a book is not an image of the world, but forms a rhizome with the world—deterritorializes the world—while the world reterritorializes the book, geocritics rethink the correlation between fictional and real places. Westphal has defined four cardinal points of geocritical approach: *multifocalization, polysensorality, stratigraphy,* and *intertextuality* that I will summarize in the following paragraphs.

By rejecting the egocentered form of imagological analysis that focuses on the subjectivity of the artist, geocriticism puts together different representations of one and the same space. Therefore, it helps to avoid fixing the referent in a monologic narrative. The spectrum of individual representations and negotiation between them allows conceiving a locus in its diversity and permanent performativity. In particular, Westphal states,

> The study of the viewpoint of an author or of a series of authors, which inevitably posits a form of identity, will be superseded in favor of examining a multiplicity of heterogeneous points of view, which all converge in a given place, the *primum mobile* of the analysis. A multifocal dynamic would be required for this analysis. Without hesitation, I would say that multifocalization is the chief characteristic of geocriticism.[46]

The multifocal perspective implies the necessity to bring together as many texts as possible, including both literary and nonliterary. The distinguishing feature of geocriticism is its concentration on understanding a given place through the problematics of representation rather than studying a given set of representations. This can be achieved through the comparative mode of analysis that presupposes dialogical understanding of the chosen place. As Westphal points out,

> geocriticism actually continues to assign supremacy to the artist, but it no longer places the artist at the center of the universe. . . . Also the bipolar relationship between otherness and identity is longer governed by a single action, but by interaction. The representation of space comes from a reciprocal creation, not simply a one-way activity of a gaze looking from one point to another, without considering the other, reciprocating gazes (as in Eurocentrism, for example). Geocritical analysis involves the confrontation of several optics that correct, nourish, and mutually enrich each other.[47]

A variety of viewpoints provides a rhizomatic paradigm for the understanding of a place. It is important to mention that multifocalization implies not only concentration on different representations of a space, but also on their intersections, as they give the possibility to figure out conflicting and concurring zones.

As far as we experience an environment through all our senses, it is necessary to consider not only visual perception, which is the dominant, but also other modes of receiving information. Yi-Fu Tuan writes in *Space and Place* that

> Experience is a cover-all term for the various modes through which a person knows and constructs reality. These modes range from the more direct and passive senses of smell, taste, and touch, to the active visual perception and the indirect mode of symbolization.[48]

The study of a polysensory perception of the world transforms and enriches our understanding of it and gives a way to escape the control of one kind of sense and open new modes of depicting a referent space.

> The endogenous, exogenous, and allogeneous points of view find equivalents in the polysensory inveigling of the world, which is perfectly heterogeneous. In terms of representation, space is subject to the infinite variety of sensory perception. We sometimes encounter "landscapes" dominated by one sense, and sometimes the "landscapes" are synesthetic.[49]

When dealing with a complex and saturated space, we need a polysensory perspective that, along with a visual, colorful, referent landscape, includes soundscape, olfactory, and haptic discourses.

The perception of the referent is relative and predetermined by the intention of the observer. In such a case, "the degree of conformity of the representation is undecidable" because each presenter is inscribed in his or her own temporal regime. In any single place we are able to perceive the diversity of temporalities synchronously, but also diachronically. In other words,

> space is located at the intersection of the moment and duration; its apparent surface rests on the strata of compacted time arranged over an extended duration and reactivated at any time. This present time of space includes a past that flows according to a stratigraphic logic. Examining the impact of time on the perception of space is therefore another aspect of geocriticism.[50]

Accordingly, heterogeneity of space is to some extent determined by a layering of several temporal curves that function similarly to Deleuze and Guattari's "strata." On the other side, heterogeneity is born from an ensemble of asynchronous rhythms that are inherent to space. The "polyrhythmic body" of space corresponds to the understanding that "a space is not *one* in a moment," just as "the city is never synchronous with itself."[51] Thus, geocriticism using the metaphor of stratification gives the notion of a referent space as a rhizome, as a stratum of non-simultaneity, and as a constellation of singularity and plurality.

Italo Calvino, in his autobiographical *Hermit in Paris,* speculates: "Before being a city of the real world, Paris for me, as for millions of other people in every country, has been a city that I have imagined through books, a city that you appropriate when you read."[52] The space is formed in our imagination as a result of intertextual construction and is first a text that is interconnected with other texts. Geocriticism aims to reconstruct the intertextual trajectory that leads to a particular representation of space. Every text about a referential space is succeeded by another text and "so on in an endless chain in which the layers of paper pile upon one another with the beautiful regularity of geological and archeological strata."[53] Accordingly, the text is not born of the space, but of other texts to which the space has been a referent.

One more dimension of geocritical intertextuality lies in the sphere of interconnectedness between space and text. They blend together and become inseparable—a unity of the real and imaginary. In such symbiosis it is impossible to search for credibility of the real, as the latter (the real) just simply does not exist. "The writer is the author of the city, the demiurge of places," who is located in myriads of geographical visions. That is why a space is always in the process of transformation, mobility, and re-actualization. Accordingly, we will look in vain for the "real" places of Dostoevsky's Saint Petersburg, Joyce's Dublin, Kafka's Prague, and Doyle's London. Reading a text influences our perceiving of a space, "the page and the stone interweave."[54]

Cultural geographers as well as literary geocritics support the idea that a "real" place is directly connected with a discursive framework. Soja deconstructs the traditional concept of urban space through figuring out the relations between what is termed "reality" and the discursive, establishing the notion of space as simulacrum. Michel Butor seeks a reconciliation between the space and a text and discusses "the city as a literary genre." In the context of geocritical intertextuality, Westphal argues:

> But intertextuality is not really a lonely walk through the woods of novels and other literary genres. Space, grasped through the representation that texts sustain, can be "read" like a novel. One reads space; one traverses a text; one reads a text as one traverses space. In this expanded view of textuality that encompasses equally bookish architexture and spatial architecture, textuality eventually escapes the closed logic that confines the text within a textual "system."[55]

In the paradigm of such intertextuality there is no radical separateness between space and text.

Drawing upon these rich traditions of spatial theory, the geocritical approach, as developed by Westphal, Tally, and Prieto, among others, can also be broadened through integrating different vistas: phenomenology, semiotics, geography, and sociology along with posthumanism, postpositivism, and New Materialism. The crossroads of these spheres of knowledge will extend the discourse on space, and make possible new spatial and critical interventions in the future.

Notes

1. Neil Smith, "Foreword," in Henri Lefebvre, ed., *The Urban Revolution*, trans. Robert Bononno (Minneapolis: University of Minnesota Press, 2003), xiii.
2. Russell West-Pavlov, *Space in Theory: Kristeva, Foucault, Deleuze* (Amsterdam and New York: Oxymoron, 2009), 17.
3. Michel Foucault, "Of Other Spaces," *Diacritics* 16.1 (1986): 22.
4. Quoted in Don Mitchell, *Cultural Geography: A Critical Introduction* (Cambridge: Blackwell Publishers, 2000), 61.
5. Barney Warf and Santa Arias, *The Spatial Turn: Interdisciplinary Perspectives* (New York: Routledge, 2009), 1.
6. Franco Moretti, *Atlas of the European Novel, 1800–1900* (London: Verso, 1998), 3.
7. Robert T. Tally Jr., *Spatiality* (London and New York: Routledge, 2013), 17.
8. Ibid., 18. Tally refers to Leonard Goldstein, *The Social and Cultural Roots of Linear Perspective* (Minneapolis: MEP Publications, 1988).
9. Tally, *Spatiality*, 18.
10. Henri Lefebvre, *The Production of Space*, trans. Donald Nicholson-Smith (Oxford: Blackwell-Wiley, 1991), 73.
11. Immanuel Kant, *Critique of Pure Reason*, trans. W. Pluhar (Indianapolis: Hackett Publishing, 1996), 397.
12. David Harvey, *The Condition of Postmodernity* (Cambridge: Blackwell, 1990), 205.
13. Lefebvre, *The Production of Space*, 299.
14. See Andrew Thacker, *Moving through Modernity. Space and Geography in Modernism* (Manchester: Manchester University Press, 2003).
15. Lefebvre, *The Production of Space*, 301.
16. Ibid., 293.
17. Edward Soja, *Postmodern Geographies: The Reassertion of Space in Critical Social Theory* (London: Verso,1989), 18.
18. West-Pavlov, *Space in Theory*, 25.
19. Fredric Jameson, *Postmodernism, or, the Cultural Logic of Late Capitalism* (Durham: Duke University Press, 1991), 16.
20. West-Pavlov, *Space in Theory*, 22.
21. Ibid., 23.
22. Ibid.
23. Lefebvre, *The Production of Space*, 175.
24. Ibid., 299.
25. Ibid., 184.
26. Edward Soja, *Thirdspace: Journeys to Los Angeles and Other Real-and-Imagined Places* (Oxford: Blackwell, 1996), 56–57.
27. Lefebvre, *The Production of Space*, 196.
28. Thacker, *Moving through Modernity*, 24.
29. Foucault, "Of Other Spaces," 24.
30. Ibid., 25.
31. Soja, *Postmodern Geographies*, 132.
32. Ibid., 61.
33. Ibid., 62.

34. Ibid., 122.
35. West-Pavlov, *Space in Theory*, 171.
36. Gilles Deleuze and Félix Guattari, *A Thousand Plateaus: Capitalism and Schizophrenia*, trans. Brian Massumi (London: The Athlone Press, 1988), 381.
37. Ibid., 480–81.
38. Ibid., 482.
39. Ibid., 485.
40. Ibid., 493–94.
41. Gilles Deleuze and Félix Guattari, *What is Philosophy?* trans. Hugh Tomlinson and Graham Burchell (New York: Columbia University Press, 1994), 96–97.
42. Ibid., 101.
43. Ibid., 103.
44. Bertrand Westphal, *Geocriticism: Real and Fictional Spaces*, trans. Robert Tally Jr. (New York: Palgrave Macmillan, 2011), 112.
45. Ibid., 113.
46. Ibid., 122. See also Eric Prieto, "Geocriticism, Geopoetics, Geophilosophy, and Beyond," in Robert T. Tally Jr., ed., *Geocritical Explorations: Space, Place, and Mapping in Literary and Cultural Studies* (New York: Palgrave Macmillan, 2011), 13–27.
47. Westphal, *Geocriticism*, 113.
48. Yi-Fu Tuan, *Space and Place: The Perspective of Experience* (Minneapolis: University of Minnesota Press, 1977), 8.
49. Westphal, *Geocriticism*, 134.
50. Ibid., 137.
51. Ibid., 138.
52. Italo Calvino, *Hermit in Paris: Autobiographical Writings*, trans. Martin McLaughlin (New York: Random House, 2007), 167.
53. Westphal, *Geocriticism*, 155.
54. Ibid., 158.
55. Ibid., 164, 168.

2 How to Do Narratives With Maps

Cartography as a Performative Act in *Gulliver's Travels* and *Through the Looking-Glass*

Emmanuelle Peraldo and Yann Calbérac

The articulation between literary text and space has been significantly redefined thanks to two major theoretical turns. Because of the *spatial turn* that marked the humanities and social sciences from the 1980s onwards, time—inherited from the Enlightenment's ideal of progress—is not the main category of analysis any longer: space has replaced it (Soja, 1989). The spatial dimension of objects is now at the core of critical and analytical preoccupations. All fields of knowledge (and not only geography) are now invited to reconsider space, places and mapping. Literary studies reflect this paradigmatic shift as can be seen in the increased usage of spatial vocabulary in critical texts to decipher the way narratives are built. As a parallel to this epistemological revolution, the beginning of the 1980s saw a *cultural turn* which questioned the positivist approach by focusing on *culture*, i.e., circumstances which constitute the specificity of human beings. All disciplines have been suggested to take into account *representations* and *discourses*. Texts, including literary ones such as those of Swift and Carroll, have become a legitimate object for both the social sciences and geography. The spatial and cultural turns have thus caused a deep transformation of the academic landscape. Objects themselves receive more attention than disciplinary methods. Current gender, urban or cultural studies departments exemplify these changes in theoretical approach as they gather researchers coming from literature, history and anthropology, to name several examples. As encapsulated in the following quotation by Robert T. Tally Jr., "literary cartography, literary geography, and geocriticism enable productive ways of thinking about the issues of space, place, and mapping after the spatial turn in literary and cultural studies" (Tally, 2013: 3). The spatial dimension of literary narratives has become an autonomous field of research at the junction of literature and geography. That said, this field is comprised of a number of various approaches determined by the disciplinary background of those who explore it. Even if they work on the same object, literary critics and geographers differ in their methods. The former focus on the poetic dimension of space while the latter question the spatiality of narratives.

Today, the major development for literary critics tackle is the poetic dimension of space, thanks to Bertrand Westphal and his translator Robert T. Tally Jr. Wesphal, who proposed the concept of *geocriticism* to define the interdisciplinary method of literary analysis that consists in using geographical space as a tool and it is defined by Bertrand Westphal in *La Géocritique. Réel, fiction, espace:* "It is the role of geocriticism to invest (partially) and to structure (a little) the crossroads between the different arts using material reality and space and time markers so as to get an aesthetic representation of it".[1] The huge success of Westphal's theory has clouded other fruitful approaches, like Kenneth White's *geopoetics*.[2] The renewal brought by these approaches lays on several objects such as landscape (Collot, 2005), environment (*ecocritics* such as Buell) and maps (*literary cartography*, a good example of which is Robert Clark and Benjamin Pauley's *mapping writing* project). Barbara Piatti also worked extensively on literary cartography, as in *The Literary Atlas of Europe*. These renewing approaches have fulfilled Franco Moretti's radical project to diversify and renew literary approaches thanks to spatial and natural sciences, as promoted in the title of his book: *Graphs, Maps, Trees* (2005).

For geographers who have taken the cultural turn, literature is a relevant source for enhancing the way people are connected to the world. From the moment of this paradigm shift, a literary geography started to rise (Mallory and Simpson-Housley, 1987; Pocock, 1988; Noble and Dhussa, 1990; Lando, 1996) whose purpose was to decipher various objects such as travel narratives or landscapes (Tissier, 1995; Brosseau, 1996; Madœuf and Cattedra, 2012). Mapping fictional spaces has become the major issue of this movement. This interest in writing is due to a return to the etymology of the word *geography*, i.e., the writing (*graphein*) of the Earth.

Now that the background is set, we would like to present the object we are particularly interested in: maps embedded in fictional narratives. Christina Ljungberg has already demonstrated the importance of maps in revealing the interrelations between verbal and visual media in fictional texts (Ljungberg, 2012). So have Pristnall and Cooper in a previous volume of *The Cartographic Journal* (2011). Our contention is that the presence of those very maps makes us realise the incapacity of a sequential text to take into account space, which has no beginning, no ending and no chapters. That has already been made clear by Perec's disappointing "attempt at exhausting a place in Paris" (Perec, [1975] 2010) insofar as he never succeeds in totally describing the Place Saint-Sulpice. A solution could be proposed to compensate for the shortcomings of the text by completing it with a specific language which has been developed to "tell" space: cartography. After all, a map is indeed "a representation founded on a language whose characteristic is to build the analogical image of a place" (Lévy, 2003: 128).

To test this hypothesis, we have decided to analyse the embedded maps of *Gulliver's Travel* by Jonathan Swift (1726) and *Through the Looking-Glass* by Lewis Carroll (1871). First, both belong to the travel narrative genre, as their complete titles—*Lemuel Gulliver's Travels into Several Remote Nations of the World* and *Through the Looking-Glass and What Alice Found There*—reveal with words such as "travels", "remote", "through" or "there", and both depict the heroes' confrontation with a radical otherness. Secondly, those texts negotiate their relation to the real differently. *Gulliver's Travels*, as a typical eighteenth-century text, is fictional but pretends not to be, repeating its truth claims that were necessary to avoid censorship (Peraldo, 2010); whereas *Alice* is a fiction which keeps claiming its fictionality, even if both texts use elements of the fantastic and the marvellous (Todorov, 1970). Thirdly, Swift and Carroll use a process which articulates text and liminal maps. In *Gulliver*, Swift reproduces the authentic maps of the great cartographer of the time, Herman Moll, but he falsifies them by adding the imaginary islands to which Gulliver goes in the blanks of the maps (Bracher, 1944; Reinhartz, 1997). In *Alice*, instead of a map, the reader finds a chessboard that can be considered a map, according to Lawrence Gasquet, who insists on the visual and graphic quality of Carroll's writing and emphasizes the role of the visual representation as a topographical tool for representing thought. For Gasquet, the chessboard thus functions as a map in that it is part of the topographical language of Carroll's text, and because it duplicates the world on a smaller scale, which is the aim of a cartographic image (Gasquet, 2000).

Those maps can best be scrutinized thanks to cartography. Maps are made of various signs that allow a semiotic reading of them (Bertin, 1967); they constitute a specific and autonomous language. Therefore, as they are a form of language, and as performativity is a property of every language (Austin, 1962), we argue that those maps embedded in fictional narratives can be deciphered thanks to this coupling of semiotics and pragmatics. As for all maps, those which are included in novels obey semiotic rules which reflect the condition and period of their production. Hence, the *performative turn* invites us to take into account the performativity of cartographic language. If, per Austin's theory, it is now possible "to do things with words", it can then be posited that it must be possible *to do things with maps*, and to act on the diegesis and characters due to the cartographic device. To test this reading grid (semiotics/pragmatics), our methodology is informed by the cross-fertilization of the two disciplines we belong to—this paper is co-written by a specialist of British literature and a geographer specializing in the epistemology of geography. This analysis is the first stage of a collaboration that questions the spatial dimensions of literary texts according to two different academic traditions that we wish to cross-fertilize: literary critics focus on the poetic dimension of space while geographers question the spatiality of narratives.

The two kinds of maps that are to be found in Swift and Carroll tend to cloud referentiality insofar as they invite their readers to go beyond the Manichean opposition between true and false, which is constitutive of *fictions*. Even if these maps are not *topographically* exact (i.e., neither Gulliver's islands nor Alice's land exist in reality), they are *fictionally* true. They do not enable readers to actually find these locations on the Earth, but they help them find their ways in the worlds of words created by the two authors. The endeavour is to go beyond the simple referentiality of maps to study the referentiality *constructed* by maps within texts. The meanings of maps depend on the way they are practiced by either novel readers or map users. These various practices define the functions of maps and invite us to focus on their peculiar statuses and to answer this crucial question: what is a map? Our argument is that maps are parts of the novels' meaning processes that the reader has to decipher, as it is a graphic and figurative inscription which combines its specific language, a semiotics, its uses and its functions (Lévy, 2003).

The stakes of Swift and Carroll's maps appear: are these maps real maps, according to the aforementioned definition? To answer this question, it might be essential to ponder the referentiality of the maps in the narratives in which they are inserted. What do these maps describe? What functions do they have in the meaning process? This opposition between what is said and what is produced echoes the distinction identified by J.L. Austin (Austin, 1962; Mondada, 2003) between stating utterances (which describe reality) and performative utterances (which transform reality), which is mirrored in literary studies by the famous opposition between *mimesis* (imitation) and *poesis* (creation of images). To what extent is it relevant to apply Austin's performativity to Swift and Carroll's maps? Are there such things as "cartographic acts" (Shusterman, 2000) similar to Austin's "speech acts"? These questions lead us to first explore the way maps can fill in the silences of the texts in order to solve the problem of referentiality. The second part of the analysis will tackle the pragmatic and performative role of maps within the writing process. The ambition of this paper is double: for the literary critic, the aim of reading extra-narrative objects such as maps is to question the textuality and literariness of external objects—such as maps—embedded in literary texts; for the geographer, these two maps reveal the opposition between space considered as a position and space defined as an interaction.

The maps under scrutiny here question the texts in which they are inserted on two different levels. First, they raise the question of textuality by interrogating the way these two travel narratives are made by maps as well as words. Secondly, they enable readers to locate the stories they are told, and referentiality anchors them in the realistic horizon. We want to start by focusing on semiotics and the "stating" dimension of maps, i.e., their mimetic function. Even if places are fictitious, their cartographic representations aim at increasing their "referential fallacy" (Riffaterre, 1982) by playing the part of a "reality effect" (Barthes, 1982).

One of the specificities of *Gulliver's Travels* is that from the very first edition of the text, maps have systematically illustrated Swift's work. In his fourth edition of *Robinson Crusoe* (London: W. Taylor, 1719), Defoe (or his publisher) also inserted a map supposedly drawn by Woodes Rogers, and even gave the latitude of the island upon which Crusoe was stranded— a latitude which was off by two degrees, reflecting either the mistakes of maps at a time when cartography was not as accurate as today, or his own poetic license in writing a story that was partly historical, partly fictional. In order to make readers believe in the reality of the events narrated, Swift and Defoe obeyed the rules of the travel account, including for instance the use of maps. As Percy G. Adams says, "the 'récit de voyage' cannot be a literary genre with a fixed definition" (Adams, 1983: 282). Indeed, it is a polymorphous genre or mode of writing, but among the major common points of travel narratives, there is the fact that the travel narrative relies and depends on the actual travelling experience it recounts; it is a means of interrogating the relationship between the self and the world, and very often it is deployed to question the known from the observation of the unknown; and it must also be useful—its aim is both to entertain and to instruct (Magetti, 2004). And indeed, in Swift's time, being real was the imperative condition for being published. In an endeavour to meet these requirements for realism, the author borrowed his maps from Herman Moll, who was the most famous eighteenth-century English cartographer[3] and revolutionized the cartographic practices by breaking with conventions which consisted of, for example, adorning maps with monsters or marvellous creatures so as to fill in blank spaces on maps.

Bracher has analysed the history of the maps of *Gulliver's Travels*. He pointed out that these maps had been taken from Herman Moll, but had been modified so as to highlight the places to which Gulliver travelled:

He had the text of the book to give approximate locations of the mythical countries, but these could only be approximate, since swift's directions are confused and inconsistent. On each map, he tried to frame the ocean surrounding Swift's mythical land with an authentic coast line copied from Moll. For the map of Brobdingnag, following Swift's hint that the peninsula was joined to America, his authentic frame is the Californian coast.

(Bracher, 1944: 62)

The presence of these maps is owed to a publisher, and Swift accepted the idea to the point that he encouraged their publication in the successive editions of his work.

Moreover, these maps anchor the text in a geographical perspective, which is reinforced by the various semantic fields. Indeed, *Gulliver's Travels* is loaded with toponyms, geographic locations and nautical terms. For example, the first letter of the first book starts with two pages accumulating real toponyms—Nottinghamshire, Cambridge, Emanuel-College, London, Leyden, Holland (p. 5), East and West Indies, Wapping, Bristol and Van Diemen's land (p. 6)—making readers forget that Lilliput, the place name which appears on page 7, is imaginary. These toponyms are completed with their accurate geographic positions and the nautical vocabulary turns this narrative into what could be Gulliver's logbook:

> We had a very prosperous gale, till we arrived at the *Cape of Good Hope* . . . We then set sail, and had a good voyage till we passed the *Straits of Madagascar*; but having got *northward* of that island, and to about *five degrees south latitude*, the winds, which in those seas are observed to blow a constant equal gale between the *north and west* . . . during which time, we were driven a little to the *east of the Molucca Islands*, and about *three degrees northward of the line* . . .
> Finding it was likely to overblow, we took in our *sprit-sail*, and stood by to hand the *fore-sail*; but making foul weather, we looked the guns were all fast, and handed the *mizen*. The ship lay very broad off, so we thought it better spooning before the sea, than trying or *hulling*. We *reefed the fore-sail* and set him, and *hauled at the fore-sheet*; the *helm was hard a-weather*. The ship wore bravely. We *belayed the fore down-haul*; but the sail was split, and we *hauled down the yard*, and got the sail into the ship, and unbound all the things clear of it.
>
> (Swift, 1998: 71–72, our emphasis)

This abundance of minute details un-places readers more than it helps them orient themselves. Hence, it questions the generic horizon to which *Gulliver's Travels* belongs, and it echoes a literary heritage, which was reactivated by the publication of Thomas More's *Utopia* in 1516. Are the islands visited by Gulliver utopic places? If one considers the utopia as a perfect place (*eu-topia*), then Lilliput, Brobdingnag and so on can absolutely not be considered as examples of those places, insofar as they are part of a satiric intention which assimilates them to dystopia more than utopia. But this term works if one refers to the second meaning of the term utopia, a place which does not exist (*ou-topia*). The geographical enumerations and the maps have the same function: to convince the reader that this utopia is real, and all the signs concur to create that reality effect.

The use of maps anchors *Gulliver's Travels* in the advent of modernity since it organises the world by organising knowledge and *vice versa*. The chorographic process (through a regional exploration of the world, bit by bit) refers to the analytical position which was developed extensively at that time. On the one hand, maps enrich that semantic field and aim at organising these descriptions by localising them on maps. However, those maps have been tampered with and the territories they represent have no real existence. Nevertheless, the fake maps, by offering a cartographic representation, give those imaginary territories an existence. Maps thus have the same function as descriptions. On the other hand, the narrative is organised around an observer who guarantees the scientificity of the ethnographic endeavour: the comparison with what readers are familiar with—"a squale you might have heard from Londonbridge to Chelsea" (p. 79)—increases the reality effect. Swift even refers to his contemporary geographers and offers to correct their maps, which he considers misleading:

> The whole extent of this prince's dominions reaches about six thousand miles in length, and from three to five in breadth: whence I cannot but conclude, that our geographers of Europe are in a great error, by supposing nothing but sea between Japan and California; for it was ever my opinion, that there must be a balance of earth to counterpoise the great continent of Tartary; and therefore they ought to correct their maps and charts, by joining this vast tract of land to the north- west parts of America, wherein I shall be ready to lend them my assistance.
>
> (Swift, 1998: 99)

This specificity can also be found in the very first pages of *Through The Looking-Glass*, which offers a *dramatis personae* completed with a chess problem,[4] which can be considered a map according to Lawrence Gasquet:

> *Through the Looking-Glass* represents Alice's peregrinations on the chessboard; Can there be a better map than a two-coloured chessboard? It can be noticed that Carroll is careful to use it in the liminal page of his second tale, as a clear and practical visual landmark to be consulted by readers whenever they need to.
>
> (Gasquet, 2000: 100).[5]

This map is completed by the evocation of landscape that Alice describes from the top of a hill:

> [Alice and the Queen] walked on in silence till they got to the *top of the little hill*. For some minutes Alice *stood* without speaking, *looking out* in *all directions* over the *country*—and a most curious *country* it was. There were a number of tiny little *brooks* running *straight*

across it from side to side, and the ground between was *divided up into squares* by a number of little green *hedges*, that reached from brook to brook.

(Carroll, 1992: 125, our emphasis)

In this Robinson Crusoe-like inaugural act, Alice—according to a classical geographical position (Calbérac, 2010)—climbs to the top of a hill in order to appropriate by her gaze what will become her territory: her looking-from-above domination is at the same time symbolic and political, as she ends up becoming the queen of this country. As a perfect positivist geographer, she describes the brooks and the hedges (reminiscent of the debate on enclosures in the eighteenth-century Britain), which were a common feature of the British countryside as painted, for example, by Constable.

The polysemy of the word "country" invites readers to mentally turn this countryside landscape into a realm, which, metonymically speaking, becomes a whole and closed universe, similar to what Paul Claudel created by writing in the very first stage direction of Paul Claudel's *Satin Slipper* (1931): "The scene of this drama is the world". Alice goes on:

"I *declare* it's marked out just like a *large chessboard!*" Alice said at last. "There ought to be some *men moving about* somewhere—and so there are!" She added in a tone of delight, and her heart began to beat quick with excitement as she went on. "It's a great huge game of chess that's being played—all over the world—*if this IS the world* at all, you know. Oh, what fun it is! How I wish I was one of them! I wouldn't mind being a Pawn, if only I might join—though of course I should like to be a Queen, best."

(Carroll, 1992: 125, our emphasis)

The landscape she observes before walking through it does not only look like a chessboard, it really *is* one, with its pawns and squares, and it is actually present in the text in the form of the chessboard-landscape drawn by Tenniel.[6] Hence, this space is now regulated by the chess pawns' moving rules, and Alice's will appears: she wants to become a queen by reaching the last line of the chessboard. By doing this, she fulfils the dream of explorers who usually want to get to the end of the world and dominate it. As nonsensical as it may appear, the liminal chessboard is indeed an efficient map not only for readers to follow Alice's adventures, but also for Alice herself to find her way in this Looking-Glass country and to understand its rules.

The map in Carroll is not to be read on the same level as in Swift. This map is not drawn according to a scale. The liminal chessboard and the chessboard landscape that Alice describes from the top of the hill are one and the same. The map is no longer a reduced representation of reality—they are two ways of representing the same thing. However, this map helps the reader understand Alice's displacements without using the usual geographic and cartographic tools, such as orientation, topography and toponymy, as employed in *Gulliver's Travels*. This enclosed universe relying on radical alterity could belong to Michel Foucault's heterotopia, i.e., spaces of otherness, in which the example of the looking-glass is appropriated by Foucault:

> Because these places are absolutely different from all the sites that they reflect and speak about, I shall call them, by way of contrast to utopias, heterotopias. I believe that between utopias and these quite other sites, these heterotopias, there might be a sort of mixed, joint experience, which would be the mirror. The mirror is, after all, a utopia, since it is a placeless place. In the mirror, I see myself there where I am not, in an unreal, virtual space that opens up behind the surface; I am over there, there where I am not, a sort of shadow that gives my own visibility to myself, that enables me to see myself there where I am absent: such is the utopia of the mirror. But it is also a heterotopia in so far as the mirror does exist in reality, where it exerts a sort of counteraction on the position that I occupy. From the standpoint of the mirror I discover my absence from the place where I am since I see myself over there.[7]

More than a mere reality effect, the materiality of maps (Moll's fake maps and the real chessboard map) is the key to imagination. Confronted by these maps, readers are in the same posture as Alice in front of the mirror. As Alice pretends she can overcome its materiality by getting through it, readers are invited to conquer the materiality of the maps drawn on the pages in order to reach imaginary regions such as Lilliput or the Looking-Glass country. Readers need to go beyond the semiotic dimension of these maps, hence discovering the active role they play in the economy of the literary texts.

Let us now explore the imaginary dimension of maps, keeping in mind what Philippe Vasset explains at the beginning of his *Livre blanc*: "I started to be interested in maps when I understood that they had only remote connections with reality" (2007: 9).[8] The pragmatic, poetic and performative functions of these maps should be examined, as Alice invites us: "'*I declare* it's marked out just like a large chessboard!' . . . if *this IS* the world at all, you know" (Carroll, 1992: 125, our emphasis). By naming the chessboard with language, she makes it real and gives new rules to the place she evolves in: the chess rules. Our contention here is that these maps do not only produce narratives, that is, action or drama, but it is within these maps—what they either show or hide—that narratives originate and develop. As Austin wondered, "how to do things with words?", we ask: "how to do narratives with maps?" To solve this question, we have to change our way of reading these two works. As Gulliver and the explorers he stands for have attempted to fill in the blanks of maps, we are going to focus on the blanks of texts and look for answers in between the lines.

Vasset's twenty-first-century inquiry into what is hidden in the blank spaces of the map is actually a reiteration of one of the questions which underwent a crucial turn in the modern era. At that time, a gap appeared between positive knowledge and imaginary knowledge. This mixture characterized the remerging modernity, and was at the origin of the distinction between science and literature (Aït-Touati, 2011). On the one hand, this thirst to discover the world—made possible by technical progress—led to a better understanding of the world in which geography and cartography contributed to bring order. Cartographer Herman Moll was emblematic of this distinction. He refused to fill in the blanks of his maps with the usual monsters, and the *terrae incognitae* remained empty. On the other hand, imagination was being rejected from scientific discourse. According to Pasquali (1994), travel narratives made contact with alterity possible, but when it was not possible, literature was there to help. Hence, literature—thanks to its poetic function—created places whose only existence was in the author's mind. It was precisely in those blanks that Swift made up the imaginary places Gulliver described: narratives obeyed a thirst for knowledge.[9]

By using Herman Moll's maps, Swift revealed a positional function of maps that presented the precise location of Gulliver's adventures that the reader was to discover. Indeed, each book opens with a map covered with topographic and toponymic elements, but no mention is made of the action unfolding. These empty maps are to be completed by the narration which occurs just after the liminal maps. This will to fill in the gaps of the map turns them into performatively creative narratives. It is therefore not surprising, as has been shown in the previous paragraphs, that each book should start with a letter saturated with geographical terms and toponyms; Swift's ambition is to articulate maps and text. But as mentioned before, when the map orders, the narrative disorders.

Nothing like that occurs in *Through the Looking-Glass*. The map is of another nature and the mapping process is more complex. The chessboard map does not mix reality and imagination; it is pure imagination, and the map does not aim at localizing any place. That is why this map is made of a game, which is the climax of the imaginary (Caillois, 1958). Carroll's fiction unfolds in a purely imaginary place—even conceptual, as the chessboard suggests—ruled by a language that opens myriad possibilities (as numerous as the moves in a game of chess) thanks to the magical sesame, "let's pretend", that enables Alice to go through the looking-glass. It is therefore a reflection on language that readers are invited to, as Deleuze suggested by theorizing on being and becoming in his developments on Alice in *The Logic of Sense* (Deleuze, 1969). There is a perfect adequacy between the liminal chessboard and the world Alice goes through, but still the chessboard is not the mere representation of that world, even if the fields and hedges that Alice describes look like the chessboard. The latter is not so much the framework of the action as what makes it possible: the characters (the players) move according to the rules of the game and the structure of the chessboard. Conversely, once they have accepted the rules, the players can operate freely and reveal the multitude of possibilities of the moves. Space is, at the same time, what makes possible and what is made possible by the practices of the players (Lussault, 2007).

In the first editions of the text, Lewis Carroll completed this map with a highly pragmatic *dramatis personae*, i.e., literally the list of the characters of the drama. Indeed, Carroll combines that list of characters with a chess problem and the list of the moves to explain how Alice wins.[10] This process can be read as a synoptic way of unfolding the plot. The list of the moves (as numerous as the chapters of the novel) is written in the language proper to chess players, and it is strictly equivalent to the novel, which is written in a literary language. Both narrate the same *drama* in its literal meaning of *action*: both are two different languages to unfold the same plot.[11] In the liminal chessboard map, the whole action is already there, virtually contained on the chessboard and precisely detailed in the consecutive list of the moves that follows, and the novel is only a literary translation of what the reader-chess player could already have guessed. From the top of the hill, Alice was right. By deciphering in the landscape the structure of a chessboard, she revealed its deep function as a producer of narratives. Alice's adventures are written in the infinite virtualities offered by the game. The chessboard works as a performative creator of narratives.

At the end of this study of Swift and Carroll's texts, we would like to return to the hypothesis we initially formulated. The maps in those texts have a performative function: they do not just illustrate the narratives, they actually trigger them. A pragmatic focus on these maps might therefore be fruitful when added to the semiotic perspective. What can this performativity of the map add to our reading and understanding of *Gulliver's Travels* and *Through the Looking-Glass*? We believe that it enables us to take the map-as-language seriously, hence finding new tools to rethink the status of cartography within the literary text.

This analysis of Swift and Carroll from a geocritical point of view opens up new, different and challenging perspectives in both literary and cartographic studies. The differences that have been highlighted between *Gulliver's Travels* and *Through the Looking-Glass* have to deal with the cartographic language more than the literary one. Indeed, those texts which were not published at the same time convey a different relationship to space. Swift possesses a positional conception of space (the map as medium to convey action), whereas Carroll makes use of a relational conception of space, in which space is as much the producer as the product of the action.

Many authors of literary texts, especially travel narratives, insert maps to either give more realism to the text, or to illustrate the journey, or—as in Swift and Carroll—to trigger the action. Stevenson, Tolkien,[12] Melville and Defoe—to mention only a few—use embedded maps in some of their narratives. Even if it would be difficult to make a typology of these embedded maps, since we have seen that they are closely related to the narratives in which they are inserted we can conclude that those maps are rarely purely decorative, and that a study on literature cannot avoid a deep reflection on space and how it can be conceptualised.

Notes

1. See Westphal (2007: 197).
2. "Geopoetics is a transdiciplinary theory and pratice that can be appled to all the fields of life and research, and whose aim is to restore and enrich the relationship between Man and Earth, which has been cut for a long time, with all the weel-known consequences on the ecological, psychological and intellectual levels". (The original quotation reads: "La géopoétique est une théorie-pratique transdisciplinaire applicable à tous les domaines de la vie et de la recherche, qui a pour but de rétablir et d'enrichir le rapport Homme-Terre depuis longtemps rompu, avec les conséquences que l'on sait sur les plans écologique, psychologique et intellectuel". Kenneth White, *La Géopoétique*. www.kennethwhite.org/geopoetique/, 25/10/13, 16h52.).
3. Dennis Reinhartz, in *The Cartographer and the Literati* writes that "although of German origin, [Herman Moll] is Great Britain's most celebrated geographer and mapmaker of the first half of the eighteenth century. The content of Moll's geographies, atlases, maps, charts and globes is diverse and sometimes, spanning the earth and its history as they were known at the beginning of the eighteenth century" (1). Jeremy Black develops a similar point of view in "Maps and History: Constructing Images of the Past".
4. In the first editions, this chessboard map came with a *dramatis personae* in which all the characters of the novel are referred to as the pawns of a chessboard. The solution to the problem—"White Pawn (Alice) to play, and win in eleven moves" (Carroll, 1992: 104)—cannot be taken for granted, and one year before he died, Carroll got rid of this *dramatis personae* that totally disappeared from the final version, which blurs the link between the chessboard map and the plot.
5. The original quotation reads: "*Through the Looking-Glass . . .* représente le parcours d'Alice sur l'échiquier. Quelle plus belle carte que le damier bicolore d'un échiquier? On note que Carroll prend bien soin de la placer en premier page de son deuxième conte; repère visuel, clair et pratique, elle doit en effet pouvoir être consultée à tout moment par le lecteur".
6. Sir John Tenniel (1820–1914) illustrated Carroll's novel from its first publication. His black-and-white drawings contributed to make Alice's adventures famous all over the world.
7. The original quotation reads: "Ces lieux, parce qu'ils sont absolument autres que tous les emplacements qu'ils reflètent et dont ils parlent, je les appellerai, par opposition aux utopies, les hétérotopies; et je crois qu'entre les utopies et ces emplacements absolument autres, ces hétérotopies, il y

aurait sans doute une sorte d'expérience mixte, mitoyenne, qui serait le miroir. Le miroir, après tout, c'est une utopie, puisque c'est un lieu sans lieu. Dans le miroir, je me vois là où je ne suis pas, dans un espace irréel qui s'ouvre virtuellement derrière la surface, je suis là-bas, là où je ne suis pas, une sorte d'ombre qui me donne à moi-même ma propre visibilité, qui me permet de me regarder là où je suis absent—utopie du miroir. Mais c'est également une hétérotopie, dans la mesure où le miroir existe réellement, et où il a, sur la place que j'occupe, une sorte d'effet en retour; c'est à partir du miroir que je me découvre absent à la place où je suis puisque je me vois là-bas". (Foucault, 1984: 47). The English translation comes from: http:// foucault.info/documents/heteroTopia/foucault.heteroTopia.en.html(consulted on March 12th, 2013).

   8. The original quotation reads: "J'ai commencé à m'intéresser aux cartes quand j'ai compris qu'elles n'entretenaient que des rapports très éloignés avec le réel" (Vasset, 2007: 9).
   9. Today, as in the eighteenth century, the reader cannot believe in the reality Gulliver describes, but back then anchoring the narrative in "reality" was a convention and a *sine qua non* condition to be published by avoiding censorship.
   10. The difficulty of this chess problems urged Carroll to delete it in the further editions.
   11. We borrow that idea from Maurice Blanchot, according to whom the original work and its translation constitute two languages to tell the very same story (Blanchot, 1959).
   12. See Habermann and Kuhn (2011).

Bibliography

Primary sources

Carroll, L. ([1871] 1992) *Through the Looking-Glass*. A Norton Critical Edition, New York, London.

Defoe, D. (1719) *Robinson Crusoe*. W. Taylor, London.

Melville, H. ([1851] 1998) *Moby Dick*. Oxford University Press, Oxford, New York.

More, T. ([1516] 1992) *Utopia*. A Norton Critical Edition, New York, London.

Stevenson, R. L. ([1883] 2011) *Treasure Island*. Oxford University Press, Oxfrod, New York.

Swift, J. ([1726] 1998] *Gulliver's Travels*. A Norton Critical Edition, New York, London.

Tolkien, J. R. R. ([1954] 2007) *The Lord of the Rings*. Harper Collins Publishers, London.

Secondary sources

Adams, P. G. (1983) *Travel Literature and the Evolution of the Novel*. The University Press of Kentucky, Lexington.

Aït-Touati, F. (2011) *Contes de la Lune. Essai sur la fiction et la science modernes*. Gallimard, Paris.

Austin, J. (1962) *How to Do Things with Words*. Harvard University Press, Cambridge.

Barthes, R. (1982) "L'effet de réel", in *Littérature et Réalité*, edited by G. Genette and T. Todorov, pp. 81–90. Seuil, Paris.

Bertin, J. (1967) *Sémiologie graphique. Les diagrammes, les réseaux, les cartes.* Mouton, Paris.

Besse, J.-M. (2003) *Les grandeurs de la Terre. Aspects du savoir géographique à la Renaissance.* ENS Editions, Lyon.

Besse, J.-M., Blais, H. and Surun, I. (ed.) (2010) *Naissance de la géographie moderne (1760–1860). Lieux, pratiques et formation des savoirs de l'espace.* ENS Editions, Lyon.

Black, J. (1997) *Maps and History: Constructing Images of the Past.* Yale University Press, New Haven, London.

Blanchot, M. (1959) *Le livre à venir.* Gallimard, Paris.

Bracher, F. (1944) "The Maps in *Gulliver's Travels*", *Huntington Library Quarterly*, 8, 59–74.

Brosseau, M. (1996) *Des Romans-géographes.* essai. L'Harmattan, Paris.

Buell, L. (2001) *Writing for an Endangered World. Literature, Culture and Environment in the United States and Beyond.* Harvard University Press, Cambridge, London.

Buell, L. (2005) *The Future of Environmental Criticism. Environmental Crisis and Literary Imagination.* Blackwell Publishing, Oxford.

Caillois, R. (1958) *Les jeux et les hommes. Le masque et le vertige.* Gallimard, Paris.

Calbérac, Y. (2010) *Terrains de géographes, géographes de terrain. Communauté et imaginaire disciplinaires au miroir des pratiques de terrain des géographes français du XXe siècle.* Doctoral dissertation in geography. Université Lumière Lyon 2. http://tel.archives-ouvertes.fr/tel-00551481

Collot, M. (2005) *Paysage et poésie; du romantisme à nos jours.* José corti, les Essais, Paris.

Cooper, D. and Priestnall, G. (2011) "The Processual Intertextuality of Literary Cartographies: Critical and Digital Practices", *Cartographic Journal*, 48(4), 250–62.

Deleuze, G. (1969) *Logique du sens.* Les éditions de Minuit, Paris.

Doiron, N. (1995) *L'art de voyager, Le déplacement à l'époque classique.* Les Presses de l'Université Laval Klincksieck, Sainte-Foy, Paris.

Foucault, M. (1984) "Des espaces autres (conférence au Cercle d'études architecturales, 14 mars 1967)", *Architecture, mouvement, continuité*, 5, 46–49.

Gasquet, L. (2000) "'A perfect and Absolute Blank': carte blanche à Lewis Carroll", in *Cartes, paysages, territoires*, edited by R. Shusterman, pp. 97–117. Presses Universitaires de Bordeaux, Pessac.

Gomez-Géraud, M.-C. and Philippe, A. (ed.) (2001) *Roman et récit de voyage.* Presses de l'Université de Paris-Sorbonne, Paris.

Habermann, I. and Kuhn, N. (2011) "Sustainable Fictions—Geographical, Literary and Cultural Intersections in J. R. R. Tolkien's *The Lord of the Rings*", *Cartographic Journal*, 48(4), 263–73.

Lando, F. (1996) "Fact and Fiction: Geography and Literature", *GeoJournal*, 38(1), 3–18.

Lévy, J. (2003) "Carte", in *Dictionnaire de la géographie et de l'espace des sociétés*, edited by J. Lévy and Lussault M., pp. 128–32. Belin, Paris.

Ljunberg, K. (2012) *Creative Dynamics: Diagrammatic Strategies in Narrative.* John Benjamins, Amsterdam and Philadelphia.

Lussault, M. (2007) *L'homme spatial, La construction sociale de l'espace humain.* Seuil, Paris.

Madœuf, A. and Cattedra, R. (ed.) (2012) *Lire les villes, Panoramas du monde urbain contemporain.* Presses Universitaires François Rabelais, Tours.

Magetti, D. (2004) "Voyage", in *Dictionnaire du littéraire,* edited by Paul Aron, Denis St Jacques and Alain Viala. PUF, Paris.

Mallory, W. E. and Simpson-Housley, P. (eds.) (1987) *Geography and Literature: A Meeting of the Disciplines.* Syracuse University Press, Syracuse.

mappingwriting.com (the Literary Encylcopedia).

Mondada, L. (2003) "Performativité", in *Dictionnaire de la géographie et de l'espace des sociétés,* edited by J. Lévy and M. Lussault, p. 704, Belin, Paris.

Moretti, F. ([1997] 1999) *Atlas of the European Novel, 1800–1900.* Verso, London, New York.

Moretti, F. (2005) *Graphs, Maps, Trees.* Verso, London, New York.

Noble, A. G. and Dhussa, R. (1990) "Image and Substance: A Review of Literary Geography", *Journal of Cultural Geography,* 10(2), 49–65.

Pasquali, A. (1994) *Le Tour des Horizons, Critique et récits de voyages.* Klincksieck, Paris.

Peraldo, E. (2010) *Daniel Defoe et l'écriture de l'histoire.* Honoré Champion, Paris, Genève.

Perec, G. ([1975] 2010) *An Attempt at Exhausting a Place in Paris.* Wakefield Press, Cambridge.

Piatti, B. (2011) *A Literary Atlas of Europe—Analysing the Geography of Fiction with an Interactive Mapping and Visualisation System.* www.literaturatlas. eu/en/

Pocock, D. C. D. (1988) "Geography and Literature", *Progress in Human Geography,* 12(1), 87–102.

Reinhartz, D. (1997) *The Cartographer and the Literati. Herman Moll and his Intellectual Circles.* The Edwin Mellen Press, Lewiston, Queenston and Lampeter.

Riffaterre, M. (1982) "L'Illusion référentielle", in *Littérature et Réalité,* edited by G. Genette and T. Todorov, pp. 91–118. Seuil, Paris.

Shusterman, R. (ed.) (2000) *Cartes, paysages, territoires.* Presses Universitaires de Bordeaux, Pessac.

Soja, E. (1989) *Postmodern Geographies: The Reassertion of Space in Critical Social Theory.* Verso Press, London.

Tally, R. T. Jr (ed.) (2011) *Geocritical explorations. Space, Place, and Mapping in Literary and Cultural Studies.* Palgrave, Macmillan, New York.

Tally, R. T. Jr. (2013) *Spatiality.* Routledge, The Critical Idiom, London & New York.

Tissier, J.-L. (1995) "Géographie et littérature", in *Encyclopédie de la géographie,* edited by A. Bailly, R. Ferras and D. Pumain, pp. 217–37. Economica, Paris.

Todorov, T. (1970) *Introduction à la littérature fantastique.* Seuil, Paris.

Vasset, P. (2007) *Un Livre blanc.* Fayard, Paris.

Westphal, B. (2007) *La géocritique, Réel, fiction, espace*. Editions de Minuit, Paris.

White, K (1994) *Le Plateau de l'albatros. Introduction à la géopoétique*. Editions Grasset et Fasquelle, Paris.

White, K. (25 October 2013) *La Géopoétique*. www.kennethwhite.org/geopoetique, 16h52.

3   Beyond Binaries and Metaphor

The Counterhegemonic Possibilities of Place

Jessica Maucione

Theoretical debates regarding space and place, their usefulness and limits, are complicated by the too often presumed "givenness" of the terms.[1] Despite their slippage into one another—conceptually, as well as a result of inconsistent or interchangeable use of space and place—many theorists in several disciplines employ spatial or placial metaphors, even as they undertake a discussion of space and/or place. On the other hand, clear designations between space and place frequently prove overly simplistic. For some, space and place are in direct opposition—Yi-Fu Tuan writes, "Place is security, space is freedom: we are attached to the one and long for the other" (3). For others, space is an expression of place or vice versa—Michel de Certeau defines *"space* [as] *a practiced place"* (117, original emphasis). According to the latter definition, then, place is dead, static, and transforms into space when animated.

In other contexts, space and place are understood together in opposition to some other entity, typically time. In *Space, Place, and Gender*, Doreen Massey sets out to salvage place from its association with changelessness, with the mother who stays home (167). As an example, in *Space and Place,* Yi-Fu Tuan describes place or homeland "as mother" who nourishes and therefore, "place is permanent and hence reassuring to man, who sees frailty in himself and chance and flux everywhere" (154). Massey draws attention to how often the "characterization of place as home comes from those who have left" and how the homeplace gets "framed around those who . . . stayed behind," the former being (traditionally) male and the latter female, so that the mother is "assigned the role of personifying a place which did not change" (167). But she later refers to *space,* too, as lacking temporality (aligned with woman as lack) along with the conception of the spatial as devoid of politics because it is atemporal and lacking in "dislocation" (Massey 257, 251). For Massey, then, the problem with understandings of space and place lies in their association with stasis, and as such, with the feminine conceived against the masculine realm of the temporal and of politics.

In order to situate this exploration of the possibilities of place within these debates, I will codify my use of the terms. First, I not only reject a space/place binary, but find that the value of theoretical work in space and place lies in its potential to cut through still operative (however anachronistic) binaries, including male/female, first/third world, self/other, as well as time/space or place. Furthermore, it is important to resist tendencies toward telos, as in the linear trajectory or continuum that posits space as a progenitor of place or place as a moment (a placial expression of a moment) in space's past. Henri Lefebvre's "representations of space" and "abstract space" inform the concept of space as distinct from place which (more tenuously) relates to Lefebvre's "representational spaces" and "absolute space"[2] and will guide this discussion.

In *The Production of Space*, Lefebvre describes "representations of space" as "conceptualized space, the space of scientists, planners, urbanists, technocratic subdividers and social engineers" and as the intentional space of the state, therefore the "dominant space in any society" (38–39). He defines "abstract space" as political, institutional, formal, and quantitative as well, but also homogenizing, repressive, and alienating—abstract space "makes a tabula rasa of whatever threatens, of differences" (Lefebvre 285). These two descriptions are useful in determining power's use of space conceptually as distinct from place as well as spaces plural. Lefebvre's "representational space," in contrast, is "directly *lived* through its associated images and symbols," and hence the space of "inhabitants" and "users," but also of artists in that it is "dominated—and hence passively experienced—space which the imagination seeks to change and appropriate" (39, original emphasis). Lefebvre aligns "absolute space" with what is often considered place—dwelling; a site of organic bonds of consanguinity, soil, language; and yet it is "religious and political" and, ultimately, "located nowhere" because its absoluteness renders its existence symbolic (236). My own definition of place is more of a "somewhere" in relation to several "elsewheres." Place coheres according to an (imagined or real) interdependence that requires its inhabitants to live in relation (however tentatively, nevertheless practiced) to one another, to the place, and with awareness of its status as place among places. To the extent that place includes a symbolic realm, its symbols may contribute to cohesion or provide sustenance; but as soon as a place becomes wholly symbolic (and thus unlocatable, nowhere), it ceases to be place and enters into psycho-social spaces that I have no interest in either celebrating or denouncing here.

While it may be tempting to attempt to carve out a transcendent both/neither category regarding the space/place question, there is greater value in working with literary texts privileging narratives of places as sites—the narratives and the places—of contestation, as counter-narratives and alternative life-ways that carry the potential to disrupt the grand, totalizing narrative of (particularly) American nationalism (and by extension, American globalism) and as humanizing, "minor" locales that present multiple, alternative ways of being American. As such, my approach privileges place, not so much over space per se as over "abstract space" or place-/spacelessness. As my idea of place makes no claims on singularity, it does not take away from the sociopolitical possibilities of postmodern spaces, but imagines the realization of these possibilities more fully, more concretely, and in opposition to the grinding down of differences toward which space moves.

Privileging place is problematic, of course, in that it is entangled in longing and desires that may as easily play out in reactionary as in revolutionary ways. To the degree that "the encroachment of an indifferent sameness of place on a global scale" incites longing for "a diversity of places," as described by Edward S. Casey in *The Fate of Place*, it also invites various approaches—communal and commercial, progressive and reactionary—to getting at or to these places (xiii). For Casey, "this is not just a matter of nostalgia," but of desire aroused by "increasingly common experiences" (Casey xiii). For others, nostalgia and desire too often work together to perpetuate the experience of place as limit; as context or justification for inward and backward attempts at reclamation of a something lost which never existed.[3]

The latter concern ought to remain at the forefront of theories of place in order to prevent places as alternative realities as well as place-as-concept from becoming counter-productive or obsolete. Thus, I will turn to the potential problems with place as presented by contemporary theorists. In *The Condition of Postmodernity*, David Harvey recognizes a "progressive angle to postmodernism which emphasizes community and locality, place and regional resistances, social movements, respect for otherness" even as he warns that "it is hard to stop the slide into parochialism, myopia, and self-referentiality in the face of the universalizing force of capital circulation" (*Condition* 351). But he later takes a more entrenched position against place and "[p]lace-bound politics" which, he says, "appeals even though such a politics is doomed to failure" ("From" 24). Harvey contends that because sentiments regarding place "lend themselves to an interpretation and a politics that is both exclusionary and parochialist, communitarian if not intensely nationalist," that "[p]laces become the sites of incommunicable otherness" defenseless against "the crass and commercial side of postmodernism" ("From" 14). Consumer culture indeed seizes on the marketability of place, especially as space precedes (or is perceived as preceding) place, as in Irit Rogoff's notion that "power produces a space which then gets materialized as place" (22). In terms of identity politics, Liz Bondi cautions that place is in danger of reinstating the essentialism of the "Who am I?" that so often gets reduced to class, nationality, ethnicity, and gender, as "Where am I?" in which "place takes the place of essence," but "does not banish essentialism" (97–98). Her concern is that "references to 'place', 'position', 'location' and so on covertly appeal to fixed and stable essences . . . in so far as [spatial] metaphors import a Cartesian conceptualization of

space as an absolute, three-dimensional grid devoid of material content"
(Bondi 98). "Geographical metaphors of contemporary politics," she
concludes, "must be informed by conceptions of space that recognize
place, position, location and so on as *created*, as *produced*" (Bondi 99,
original emphasis). Bondi's critique, then, supports Harvey and Rogoff's
as well as echoes each in granting space as a condition that gives rise to,
or allows the production of, place.[4]

The view of space as *a priori* in relation to place as *a posteriori* lies
at the crux of what theories that privilege place, or undermine space as
such, seek to combat.[5] If space is self-evident or presupposed, place easily
becomes incidental and atemporal. Space's privilege becomes its relationship to time—as in Tuan's notion that associates space with movement,
place with pause. It follows that "[s]pace is a common symbol of freedom in the Western world," while place can elicit images of confinement
(Tuan 54). Space as given—an abstraction like "freedom"—facilitates its
use by the powerful to perpetuate structures of power that rely on such
abstractions which already lead from problems with place, to problems
with space. Mainly, I am concerned here with the particular understanding of space as "the first and the last."

While earlier societies were organized around absolute space, Lefebvre
contends that with the Roman Empire "[a]bstraction was introduced—
and presupposed—by the Father's dominion over the soil, over posses-
sions, over children, over servants and slaves, and over women" (243).
The introduction of the principle of private ownership signals a shift into
abstract space as imperial space that "dissolves and incorporates [as well
as replaces] such former 'subjects' as the village and the town" (Lefebvre 51–52). This impulse to devour, furthermore, is "backed up by a
frightening capacity for violence," a mode of aggression that he argues is
"intrinsic to abstraction" (Lefebvre 289). If this seems to imply (in opposition to the view of space as *a priori*) that place was first, and then space
came and destroyed it, Lefebvre qualifies: "what came earlier continues
to underpin what follows" and "[n]o space [i.e. place] disappears in the
course of growth and development: the worldwide does not abolish the
local" (229, 86). In other words, "[a]bstract space is not homogenous;
it simply has homogeneity as its goal, its orientation, its 'lens' . . . it renders homogenous" (287). More importantly, the contradiction within
abstract space between its multiplicity and its intended homogeneity
could lead to "differential space"—a potential site for resistance, social
transformation, and revolution (Lefebvre 52).[6]

Lefebvre's "abstract space" describes the political realization of Neil
Smith and Cindi Katz's "absolute space"—"a conception of space as a field,
container, a co-ordinate system of discrete and mutually exclusive locations—the space that is broadly taken for granted in Western societies—
our naively assumed sense of space as emptiness" (75). They hold that
it is precisely "that thoroughly naturalized absolute conception of space

that grew up with capitalism" that "expresses a very specific tyranny of power" (Smith and Katz 76). It is as if, then, Lefebvre's abstract space of empire has undergone a naturalization process that allows it to claim an absoluteness and thus become the absolute space that Smith and Katz relate to late capitalism/neo-imperialism. Elsewhere, Smith's work parallels Lefebvre's more closely. In *Uneven Development*, Smith writes of the "abstraction of space from matter" in terms of a break from earlier ways of being and the Western concept of space as a "product of continual abstraction" (69, 72). According to Lefebvre, Smith, and Katz, then, capitalist or imperial space works to sever individuals and communities from the more tangible, grounding features of habitation.

This in turn indicates space's volatile relationship with time, as well as place. In Lefebvre's absolute space, "time was not separated from space; rather it oriented space" in that rituals performed in absolute space punctuated time (267).[7] But he appears to describe this orientation as a characteristic of a lost civilization. It follows that when place is not time stopped or a temporary product of space in contemporary thought, it is often conceived of as an entity in an earlier stage in the process of becoming space. The latter is the capitalist version of space and serves multinational capitalist/neo-imperialist aims. American neo-imperialism acquires a rhetorical naturalization by way of inevitability—suggested by the terms pre-capitalist and capitalist—of capitalism's (often collapsed rhetorically with "democracy's") spread. This move assigns a telos to place with its absorption into space as its teleological end. But, as Smith points out in *American Imperialism*, clearly "there is nothing inevitable about the global geographies that accompanied and facilitated U.S. hegemony" (24). Abstract space draws postcolonial emergent nations into its system of power without sacrificing its rhetorical promotion of the very "freedom" implied in the term postcolonialism. Smith reports, for example, that Roosevelt "saw no contradiction between . . . declarations of sovereignty and self-government on the one side and a paternalistic appeal that the 'minor children among the peoples of the world' be placed under the 'trusteeship' of the 'adult nations' on the other" (*American* 351). Roosevelt's view thus characterizes American power as inevitable (perhaps burdensome) and presents an adult-child relationship between the "first" and "third" world that corresponds to (neo-imperialist) space's relationship with place.

As per usual, this imperial paradigm embraced by the "first world" serves political ends as well as plays into global consumer culture. Amy Kaplan argues in *The Anarchy of Empire* that "underlying the dream of imperial expansion is the nightmare of its own success, a nightmare in which movement outward into the world threatens to incorporate the foreign and dismantle the domestic sphere of the nation" (12). Thus, the "foreign" "third" world's relegation to childhood in relation to the paternal "first" world keeps difference and its threats at bay. In that "modernism always posits a progressive development that erases the past" (Kaplan, C. 59), this paternal rhetoric transports the linearity associated with modernism into the postmodern era. The commercialization of place that grows out of this, then, involves the marketing of pastness integrated with place. In *Questions of Travel*, Caren Kaplan explains that "[t]he 'vanishing' native, the 'lost' ideal culture, the end of 'pristine' experiences: all these tropes of the modern era reflect the conviction that modernity destroys or cannot salvage the traditional or nonmodern aspects of the past;" so that only "[o]nce the destabilizing or resisting elements of culture are fixed as 'vanishing,' 'endangered,' and local' [may they] be visited" (59). Thus (primarily European and American) tourism. This converts the sense of timelessness as a "quality of distant places" that feeds the "belief that exotic peoples have no history" (Tuan 122), into an interpretation of place as an expression of a former historical moment—an arrangement that allows movement in space to become equal to movement in time.

In a macrocosmic version of the scenario in which the homeplace becomes associated with the past or stasis, the tourist industry works with multinational corporations to provide an experience of backward time travel afforded by place. Lefebvre contends that

> neo-capitalism and neo-imperialism share hegemony over a subordinated space split into two kinds of regions: regions exploited for the purpose of and by means of *production* (of consumer goods), and regions exploited for the purpose of and by means of the *consumption of space.*
>
> (353)

One of the most obvious examples of this (and one that relates to current trends in literary studies to map out transatlantic and global contexts) is Western tourism in the Mediterranean. While the "transformation of the Mediterranean into a leisure-oriented space for industrialized Europe" (58) enshrines "both the illusion of transparency and the illusion of naturalness," the "seemingly nonproductive" places of the region are yet "centralized, organized, hierarchized, symbolized and programmed" by and in service of the multinational tour-operators (Lefebvre 58–59). Under the current neo-capitalist/-imperialist regime, then, the arbiters of space manipulate place by commercializing it and then attempting to hide that commercialization.[8] This involves a continuation, however implicit, of the rhetoric of racial inequality as well. Put another way, this is the contemporary answer to Antonio Gramsci's *Southern Question* that recognizes in the logic of nineteenth-century industrial capitalism the belief that "Southerners are biologically inferior beings, either semi-barbarians or out and out barbarians by natural destiny" so that "if the South is underdeveloped it is not the fault of the capitalist system, or any other historical cause, but of the nature that has made Southerners lazy, incapable," and so on (20). Thus, the Mediterranean as Europe's (and by extension America's) past becomes holiday spot as past-time in a way that echoes Roosevelt's infantilization of the "third world."

The question of whether it is possible to rescue place from the trap of neo-capitalist, neo-colonial, neo-imperial commercialization is perhaps the most important of the inquiries into the use or value of place in contemporary theory. Theoretical works built upon place ultimately rest upon the conviction that specific places somehow escape or survive the fragmenting effects of industrialization and global capitalism "intact— and not merely in the folkloric sense, not as relics, not as stage management for tourists, not as consumption of the cultural past, but indeed as immediate practical 'reality'" (Lefebvre 123). This further gives rise to a question of scale. It does not benefit my argument in favor of place to impose size guidelines. Place, typically associated with "the village" (which *is* still in existence), may occur at urban or global levels as well. Fredric Jameson argues that

> [d]isalienation in the traditional city . . . involves the practical reconquest of a sense of place and the construction or reconstruction of an articulated ensemble which can be retained in memory and which the individual subject can map and remap along the moments of mobile, alternative trajectories.
>
> (51)

Beyond the city, environmentalists posit place as a way of thinking. They ask us to inhabit the Earth not as empty or endless space, but as place, and therefore with cognizance of the vulnerabilities and responsibilities place implies. Likewise, Massey advocates "a global sense of the local" as a way to break out of the more confining aspects of place (155). Conceiving of place on these variant scales helps prevent theories on place from being locked into nostalgia for irretrievable or unreachable ways of being. Regarding the contemporary era, Jameson concludes that "[t]he political form of postmodernism, if there ever is any, will have as its vocation the invention and projection of a global cognitive mapping, on a social as well as a spatial scale" (54). While I am wary of some of the language employed in parts of Jameson's *Postmodernism* (allusions to conquest, cartography, etc.), it does propose a politics that begins to overcome the dichotomy of space/place even as it recognizes the importance of both. Furthermore, this local-global conception signifies heterogeneity, if only through the impossibility/impracticability of homogeneity.

The survival of place depends at least as much on practices committed to inclusion as to exclusion. While the community belonging to a place may need to exclude permanent marks or representatives of the structures that threaten its existence, it is maintained according to a certain flexibility that permits incorporation of "others" or otherness into the fabric of the place. Indigenous tribes in the U.S. were traditionally porous in this way—membership was based on participation in cultural practices and incorporation into the community by outsiders was always a possibility. The current exclusionary measurement of blood quantum to determine membership is a colonial mechanism, bent on destruction of these communities. While I have drawn upon Lefebvre's notion that abstract space has homogeneity as its goal, place is only useful and sustainable as long as it does not share this objective—which at the level of place, may lead to a politics of ethnic or racial purity, among other exclusionary practices. In addition to the obvious political problems with the latter, it is also dysfunctional as a practice—as Toni Morrison's historical novel *Paradise* shows in terms of a mid-twentieth-century all-black community in Oklahoma. Place, and the community that it makes possible, remains politically viable only in so far as race, ethnicity, gender, sexuality, religion, and all "marks" of otherness are not subjected to erasure nor to a begrudging or selective homogeneity, but incorporated into the heterogeneity that place, in its sustainable form, *is*.

My own theoretical move away from the "imagined community" that is the nation as well as the imagined hospitality of places that have been designated holiday escapes from a contemporary moment or space (in terms of present/past, developed/underdeveloped, adult/child, and other power-based and power-serving binaries) leads me to endorse a different kind of hospitality. Place coheres according to the permeability of its boundaries. As such, place in its best possible form recognizes what Jacques Derrida deems a "duty to hospitality." In *On Cosmopolitanism and Forgiveness*, Derrida puts forward a new "cosmopolitics" that would transform urban locations into "cities of refuge" dedicated to offering the "right to asylum" to all displaced peoples (Derrida 16). Although this sounds utopian, *On Cosmopolitanism* does not claim to posit an ideal, ungraspable cultural reality; rather, "one cannot speak of cultivating an ethic of hospitality. Hospitality is culture itself" and "ethics is hospitality," according to Derrida (16–17). This notion extends the concept of interdependence I have associated with place. Being a member of a local community or belonging to a place, in Derrida's sense, depends on the community's commitment to incorporating arrivals—offering place to the displaced. Social responsibility of this kind can be abused or become abusive, but it also speaks to the possibility of place to serve as a site of humility and reciprocity. In the same way that fear of the other can translate into fear of being/becoming the other,[9] so the displaced come to represent the possibility of all people's displacement. A shared cognizance of this particular vulnerability may lead to the conception, perhaps actualization, of place as a site of multiple and fragmentary subjectivities in functional relations with one another and their surroundings.

This conception of place allows for movement, but does not celebrate "mobility" as innately good. It is important to first recognize the ways that place can become confinement. Feminist discourses address this issue in terms of the cultural conceit of the vulnerability of the female body that renders staying in one's "proper" place synonymous with safety. Gillian Rose writes that "[s]pace [the 'empty' street, for example] almost becomes like an enemy itself" (Rose 143). But place in this scenario is no less an enemy.

Rose points to "a desire to make ourselves absent from space" that can lead women to "participate in our own erasure" (143). The experience of being erased as such is akin to being "placed"—again, in terms of a propriety engendered by patriarchal and hegemonic systems.

Mobility—the experience of being unplaced—warrants critique as well. Mobility, in its often revered form, is class privilege. The two kinds of gated communities that arose in America after the Second World War—those designed to keep people in (another example of place as confinement), and those designed to keep the same (undesirables) out— lend physical form to this concept. Who and what moves as a result of mobility afforded by late capitalism's shrinking world? Two of Don DeLillo's novels answer this question on both counts: the who is the neo-cosmopolitan, white, male, heterosexual, multinational corporate officers of *The Names* (1982); and the what is capital, as that which is moved by a relatively stationary, multinational corporate officer in *Cosmopolis* (2003). At the macrocosmic level, then, mobility awards a form of freedom that defies freedom to others—that restrains the movement of the disenfranchised and expands the domain of those in power.

But in addition to this sociopolitical understanding of mobility, there is also the psychosocial form that warrants much attention from postmodernists. The urge or freedom to remake oneself is often expressed in movement across and through different spaces (which are also constantly being "remade" according to similar desires). Postmodernism/ity extends the *Bildungsroman*'s requirement that its protagonist leave home in order to find himself and to require or impose seemingly constant motion in order to come to terms with a fragmented and/or multiple subjectivity.[10] Paul Auster's *City of Glass* exemplifies this approach to navigating the postmodern condition. The protagonist's primary activity is walking the streets of New York. He stays in motion and in solitude not to know himself, but to lose himself; not to experience New York, but to experience placelessness (the city as nowhere). This is the expression of the protagonist's (ultimately if not futile, then contradictory) attempt to escape, or perhaps just bear, a tragic past. But the reversal of the *Bildungsroman*— the proposition of a connection between staying home and personal growth—offers another approach to negotiating postmodern conditions. In contrast to the traditional *Bildungsroman* (as well as women's narratives of confinement in relation to familial or ethnic enclaves), for example, Tina DeRosa's *Paper Fish*—a 1980 novel that resurrects Chicago's Little Italy of the 1940s and '50s—presents a protagonist whose self-discovery hinges upon her ability to define herself *within* her family and community. DeRosa's novel speaks to the inaccuracy of reducing place to confinement and mobility to freedom by describing an experience of place that exposes the limits of the American constructs of individualism and self-containment. It recognizes the harm that may arise out of the local community's impulse for self-preservation and its tenuous hold on an inside/outside binary; but the more insidious violence comes from outside—the flattening forces of the state in the form of urban renewal. The fact that experiences of place that achieve some level of interdependent collectivity pose a potential threat to state power hints at the possibility that staying in a place, or maintaining a dynamic relationship to a place, might be counter-hegemonic. The idea, furthermore, that care of the self is inextricable from some form of loyalty to others and to shared surroundings is, arguably, the foundation of all revolutionary ideas and actions. Although "staying put" may in some cases serve a hierarchical structure or agenda, there are instances in which staying can signal nonconformity to, or a rejection of, individualism and other constituents of the politics of domination and exploitation.

American nationalism and internationalism alike, therefore, rest upon a "placelessness" that provides an endless frontier-space. In Smith's words, the "emptiness of the continent was the 'crucial founding fiction'" while "internationalism was the fruition of American nationalism, a global manifest destiny underpinned by growing economic dominance" (*American* 9, 455). Imperialism impinges on the discreteness of places, in one way, by folding them into its abstract space. Massey denies that homogenization is a characteristic of globalization in that "[t]he spanning of the globe by economic relations has led to new forms and patterns of inequality" (160); however, these inequalities are increasingly measured with the same instruments and conditioned under the same rubric (i.e., exchange value trumps use value on a global scale). Furthermore, neo-imperialism's economy-based (rather than directly land-based) extension of influence goes beyond a denial of place and arrives at a denial of space, too. According to Smith, "the 'universalizing tendency of capital' represents an inherent drive toward spacelessness, in other words toward an equalization of conditions and levels of production" (*Uneven* 94). The supposedly spaceless manifestation of the global market thus compels a form of "cooperation" that proves more menacing even than the proliferation of McDonald's around the world. In that the "contention of a spaceless globalization" takes for granted the obsolescence of space and place, it also "occlude[s] alternative political futures" and "depoliticize[s] history, albeit the history of the present and near future" (*American* 23). It is useful, then, to combat America's neo-imperial "antispatial imagination" not only with attention to places, but also spaces (*American* 15).

Just as it is necessary to conceive of place among or beside other places (rather than reduce place to a singular or former entity within space), considering spaces as multiple and multiform can lead to constructive insights into social and cultural realities. Theories that privilege space(s) in terms of multiplicity rather than abstraction work with rather than against theories about place that recognize place's heterogeneity. As feminism and postcolonialism insist on multi-subjectivity, "so does the critical process of geographical spatialization insist on the multi-inhabitation of spaces through bodies, social relations and psychic dynamics" (Rogoff 23). Rogoff's "multi-inhabitation" implies that place is integral to the liberating potentialities of spatial conceptions and practices. Edward Soja and Barbara Hooper instead combine place with an interstitial, alternative space that recalls Homi Bhabha's " 'in-between' space" in which "[t]he past-present becomes part of the necessity, not the nostalgia, of living" (7). For Soja and Hooper, "the distinctions between real and imaginary spaces and places, between spatial metaphors and materialized geographies, dissolve emphatically into what might be described as a 'thirdspace' of political choice" (192). The dissolution proposed by "thirdspace" serves psychological, perhaps psychosocial, and certainly metaphorical constructions of locatedness, as in bell hooks' naming "the margin" the " 'space of resistance' " (qtd. in Soja and Hooper 200). The juxtaposition, on the other hand, of spaces and places provides a mode of grounding theoretical work in the sociopolitical realm.

Rhetorical constructions of place prove nearly as important as practical ones. As Michael Keith and Steve Pile argue, "new radical geographies must demystify the manner in which oppressions are naturalized through concepts of space and spatialities and recover progressive articulations of place and the politics of identity" (225). Recovery in this sense refers to the need for a rhetorical, rather than physical, return—based again on the (admittedly tenuous) premise that place, in some form, exists. I contend not only that places endure, but also that theory and art on place potentially offer the most viable imaginaries of collective political action from the margins. To responsibly inhabit place and recognize in place-based relations the liberating, transformational possibilities of collaborative ways of being is to conduct an initial step toward becoming receptive to and potentially addressing deeply held human desires for belonging and place.

Notes

1. Neil Smith and Cindi Katz problematize this concept in terms of over- or misuse of spatial metaphor: "the apparent familiarity of space, the givenness of space, its fixity and inertness . . . make a spatial grammar . . . fertile for metaphoric appropriation" (69).
2. I have left out Lefebvre's "spatial practice" despite its everydayness that appeals to my sense of place because it sort of reverses my conceptions of

place and spaces in that it assumes "the most extreme separation between the places it links together" in such a way that necessitates some cohesiveness, but does not really allow for the kind of coherence—or attempt at coherence—that, for my argument, belongs to place.

3. Anthony Vidler calls this the "paradox of all nostalgia, that consciousness that, despite a yearning for a concrete place and time, the object of desire is neither here nor there, present or absent, now or then" (66).

4. Although this critique is concerned more with applications of place (or space) through metaphor as determinant of identity than with place itself, it belongs in this discussion because of its concern with the usefulness or not of place in theoretical work.

5. A semi-reversal of this notion that aligns space with present and future and place with past (to be discussed in further detail later) is equally problematic; and, rather than opposed to the view of space as a priori, it too lends itself to a reductive conception of place as incidental to space.

6. Lefebvre's "differential space" corresponds to Gillian Rose's feminist "paradoxical space" which, she contends, is necessary "in order to articulate a troubled relation to the hegemonic discourses of masculinism" (159).

7. This almost sounds like a "primitive," slowed-down version of Harvey's postmodern conception of "time-space compression" that "revolutionize[s] the objective qualities of space and time" (*Condition* 240). But instead of "annihilating time," Lefebvre's absolute space is a context in which time is incorporated into lived experience.

8. Lefebvre notes further that "no sooner does the Mediterranean coast become a space offering leisure activities to industrial Europe than industry arrives there" (353). "But," he continues, "nostalgia for towns dedicated to leisure . . . continue to haunt the urbanite of the super-industrialized regions. Thus the contradictions become more acute—and the urbanites continue to clamor for a certain 'quality of space' " (Lefebvre 353).

9. As Julia Kristeva points out in *Strangers to Ourselves*, "[l]iving with the other, with the foreigner, confronts us with the possibility or not of *being an other*" (13, original emphasis).

10. The gender-exclusive pronoun is purposeful here.

Works Cited

Bhabha, Homi. *The Locations of Culture*. New York: Routledge, 1994.

Bondi, Liz. "Locating Identity Politics." *Place and the Politics of Identity*. Eds. Michael Keith and Steve Pile. London and New York: Routledge, 1993.

Casey, Edward S. *The Fate of Place: A Philosophical History*. Berkeley: U of California P, 1997.

DeCerteau, Michel. *The Practice of Everyday Life*. Berkeley and Los Angeles: U of California P, 1984.

Derrida, Jacques. *On Cosmopolitanism and Forgiveness*. Trans. Mark Dooley and Michael Hughes. London and New York: Routledge, 2001.

Gramsci, Antonio. *The Southern Question*. Trans. and Intro. Pasquale Verdicchio. West Lafayette, IN: Bordighera Inc., 1995.

Harvey, David. "From Space to Place and Back Again: Reflections on the Condition of Postmodernity." *Mapping the Futures: Local Cultures, Global Change*. Eds. Jon Bird, et al. London and New York: Routledge, 1993.

Jameson, Fredric. *Postmodernism, or the Cultural Logic of Late Capitalism.* Durham: Duke UP, 1991.

Kaplan, Amy. *The Anarchy of Empire in the Making of U.S. Culture.* Cambridge: Harvard UP, 2002.

Kaplan, Caren. *Questions of Travel: Postmodern Discourses of Displacement.* Durham and London: Duke UP, 1996.

Keith, Michael and Steve Pile. "Towards New Radical Geographies." *Place and the Politics of Identity.* Eds Michael Keith and Steve Pile. London and New York: Routledge, 1993.

Kristeva, Julia. *Strangers to Ourselves.* Trans. Leon S. Roudiez. New York: Columbia UP, 1991.

Lefebvre, Henri. *The Production of Space.* Trans. Donald Nicholson-Smith. Oxford: Blackwell Publishers, 1974.

Massey, Doreen. *Space, Place, and Gender.* Minneapolis: U of Minnesota P, 1994.

Rogoff, Irit. *Terra Infirma: Geography's Visual Culture.* London and New York: Routledge, 2000.

Rose, Gillian. *Feminism and Geography: The Limits of Geographical Knowledge.* Minneapolis: U of Minnesota P, 1993.

Smith, Neil. *Uneven Development: Nature, Capital and the Production of Space.* New York: Basil Blackwell, Inc., 1984.

———. *American Empire: Roosevelt's Geographer and the Prelude to Globalization.* Berkeley: U of California P, 2003.

Smith, Neil and Cindi Katz. "Grounding Metaphor: Toward a Spatialized Politics." *Place and the Politics of Identity.* Eds. Michael Keith and Steve Pile. London and New York: Routledge, 1993.

Soja, Edward and Barbara Hooper. "The Spaces that Difference Makes: Some Notes on the Geographical Margins of the New Cultural Politics." *Place and the Politics of Identity.* Eds. Michael Keith and Steve Pile. London and New York: Routledge, 1993.

Tuan, Yi-Fu. *Space and Place: The Perspective of Experience.* Minneapolis: U of Minnesota P, 1977.

Vidler, Anthony. *The Architectural Uncanny: Essays in the Modern Unhomely.* Cambridge: The MIT Press, 1992.

Part II
Geographies of the Text

4 Mallarmé, Poet of the Earthly World

On Spatiality in *L'Après-midi d'un Faune*

Rogério de Melo Franco

To observe how a notable self-declared detractor of description and realism describes nature may sound like a rather arbitrary or irreverent way of reading. Nonetheless, besides being a body of texts, Mallarmé is also the result of his interpreters; as much as any other literary authority, readings of his works have been negotiated by different groups, which must not be seen as untouchable or unmovable entities. Enthroning the author by accepting his considerations about his work without question and reasoning might deserve objections as well. In any case, would it be worthwhile to hold an investigation about a poem by Mallarmé whose foundations imply the consideration of landscape description as its expressive backbone? That is the tentative question this essay is committed to.

The poetry of Mallarmé has a history of reception that has frequently focused upon rather centripetal[1] approaches to his oeuvre. In other words, a particular kind of criticism regarding this French poet has given rise to what could be called a purifying tendency toward the understanding of his use of artistic discourse. This productive, traditional perspective concerning Mallarmé had an undeniable influence on intellectual and literary thought throughout the twentieth century. For instance, German theorist Hugo Friedrich, in his famous work *The Structure of Modern Poetry*, has condensed a number of principles which shaped (and still shapes) the most widespread regimen of reading regarding Mallarmé's work. If I were to restrain myself to some of the most influential critical landmarks, I would add that Michael Hamburger's *The Truth of Poetry*, to some extent, follows Friedrich's path in consideration of Mallarmé's writing, much like many other representatives of that distinctive interpretive community.[2]

While the aforementioned way of reading is as legitimate as it is highly persuasive, I will conduct a reflection upon Mallarmé's poem *L'Après-midi d'un Faune* in a more open fashion. As mentioned before, this essay aims to examine the centrality of landscape as a literary means within this piece of poetry, insofar as the author resorts to a particular use of spatial description. That piece of poetry is especially resourceful regarding the relationship between narration and description and has, hence, an unusual place in Mallarméan body of work. Although numerous theoretical understandings of description have been formulated, the perspective assumed in this essay connects descriptive features preferably with visual aspects of reality (or imagination) and the linguistic expedients concerned with writing them down/up (*de-scribere*, to transcribe). Description would be a mode of being of writing, as it brings a verbal utopia where language is celebrated in its strength as nomenclature (Hamon, 1993: 6). The question of nomenclature reminds us how the poet famously advocated in favor of suggestive writing in preference of direct naming; in my estimation, this general disposition against naming is precisely what makes Mallarmé's descriptive procedures worthy of inquiry.

Following the Tournon's crisis,[3] the poet moved to Southern France for a couple of years, and his contact with the Mediterranean had a quite considerable impact on his overall motivation, which is well documented through the letters sent by him during that period. Inasmuch as *The Faun* is fictionally set in Sicily, Mallarmé has chosen an exemplary Mediterranean island as a *locus* for this solar poem, considered by his close friends to be one of his finest.[4] The existence of this biographical detail should not be perceived as a psychological explanation of the poet's creative mind or any type of quality warranty for his poem. It is not because Mallarmé moved to the south that his piece has aesthetic values. My reading does not rely on that contingency, even though it may have its contextual interest when approaching to the poem.

L'Après-midi d'un Faune belongs to the *églogue* genre, according to its author.[5] The Romans derived their fundamental precepts for eclogues from Virgil's *Book of Bucolics*, whose pieces were called *eclogae*. It is not by chance that a Sicilian Greek, Theocritus, is recognized as the founder of bucolic poetry. That being said, it would certainly be a mistake to observe Mallarmé's poem in the light of ancient precepts; however, it would be equally unsuitable to erase the bucolic undertones of his poetic elaboration. *The Afternoon of a Faun* lyrically mobilizes a reimagined Sicilian wilderness intertwined with a dense, restricted narrative.

Mallarmé *Terre à Terre*

Prudence is advisable when it comes to read Mallarmé, especially when addressing the issues of representation. Some authoritative commentators have stressed the idea of an obscure literary art, articulated with the poet's uncommon approach to fiction and language. The (quasi-) absence of outward attention, or centrifugal disposition, is a perspective supported by Mallarmé in a substantial number of his own critical texts. Moreover, Mallarmé's vocabulary and style is an affluent source for recent compelling intellectual enterprises;[6] this fact grounds a distinctive body of readers who see Mallarméan production primarily as writing turned toward itself and a celebration of inaccessibility to the outside of the text (*hors-texte*).[7]

Apparently, Mallarmé has contrived his theory of fiction, pertinent in this context, under the impact of Cartesian thinking.[8] The hypothetical procedure conducted by the philosopher of the *Discourse on the Method* might have been a source to a sort of desertion sentiment when it comes to Mallarmé's representation of reality. Descartes imagines a depleted existence[9] whose last necessary foundation would be the *cogito*; one could suggest that Mallarmé's suspicion regarding representation adopts a similarly abstractive attitude. In any case, this fundamental approach should be understood, above all, as a sensibility of thought: It naturally does not mean, in any respect, that Mallarmé's poetry doesn't describe or narrate anything through the descriptive or narrative aspects it is endowed with.[10]

This last reflection is not a gratuitous digression; it emphasizes the defense of a *reasoned* reception of the poet's own critical discourse and an effort to broaden the understanding of representation in his oeuvre. It is worth noting the fact that, according to etymology, "to suggest" (a very Mallarméan verb) is indeed a way of generating something (*sub-genere*).[11] In this regard, I would readily state that, by means of representation, the author of *The Faun* is a creator of spaces.

As a general rule, a verbal material selection concerning representation is bound to be thought of as the avoidance of every other paradigmatic possibility; what does it mean, then, to represent a specific countryside in detriment of others? Furthermore, what does it mean, in this particular piece of poetry, to represent the aforesaid natural environment in a particular manner, as though the poem stood against the grain of description? In this vein, Jacques Rancière's perspective on the poet of the constellations is a source related to a movement that brings the reading of Mallarmé back to social landscapes. If it is true that his poetry is also a sort of politics, a peculiar assessment of distribution of the sensible is crucial to Mallarmé's oeuvre, if I were to adhere to Rancière's lexicon. Hence, inasmuch as the poet produces the space represented within his piece of literary art, his poetic suggestion (or sub-generation) of landscape is a power grab, so to speak, by a particular sensibility concerning Sicily and the cultural tradition related to it. In fact, I hold that Sicily and mythology blend one with another by means of landscape description, which concerns the culture-nature relationship forged by an inhabitants-habitat link.

A number of Mallarméan quotations have attained extensive publicity. Their sources are diverse. Parts of them came to be known through witnesses, or were originally extracted from letters and writings. At any rate, without enough care, those axioms would pass for the "symbolist" version of an *Ars Poetica*. In this regard, had the poet conducted the elaboration of such a prescriptive, lengthy endeavor, in the manner of Horace or Boileau, Mallarmé's alleged difficulty would be probably less shocking. Indeed, some would maintain, his self-imposed task as a poet had little to do with the easy exposition of his artistic intentions—and these, in fact, seemed to be astronomically ambitious.[12]

Among the most known Mallarméan *dicta* (1956: 869) are the following formulas: "To name an object is to suppress three quarters of the poem's pleasure, which comes from guessing little by little: To suggest, that's the dream";[13] "To paint, not the thing, but the effect it produces";[14] and "It's not with ideas that one composes verses . . . It's with words."[15] The ideas that sustain these mottos are modern pills of wisdom, according to some artistic tendencies that frequented the last centuries, such as the focus on the subjective effect and the avoidance of straightforward representation. For a long time now the crystal clear mimesis of nature has been the victim of suspicion, to say the least. Amid the fog of numerous narrations of this process, Monika Schmitz-Emans formulates it in an interesting way in a chapter regarding the relationship between landscape and literature, while mobilizing a quotation from the philosopher Hans Blumenberg:

> Art in the modern era is largely marked by the "surpassing, disempowerment, and deformation [Entstaltung] of nature, a deep dissatisfaction with the given" (Blumenberg, 1957: 56), and it is for that very reason an exemplary expression of the relationship of modern man to the given reality. The works of art demand originality. Nature as the former basis of the work's instance is replaced by other instances.[16]

It is debatable whether we are still in an era presided by originality, but *The Afternoon of a Faun* fits this state of things as a classic example. So, a central question must be, with regard to Mallarmé, the reason why nature and landscape should hold a privileged placed in the question of literary representation. Nature is utterly present in the poem's lexical stock, but it is used in a way that defies traditional mimetic patterns.[17] Henri Meschonnic has mentioned the issue of description in Mallarméan *corpus*.[18] However, I would define its role, objecting to the great critic in this matter, as a linguistic strategy frequently correlated with—and not necessarily opposed to—the avoidance of naming.

For the sake of theoretical cohesion concerning the present inquiry, I have to advocate for the flexibility of description, a feature deeply involved with the nature of language regarding verbal representation of visual features. On a book about representation, Louis Marin quotes Blaise Pascal, who points out this descriptive property, which I'd loosely call elasticity, in a paragraph of his *Pensées*: "A city, a countryside, from a distance, are a city and a countryside, but whenever one gets nearer, they are houses, trees, roof tiles, leaves, grass, ants, ant legs, *ad infinitum*. Everything is wrapped by the noun *countryside*."[19]

In this passage, Pascal is probably concerned with other branches of knowledge, such as anatomy, theology, and the nature of sciences; however, his linguistic consideration may provide assistance to our reflection: How is Mallarméan "suggestion" associated to descriptive flexibility of the countryside, for instance? That's what I will try to pursue in the case of *The Afternoon of a Faun*.

The properly descriptive play of so-called "denomination" and "expansion" has been well investigated by structuralism specialists such as Michael Riffaterre.[20] This play embodies the faun's dissemination of descriptive features from end to end, which include a little bough (*"rameau subtil"*) and the whole island's coastline (*"ô bords siciliens !"*). There's indeed a conflict taking place in Mallarméan descriptions, which a commentator identified as a tension between a "temptation of the detail" and a "temptation of the whole [*ensemble*]."[21] So to speak, word-wise, the description is derived in order to cover both minimal and huge visual features of the insular countryside. The issue of a necessary linearity of verbal signs has been extensively revised since Lessing.[22] There is no natural order for the description of a literary landscape, except the submission of the eye to the reading and its temporal regimen—even if literature, of all things, is frequently an effort to subvert temporal (and spatial) regimens, as in Proust or concrete poetry. Mallarmé employs this submission to temporal regimen so that it composes lively descriptions which are interlaid with a very unusual narration whose foundations may rest upon a conception of nature, divinity, and religion.

As a matter of fact, Mallarmé's work *Les Dieux antiques* (*The Ancient Gods*) is a partial translation of a book by George William Cox, a follower of Max Müller's comparative religion. According to Bertrand Marchal,[23] the idea of a "tragedy of nature" (*"tragédie de la nature"*) is not an expression among others to be found in Mallarmé's translation, but also the symbol of a major tendency expressed by intellectual celebrities from French nineteenth-century *milieu*. One of them is Edgar Quinet, who held (via German philology, mainly Creuzer) that mythology would be a kind of a byproduct of a much simpler cult of stars, elements, and first principles of nature—an archaic fusion of nature and divinity.

Mallarmé's *Les Dieux antiques* cites the solar drama of daily sunrise and sunset as a sample of the tragedy of nature. I have the opinion that it may be productive to look at *L'Après-midi d'un Faune* in this particular light: in this perspective, the horizon of the tragic flaw of nature [24] would be established since the very first verses, as soon as the faun mentions "the ideal error of roses" (*"la faute idéale de roses"*), or even earlier, as he expresses his desire for perpetuating the nymphs.[24]

L'Après-midi as a Chronotope

The French temporal expression *après-midi* has geographic undertones. Literally, it means *afternoon*, and morphologically, it is the combination of *après* and *midi*. The latter, in its appearances in a number of languages,[25] is a common word meaning south. The reason for this is a conventional one: From the perspective of the Northern Hemisphere, during midday (noon), the Sun points to the south. The fact that Sicily is a southern island (from a Parisian or Roman perspective, for example) is manifested in both Italian and French by that spatiotemporal catachresis: Sicily is located *nel mezzogiorno* or *dans le midi* of the European continent.

Analogically, I think that the poem's *midi* could be conceived in regard to what Bakhtin would call a chronotope of the artistic discourse:

> What counts for us is the fact that it [chronotope] expresses the inseparability of space and time (time as the fourth dimension of space). We understand the chronotope as a formally constitutive category of literature; we will not deal with the chronotope in other areas of culture.' In the literary artistic chronotope, spatial and temporal indicators are fused into one carefully thought-out, concrete whole. Time, as it were, thickens, takes on flesh, becomes artistically visible; likewise, space becomes charged and responsive to the movements of time, plot and history. This intersection of axes and fusion of indicators characterizes the artistic chronotope.[26]

Robert T. Tally Jr., a scholar dedicated to spatiality in literary art,[27] points out that Bakhtin's chronotopic conception "elevates space to a level equal to (and, in fact, inseparable from) time," which puts Bakhtin's ahead of spatial turn in literary studies as a sort of forerunner critic of literary historicism (the Russian essay conveying the chronotope conceptualization was first published in 1937–1938).[28] The continuity of time and space is bound to be recognized as a manifestation of a spatial turn in the sense that it questions historicism and the repression of space.

What I am willing to elaborate on in this paper is that the inseparability of space-time whose linguistic expression would be the *après-midi* reverberates throughout Mallarmé's composition of the poetic piece. The sign of time is present since the famous *incipit* of the definitive version of *The Faun*, related to the desire of perennial presence, or extended lastingness: "*Ces nymphes, je les veux perpétuer.*"[29] Many readers pointed out the latent word *tuer* (to kill) *suggested* by *perpétuer* (perpetuate).[30] I should recall, for that matter, a remarkable distich by Schiller (famously quoted by Hegel, Freud, and others): "*Was unsterblich im Gesang soll leben/Muß im Leben untergehn*" ("What must live immortally in the song has to perish in life"), the ending verses of *Die Götter Griechen-lands* (*The Gods of Greece*).[31] Both poems, Schiller's and Mallarmé's, are grounded in an unrecoverable past; in substance, the "*Blüthenalter der Natur*" ("blossom-time of Nature") and the nymphs function as a sort of consumable raw material, such as ink or paint, whose loss is necessary for artistic perpetuation.

Mallarmé's verses weave the faun's soliloquy, whereby a mourning of a memory arguably takes place.[32] The capitalization of memory ("*O nymphes, regonflons des SOUVENIRS divers,*"[33] sixth stanza) and narration ("*CONTEZ,*" second stanza) ingeniously stresses a frustrated, merely tenta-tive recollection of unsure past events. In the absence of certain remem-brance, the faun richly thematizes the countryside, inasmuch as natural spatiality stands for the nymphs themselves.

The Mallarméan *midi* is frequently composed by means of descriptive effect of the nymphs: The brunette is "warm breeze"; the other one has eyes "blue and cold as a weeping fountainhead." The presence of the Etna volcano at the very end of the poem is what some narratologists would call a *realeme*.[34] Etna, the geographical monument, is a natural landmark, and Mallarmé mentions its magmatic activity. It is possible to look at the volcano's influence at the full length of Sicilian history like a recurrent tragedy of eruption ("Treading your lava with innocent feet")[35] which closes the eclogue.

The *locus amoenus*[36] is the scenery intended for the soliloquy since the first versions of the poem, initially thought of as a dramatic work.[37] It is sustainable that Mallarmé's spatial metaphors are not conceived, in his poetic discourse, as a traditional resort to the figure of speech which relates to an object in order to represent another object. I hold that the spatial descriptions create a bond between culture and space, for instance, insofar as they refer to both the natural objects and the mythological entities identified with them. So to speak, the landscape is unfolded and saturated of mythological density by poetic elaboration.

Hence, the poetic power of metamorphosis, as it were a kind of narra-tive metaphor, or metaphor, as it were a kind of verbal metamorphosis, is manifested by the habitat/inhabitant intertwinement.[38] The avoidance of a one-sided, inert concept of landscape is not something unprecedented in the nineteenth century, as a famous quotation by Hölderlin witnesses: "*Voll Verdienst, aber dichterisch wohnet der Mensch auf dieser Erde*" ("Full of merit, but poetically, resides man on this Earth").[39] Mallarmé's circumscription of the poet's only craft, "*l'explication orphique de la terre*" ("orphic explanation of the earth"),[40] reverberates the poet's duty, which is to explain or sing the land (or the planet). Lloyd James Austin states that what charmed Mallarmé's mind concerning the orphic myth is its effective relationship with the artistic ideal of immortality, among other powers of poetry.[41] As the author correctly observes, Mallarmé is not especially inclined toward already-existing mythology,[42] and *The*

Faun would be an important exception to this tendency. It follows, pursuant to Austin:

> What means, then, the famous "orphic explanation of the earth"? There's nothing "orphic" in the strictest sense of the word. . . . [W]e may conclude that what Mallarmé meant by "orphic" is merely "poetic", since Orpheus was for him the quintessential poet.[43]

Contez, Souvenirs: On Narration of Memory

Much has been written and said, from the perspective of memory, about the time-space relationship. In his extensive work, *Les Lieux de Mémoire* (translated by Arthur Goldhammer as *Realms of Memory*), Pierre Nora (1984: 955) recalls the density of the landscape concerning its relationship with time and culture:

> The landscape, this "historical monument," following the formula from a prisoner of the aerial archeology (Roger Agache) . . . . But the landscape belongs to whom, this space developed by the combined forces of nature, man, and time? The geographer, who turns toward the historian? The traveler? The surveyor, the photographer, the writer?[44]

I would add: the mythologist, let alone the creator of mythologies?

In his *Handbook of Inaesthetics*, Alain Badiou's reading of *The Afternoon of a Faun* is decidedly devoted to what he calls the "narration of the place" and its relationship with doubt and mystery. Badiou (2006: 128) understands that *The Faun*'s landscape presents "indubitably" the "most general movement of Mallarmé's poems," which is "[t]he presentation of the place, followed by the attempt to discern within it the proof of some vanished event."[45]

There are undeniable similarities between Badiou's interpretation of the role of landscape in Mallarméan poetry and the approach undertaken in this paper. It may be productive, however, that some of his suggestions be deepened. I would hold that some of Badiou's assertions concerning the very nature of *The Faun* may be looked at in an equally fertile—yet different—light. The French philosopher states that "the operation of the poem is that of thought, not of remembrance or anamnesis."[46] I don't agree with every corollary derived from that particular statement; nevertheless, he concedes the following:

> However, there still lingers a nostalgia for the void itself, such as it had been summoned up in the flash of the event. This is the tempting nostalgia of a full void, an inhabitable void, a perpetual ecstasy. Of

course, this nostalgia demands the blindness of intoxication. This is what the faun abandons himself to and against which he finds no other resort than the brutal resumption of narrative memory.[47]

This nostalgia, in my estimation, is what Fredric Jameson has defined as nostalgia for nostalgia[48] on the occasion of a reading on J. G. Ballard's "displacement of time, the spatialization of the temporal": "what is mourned is the memory of deep memory; what is enacted is a nostalgia for nostalgia." Even though the literary pieces (Mallarmé's and Ballard's) are rooted in different traditions and conditions of production, this perspective may be true about a number of works from a number of traditions. Seeing that contemporary sensibility pays attention to the loss of deep memory and spatialization of temporality, the nostalgia of nostalgia is to be found in a wide range of literary works.

The *midi* chronotope is the artistic alchemy which the faun takes as a doubtful scenery of a memory, perhaps a dreamed one ("Did I love a dream?/My doubt, a heap of ancient night, is finishing/In many subtle branches")[49] or a fruit of his own craft ("You, instrument of flight, Syrinx malign,/At lakes where you wait for me, bloom again!"). For that matter, as Badiou reasons, the idea of absolute fiction is not at all unrelated to Mallarméan thought.[50] A piercing abstract of Mallarmé formulated by Richard may come to mind: "*La beauté n'est qu'une fiction*" ("beauty is nothing more than a fiction").[51]

At any rate, in both hypotheses, the landscape is a supportive nature that bestows its permanence to the faun's pensive song about a dubious past event. This idea is inscribed in Mallarmé's polysemic verse "*rien/n'aura eu lieu/que le lieu*" ("nothing/will have taken place/but the place") from his *A Throw of the Dice*.

Badiou's "proof of some vanished event" within a place has been observed by theorists connected to the spatial turn. The idea of a connection between what has been (*das Gewesene*) and spatial settings may be identified with the Benjamin concept of the past metamorphosed into space (*raumgewordene Vergangenheit*). This notion was articulated by Walter Benjamin in his *Arcades Project*, which dealt with Parisian urban features and its attachment to time.[52] The German philosopher states that distortion (*Entstellung*,[53] a word whose etymology leads to displacement) is the form things assume when they are forgotten[54] and that there are "places (*Stellen*) where dreams open out onto waking existence."[55] So, it follows that past and dream are distortable into space. That idea, which might be a reinterpretation of Benjamin's work, is apparently analogous with Mallarméan, so to speak, "chronotopic" lyrical elaboration.

Benjamin implies similarities between the *flâneur* of the modern city and the former wanderer of the forest.[56] In fact, it is conceivable that landscapes work as spaces of memory (*Gedachtnisräume*) in a manner similar to the Parisian passages. Numerous contributions from memory studies have already explored the mnemonic dimension of spatial set-tings.[57] As Jameson noted, even Frances Yates's project dealing with the spatialization of memory in Renaissance architecture, for instance, may be interpreted within this specific aspect of spatial theoretical turn.[58]

Jean-Pierre Richard, whose investigation of Mallarmé's poetry is as extensive as it is influential, did not lose sight of the metamorphoses of nature and fiction that takes place in the faun's song of uncertain mem-ory. Richard observes the Mallarméan taste for foliage and vegetal life in general.[59] The sensual aspiration of greenery is possibly connected to the "penetrability of foliage" and the desire to "become one with the forest" according to the same critic, which implies that Mallarmé's relationship to memory is a mystical one. Likewise, the faun's lust for the natural *midi* is accordingly a lust for the nymphs and the dreamlike rendezvous with them. The empty grape berries, of which the soliloquist speaks with sor-row, may stand for the absence of nymphs in their supposed habitat. The consumable nature of the grapes leaves a trace: the skin is their durable vestige. This polysemous elaboration belongs to synecdoche and meta-phor figures of speech, inasmuch as the grape skin arguably represents both its own whole habitat and the nymphs.

> So when I've sucked the clarity of grapes
> To banish, laughing, rue my ruse escapes,
> I, raising empty bunch to burning sky,
> Blow up the shining skins, and yearn to lie
> Dead drunk, 'til evening I see through it all.[60]

The last verses of the poem relate the drinking of the wine of stars, which has to do with another kind of metamorphosis that connects the transmutation of the nymphs (or their memory) to natural elements of this worldly space (grapes) and the outer space (the stars, a typical theme of the later Mallarmé).[61] All in all, grapes and stars are uncanny spaces in their ability to invoke intoxication and mysticism.

In fact, the idea that space's durability surpasses the time span of an experience or phenomenon housed within it grounds the foundations of the relationship between space and memory. Halbwachs, one of the founders of memory studies, notes:

> It is only the image of space that, due to its stability, creates the illu-sion of never changing at all through time and regaining the past in the present; yet this is how one might define memory; and only space is sufficiently stable in order to long without growing old nor losing any of its parts.[62]

Halbwachs gives samples of literary spatial description in the work-ings of social memory, such as Dickens's and Balzac's. These authors chiefly belong to a "legible-realist dominant,"[63] which is naturally not the case when it comes to Mallarmé, but he certainly deals with issues of representation and memory as well, even if in a specific manner. This specificity is parallel to that of his suggestive doctrine, opposed to realist regimen, so that he would avoid directness both in its lexical-syntactical and representative expressions. If the faun's memory is not crystal-clear, accordingly, his language is not direct at all: there are deformations (*Entstaltungen*) as in a dream or a repressed memory.

The Joy of Perceiving Oneself as Simply and Infinitely on the Earth

The passage "joie . . . de se percevoir simple, infiniment, sur la terre" closes one of Mallarmé's divagations devoted to landscape and bucolic countryside.[64] The proposal of inquiring about Mallarmé's spatial conception is not at all undiscovered, but it may presently find new outcomes, as the collection of writings by Mallarmé and about Mallarmé are subjected to the historical horizon of their endlessly renewable readers. The turnabouts of a body of works from the last decades have revived the interest of thinking about space, spatialization, and spatiality.

This attention is what guided French scholar Bertrand Westphal in his interesting book *La Géocritique* (translated as *Geocriticism* by Robert T. Tally Jr.) when it comes to the interpretation of Auerbach's classic contribution on Dantesque poetry, *Dante als Dichter der irdischen Welt*. For a long time, a sort of unintentional historicist catachresis has translated the word *irdisch* as secular, so that *Dante, Poet of the Secular World* is a very influential title for Auerbach's work in English-speaking countries. However, *irdisch* is evidently connected to the English word *earth*, which is much closer to the spatial lexicon than secular, even though secular effectively relates, by means of catachresis, to worldly or lay matters. After all, Dante's *Commedia* is blatantly affiliated with geography and space. The Dantesque depiction of afterlife has a lot do with his understanding of earthly life, especially Florentine spiritual and political behavior. In that light, bringing Mallarmé back to Earth from a pure poetry of fictional constellations is something comparable to that perspective on the *Commedia*.

What is yet to be shown is that Mallarmé has his share of creative spatial thinking—not only paper space, a facet which has been extensively observed, but also in a properly earthly sense of space. The conciliation of this earthly Mallarmé (from *The Faun* and some divagations, for instance) and the Mallarmé of the constellations (chiefly the Mallarmé of the unfinished *Livre* and of *A Throw of the Dice*) is not that impossible a task if we understand space in a rather multilayered interpretation.[65] Foucault's heterotopia, for instance, which has informed contemporary geography, conceptualizes the coexistence of a number of spaces within a single space that opens itself to Otherness. This idea may be paralleled to the following verses from *A Throw of the Dice*: "EXCEPT/at the altitude/ PERHAPS as far as a place fuses with beyond" ("EXCEPTÉ/à l'altitude/ PEUT-ÊTRE/aussi loin qu'un endroit // fusionne avec au delà").[66]

The idea of a sort of place (connected to Foucauldian heterotopia? Or to Lefebvre's *espace vécu*?) that is fusible with beyond has affinities with Soja's thirdspace concept, for instance—represented paradigmatically by Borgesian aleph, the fusion of every worldly spatial possibility within itself. As the conclusion to his text about the mystery in letters, Mallarmé makes it clear: "the melody or song beneath a text convoys the *divination* from *here* to *there*."[67]

One might hold that focusing on the earthly and descriptive writing features of an author who considers himself against description and realist representation is to read his production in a contrived fashion, but this perception depends on a possible Mallarmé, historically formulated by some tendencies of a number of interpretive communities. I would advocate that this is where the interest of such inquiry lies. Some of Mallarmé's literary heroes were masters of description, such as Aloysius Bertrand,[68] Victor Hugo, and Théophile Gautier. Moreover, to read an author in a contrived manner may produce a fruitful interpretation, as long it is historically reasonable and well-informed. As Walter Benjamin stated on a different occasion, one should read the history against its grain.[69] The same disposition may have interesting outcomes when it comes to reading literary history and its unending turnarounds against the grain. The "explanation of the earth" and the idea of "[living] infinitely on earth" must not remain as sort of historical repressions of Mallarméan thought. I hold that such a perspective opens the horizon to an interesting reading of his writing. I think that conceiving the *après-midi* as the linguistic materialization of a chronotope and the spatialization of memory is a good place to start.

Notes

1. When using this expression, I'm employing a concept articulated by Northrop Frye in *Anatomy of Criticism* and *The Critical Path*. According to the Canadian critic Frye (1957: 73), "[w]henever we read anything, we find our attention moving in two directions at once. One direction is outward or *centrifugal*, in which we keep going outside our reading, from the individual words to the things they mean, or in practice, to our memory of the conventional association between them. The other direction is inward or *centripetal*, in which we try to develop from the words a sense of the larger verbal pattern they make. . . . Verbal elements understood inwardly or centripetally, as parts of a verbal structure, are, as symbols, simply and literally verbal elements, or units of a verbal structure" (underlining mine). Unless otherwise stated, all translations are also mine.
2. The concept of interpretive communities is connected to German reader-response criticism and was elaborated in a classic work called *Is there a text*

in this class? The authority of interpretive communities, by Fish (1980). Fish supports that reading is not an entirely subjective process; diversely, it works under the influence of a body of beliefs about languages and writing whose presence is repeated and conserved by certain communities of culture agency.

3. "Tournon crisis" is how some biographers and other scholars have baptized a series of professional and artistic crises which took place when Mallarmé taught English in a number of provincial cities, including Tournon and Besançon, and led to a more mature phase of his thought. Mallarmé (1995: 157–58), in his Letter from December 30, 1863, has deplored Tournon's gusty environment and its "hideous Northern wind" (*"l'affreuse bise"*), having described to Cazalis that "The weather here is gray and glacial, it's the only thing that leaves me gloomy. Tournon is on the road of every wind from Europe: it's an interstation and their meeting point" (*"Le temps est gris et glacial, ici, cela seul me rend maussade. Tournon est sur la route de tous les vents de l'Europe: c'est un relais et leur rendez-vous."*). Some months later, in his Letter from August 30, 1864, he wrote again to his confidant: "My friend, I'm absolutely dispirited. I think I have one year of Tournon in my spirit. . . . Tomorrow I'll flee from Ardèche. This name horrifies me" (*"Mon ami, je suis éteint absolument. Pense que j'ai un an de Tournon sur l'esprit. . . . Demain, je fuirai L'Ardèche. Ce nom me fait horreur."*). Steinmetz (1998) follows Mallarmé's itinerary through England, Tournon, Besançon, and Paris, and connects it with the poet's difficulties and crises until his fortunate residence in Paris and Fontainebleau. Mondor (1943) pays particular attention to the Tournon years and his correspondence with Cazalis and other friends, as well as his connection with Valéry. Gallardo (1998) also addresses the Tournon crisis and depicts a very compelling role when regarding this phase in Mallarméan conception of his aesthetic novelty.

4. In fact, it is a much diffused opinion from Paul Valéry (1952: 46) that *L'Après-midi* is the greatest poem of French tradition. A number of reception tendencies regarding Mallarméan oeuvre were distilled taking Valéry's Mallarmé into account, in variable degrees. His Letter to Mallarmé from 04/18/1891 states: "Thus, what is imperative is the supreme conception of an elevated symphony that unifies the world that surrounds us and the world that haunts us, built according to a rigorous architecture. . . . *The Afternoon of a Faun* is the only [poem] in France to achieve this aesthetic ideal, and the perfection unheard of that it demands displays the future disappearance of the infuriated false poets, annihilating their mediocrity in a sort of mechanical fashion" (*"Alors s'impose la conception suprême d'une haute symphonie, unissant le monde qui nous entoure au monde qui nous hante, construite selon une rigoureuse architectonique. . . . L'Après-Midi d'un Faune est seule en France à réaliser cet idéal esthétique, et la perfection inouïe qu'elle exige démontre la disparition future des faux poètes exaspérés, et que leur médiocrité anéantit en quelque sorte mécaniquement."*).

5. It is persuasive that the definitive version of the piece has the noun *"églogue"* under its title.

6. I would name Derrida's reading, for instance. In *"La Double Séance"* ("The Double Session" in Barbara Johnson's translation) Derrida compares Mallarméan fiction to the Platonic views on representation, which produces a coherent and influential reading of a contemporary philosopher on a specter poet of the twentieth century. I mean that Mallarmé was quite elderly to be considered an initiator of what a portion of literary historians came to call symbolism, even though he acted as an ancestor of younger symbolist poets. A hundred years later, he received a renewing reception

by the nouvelle critique Tel Quel, and structuralism approaches. So, Mallarmé had a sound moment of his reception history at that time (it would be precise to add that concrete poetry played a part on this). Mallarméan approach to representation is read in a doubtful manner that doesn't deny nor reaffirm Plato's critique of a copy of a copy: Mallarmé, according to this reading, plays with the ambiguity of representational discourse. Derrida is to be recalled as well in order to underline his affinity with my enterprise in this essay: The ambiguity of representational discourse has affinities with our point of view on Mallarmé, both geographical and mythical and written by someone who resists naming, but does so. Cf. Derrida, 1974: 376; Siscar, 2010: 83–102.

7. This controversial quotation (*il n'y a pas d'hors texte*) which figures in Derrida's most famous work, *De la Grammatologie* (1967: 227) is probably meant to be understood with a grain of salt. As he advocated later, "Certainly, deconstruction tries to show that the question of reference is much more complex and problematic than traditional theories supposed. It even asks whether our term 'reference' is entirely adequate for designating the 'other.' The other, which is beyond language and which summons language, is perhaps not a 'referent' in the normal sense which linguists have attached to this term" (Derrida, 1984: 123–24).

8. It is useful to remember that Marchal (1988: 97) composes an interesting outline about Mallarmé's dismissed thesis that would have dealt with the problematic of language and fiction. Apparently, Cartesian thought was the prevalent motivation of these preliminary scholarly drafts.

9. Richard (1961: 376) stresses Mallarmé's "nausea of the material."

10. We may ponder that this sensibility is also historical, for it might be related to the then recent visual revolution brought by photographical breakthroughs.

11. The word "*poésie*" and its cognates, such as "poetry," are etymologically connected to the idea of production as well: The Greek verb *poieō* (ποιέω) means, literally, "I make." Accordingly, it is not inaccurate to state that "to suggest," as to generate, and "to poetize," as to make, are (diachronically) semantically connected. The aforementioned etymological fact (the connection between poetry and *poiesis*) is important for a plethora of aesthetic reflections over the last centuries.

12. Undoubtedly, Mallarmé's self-imposed task is incommensurable if one takes some of his writings into account. As a sample, I would note his particular reading of Émile Montégut. Mallarmé formulates a cultural history divided into three eras and their corresponding representatives: Phidias, Leonardo da Vinci, and the modern poet. The third era would be that of the *Oeuvre*, succeeding the lineage formed by the Venus de Milo and the Mona Lisa. A new kind of beauty would be forged by Mallarmé's work, which would be the most appropriate for the modern, godless world. A keen interpretation of those issues may be found in Marchal (1988: 72–76).

13. "*Nommer un objet, c'est supprimer les trois quarts de la jouissance du poème qui est faite de deviner peu à peu: le suggérer, voilà le rêve.*" (Mallarmé, 1956: 869).

14. "*Peindre, non la chose, mais l'effet qu'elle produit.*" (Mallarmé, 1995: 206). According to the editor's note, this new poetic may be read as an extension of Edgar A. Poe's conception of literary composition, an undeniable influence emphasized by Baudelaire's association with the American author.

15. "*Ce n'est point avec des idées que l'on fait des vers . . . C'est avec des mots.*" This motto was spread by Paul Valéry, who was intimate friends

with both Mallarmé and Degas, in his *"Poésie et pensée abstraite"* (1945: 141). According to Valéry, Mallarmé gave this piece of advice to Degas, who complained about his own inability to write verses, even though he effectively had ideas. As an answer from a poet to a painter full of ideas but lacking poems, it is a verisimilar fragment of a dialogue; still, one should always keep in mind that Valéry must be the ultimate author of the statement, since Mallarmé never published or gave notice of this particular literary conviction. Similar to the Platonic Socrates, this quotation belongs to Valéry's Mallarmé.

16. *"Die Kunst steht in der Moderne weitgehend im Zeichen der 'Überbietung, Entmachtung und Entstaltung der Natur, eines tiefen Ungenügens am Gegebenen'* (Blumenberg, 1957: 56), *und sie ist gerade darum exemplarischer Ausdruck der Beziehung des modernen Menschen zur gegebenen Wirklichkeit. Die künstlerischen Werke beanspruchen für sich Ursprünglichkeit. Die Natur als einstige Begründunginstanz des Werks wird durch andere Instanzen abgelöst"* (Schmitz-Emans, 1999: 111).

17. Indeed, these patterns coincide with Frye's very pragmatic definition of literary realism: "representative likeness of life" or "lifelikeness" (See Frye, 1957: 134).

18. Cf. Meschonnic (1999): "A poem transforms. That's why to name, to describe are worth nothing for the poem. And to describe is to name" (*"Un poème transforme. C'est pourquoi nommer, décrire ne valent rien au poème. Et décrire est nommer."*). The French scholar and poet insisted on the attention to the opposition between *nommer* (to name) and *suggérer* (to suggest) in Mallarméan poetic thinking. On another occasion, after presenting his disagreement with Michel Deguy about this subject, Meschonnic advocates its importance for modern poetry in the following interview: www.editions-verdier.fr/v3/auteur-meschonnic-2.html.

19. *"Une ville, une campagne, de loin, c'est une ville et une campagne, mais à mesure qu'on s'approche, ce sont des maisons, des arbres, des tuiles, des feuilles, des herbes, des fourmis, des jambes de fourmis, à l'infini. Tout cela s'enveloppe sous le nom de campagne."* (*Apud* Marin, 1992: 245).

20. Riffaterre's role in this itinerary is quickly summarized in Hamon, 1993: 127.

21. Richard, 1961: 433.

22. As to this everlasting issue concerning the relationship between words and images, I would refer to Vouilloux, 2005 (1994): 63.

23. Marchal, 1988: 114, 344.

24. The concept of the tragic flaw is connected to the Ancient Greek idea of *hamartia* (ἁμαρτία), most known in cultured practices via Aristotelian interpretation. Its role in drama would be connected to catharsis, a sort of emotional purgation attained through the representative arts. The concept plays a role in a great many theorizations, from Christian hermeneutics to Frye's "theory of modes" and Augusto Boal's "theater of the oppressed."

25. Anglic Germanic languages, such as Scots and English, derived words for *après-midi* from the Latin *nona hora*, rather than *meridies*. The *nona hora* (noon) concerned the midway of a monastic day, which started at what is modernly 6:00 a.m.; the ninth hour would be 3:00 p.m.; the noon was eventually retracted in order to fit the midday. The English "afternoon" and Scots *"efternuin"* reflect this.

26. Bakhtin, 1982: 84.

27. Tally, 2013: 58.

28. Actually, the notion of forerunning is relative (besides being both a spatial and temporal metaphor), since others may be bestowed with that honor before Bakhtin, such as Wyndham Lewis over and against Bergson and Joyce.

29. A very literal translation would be: "Those nymphs, I want to perpetuate them." Every mention to the poem, unless otherwise stated, refers to Mallarmé, 1989: 75–79.
30. This reading is currently widespread. For instance, a Portuguese translation influential in Brazil by the critic and poet Augusto de Campos propounds the neologism *perpematar*, as it combines *perpetuar* (to perpetuate) and *matar* (to kill). Something close I would think of is the English neologism "perpetuerase."
31. "*Die Götter Griechenlands*" in Schiller, 1972: 173.
32. I will go further on this matter in the following pages.
33. A translation I would sustain is: "Oh, nymphs, let us reinflate various REMEMBRANCES."
34. Cf. Even-Zohar, 1980: 65–74, 1985: 109–18.
35. Mallarmé, 1994: 41 (translation by Henry Weinfield).
36. The most widespread description of the *locus amoenus* as a literary *topos* is found in a classic work by Curtius called *Europäische Literatur und lateinisches Mittelalter* (1973: 197–206). Bakhtin (1982) also exposes the literary productivity of the idyllic chronotope in the eighteenth and nineteenth centuries, even if mostly in regard to fictional prose.
37. Actually, Mallarmé (1995: 242) has even stated to Cazalis that the Faun would "call for a stage." Still, one must concede that the definitive version is a full-fledged poem and its primary reception was, for the most part, dependent on reading. On the other hand, the genetic account of the poem instills it with dramatic powers, so much so that a soliloquy aspect is legitimated by presence of the noun "FAVNE," as it were above the faun's solitary speech, or theatrical line.
38. The metamorphosis into natural elements is highly frequent in Ancient Greek and Roman mythologies (to think of the metamorphosis of the nymph Syrinx into reeds and its use for the handcraft of pan pipes is an immediate reaction when it comes to elucidate the *Faun*, but I think this approach is intellectually unsatisfactory, as Mallarmé's own mythology has its peculiar strengths and subtleties as a poetic tale from a sound thinker of language and fiction). Another kind of metamorphosis that is quite easily found in Ancient mythology is the particular conversion into a constellation. This last idea is very close to the Mallarméan universe and may have to do with the last verses of the *Afternoon of a Faun*; see the following.
39. These verses were famously interpreted by Heidegger (1967: 61–78) in the context of his lectures on Hölderlin during his late career. Michel Deguy (2012) has extended his interpretation and put Hölderlin's verses side by side with our renewed attention for ecology and what Westphal (2007) calls the reign of the geocentric literary approach (a literary perspective based on earthly matters, rather than an egocentric perspective, based on individual standpoints).
40. A more extended quotation is: "The orphic explanation of the Earth, which is the only task of the poet and the prevalent literary play" ("*L'explication orphique de la Terre, qui est le seul devoir du poète et le jeu littéraire par excellence*"). Mallarmé (1995: 586) is mentioning aspects of the *Livre*, his conjectural *grand oeuvre*.
41. Austin, 1970: 169–80.
42. Mallarmé richly displays his reservations concerning national mythology in his text about Richard Wagner: "*Rêveries d'un poète Français*" in Mallarmé, 1998: 363–68.

43. "*Que signifie alors la fameuse 'explication orphique de la terre ?' Rien 'd'orphique' au sens strict du mot.* . . . *[O]n peut conclure que Mallarmé voulait dire que Mallarmé voulait dire par 'orphique' tout simplement 'poétique', puisque Orphée était pour lui le poète par excellence.*" Austin, 1970: 179.

44. "*Le paysage, ce 'monument historique', selon la formule d'un prisonnier de l'archéologie aérienne (Roger Agache)* . . . . *Mais à qui appartient le paysage, cet espace élaboré par les forces conjuguées de la nature, de l'homme et du temps ? Au géographe, qui se tourne vers l'historien ? Au voyageur ? A l'arpenteur, au photographe, à l'écrivain?*" (Nora, 1984: 955).

45. Badiou, 2006: 128.

46. Ibid: 127.

47. Ibid: 132.

48. Cf. Jameson, 1991: 156.

49. Mallarmé, 1937; translated by Roger Fry.

50. Badiou, 2006: 132.

51. Cf. Richard, 1961: 295. Much of French (and generally European continental, seemingly) thought may be overheard in this strong statement, which would be fiercely confronted with Keats's lapidary verse "beauty is truth, truth beauty—that is all."

52. Apud Weigel, 1996: 112.

53. The word, traditionally psychoanalytic in nature, has found an important reception by Homi Bhabha's cultural theory (cf. Bhabha, 1985: 102–22, 105).

54. Weigel, 1996: 113.

55. Ibid: 103.

56. Ibid: 137.

57. "To repeat a particular past in present time is the specific task of sites of memory in space and time. . . . People store their remembrances not only in signs and objects, rather in sites, in rooms, courtyards, cities, public spaces, and landscapes. . . . Specific locations form a contact zone between present and past, so as in these places a mysterious door opens to a bygone world. Pausanias mentions that there were places in the ancient world which were pointed out as though they led to the underworld. Odysseus receives from Circe the reference to the exact place where he could descend to the realm of the dead. Space and time, past and present, are connected in such sites" ("*Es ist die besondere Aufgabe von Gedächtnisorten in Raum und Zeit, eine bestimmte Vergangenheit in die Gegenwart hereinzuholen.* . . . *Menschen lagern ihre Erinnerung nicht nur in Zeichen und Gegenstände aus, sondern auch in Orte, in Zimmer, Innenhöfe, Städte, öffentliche Plätze und Landschaften.* . . . *Bestimmte Orte eine Kontaktzone zwischen Gegenwart und Vergangenheit bilden, dass sich an diesen Orten ein geheimnisvolles Tor öffnet in eine vergangene Welt. Pausanias erwähnt, dass man in der antiken Welt Orte zeigte, an denen es in die Unterwelt hinabging. Odysseus erhält von Kirke den Hinweis auf den genauen Ort, wo er ins Totenreich hinabsteigen kann. An solchen Orten verbinden sich Raum und Zeit, Gegenwart und Vergangenheit.*"), Assmann, 2006: 217, 218.

58. The influential work (Yates, 1966) is an important case of a spatial turn on memory studies.

59. Richard, 1961: 103ff.

60. Translated by Winslow Shea. www.ancientworlds.net/aw/Article/1269922.

61. An interesting reading on this matter concerning the grapes and their relationship with the nymphs is to be found in Thibaudet, 2006: 363.

62. "*C'est l'image seule de l'espace qui, en raison de sa stabilité, nous donne l'illusion de ne point changer à travers le temps et de retrouver le passé dans le présent; mais c'est bien ainsi qu'on peut définir la mémoire; et que l'espace seul est assez stable pour pouvoir durer sans vieillir ni perdre aucune de ses parties,*" Halbwachs, 1997: 236.
63. This descriptive typology is employed by Hamon (1993: 52) in order to classify the highly mimetic-oriented writing of fiction authors like Zola, Balzac, Dickens, and Walter Scott.
64. Mallarmé, 2003, 318.
65. Foucault, 2009 proposes the idea of heterotopias, with which this text will deal in the next lines. Lefebvre, 1974, formulates the proposition of a socially produced space. If I were to loosely and roughly resume it (since my lines are not infinite), his "trialectic" conception comprises the *espace perçu* (perceived space), which has to do with everyday space; *espace conçu* (conceived space) which deals with representations of space, with its languages, signs, and sights; and the *espace vécu* (lived spaces) which is derived from those different instances of spatiality and resists simplifications and is linked with the most hidden, private, and subversive side of social production of space. Soja conceives his thirdspace from Foucault's and Lefebvre's conceptions of a multilayered and extremely dense spatiality (real-and-imagined space). Cf. Soja, 1989, 1996.
66. Mallarmé, *Un coup de dés jamais n'abolira le hazard*. Translated by A. S. Kline, 2007 (digitally republished at www.poetryintranslation.com/PITBR/French/MallarmeUnCoupdeDes.htm).
67. Mallarmé, 2003: 288.
68. Studies on Mallarmé's reading of Bertrand may be found in Melo Franco (2010), Richards (1998), and Palacio (1973).
69. "*Der historische Materialist rückt daher nach Maßgabe des Möglichen von ihr ab. Er betrachtet es als seine Aufgabe, die Geschichte gegen den Strich zu bürsten.*" The historical materialist thus moves as far away from this as measurably possible. He regards it as his task to brush history against the grain. (Original German: *Gesammelten Schriften* I:2. Translation by Dennis Redmond. Suhrkamp Verlag: Frankfurt am Main, 1974. Available at www.marxists.org/refer).

Bibliography

Primary Sources

Mallarmé, S. *Poems*. Translated by Roger Fry with commentaries by Charles Mauron. New York: Oxford University Press, 1937.
———. *Œuvres complètes*. Paris: Gallimard (Pléiade), 1956.
———. "L'Après-midi d'un Favne, Églogve", in *Poésies*. Édition de Lloyd James Austin. Paris: GF Flammarion, 1989.
———. *Collected Poems*. Translation by Henry Weinfield (a bilingual en face edition). Berkeley, CA: University of California Press, 1994.
———. *Correspondance complète 1962–1871 suivi de Lettres sur la poésie 1872–1898*. Édition de Bertrand Marchal. Paris: Gallimard, 1995.
———. *Écrits sur l'art*. Présentation Michel Draguet. Paris: GF Flammarion, 1998.
———. *Igitur, Divagations, Un Coup de dés*. Édition de Bertrand Marchal. Paris: Gallimard, 2003.

Secondary Sources

Assmann, A., *Der lange Schatten der Vergangenheit. Erinnerungskultur und Geschichtspolitik*. München: C. H. Beck, 2006.

Austin, L. J., "Mallarmé et le mythe d'Orphée", *Cahiers de l'Association internationale des études francaises*, Vol. 22, 1970.

Badiou, A.,"Philosophy of the faun", in *Handbook of Inaesthetics*. Translation by Alberto Toscano. Stanford, CA: Stanford University Press, 2006.

Bakhtin, M., *The Dialogical Imagination*. Austin: University of Texas Press, 1982.

Benjamin, W., *Gesammelten Schriften I:2*. Translation by Dennis Redmond. Suhrkamp Verlag: Frankfurt am Main, 1974. www.marxists.org/reference/archive/benjamin/1940/history.htm

Bhabha, H., "Signs Taken for Wonders: Questions of Ambivalence and Authority under a Tree Outside Delhi, May 1817", *Critical Inquiry*, Vol. 12, No. 1: "Race", Writing, and Difference, 1985.

Blumenberg, Hans., "Nachahmung der Natur: Zur Vorgeschichte der Idee des schöpferischen Menschen", *Studium Generale*, Vol. 10, No. 5: 266–283, 1957.

Curtius, E. R., *Europäische Literatur und lateinisches Mittelalter*. Bern und München: Francke, 1973.

Deguy, M., *Écologiques*. Paris: Hermann Éditeurs, 2012.

Derrida, J., *De la Grammatologie*. Paris: Les Éditions de Minuit, 1967.

_____. "Mallarmé", in *Tableau de la littérature française: de Madame de Staël à Rimbaud*. Paris: Gallimard, 1974.

_____. "Deconstruction and the Other", in *Dialogues with Contemporary Continental Thinkers: The Phenomenological Heritage*. Edited by Richard Kearney. Manchester: Manchester University Press, 1984.

Even-Zohar, I., "Constraints of Realeme Insertability in Narrative", in *Poetics Today*. Special Issue: Narratology I: Poetics of Fiction. Duke University Press, Vol. 1, 1980.

_____., "Les règles d'insertion des 'réalèmes' dans la narration", in *Littérature* 57, (digitally republished www.tau.ac.il/~itamarez/works/papers/translated/realemes_narration.pdf), 1985.

Fish, S., *Is there a Text in this Class? The Authority of Interpretive Communities*. Cambridge: Harvard University Press, 1980.

Foucault, M., *Le corps utopique suivi de Les héterotopies*. Présentation de Daniel Defert. Paris: Nouvelles Éditions Lignes, 2009.

Frye, N., *Anatomy of Criticism. Four Essays*. Princeton, NJ: Princeton University Press, 1957.

Gallardo, J., *Mallarmé et le jeu suprême*. Orléans: Paradigme Publications Universitaires, 1998.

Halbwachs, M., *La mémoire collective*. Edition critique établie par Gérard Namer. Paris: Albin Michel, 1997.

Hamon, P., *Du Descriptif*. Paris: Hachette, 1993.

Heidegger, M., *Vorträge und Aufsätze. Zweite Teil*. Tübingen: Neske, 1967.

Jameson, F., *Postmodernism, or, The Cultural Logic of Late Capitalism*. Durham: Duke University Press, 1991.

Lefebvre, H., *La Production de l'espace*. Paris: Anthropos, 1974.

Marchal, B., *La Religion de Mallarmé*. Paris: José Corti, 1988.

Marin, L., *De la représentation*. Paris: Gallimard, 1992.

Melo Franco, R., "O primeiro ancestral pequeno romântico do surrealismo", *Lettres Françaises* (UNESP Araraquara), Vol. 10, pp. 149–69, 2010.

Meschonnic, H., *Manifeste pour un parti du rythme* (digitally republished www. berlol.net/mescho2.htm), 1999.

Mondor, H., *Vie de Mallarmé*. Paris: Gallimard, 1943.

Nora, P., *Les Lieux de mémoire*. Paris: Gallimard (Bibliothèque illustrée des histoires), Vol. 1, 1984.

Palacio, J., " La posterite du Gaspard de la Nuit: de Baudelaire à Max Jacob ", *Revue des lettres modernes*, Vol. 336, pp. 157–89, 1973.

Richard, J. P., *L'Univers imaginaire de Mallarmé*. Paris: Editions du Seuil, 1961.

Richards, M. *Without rhyme or reason, Gaspard de la Nuit and the dialectic of the prose poem*. London: Bucknell University Press, 1998.

Schiller, F., *Sämtliche Werke*. Edited by G. Fricke and H. G. Göpfert München: Hanser, Vol. 1, 1972.

Schmitz-Emans, M., "Gemalte Landschaften im Spiegel literarischer Texte", in *Das visuelle Gedächtnis der Literatur*. Edited by M. Schmeling, M. Schmitz-Emans and W. Eckel. Würzburg: Königshausen und Neumann, 1999.

Siscar, M., *Poesia e crise*. Campinas: Editora da Unicamp, 2010.

Soja, E. W., *Postmodern Geographies*: The Reassertion of Space in Critical Social Theory. Nova York, Londres: Verso, 1989.

_____., *Thirdspace*: Journeys to Los Angeles and other Real-and-Imagined Spaces. Malden, MA, Oxford, OX and Carlton Victoria: Blackwell, 1996.

Steinmetz, J., *Stéphane Mallarmé: L'absolu au jour le jour*. Paris: Fayard, 1998.

Tally, R. T., *Spatiality*. London and New York: Routledge, 2013.

Thibaudet, A. *La Poésie de Stéphane Mallarmé*. Paris: Gallimard, 2006.

Valery, P., "Poésie et pensée abstraite", in *Variété V*. Paris: Gallimard, 1945.

_____., *Lettres à quelques-uns*. Paris: Gallimard, 1952.

Vouilloux, B., *La peinture dans le texte. XVIIIe—XXe siècles*. Paris: CNRS Éditions, 2005 (1994).

Weigel, S., *Body-and Image-space: Re-reading Walter Benjamin*. Londres: Routledge, 1996.

Westphal, B., *La Géocritique. Réel, fiction, espace*. Paris: Les Éditions de Minuit, 2007.

Yates, F. A., *The Art of Memory*. Chicago: University of Chicago Press, 1966.

5 Zola's Spatial Explorations of Second Empire Paris

Julia Kröger

Literary criticism now has several decades of intense research on spatiality behind it. Yet it was only with the paradigm shift of the so-called "spatial turn" (Soja 1989: 39; Jameson 1991: 154; see Döring and Thielmann 2008) that new ideas regarding the interrelation of space as both conceived and perceived, the dialectics of space and place, and the significance of both to human experience began to be systematically developed (see Foucault 1984; Lefebvre 2000 [1974]; Relph 1976; Detering et al. 2012: Lotman 1972; Bachtin 2008). The central premise of much of this work is that space and place are produced through a dialectical interaction of our practical experience of place with our mental conceptions thereof (cf. Relph 1976). It is important to note, however, that literary studies (at least on the continent) have generally failed to take into account both sides of this dialectic (space as a mental *and* physical entity). By focusing on the translation of cognitive space alone into literature, literary criticism has tended to omit actually perceived, real-life geographical space, thus rendering impossible an understanding of "lived space" (Lefebvre 2000).[1]

The aim of this article, then, is twofold: Firstly, I shall attempt to demonstrate the ways in which Lefebvre's triad of space lends itself to the analysis of the construction of space in Zola's preparatory work and its subsequent expansion into the "lived space" of the novels. In doing so, I hope to show, secondly, that the constructed "lived space" of Zola's fiction can be seen as the result of the author's physical and cognitive real-life encounter with Parisian space, i.e., in this case, the Paris Halles.[2] Zola offers us a unique opportunity in this respect, since his process of literary production involved a transformation of *conceptions* and *perceptions* of space into the *lived space* of the novel's storyworld. His notebooks consisted of, on the one hand, a series of documents and maps which enabled him to construct a conception of Parisian space, and, on the other, his jottings based upon his direct perceptions and observations of city life. He depicts the Paris Halles as more than just an architectural infrastructure; via his notes we become aware of the emotive and affective quality of the atmospheric market quarter. Thus, I intend to show that Zola's work is not only a rich source of historical and topographical knowledge, but also that it offers a crucial insight into past urban experience. It enables its readers to experience the created world from an interior perspective, rather than a didactic external perspective.[3] The article concludes by examining the ways in which Zola transposed his preparatory notes into novels by employing various strategies of narrativization and by organising space within the text.[4]

Encountering Paris—Zola's Scientific Observations— Conceived Space

Zola's notebooks—*les carnets d'enquêtes*—are part of the preparatory dossiers [*dossiers préparatoires*] which contained the research that formed the basis of each novel in the Rougon-Macquart cycle; they thus played an essential role in the genesis of his works.[5] Henri Mitterand (2007: 1) divides the content of the notebooks into "things seen" [*choses vues*] (Zola's direct observations) and "things read" [*choses lues*] (including heterogeneous documents such as photographs, indexes of names, hand-drawn maps and drafts) (cf. Pierre-Gnassounou in Nelson 2007: 86). The dossiers thus consisted of a whole range of material which reflected the scientific culture of the 19th century in general and Zola's principles of a naturalistic fiction in particular:[6] in line with Lefebvre's triad, I claim that this culture informed Zola's *conceptions* of space. This is the space of "*savoir* (knowledge) and logic, of maps, mathematics, the instrumental space of social engineers and urban planners, of navigators and explorers" (Elden 2004: 191). Conceived space (*l'espace conçu*) is thus the abstract space of geometry and measurement which inscribes itself in social practice (and thereby informs it).[7] As we shall see, Zola approached the city of Paris not only from the standpoint of the literary scholar, but also with the architect's systematic gaze in order to render urban complexity measurable and mappable.

The conceptual discourses which influenced Zola most were those originating in the natural sciences and positivism; his combination of these ideas with a literary method is set out most prominently in his book *The Experimental Novel* (1880). Drawing on Claude Bernard's theory of physiology and Prosper Lucas's theory of heredity, Zola attempted to introduce observation, experimentation and genealogy into literature, and in doing so, to transform the writer into a scientist who not only entertains his readers, but actually educates them (cf. Mitterand 2007: 2).[8] The naturalist doctrine is thus characterized by its strong focus on societal reality, its belief in people being conditioned by their environments and its determinist theory of causality. It aimed to test out hypotheses in the story that were first formulated on the basis of *documents humains* (cf. Zola 2003: 49).[9] Consequently, literature was seen as needing to provide universal, practically applicable knowledge that not only contained information about physical human particularities, but which also furnished insights into people's emotional and mental states.

What does this seemingly scientific approach tell us about Zola's conception of Second Empire Paris?[10] I claim that Zola contributed to the production of a conceived space of Paris via the creation of a mental map which was the result of his own theoretical and empirical research.[11] In the notebooks for his novel *The Belly of Paris*,[12] for example, one can find information about the urban built environment and sketches of the pavilions and streets adjoined to the market halls. These sketches often attested to the author's highly developed spatial sense, a capacity that brought him close to the work of 19th-century architects.[13] Zola's positivist leanings thus informed his cognitive map of Paris. Taken as a whole, it amounts to nothing less than "the building of a theoretical apparatus" which helped him (and the reader) "to possess the city in imagination" (Harvey 1989: 2).

As well as being mediated through the powerful scientific discourses of his time, Zola's experience was also influenced by the increasingly complex literary discourse on Paris.[14] Throughout the 19th century, positive attributes of the city—such as its cultural and intellectual diversity—were often overshadowed by the idea of the city as an "abyss", "hell" or "Babylon" (see Rousseau, Diderot, Mercier); as "unreal", "mythical", "labyrinthine" or "a black ocean" (see Hugo, Poe, Baudelaire)—to cite only a few examples. The underlying presuppositions of this literary discourse were that the city was legible and that the expression of urban experience in language was possible. In a cyclical process, the urban experience was translated into a multiplicity of metaphorical images which in turn became elements of actual urban experience. Many authors' main aim, however, beyond this "metaphorisation" of the city, was to produce a total representation of it (hence the gargantuan efforts embodied in Zola's Rougon-Macquart cycle or Balzac's *Comédie humaine*)—an attempt that was doomed to fail because of the impossibility of capturing the full complexity of urban experience. The substantial and dynamic transformation of 19th-century Paris—whether driven by Haussmann or capital accumulation or both—was almost by definition unrepresentable.

In short, taken together, the scientific and literary discourses were central in the formation of Zola's conception of space.

Zola's Sensorial Perception of the Market Quarter— Perception of Space

It is worth bearing this in mind when we now turn to his research methods and notes, i.e., his literal, affective encounter with the urban environment. In the spirit of Lefebvre's triad, I shall name this aspect of Zola's work his *perception* of space. Whereas conceived space is a mental construct, perceived space (*l'espace perçu*) is concrete, "the space of gestures and journeys, of the body and memory . . . the space that is generated and used [by its inhabitants]" (Elden 2004: 188f.).[15] It is precisely the observation of people's use of space, their movements and actions within it, and their appropriation of it that attracted Zola's interest. Because it has gone largely unnoticed, I shall spell out at some length the exact functions of spatial sense-perceptions in the notebooks.

Zola collected his data—those "things seen"—over days of time-consuming fieldwork at particular locations (mainly in order to inform his creation of characters and setting). He spent days and nights in the market halls observing the bustling activity around him.[16] Thus, his conception of space was extended and enriched by his personal experiential appropriation of *Les Halles*.[17] Like an ethnographer, Zola thereby sought to produce a "thick description" (Geertz 1999) of the city—an account of human behaviour enhanced by a supplementary description of that behaviour's context (cf. Lumbroso 2017). What is important here is that he experienced the context himself in order to gain knowledge. It is at this preparatory stage in Zola's work that he came closest to what we might call the perception of "material and physical" space (Elden 2004: 189)—that is, that aspect of space which the so-called "spatial turn" in literary studies has tended to ignore.

Ethnographical fieldwork often stresses the preponderant role of the senses of sight and hearing. The remarks in the notebooks concerning the topography of the market halls, as well as the streets, commodities, shops, etc. also attribute an importance to visual and auditory perceptions. Let us consider two examples—the first taken from Zola's nightly observations of the market halls. Here, the unloading of vegetables:

> Market halls at night. Each pavilion forms a square, with interior gas-lights (. . . rising in clouds); . . . Hardly any one there, noise muffled. . . . An employee—fat, large jacket, flabby hat, side whiskers, cane—gives out paperwork: "Oi! Over there, let's get moving . . . How many metres you got? . . . Five?"
>
> [*Les Halles la nuit. Le carré que forme chaque pavillon, avec les gaz intérieurs (rangés pour certains, poudroyant pour les autres) . . . Peu de monde, bruit sourd. . . . Un employé, gros, grand paletot, chapeau mou, favoris, une canne, distribue les bulletins: « Eh! Là-bas, avançons . . . Combien avez-vous de mètres ? . . . Cinq ?"*]
>
> (Carnets [henceforth C.]: 364)[18]

The second example is a compilation of impressions taken from different parts of the notebooks:

> There are coconut-sellers. Cock cry, afternoon; mud on the pavement. Hansoms pass by more rapidly and noisily. Sweepers, taking a break, with their big brushes;

Afternoon, church silent, people are confessing but you can hear the hubbub of the market halls, and especially the carriages rolling by the Saint-Eustache clock. The church has stoves;

At the barrier, overload, customs officers sounding people out. Noise of the jolts, in the great silence, with echoes against the houses, on the pavement strip;

[*Il y a des marchandes de coco. Un chant de coq, l'après-midi; Boue sur les pavés. Les fiacres passent plus rapides et plus sonores. Des balayeurs dans une éclaircie, avec leurs grandes brosses*] (C.: 349, *Notes générales*);

[*L'après-midi, l'église silencieuse, on confesse et l'on entend le brouhaha des Halles, et surtout le roulement des voitures à la pointe Saint-Eustache. L'église a des calorifères*] (C.: 359, *Les rues autours des Halles*);

[*A la barrière, encombrement, les gabelous sondant. Le bruit des cahos, dans le grand silence, avec échos contre les maisons, sur la bande de pavés*]

(C.: 364, *Une Nuit aux Halles*)

The visual descriptions are linked to the topographical, geometrical or architectural properties of space ("square"; "by the Saint-Eustache clock"; see also p. 349: "One angle of the market halls, oblique views of Montmartre street" [*Un aspect des halles, vues de biais, de la rue Montmartre*]) and serve the needs of a true-to-original conception of characters ("coconut-sellers"; "An employee—fat, large jacket, flabby hat etc.").[19] The auditory impressions register snippets of conversation ("Oi! Over there", etc.) in their temporal unfolding, snapshots of daily urban life ("Cock cry") and the contrast between silence and noise ("Noise of the jolts, in the great silence"). This linking together of sight and hearing is quite typical of the notebooks.[20] Since both senses were related to rationality and knowledge in scientific discourses of the 19th century, one might argue that Zola, the naturalistic author, consciously foregrounded the primacy of sight and hearing in his observations in order to connote the precision and transparency of his work.[21]

But there is an alternative explanation. Zola was close to the impressionist painters Monet and Cézanne, and once wrote: "I have translated them into literature by the touches, notes, and colorations, by the palette of many of my descriptions" [*Je les ai traduits en littérature, par les touches, notes, colorations, par la palette de beaucoup de mes descriptions*] (cited in Lethbridge in Nelson 2007: 67). Nelson (2007: 4) rightly states that "[h]e combines the vision of a painter with the approach of a sociologist and reporter in his observations". It thus comes as no surprise that various pictorial impressions in the notebooks stand in the tradition of impressionist painting. Just as these painters emphasized the role of light and colours in their (urban) motifs, Zola examines the effects of light on substances throughout his notes.[22]

And yet, even though visual and auditory perceptions are numerous in the notebooks, one cannot but stress the equal importance of the so-called "lower" senses of smell and touch in Zola's perception and construction of material space. Touch is mentioned at various points and is mainly associated with narrowness and the crowd ("narrow paths" [*étroits sentiers*] [C.: 366], "They [the eels] slide over one another" [*Elles [anguilles de mer] glissent l'une sur l'autre*] [C.: 389], "Massive crowd gathers around the sales offices" [*Une foule énorme se presse autour des bureaux de vente*] [C.: 390]). However, those passages in which smell is perceived are more striking still: the Vauvilliers street is described as "stinking" [*puante*] (C.: 355), and the vegetable market as follows: "In terms of odour what dominates is the sour smell of the carrots, and the perfume of parsley and celery" [*Ce qui domine comme odeur, c'est la senteur âpre des carottes, et le parfum du persil, et du céleri*] (C.: 364). Unsurprisingly, the flower market also has olfactory connotations: "Extremely penetrating and delicate smell" [*Odeur très pénétrante et très délicate*] (C.: 367); the cheese displayed in the cheese dairy has a "strong odour" [*odeur forte*] (C.: 396), each cellar "its own smell" [*son odeur propre*] (C.: 400), and the descent into the poultry storeroom is rendered thus:

> On entering, strong smell, penetrating and as if warm. It's the smell of feathers, of poultry excrement where the alkalis grab you by the throat, and the smell stays on your clothes for a long time. It must be very unhealthy to live in this enclosed air, full of living scents.
>
> *En entrant, odeur forte, pénétrante et comme tiède. C'est une odeur de plume, de fiente de volaille où les alcalis vous prennent à la gorge, et l'on garde longtemps l'odeur dans ses vêtements. Ce doit être très malsain de vivre dans cet air renfermé plein de senteurs vivantes.*
>
> (C.: 402)[23]

Zola seems to be very sensitive to "those qualities of the physical and geographical formations that are most difficult to detect" (Prieto in Tally 2011: 14). The passage quoted previously is only one example of how Zola detects and describes the affective qualities of an environment, or the effects of a perceived space. It shows how odours emanate within a closed space, becoming interiorised; Zola's stressing that it "grabs you by the throat" creates an atmosphere of malaise and imprisonment. In each case, one can sense what Kraft and Adey (cited in Rose et al. 2010: 339) call the "push that the particular relationship between a body and a building could bring about: an affect" (see Tuan 2001; Thrift 2004). This push is initiated by the fusion of bodily behaviour and sensory perception (of light, bodies in motion, e.g., merchants, crowds, etc.), and it results in an affective "feeling of buildings" (cf. Rose et al. 2010) or sense of place.[24]

In short, Zola's notebooks are full of sensory impressions, all of which help us to reconstruct at least a working hypothesis of the author's actual *perception* of space. And yet, this perception, as we have seen, is always already informed or mediated either by his *conceptions* of space or by the prevailing artistic discourses of his time. It is crucial to bear this in mind since Zola's notebook perceptions all seem non-reflexive: we enter a realm that appears to reside outside consciousness, constituted by the senses and various "reflexes and automatisms . . . which account for the bulk of [the city's] activity" (Amin and Thrift 2002: 28). The notebooks only include very few consciously formulated valuations of, or opinions about, the effect of the urban encounter. In fact, there is no verbal elaboration of Zola's cognitive or emotional state whatsoever—on the contrary, the notes consist solely of spontaneous, off-the-cuff perceptions. Through the author's intermittently shifting observations in the present tense, the reader gets the impression of experiencing Parisian space in all its immediacy. Nevertheless, this immediacy is never disinterested: Zola's approach to the urban is selective; he views the terrain, not only through the eyes of an impressionist painter, but also those of a (naturalist) novelist actively seeking out those locations or events which could eventually be exploited in the composition of the novel (cf. Mitterand 1987: 82).[25] Moreover, it is important to note that even if the olfactory and tactile, visual and auditory explorations of the Paris Halles are recorded without detailed emotional commentaries, the reader can sense the unease or pleasure Zola must have felt at certain places. Indeed, the emotive quality of the physical environment, as insignificant as it might seem in the notebooks, will become no less than the motivation for the overarching structures of symbolic and metaphorical meaning in the lived space of the novels.

The Belly of Paris—Lived Space

The last section of this article will focus precisely on how Zola brings together his *conceptions* and *perceptions* of space in the "lived space" (i.e., the third and final element of Lefebvre's conceptual triad) of the novel itself.[26] This third space (*l'espace vécu*) is the space of inhabitants, of artists and philosophers, etc.; [it is] "invested with symbolism and meaning. . . *real-and-imagined*" (Elden 2004: 190). Lefebvre describes it as a layer which covers material space by adding a symbolic connotation to its objects which thereby become signs decipherable by its inhabitants.[27] It is at the level of lived space, then, that subjective experiences, people's imagination and feelings are registered. In Zola's case, we can witness the creation of a fictionally represented lived space invested with symbolism and meaning which still contains his mental conceptions of space as well as his concrete and personal observations. This entails a process of translation of the elements of *espace perçu* and *espace conçu* into the fictional realm of the storyworld.[28]

At a very basic level, *The Belly of Paris* (henceforth B.) (*Le Ventre de Paris* [henceforth V.]) translates Zola's *conceived* space in several ways. Firstly, the whole structure of the book mirrors the spatial organization of Baltard's market halls; that is, there exists a structural homology between the concrete physical environment of *Les Halles* and the textual distribution of spatial information in the novel. Each chapter introduces a different pavilion (vegetables, fish, etc.) and explains how it functions. Secondly, the narrative distribution of information is always linked back to topographical reference points which specify a character's location: "Florent glanced up at the luminous clock of Saint-Eustache" [B.: 10]; "All the way down the Rue du Pont-Neuf " [B.: 13]; [*Florent . . . levait les yeux sur le cadran lumineux de Saint-Eustache* (V.: 24); *Tout le long de la rue du Pont-Neuf* (V.: 28)]. However, the communication of such empirical information through the medium of the novel is only one of the novel's functions. If Zola, in true naturalist guise, saw himself as a scientist whose job was to educate and enlighten the masses, he was also a novelist who wanted to tell a story about the city of Paris and its inhabitants. One might even go as far as to say that the novel itself is structured by these dual desires: to inform and to entertain, to describe and to narrate.

How did Zola go about doing both at once? He uses two main strategies. Firstly, he distributes both his *conceptions* and *perceptions* of space across several characters throughout the novel. The mental map of the Parisian market halls, for example, is deployed via character guides like Claude the painter or Madame François (or—another ploy—reconstructed through Florent's memory of places from before his exile). Because of the large variety of his personal data, Zola uses several characters, each of whom might be said to represent one facet of his urban experience, thus creating overlapping layers or multiple "senses of place". His characters are thereby often reduced to what Philippe Hamon (1983) has called "functionaries" [*fonctionnaires*]—mere conduits through which Zola can pour his perceptions and research. What is important to note here is that the diverse and multiple materials of the notebooks could potentially be spread across an infinite number of characters; thus, to prevent this boundless proliferation, Zola must limit them to the parameters of a fictional narrative. He cannot make use of the well-known 19th-century tradition of the Parisian *tableaux*, which consisted of non-narrative descriptions of particular locations and urban physiologies, precisely because this form is itself potentially infinite (after all, how many *tableaux* is too many *tableaux*?). In line with the need for closure inherent to the classical novel form, Zola thus had to find some way of producing an ordered narrative whole. He did so, firstly, via the imposition of a more or less enclosing spatial unit (the market quarter) on the multiple characterological perspectives, thus limiting them to a finite number. Then, secondly, he subordinated the individual lives and perceptions of the characters to an overarching narrative leitmotif: the battle between the fat [*les Gros*] and the skinny [*les Maigres*]. Thus, the first strategy for combining information and narration consists in distributing his research material across a cast of characters whose respective perspectives are unified by the space of the market halls and the overarching plot of *les Gros* versus *les Maigres*.

The second strategy for the narrativization of his research material was to include an abundance of descriptions. The novelist translates his material through long descriptive passages that function as an illustration of the determining milieu. It is the senses which filter this environment, hence why they play a significant role in the stylistic deployment of the story. As Philippe Hamon has shown:

> By definition a description is an interruption in the syntagmatics of the narration due to a paradigm (a catalogue, an enumeration, a lexicon), and thus a prolongation of the act of looking of the character who is assigned the description.
>
> (1983: 312)

The longer and more technical these passages become, the more the reader gets the impression that the writer's authorial voice is taking over, thus undermining the character's independent act of perception. Internal focalization (characters as reflectors, cf. Stanzel 1995) contrasts with the external focalization of the heterodiegetic narrator, meaning that we sometimes cannot abstract the multiplicity of perceptions from Zola's overriding standpoint. The consequence is that the feeling of immediacy the reader experienced when consulting the notebooks is now diluted because of its being channelled through a specific character's perspective.

There is then a second aspect to this process of translation between the notebooks and the novel: what, in the notebooks, was primarily denotative becomes, in the descriptions contained in the novel, connotative (that is, broadly speaking, *symbolic*). And it is precisely through this use of symbolic language that a creation of a meaningful, coherent sense of place occurs. Let us look at one of the translations of the notes into a descriptive passage. Here is the notebook version: "Bit by bit, however, day rose. At the end of Rambuteau street, in the sky, white tears. Then all becomes a tender grey. The gas-lights grow pale". [*Peu à peu cependant le jour grandit. Au fond de la rue Rambuteau, dans le ciel, des déchirures blanches. Puis tout devient d'un gris tendre. Les gaz pâlissent*] (C.: 367). These impressions are altered and prolonged in the novel:

> In the bars at the end of the neighbouring streets, the gas jets went out one by one, like stars dimming with the coming of day. Florent

watched Les Halles emerge slowly from the shadows, from the dreamland in which he had seen them, stretching out like an endless series of open palaces.

(B.: 24–25)

[Chez les marchands de vin, au fond des rues voisines, les becs de gaz s'éteignaient un à un, comme des étoiles tombant dans la lumière. Et Florent regardait les Halles sortir de l'ombre, sortir du rêve, où il les avait vues, allongeant à l'infini leurs palais à jour.]

(V.: 41)

It is not only the comparison of the street lamps with falling stars that seems poetic; above all, it is the awakening of the market halls from a dreamland that dramatizes the dawn. The contrast between nature and culture is also illustrated in another passage in which a *tableau* of fish is aestheticized through its visual and auditory comparison to jewellery. A "broad sunbeam [which, J.K.] falls from the windows of the large, covered street and [which, J.K.] makes the fish sparkle" [*large rai de soleil* [*qui*, J.K.] *tombe des vitres de la grande rue couverte et* [*qui*, J.K.] *fait resplendir tout le poisson*] (C.: 388) becomes

A shaft of light suddenly came through the glass roof of the covered avenue, illuminating all these precious colours, toned and softened by the waves—the iridescent flesh-tints of the shellfish. . . . It was as if the jewel boxes of some sea nymph had been emptied out on dry land—a mass of fantastic ornaments, heaps of necklaces, fabulous bracelets.

(B.: 91–92)

[Une barre de soleil, tombant du haut vitrage de la rue couverte, [qui, J.K.] vint allumer ces couleurs précieuses, lavées et attendries par la vague, irisée et fondues dans les tons clairs des coquillages . . . . C'était comme les écrins, vidés à terre, de quelque fille des eaux, des parures inouïes et bizarres, un ruissellement, un entassement de colliers.]

(V.: 128)

This excessive stylization produces clusters of affect; a type of writing which Katherine Ashley has labelled *écriture artiste*:

Like the Impressionist Painters of the 19th century who, to a large extent, neglected or rejected the moralizing narrative function of art in favour of perception and immediacy, *écriture artiste* draws attention not so much to the object being described as to its sensory effect.

(Ashley 2005: 25)

Here resides the most fundamental difference between the notebooks and their literary translation: the staccato-like notes of the writer's perceptions which retained the urban reality as their reference point are transposed into semiotically poeticised impressions where the fictional urban world is combined with a layer of myth. Through this multisensory aesthetic Zola transforms the abbreviated, pseudo-objective observations of the notebooks into descriptions whose affective intensity is a key component in the novel's representation of "lived space"—that type of space in which, as urban geographers have taught us, the real and the imagined combine.

These two strategies of narrativization come together to produce, at the level of the actual storyworld, an extremely nuanced sense of "lived space". The space of the novel is more than simply a setting in which the action takes place. As Bertrand-Jennings (1987: 11) argues: "symbolic or anthropomorphic, Zolian places live their own lives, shelter, crush, oust their occupants, and even tend to substitute themselves for these latter: they transform themselves into the protagonists of the great conflicts which traverse *Les Rougon-Macquart*". [*symboliques ou anthropomorphes, les lieux zoliens vivent de leur propre vie, abritent, écrasent, évincent leurs occupants, et tendent même à se substituer à eux pour se métamorphoser en acteurs des grands conflits qui traversent* Les Rougon-Macquart.] On several occasions, Paris is described as a living organism.[29] It is in the imaginative fusion of external and internal *milieux* where Zola's strength lies. Nelson (2007: 5) explains that the resulting atmospheres in his novels are "always presented through the eyes of individuals, and are never separate from human experience". The multiplicity of atmospheres and fictional urban experiences presented in *The Belly of Paris* always take as their starting point the physical interaction of characters with their environment, and in that sense they embody that very modern conception of the "production of space" about which Lefebvre wrote in such great detail. Indeed, the milieu is so closely interwoven with the characters that there would be no such space as *Les Halles* without the social groups inhabiting it. Thus, this type of literature contains *representations of the production of lived space*, ones which reproduce in fictional guise the simultaneously bodily and ideological dynamics of spatial production.

In the following, I would like to sketch out in more depth the precise nature of the "lived space" which is produced in the fictional world of Zola's novels. I have already referred to the distribution of the documentary material amongst the characters of the novel. This distribution allows the novelist to explore imagined affective worlds that are based on his actual "feeling of place" as previously described. In the case of *The Belly of Paris,* Zola presents four versions of space, which together form the totality of the novel's "lived space":[30] the space of artistry (1) (Claude), the space of spectacle (2) (Madame Saget, La Sarriette,

Madame Lecœur), the space of abundance and power (3) (Lisa, Quenu, Les Méhudins), and the space of nature (4) (Mme François, Marjolin & Cadine). All four belong to one or another of the two main collective protagonists of the novel: the Fat and the Skinny.[31]

These multiple affective topoi are partially unified through the perspective of Florent, whose alienation from his surroundings provides Zola with an excuse to have him constantly wander through the market halls. In contrast to Florent, whose unease regularly manifests itself in bodily form,[32] Claude's "space"—the space of artistry (space 1)—can best be described through fascination and curiosity.[33] His relation to the halls stands for the attitude of *les Maigres* in general: he is well aware of the present injustices and often complains about them, but he dare not act on this awareness because of his fear of being quite literally digested by the market.[34] His painterly vision—sight is the most cerebral and distancing of the senses in Zola's eyes—enables him to separate himself from his lived environment to a greater extent than other characters in the novel. But unlike Florent the political rebel, Claude remains ultimately just as trapped by the space of the market halls. The space of spectacle (space 2) also contrasts with Florent's negative experience of *Les Halles*; while the three ladies eagerly scour the market halls in search of scandals, exploiting the architectural peculiarities of the building the better to snoop and pry, Florent is repulsed by the excessive sensuality of the very spectacles they desire. Indeed, Lefebvre's explanation of the body as a site of resistance becomes pertinent here as a way of interpreting Florent's somatic unease as a mode of political resistance to the market system. No place, however, embodies these sensuous excesses more than the fishmonger's and the butcher's shop (the space of abundance and power—space 3),[35] places whose olfactory and tactile (not to mention sexual) overabundance are of truly Rabelaisian proportions. If Claude could at least partially distance himself from his *milieu*, some of the *Gros* are almost physically embedded in it.[36] It is only when Florent enters the space of nature (space 4) that he experiences feelings of homeliness and peace. This is the space of tradition or provinciality where, in a somewhat idealized manner, the senses come to rest.[37] This space, too, manages to achieve a certain distancing from the dominant space of the market hall, located as it is on the periphery between country and city.

The interaction of these four competing spaces—each of which embodies one or another aspect of Zola's spatial conceptions or perceptions—constitutes the *lived space* of the novel. And yet one of them is dominant: the space of abundance and power is the *place* of *les Gros* and it is this place which, because of the economic and political power of that class, constitutes the overarching *space* within which the other characters must function—whether that be simply to acquiesce, to create a pocket of resistance or, like Florent, to openly rebel. Lisa is the only character who seems to develop throughout the novel, ultimately becoming the incarnation of the successful *petite bourgeoise*. Following Lefebvre's *Production of Space*, one might argue that she represents the class which owns space and controls its production from a central position. It is Lisa who eventually unveils her hypocritical character and puts an end to the spatial disorganisation produced by Florent. Space thus becomes an active force, "the main issue in the conflict being related" (Pierre-Gnassounou in Nelson 2007: 95). The great narrative antagonism between *les Gros* and *les Maigres*, that same antagonism which we recognized as one of the formal organizing principles of the novel, is thus unveiled as a simultaneously *spatial* and *affective* antagonism. It is condensed in the ideological force field of the "lived space" produced by Zola's work in which senses of space, when drawn into the gravitational field of fiction, become constitutive elements of the novel's literary form.

Conclusion

The article demonstrated that the Parisian space in Zola's work in general, and in his novels in particular, is much more than just a simple necessity or décor, but on the contrary a highly researched, explored and elaborated spatial unit. Using Henri Lefebvre's theory, I have distinguished the various types of space that come into play during the genesis of Zola's novels—in this case, *The Belly of Paris*. The notebooks evidence that Zola's physical encounter with the market halls left a lasting impression on him—one that helped structure the whole narrative not only on the basis of his (mental) map or plans (conceived space), but of the actual physical space of *Les Halles*. This overarching frame, linked to the battle between *les Gros* and *les Maigres*, is then filled with the author's real-life experiences (perceived space), distributed among various characters' individual senses of space and enriched by metaphor and symbolicity (lived space). The arrangement of these elements results in a dialectical movement between conceived, perceived and lived space, between the real and the imagined: the layers merge without fully dissolving into an indistinct whole. One must bear in mind, however, that the representations of space in literature cannot be abstracted from the very literariness of the genre; the novel brings together real-life experiences with the levels of style, form and narrative. It is a medium which brings us close to the actual sensory and affective aspects of spatial experience, and one that captures the complex interweaving of practices, conceptions, perceptions and symbols in Zola's production of space.

Notes

1. "Lived space" is a fusion of physical and mental constructs, symbolism and meaning. It can be usefully compared with the notion of "real-and-imagined" space (in literature) (Detering et al. 2012: 263; see Soja 1996). Weigel (2002)

coined the term "topographical turn" to refer to the interdisciplinary work of cartography and literature, i.e., literary criticism's use of non-literary topographical knowledge for its analysis of space in texts. But because the notion implies an approach that works with already mediated materials (maps, etc.), it lent itself to a substantial extension. Consequently, it has since accrued a much wider scope and now designates diverse types of spatial representations (cf. Detering et al. 2012: 258). Even if Detering et al. concentrate their critiques on continental literary studies, Hones (2011) stresses that Anglo-American narrative theory also needs to revise its limited conception of space—a demand that she sees as being answered by literary geographers.

2. Victor Baltard designed the central market in Paris, consisting of twelve pavilions to be built from the then modern materials of glass and iron, and which were subsequently constructed between 1852 and 1936 (cf. Woollen 2000: 24).

3. We must, of course, always remain aware that this experience is overdetermined by the literary forms in and through which authors compose their works. Moreover, fictional storyworlds are obviously not always mediated through internal focalization; nevertheless, reader involvement is generally higher in those passages that are, for example, internally narrated from a single viewpoint (cf. Hillebrandt 2011: 87).

4. A more elaborate version of this approach can be found in my forthcoming book on "constructions of space" in selected preparatory dossiers and novels (*La Curée, Le Ventre de Paris, Au Bonheur des Dames*) by Émile Zola. It develops a theory of space in literature based on Henri Lefebvre's threefold dialectic of space which helps to overcome long-standing assumptions on Zola's alleged deterministic milieu theory by taking into account the character's involvement in the production of space.

5. A significant part of Zola's notebooks has already been published under the direction of Colette Becker, who extracted incoherent excerpts of the dossiers and arranged them into thematic groups. In the case of *The Belly of Paris*, these include: "General notes on the market halls" [*Notes générales sur les Halles*], "Streets adjoined to the halls" [*Les rues autour des Halles*], "A night in the market halls" [*Une Nuit aux Halles*], "Sales" [*La vente*], "The pavilions" [*Sous les pavillons de Baltard*], "The basements" [*Les caves, les resserres*] and Les Quenu-Gradelle (a family in the story).

6. The subtitle of his magnum opus, *The Natural and Social History of a Second Empire Family,* already hints at the aim of a cultural anthropology on the one hand and at the association of literature and science on the other (cf. Kaiser 1990: 37).

7. See Lefebvre (1991: 38f.): "Representations of space: conceptualized space, the space of scientists, planners, urbanists, technocratic subdividers and social engineers, as of a certain type of artist with a scientific bent—all of whom identify what is lived and what is perceived with what is conceived. . . . This is the dominant space in any society (or mode of production). Conceptions of space tend, with certain exceptions to which I shall return, towards a system of verbal (and therefore intellectually worked out) signs."

8. See in particular: Claude Bernard: *Introduction à l'étude de la médecine expérimentale.* Paris: B. Baillière et Fils, 1865; Prosper Lucas: *Traité philosophique et physiologique de l'hérédité naturelle.* Paris: Baillière et fils, 1847–1850. Likewise, the dossiers attest to a strong affiliation with Hippolyte Taine's social environmentalism which aimed at the analysis of the context of literary works based on "race", "milieu" and "moment". Zola was equally influenced by positivism (Auguste Comte), degeneration theory (Bénédict

Augustin Morel), evolution theory (Charles Darwin), chemistry (Antoine L. de Lavoisier) and temperament theory, to name but the main sources of inspiration.

9. Ashley (2005: 71) defines the notion *document humain* as follows: "the process of literary creation and the status of the document as material to be exploited in a novel [and] the result of the process of observation and the accumulation of data. . . . The document is, on the one hand, a material trace of a present or past empirical reality . . . and generate[s] what can, given the dual meaning of the term, be considered a new document: the novel."

10. For the purposes of this short article, I am going to concentrate on the preparatory notes (*Carnets*) of *The Belly of Paris* and their translation into the final novel. My conclusions can, however, be adapted to his other novels even though the content and location may vary.

11. The works mentioned in the dossiers include: Du Camp, M.: *Paris, ses organes, ses fonctions et sa vie dans la seconde moitié du XIXᵉ siècle*. Paris: Hachette et cie, vol II, 1870; Delord, T: *Histoire du second Empire*. 6 vols. Paris, 1869–1875; Delescluze, Ch.-L.: *De Paris à Cayenne, journal d'un transporté*. Paris: Le Chevalier, 1869 (cf. Scarpa 2000: 17).

12. *The Belly of Paris* is set in 1858–1859 and depicts the story of the Quenu-Gredelle, a branch of the Macquart family. Its protagonist is Florent, who returns to Paris after escaping from the island of Guyana where he had been wrongly imprisoned. No one knows his secret except for his brother Quenu and his wife, Lisa. The latter couple own a well-run butcher's shop within the market halls [*Les Halles*] of Paris. The situation worsens when Florent seeks to overthrow the ruling order of the market hall, thus endangering the existence of his brother's family.

13. Zola's friend, the architect and author Frantz Jourdain, went so far as to call him "the architect of Médan" [l'architecte de Médan] because of his precise rendering of the department store building in *Au Bonheur des Dames* (1884), thus confirming Zola's proximity to the architectural discourse of his time (cf. Nakai 2000: 556).

14. The elaboration of this discourse coincided with the very emergence of modern Paris itself (cf. Stierle 1993: 48).

15. See Lefebvre (1991: 38): "The spatial practice of a society secretes that society's space; it propounds and presupposes it, in a dialectical interaction; it produces it slowly and surely as it masters and appropriates it. From the analytic standpoint, the spatial practice of a society is revealed through the deciphering of its space".

16. Cf., for example, the entry "A night in the market halls" [*Une Nuit aux Halles*] in the notebook.

17. This included useful observations on the day-to-day functioning of this specific quarter, i.e., the flows of commodities and people as well as the mechanisms of control and administration (cf. Harvey 1989: 262; see also Harvey 2006).

18. Daniel Hartley deserves a special thanks for translating the original French passages and for reviewing an earlier version of this article.

19. There are other examples that testify to Zola's precision in topographical information: a whole chapter in the notebooks is devoted to the naming and description of streets in the market quarter.

20. One can find traces of this linking together in the *Experimental Novel* as well: "Here it is nearly always an experiment "pour voir" ["to see"], as Claude Bernard calls it."; "The observer relates purely and simply the phenomena which he has under his eye. . . . He should be the photographer of

phenomena, his observation should be the exact representation of nature . . . He listens to nature and he writes under its dictation" (Zola 1934: 7f.).

21. Recent research on the social and cultural history of the senses shows, however, that such a derivation is mistaken. Smith explains that the dominance of the eye traces back to "a particular style of . . . historical writing on the history of the senses . . . by intellectual historians" (2007: 13). He sees it as a cultural product of a particular social class that does not necessarily tell us something about the actual use of the senses. David Howes (1991, 2003, 2005), Constance Classen (1993, 1994, 1998) and Alain Corbin (1986, 2000) offer useful overviews of the range of cultural and social research on the senses.

22. Cf. "Only the streets' supine glass roofs give off rays of sunlight in the general gloom" [*Les verrières allongées des rues jettent seules des rais de soleil, dans le gris général*] (C.: 348, *Notes générales*); "The play of the light changes at every moment the face of the market halls. Sunset over the halls, the glass shines on high" [*Les jeux de lumière changent à chaque instant l'aspect des Halles. Un coucher de soleil sur les halles, les vitres brillent, en haut*] (C.: 349, ibid.); "Effect of a lantern beam on a heap of vegetables" [*Effet d'un coup de lanterne sur un tas de légumes*] (C.: 365, *Une Nuit aux Halles*). Alternatively, one might also explain this interest in light as a consequence of the use of steel and glass as building material in Haussmann's Paris. New architectural conditions—vast visual axes (streets, boulevards), the apparent annihilation of boundaries between inside and outside (market halls), and so forth—enabled new ways of perceiving which stressed the visual (cf. Palmbach 2001: 25–64).

23. The last sentence may refer to the idea that malicious smells cause diseases. This reasoning was common in France before the insights brought about by Louis Pasteur's bacteriology.

24. The distinction between space and place has been studied in various disciplines. I understand place as the result of a transformation of conceptual space into a factual, i.e., humanised and enclosed, centre of established values (cf. Westphal 2011: 5).

25. Colette Becker emphasises the fact that a first plan of the novel existed prior to Zola's fieldwork (cf. Becker 2003: 11). There are passages in the *Carnets* which prove this, for example: "It is in the poultry storeroom that I will have the rape scene take place" [*C'est dans la resserre aux volailles que je fera passer ma scène de viol*] (C.: 403); "I could make them love Cadine by holding a beautiful soiree there [in the auction pavilion]" [*Je pourrais y [dans le pavillon des criées] faire aimer Cadine par une belle soirée*] (ibid.). The observations could nevertheless influence the general plan (cf. Mitterand 1987: 84f.).

26. I argue in my forthcoming book that traces of "lived space" can already be found in the dossiers and that those layers interact with the conceptions and perceptions of space noted here. There exists thus an interplay of *espace conçu*, *perçu* and *vécu* in both the preparatory stage and the final stage of the novel which cannot be discussed at length here.

27. See Lefebvre (1991: 39): "Representational spaces: space as directly lived through its associated images and symbols, and hence the space of 'inhabitants' and 'users', but also of some artists and perhaps of those, such as a few writers and philosophers, who describe and aspire to do no more than describe. This is the dominated—and hence passively experienced—space which the imagination seeks to change and appropriate. It overlays physical space, making symbolic use of its objects. Thus representational spaces may be said, though again with certain exceptions, to tend towards more or less coherent systems of non-verbal symbols and signs".

28. Even if the dossiers prove his systematic approach to writing—Zola sketched a first plan for each novel (brief notes on the story's chapters) and then reviewed this plan with the help of his documentation—the actual genesis of the novel, i.e., the configuration of the research material, was a complex process of adaption and transformation of information (cf. Becker 2003: 11).

29. For example: "They seemed like some satiated beast, embodying Paris itself, grown enormously fat, and silently supporting the Empire" (B.: 124) or "The great voice of the markets grew louder" (translation modified), (B.: 20) [*Paris entripaillé, cuvant sa graisse, appuyant sourdement l'Empire*] (V.: 169) or [*La grande voix des Halles grondait plus haut*] (V.: 36).

30. It is important to note that these four "spaces" are theoretical constellations that I, as a reader, have abstracted from my experience of reading the novel. The whole point is that, from the fictional perspective of the characters in the storyworld, these four "spaces" are experienced as *place*.

31. Claude the painter, the political friends and the two gossips, Mme Saget and Mme Lecœur, belong to the Skinny with Florent as their "king" whilst the Quenu, the Méhudins, Monsieur Lebigre (a pub owner), Gavard, the young lovers Marjolin and Cadine, and La Sarriette, a fruit merchant, are part of the Fat (cf. V.: 252–54).

32. Florent's growing unease is generally rendered via the visual sense: "He wished he could no longer see; he turned towards Saint-Eustache, which he could now see. . . . The tide was still rising. He had felt it round his ankles, then on a level with his stomach, and now it threatened to drown him altogether. Blinded, submerged, his ears ringing, his stomach crushed by everything he had seen, feeling the presence of new, endless quantities of food, he prayed for mercy", (B.: 26ff.). [*Il ne voulait plus voir, il regardait Saint-Eustache. . . . Il l'avait senti à ses chevilles, puis à son ventre; elle menaçait, à cette heure, de passer par-dessus sa tête. Aveuglé, noyé, les oreilles sonnantes, l'estomac écrasé . . . il demanda grâce*] (V.: 42ff.).

33. Cf. "Claude had enthusiastically jumped onto the bench", (B.: 25). [*Mais Claude était monté debout sur le banc, d'enthousiasme*] (V.: 43).

34. Cf. "Paris was chewing over the daily food of its two million inhabitants", (B.: 29). [*Paris mâchait les bouchées à ses deux millions d'habitants*] (V.: 49).

35. Both places are described visually, but receive their characteristic stamp from tactile and olfactory impressions. The fish market is presented as a rude and malicious milieu that has generally negative connotations: "penetrating smell; the stench of rotting flesh mingled with the smell of mud in the neighbouring streets . . . the stench rose and the air grew heavy with the hot air of plague", (B.: 121). [*odeur pénétrante; des senteurs de chairs tournées se mêlèrent aux souffles fades de boue . . . la puanteur monta, alourdit l'air d'une buée pestilentielle*] (V.: 164). The butcher's shop is a place of abundant nutrition; it is place and space at the same time since it is a miniature version of the overall structuring space of the Fat and the Skinny.

36. Cf. "She had the fine skin and pinky-white complexion of those who spend their lives surrounded by fat and raw meat", (B.: 35). [*Sa chair paisible avait cette blancheur transparente, cette peau fine et rosée des personnes qui vivent d'ordinaire dans les graisses et les viandes crues*] (V.: 57, my italics).

37. Which is not to say that Zola *always* idealised nature. On the contrary, in true Enlightenment spirit, he believed it was necessary to domesticate it. Take the characters Marjolin and Cadine, for example. They are creatures born in the market halls and seem to respond to their environment in a naïve and intuitive way. They explore the subterranean spaces via vertical movements,

climbing up on the roofs of the halls or hiding in the basements. And yet this potentially transgressive force must always be tamed: when Marjolin attacks Lisa with "the strenght of a bull" (B.: 182) [*une force de taureau*] (V.: 239), she fights back and thus re-establishes order.

Bibliography

Amin, Ash and Thrift, Nigel: *Cities. Reimagining the Urban.* Cambridge: Polity Press, 2002.

Ashley, Katherine: *Edmond de Goncourt and the Novel: Naturalism and Decadence.* Amsterdam and New York: Rodopi, 2005.

Bachtin, Michael M.: *Chronotopos.* Frankfurt and Main: Suhrkamp, 2008.

Becker, Colette: "Préface", in: Zola, Émile, edited by Becker, Colette: *La Fabrique des Rougon-Macquart: Édition des dossiers préparatoires.* vol. 1. Paris: Champion, 2003, 7–19.

Bernard, Claude: *Introduction à l'étude de la médecine expérimentale.* Paris: B. Baillière et Fils, 1865.

Bertrand-Jennings, Chantal: *Espaces romanesques.* Collection Etudes 47, Sherbrooke: Naaman, 1987.

Classen, Constance (ed.): *Worlds of Sense: Exploring the Senses in History and Across Cultures.* New York: Routledge, 1993.

———: *Aroma: The Cultural History of Smell.* New York: Routledge, 1994.

———: *The Colour of Angels: Cosmology, Gender and the Aesthetic Imagination.* New York: Routledge, 1998.

Corbin, Alain: *Le Miasme et la jonquille—l'odorat et l'imaginaire social 18–19ème siècle.* Paris: Flammarion, 1986.

———: *Les cloches de la terre—Paysage sonore et culture sensible dans les campagnes au XIXème siècle.* Paris: Flammarion, 2000.

Delescluze, Ch.-L.: *De Paris à Cayenne, journal d'un transporté.* Paris: Le Chevalier, 1869.

Delord, T: *Histoire du second Empire.* 6 vols. Paris: Baillière, 1869–75.

Detering, Heinrich, Seifert, Kim and Winkler, Kathrin: "Die Literaturwissenschaften im Spatial Turn. Versuch einer Positionsbestimmung", *Journal of Literary Theory* (1) (2012), 253–69.

Döring, Jörg and Thielmann, Tristan (ed.): *Spatial turn. Das Raumparadigma in den Kultur- und Sozialwissenschaften.* Bielefeld: Transcript, 2008.

Du Camp, M.: *Paris, ses organes, ses fonctions et sa vie dans la seconde moitié du XIXe siècle.* vol. II. Paris: Hachette et cie, 1870.

Elden, Stuart: *Understanding Lefebvre. Theory and the Possible.* London and New York: Continuum, 2004.

Foucault, M.: "Des espaces autres. Une conférence inédite de Michel Foucault", *Architecture, Mouvement, Continuité* 5 (1984), 46–49.

Geertz, Clifford: *Dichte Beschreibung. Beiträge zum Verstehen kultureller Systeme.* Frankfurt and Main: Suhrkamp, 1999.

Hamon, Phillipe: *Le personnel du roman. Le système des personnages dans 'Les Rougon-Macquart'.* Geneva: Droz, 1983.

Harvey, David: *The urban experience.* Baltimore: The Johns Hopkins University Press, 1989.

———: *Paris, capital of modernity.* New York: Routledge, 2006.

Hillebrandt, Claudia: *Das emotionale Wirkungspotenzial von Erzähltexten. Mit Fallstudien von Kafka, Perutz und Werfel.* Berlin: Akademie Verlag, 2011.

Hones, Sheila: "Literary Geography: setting and narrative space", *Social & Cultural Geography* 12 (7) (2011), 685–99.

Howes, David (ed.): *The Varieties of Sensory Experience: A Sourcebook in the Anthropology of the Senses.* Toronto: University of Toronto Press, 1991.

——, *Sensual Relations: Engaging the Senses in Culture and Social Theory.* Ann Arbor: University of Michigan Press, 2003.

——: *The Empire of the Senses: The Sensual Culture Reader.* Oxford: Berg, 2005.

Jameson, Fredric: *Postmodernism, or, The Cultural Logic of Late Capitalism.* Durham: Duke University Press, 1991.

Kaiser, Elke: *Wissen und Erzählen bei Zola.* Tübingen: Narr, 1990.

Lefebvre, H.: *The Production of Space.* Oxford [u.a.]: Blackwell, 1991.

——: *La production de l'espace* (1974). Paris: Anthropos, 2000.

Leroux, Pierre and Neveu, Erik (Hg.): *En immersion —Expériences, pratiques, représentations de l'immersion en sciences sociales et journalisme et littérature.* Institut d'Études politique de Rennes: PUR, 2017.

Lethbridge, Robert: "Zola and Contemporary Painting", in: Nelson, Brian: *The Cambridge Companion to Emile Zola.* New York: Cambridge University Press, 2007, 67–85.

Lotman, Jurij M.: *Die Struktur literarischer Texte.* München: Fink, 1972.

Lucas, Prosper: *Traité philosophique et physiologique de l'hérédité naturelle.* Paris: Baillière et fils, 1847–50.

Lumbroso, Olivier: "La sociologie pratique d'Émile Zola: ,L'immersion émergente' en régime naturaliste", in: Leroux, Pierre and Neveu, Erik (Hg.): *En immersion —Expériences, pratiques, représentations de l'immersion en sciences sociales et journalisme et littérature.* Institut d'Études politique de Rennes: PUR, 2017, S. 79–92.

Mitterand, Henri: *Le regard et le signe. Poétique du roman réaliste et naturaliste.* puf Écriture, 1987.

——: "Intertexte et avant-texte: la bibliothèque génétique des Rougon-Macquart", 2007. Available online at: www.item.ens.fr/index.php?id=172739 (22.02.2019).

Nakai, Atsuko: "Architecture et Littérature. L'influence réciproque entre Émile Zola et Frantz Jourdain", *Doshisha Studies in Language and Culture* 2 (4) (2000), 547–83.

Nelson, Brian: *The Cambridge Companion to Emile Zola.* New York: Cambridge University Press, 2007.

Palmbach, Barbara: *Paris und der Impressionismus.* Weimar: VDG, 2001.

Pierre-Gnassounou, Chantal: "Zola and the art of fiction", in: Nelson, Brian: *The Cambridge Companion to Emile Zola.* New York: Cambridge University Press, 2007, 86–104.

Prieto, Eric: "Geocriticism, Geopoetics, Geophilosophy, and Beyond", in: Tally Robert T.: *Geocritical explorations: space, place, and mapping in literary and cultural studies.* New York: Palgrave Macmillan, 2011, 13–28.

Relph, Edward: *Place and Placelessness.* London: Pion 1976.

Rose, Gillian, Degen, Monica and Basdas, Begum: "More on 'big things': Building Events and Feelings", *Transactions of the Institute of British Geographers* 35 (3) (2010), 334–49.

Scarpa, Marie: *Le Carnaval des Halles. Une ethnocritique du Ventre de Paris de Zola.* Paris: CNRS Éditions, 2000.

Smith, Mark M.: *Sensing the Past. Seeing, Hearing, Smelling, Tasting and Touching in History.* Los Angeles and Berkeley: University of California Press, 2007.

Soja, Edward W.: *Postmodern Geographies. The Reassertion of Space in Critical Social Theory.* London and New York: Verso, 1989.

————: *Thirdspace. Journeys to Los Angeles and other Real-and-Imagined Places.* Cambridge: Blackwell, 1996.

Stanzel, Franz K.: *Theorie des Erzählens.* Göttingen: Vandenhoeck & Ruprecht, 1995.

Stierle, Karlheinz: *Der Mythos von Paris. Zeichen und Bewusstsein der Stadt.* München: Hanser, 1993.

Tally, Robert T., Jr. (ed.): *Geocritical explorations: space, place, and mapping in literary and cultural studies.* New York: Palgrave Macmillan, 2011.

Thrift, Nigel: "Intensities of Feeling: Towards a Spatial Politics of Affect", *Geografiska Annaler* 86B (1) (2004), 57–78.

Tuan, Yi-Fu: *Space and Place. The Perspective of Experience.* Minneapolis: University of Minnesota Press, 2001.

Weigel, Sigrid. (2002) "Zum 'topographical turn': Kartographie, Topographie und Raumkonzepte in den Kulturwissenschaften." *KulturPoetik* 2.2. pp. 151–165.

Westphal, Bertrand: *Geocriticism: Real and Fictional Spaces.* Basingstoke: Palgrave Macmillan, 2011.

Woollen, Geoff: "Zola's Halles, A *Grande Surface* Before Their Time", *Romance Studies* 18 (1) (2000), 21–30.

Zola, Émile, edited by Sherman, Belle: *The Experimental Novel* (1880). New York: The Cassell, 1934.

————, edited by Becker, Colette: *La Fabrique des Rougon-Macquart: Édition des dossiers préparatoires.* vol. 1. Paris: Champion, 2003.

————, edited by Mitterand, Henri: *Carnets d'enquêtes. Une ethnographie inédite de la France* (1986). Paris: Terre Humain and Plon. 2005.

————: *The Belly of Paris.* New York: Oxford University Press, 2007.

————: *Le Ventre de Paris* (1873). Paris: Librairie Générale Française, 2010.

6 "Dr. Livingstone, I presume?"

The Demonic Grounds of M. NourbeSe Philip's *Looking for Livingstone: An Odyssey of Silence*

Kate Siklosi

Traditionally, the study of geography is largely concerned with mapping and organizing the land according to Euclidean distances and measurements. More recently, however, the material and physical tenets of geographical discourse have been fused with the semiotic—spaces are no longer meaningful in terms of strict calculation alone but are also considered human, semiotic planes that are imbued with history and signification beyond the physicality of the landscape. This lens offers promising possibilities for the ways in which literature can reimagine historical geographical narratives and propose alternative ways of moving through and being in space. In *Demonic Grounds: Black Women and the Cartographies of Struggle* (2006), feminist human geographer Katherine McKittrick argues for such a revisioning and restructuring of geographic discourse along humanist lines. As she points out, "racial-sexual domination is an ongoing spatial project" (121), for the production of geographical space is inextricably linked with racial ideologies and experiences. According to McKittrick, black geographies have largely been rendered invisible by traditional geographical discourses, which are built on capitalist systems of value and metanarratives of dispossession that "*require* black displacement, black placenessness, black labour, and a black population that submissively stays 'in place'" (9; original emphasis). Such metanarratives of domination operate from a singular vantage point, one that serves to "naturalize both identity and place, repetitively spatializing where nondominant groups 'naturally' belong" (xv).

In order to "rethink the complex linkages between history, blackness, race, and place" (143) as sites of spatial production, McKittrick borrows the term "demonic" from Caribbean cultural critic Sylvia Wynter.[1] The demonic demarcates oppositional spaces and places for black geographies that are rendered invisible by traditional geographic epistemologies. It involves interpreting the landscape with a tripartite epistemological, linguistic, and spatial lens; as McKittrick puts it, this provides

> a very different geography; one which is genealogically wrapped up in the historical spatial unrepresentability of black femininity and . . . one that thinks about the ways in which black women necessarily contribute to a re-presentation of human geography.
>
> (xxv–xxvi)

This multiscalar geographic approach disrupts the colonizer's view of the land and its inhabitants as transparent and objectively knowable. That is, the demonic alters the very notion of territory: rather than existing as a stable marker of naturalized "place," territory becomes a fluid and local ground that develops with, rather than against, the subjectivities that inhabit the land.

One of the tools of this alternative geographic and cartographic mode is language—the human resonances and reverberations of the landscape, and the lived experiences and accumulated stories humans tell. In Tobagan-Canadian poet M. NourbeSe Philip's poetic novella *Looking for Livingstone: An Odyssey of Silence* (1991), demonic grounds are established through the protagonist, known only as "The Traveller," moving through the African landscape by memory, feel, and language. Over the course of the work, The Traveller ventures into the interior of Africa to challenge the "discoveries" of Scottish missionary and explorer Dr. David Livingstone. Livingstone's legacy of exploration represents Africa's mythological place in the European imaginary as an "uncharted," "virginal" frontier that, with its perceived lack of origin and geographical arrangements, was seen to need European intervention to "discover" the land and "civilize" its people. Livingstone is said to have been the first European to see "the falls of Mosiotunya," which he then renamed "Victoria Falls" (Philip, *Looking for Livingstone* 7). He was also shown other African sites by Indigenous Africans, such as the local main river systems, which he afterwards claimed to have also discovered. The Traveller sets out to reinstate the silence created by Livingstone's imperialist exploits, while also venturing across the land to reclaim the stolen inherited silences of her foremothers.

The Traveller's journey takes place across time and space, as her creation narrative spans thousands of years. The mock-Biblical style of the text, as well as its self-reflexive appropriation of the travel narrative (the book is constructed in a series of dated diary entries of her "discoveries"), represents a counter-hegemonic reimagining of historiography and geographic conquest. This allegorical journey into the African interior is mirrored by The Traveller's own exploration of her inner geography, the mapping of her own silence, "not a thing to be discovered, so much as recovered" (10). As such, the work destabilizes imperialist assumptions about the "silence" of Africa and its people by threading intricate accounts of people's physical, spiritual, and geographic resistance to colonization. Livingstone's quest through Africa is thus paralleled by The Traveller's journey, and whereas Livingstone's quest to "discover" Africa imposes European meaning and authorial word—the patriarchal "father tongue"—upon the land and its peoples, The Traveller's quest recovers the rich meanings of silence outside Eurocentric systems of signification.

For McKittrick, both the material reality and imagined potential of space are integral to our understanding of geographical discourse; and because black women, in particular, are largely absent from the geographies of patriarchal power, we must work towards "more humanly workable" lenses and conceptual frameworks (McKittrick xii). Philip's work in *Looking For Livingstone*, and throughout her entire oeuvre, answers this call by shedding light on the ways in which literature can imbue the study and practice of geography with a linguistic, human focus—one that resists or provides an alternative to the calculating rationality of "mapping" and "naming" that upholds the colonial project. Along The Traveller's journey, a demonic ground is established by means of her haptic interaction with the land and her relations to and interactions with the people and objects in the local landscape, and a language, practice, and geography of silence surfaces. And in her final confrontation with Livingstone—which I will turn to later in this discussion—The Traveller demonstrates the way in which language can produce space in the face of erasure in historical narratives. In other words, her journey "reveal[s] new and innovative spatial practices: if one moves through, rebuilds, contests, or even 'says' space, 'natural' geographic arrangements are called into question" (McKittrick 145–46). In her book *Frontiers*, Philip also attests to this profound "sayability" of imagined geographies from occupied centres instead of outside margins. As she writes,

> dreaming—the imagination—the one faculty of the human that can resist colonization. To construct imaginative and poetic worlds AS IF we were at the centre. To design imaginative and poetic scapes with us at the centre. We speak from the centre and are whole.
>
> (69–71)

Philip's work thus unites the imaginative possibilities of space with "a flesh-and-blood worldview implicit to the production of space" (McKittrick 122).

In light of Philip's geographical allegory and McKittrick's discussion of demonic grounds—with their common focus on oppositional methodologies and linguistic constructions of space—Deleuze and Guattari's framework of nomadology in *A Thousand Plateaus*, figured by the rhizome, is also a useful tool for considering the ways in which Philip intervenes on imperialist geographic schemas and narratives. Deleuze and Guattari use the concept of the rhizome as a trope to characterize the movements and ideology of nomadic cultures.[2] As opposed to the vertical hierarchy of the State (in which the upwards growth of a tree is symbolic) the nomad negotiates space horizontally, arriving and departing between various paths as opposed to a fixed point. To be sure, their theory has been rightly criticized for its tendency to romanticize the rhizome/nomad, figuring it as a radical, transgressive figure that moves about "unscripted." However, in Philip's narrative, and in McKittrick's theory, there are very real and entrenched scripts in place that are meant to contain, control, and silence bodies, and so the rhizome/nomad can be a helpful metaphor for the ways in which The Traveller renegotiates movement and spatial production outside of these bounds.

In applying the geographic theories of demonic grounds and nomadology to Philip's narrative, certain binaries surface—namely, the confrontation of *nomos* and *logos* (figured as "nomad" versus "royal" science), and "smooth" versus "striated" space—that highlight the friction between hegemonic and alternative spatial practices. By means of what I call The Traveller's *intensive mapping* of smooth space—my term for a non-Euclidean measure of geography that expands upon McKittrick's notion of demonic geography by inflecting it with the Deleuzoguattarian notion of nomadic *intensity* (as opposed to statist *extensity*)—as well as The Traveller's displacement of colonial *logos* with localized *nomos*, a demonic ground is established from which she resists colonial sanctions of geographical, corporeal, and epistemological space.

Before going further, however, it will be helpful to flesh out what I mean by "intensive mapping" and how it characterizes The Traveller's movement through space and her creation of demonic grounds in imperialist Africa.

"Geography," as Deleuze argues, is "no less mental and corporeal than physical in movement" (*Dialogues II* 38) and thus becomes a discipline of various intensities rather than of static substances. Intensity is closely linked to nomadology—the movement of agential vectors across planes of "smooth space." Smooth space stands in contrast to striated space, wherein the landscape is viewed as a planiform, homogenized surface consisting of fixed points that are assigned definite values and can be "counted" according to traditional geographic and cartographic means. Land so precisely calculated and lineally striated, and viewed from a universalized external perspective, allows for space to be readily reproduced. Smooth space, on the other hand, resists such totalizing impulses by disallowing an externalized point of view. As Deleuze and Guattari explain,

> Smooth space is a field without [parallel] conduits or channels. A field, a heterogeneous smooth space, is wedded to a very particular type of multiplicity: nonmetric, acentred, rhizomatic multiplicities

that occupy space without "counting" it and "can be explored only by legwork." They do not meet the visual condition of being observable from a point in space external to them; an example of this is the system of sounds or even of colours, as opposed to Euclidean space.

(*A Thousand Plateaus* 409)

Moving through smooth space "by legwork" thus involves traveling *intensely* as opposed to *extensively* (528). With this lens, not just physical coordinates but colours, sounds, sights, rituals, and voices all become a way of signalling the human in and through space. Such a cartographic mode presents a challenge to the historical fixity of origin, for drifting between multiple sites on the land reterritorializes the landscape beyond its sited/sighted bounds; or, as Deleuze and Guattari put it, "Here the absolute is local, precisely because place is not delimited" (494). Their theory helps expound the ways in which human history and traditional geography has entrenched measured coordinates and specific sites as the markers of place; rather, they propose that entire regions and landscapes can also be considered places that are full of movement, meaning, and being.

As an epistemological mode, *nomos* is embodied and based on proximities rather than precision and empirical validation. Moving through the landscape by means of intensive mapping creates unpredictable and objectively unknowable pathways that both resist and permeate the controlling order of State-instituted boundaries of human movement. Philip's Traveller navigates the African interior haptically and spiritually: as she tells Livingstone at the end of the text, "what I did, I did all by myself— no guides, no artificial horizons, no compasses" (62). This is opposed to the luxuries of the well-equipped Livingstone, the explorer-missionary:

> His supplies alone would have kept me going for centuries—a thermometer; quinine for malaria; a magic lantern to frighten and impress the "savage heathen" with God; guns for killing . . . Thomson's Logarithm Tables; and, of course, the "good book" . . . as well as sugar, coffee, and tea—"elevenses" in the deep, mysterious African jungle! . . . And finally his arrogance—his insurmountable arrogance.
>
> (16)

As opposed to Livingstone, The Traveller moves through the landscape by means of intensive mapping—using nomadic movement, local rituals, and linguistic interventions to find her way. And in so doing, she ruptures the imperialist "word" imposed on the land by Livingstone's maps and "discoveries."

Philip's work is undergirded by a word/silence dichotomy that becomes a spatial metaphor for the struggles between colonizer and colonized from the past through to the present. The word/silence dichotomy points to the historical rendering of silence as invisible and immaterial, and subject to displacement by the patriarchal power of the word.[3] Over the course of The Traveller's journey, silence is retrieved from its colonial circumscription as immaterial and ungeographic; no longer categorized as stagnant or passive, the "travelling silence" embodied by The Traveller destabilizes the word as *the* authorial colonial tool. This conception of the land as a material and semiotic assemblage of vibrant forces comes together in what Philip elsewhere theorizes as the "word/i-mage equation":

> The power and threat of the artist, poet or writer lies in this ability to create new i-mages, i-mages that speak to the essential being of the people among whom and for whom the artist creates. If allowed free expression, these i-mages succeed in altering the way a society perceives itself and, eventually, its collective consciousness . . . This can only be done by consciously restructuring, reshaping and, if necessary, destroying the language.
>
> (Philip, "The Absence" 12, 21)

Philip's bifurcation of the term "image" into "i-mage" references "the Rastafarian practice of privileging the 'I' in many words" (12) and serves to overturn the denial of African subjectivity in colonial historiography. In Philip's work, the historical dislocation of the i-mage from the word is marked by spatial dispossession and forced oppression under the foreign tongue of the colonizer. Both the linguistic and geographical violence of the imperialist project is underscored by a displacement of being that must be revived by "reshaping" or even "destroying the language."

Philip's Traveller reconstructs the i-mage based on a series of linguistic and spatial movements that are guided by mystic rituals that oppose the *logos* inscribed by the State. Throughout her journey, The Traveller pivots based on the wisdom she gains from the women in the African tribal communities that she encounters, whose names are different anagrams of the word "SILENCE." For instance, she visits the Museum of Silence that houses the various "labelled, annotated, dated, catalogued" silences of the anagram tribes (Philip, *Looking for Livingstone* 57). When leaving, The Traveller sprinkles white "powder of unforgetting" (58) in the manner of the voodoo *vèvè* outside the museum doors. The *vèvè* is an African-Haitian ritual in which specific deities are invoked by drawing on the ground using chalk or corn flour. As Harold Courlander explains, "the *vèvè* is not a permanent record . . . In the ensuing ritual and dance, the *vèvè* is obliterated by the feet that pass across it" (125). The impermanence of the *vèvè*, with its impetus of improvization, subverts European claims to stable, static truths about the land. Lamenting the silencing of these voices by the museum, The Traveller (re)inscribes the space with the ancestral silences represented by the sacred drawings—she reterritorializes the ground by invoking the silenced spirits of her foremothers. The reclamatory signature of the *vèvè* undermines the authorial possession of the "word," embodied by the "royal science" of the museum—and by extension, Livingstone. The Traveller's redrawing encroaches on the territory of the museum by improvising space with specific ancestral locality.

The Traveller must negotiate these demonic grounds using *nomos*—the learned local wisdom of the African women and her inner silence—as her epistemological guide. As mentioned previously, the names of the tribal communities she encounters all form anagrams of the word "SILENCE"—a rhetorical move on Philip's part that subverts the colonial circumscription of African silence as singular, transparent, and unvarying. While visiting the CESLIENS tribe, The Traveller is put into the centre of a circle drawn in the dirt and given a string with which she attempts to measure the circle's circumference using the mathematical constant "pi." Each attempt to measure the circle in this traditional scientific manner fails, as the string transforms into a snake and an umbilical cord in her hands. Recalling both the Fall of Eden and The Traveller's own birth, the string symbolizes the word, creating a circle of memory that circumscribes history. The string—the word—proves to be no more than an empty illusion, useless to The Traveller aside from reminding her of what is within—her memory and her silence. The calculative, linear measurements of royal science do not serve The Traveller in this space; she remains caught in the circle until a thought comes to her to draw her own circle inside of the one drawn by the other women. While inside this other circle, she is enlightened as to the anagram puzzle given to her by a previous tribe, which, when solved, would tell The Traveller something about the object of her quest. By means of this mystical methodology, the words "SURRENDER and WITHIN" (38) surface, symbolizing the need to give herself to her own history, to her own memory of silence.

As this episode demonstrates, The Traveller must negotiate space demonically without the use of traditional tools of objective measurement by relying on the relations between herself and the intensities in her environment. As Deleuze and Guattari remind us, smooth space is "a space of affects, more than one of properties" (528), and so The Traveller must proceed by "haptic rather than optical perception . . . intensities, wind and noise, forces, and sonorous and tactile qualities" (528). Trapped in the mystical circle, the Traveller must forge new connections between her body and the physical environment, engaging with a "topology that relies not on points or objects but rather on haecceities, on sets of relations" (421). This movement through space involves a spiritual connection to one's surroundings, one that is also entrenched in the concept of the demonic, which

> invites a slightly different conceptual pathway—while retaining its supernatural etymology—and acts to identify a system . . . that can only unfold and produce an outcome if uncertainty, or (dis)

organization, or something supernaturally demonic, is integral to its methodology.

(McKittrick xxiv)

The Traveller must create her narrative from memory, from the mystical intensities of the landscape, and from communing with other women in ritual—it is this intensive, spiritual mapping that disarticulates the "word" of Livingstone and evades his knowledge and possession. These creative and linguistic relations between the body and the landscape open concealed subjectivities within geographical spaces that have been overwritten in historical record, for as McKittrick argues, " 'saying,' imagining, and living geography locates the kinds of creative and material openings traditional geographic arrangements disclose and conceal" (144).

Further opposing the linearity and causality of patriarchal historical record, The Traveller's journey itself takes place across various "circles" of history, for she "travels in circles . . . circles upon circles" (10) in a manner that mimics the encircled nature of the world's various historical narratives, both written and unrecorded. As Philip declares in the text,

> The traveller seeks
> contentment
> in silence
> containment
> of press of circle upon circle
> that cleanses
> the pollute
> the profane in word

(39; original spacing)

Formally speaking, the narrative of the text is repeatedly broken by these commentaries on the nature of the relationship between word and silence in historiography. Philip constructs the majority of these poetic passages in a divisive line structure that mimics a ledger which poetically enacts the process of balancing the word/silence equation. Uniting form and content, these intermittent poetic passages disrupt the circular continuity of traditional historical narratives by inserting hermeneutical circles of silence. The circular motifs in Philip's work thus render both time and history as alterable sites and cites, changeable by memory and the intensity of silence against the extensive word. In her discussion of Philip's work, McKittrick also employs the circle as a somatic symbol, for she asserts that the "geography of the body touches elsewhere—it moves between the local (the inner space between the legs), the outside (the place of oppression, the plantation) the New World, and circles back again to reinvent black (female/New World) diaspora histories" (50).

Philip's circular motif also challenges the "either/or" logic of Western colonial geographic narratives by allegorizing the conflict between the *nomos* embodied by The Traveller and her silence, and the *logos* embodied by Livingstone and his imposed "word." Whereas the "word" represents the violence of the colonial historical record and its erasure of African peoples' subjective and geographical agency, silence becomes representative in the text of stolen African history, culture, language, and place. For example, Livingstone's "naming" of Victoria Falls according to *logos* is an attempt to rationalize and impose colonial boundaries, to encamp the land as a found "site" in the authorized fiction of history. The Traveller's demonic negotiations of geography, on the other hand, subvert the colonial ideas of black presence and place as symbolic; as McKittrick writes, "Sanctioned geographic knowledges position the black subject, and her/his [sic] politics of location, as symbolic (rather than real) interruptions in the landscape" (14, 19). In Philip's work, The Traveller does not only interrupt the colonial landscape, she commands it and seeks vengeance through breaking down Livingstone and his frail colonial logic. In her final exchange with Livingstone, which spans several pages and hundreds of years, The Traveller addresses Livingstone and states:

> "You captured and seized the Silence you found—possessed it like the true discoverer you were—dissected and analysed it; labeled it— you took their Silence—the Silence of the African—and replaced it with your own—the silence of your word."

> (70)

It is important to note that The Traveller exposes the epistemic violence of colonial record without simply *replacing* it with the metanarrative of silence. As Eva C. Karpinsky observes, by seeking "not to fill the silences in the historical record but to testify to their presences," The Traveller "undermines the record, as well as the way of reading other people's histories and cultures presumed to be represented" (189).

Indeed, in her Socratic-like final exchange with Livingstone, The Traveller challenges the master narratives and claimed "truths" of Livingstone's legacy by paralleling them with her narrative of silence. Here, the volatile binaries in the text between *nomos* and *logos*, smooth and striated space, silence and the word, come to a head and imperial power structures are dramatized, plundered, and destabilized in the process. In the heated confrontation, The Traveller challenges Livingstone's accolades— the "royal" honorariums of books, awards, and keys to cities—as markers of "fact" and "proof." The Traveller exposes "fact" as a construction that is supported by power structures, for as she explains to Livingstone, "a fact is whatever anyone, having the power to enforce it, says is a fact" (Philip, *Looking for Livingstone* 67). In the exchange, Livingstone and The Traveller debate the validity of silence compared to the word. The Traveller reveals that she has discovered her silence throughout her journey, yet Livingstone denies such a possibility based on its immateriality: "I don't understand how you can do that—discover silence, I mean. It's not a thing like a river, or a waterfall, or a country" (69). Livingstone characteristically renders African silence "ungeographic," for it does not adhere to the traditional Eurocentric "sanctioned geographic knowledges" (McKittrick 14) that uphold his life's work. The Traveller's silence is thus "unknowable" to Livingstone—its underlying local intensities, rituals, and epistemologies do not fit into his tidy narrative of knowledge and discovery.

In their exchange, Livingstone denies both the material and semiotic validity of silence, for he has "dissected and analysed" the silence of the African people with his "word" and silence cannot be circumscribed in the royal science of his trade as explorer and missionary. The Traveller's interrogation of Livingstone dramatizes these competing discourses:

> "You captured and seized the Silence you found—possessed it like the true discoverer you were—dissected and analysed it; labelled it—you took their Silence—the Silence of the African—and replaced it with your own—the silence of your word."
>
> "No, no—I insist . . . I broke the silence that was there before and that was a good thing—silence is never a good thing."
>
> (69–70)

In the face of the erasure and replacement of silence by Livingstone's word, The Traveller nonetheless persists and asserts the materiality of her silence as a fully quantifiable parallel: "I assure you I have mapped and measured my own Silence to the last millimeter, and it exists . . . so tangible I can even touch it at times" (70). Earlier in the narrative, the NEECLIS tribe challenges The Traveller to weave a tapestry of her silence using word as the suturing thread (51). After first denying that silence has words and tangible materiality, The Traveller learns that silence and word share a symbiotic relationship, and she finally succeeds in weaving her tapestry, "a multicoloured quilt—of Silence—[her] many silences—held together by the most invisible of stitches—the invisible but necessary word" (55). After discovering the materiality of her silence, The Traveller enters the Museum of Silence, where the stolen African silences are put on display, and she perceives the silences as material and tangible objects with obvious spatial parameters, "a structure, an edifice I could walk around, touch, feel, lick even" (57). The Traveller confronts Livingstone with the very materiality of her inherited silence, which forces him to encounter its "unimaginable" presence as a producer of space and being.

Repeatedly throughout the exchange, The Traveller undermines Livingstone's linear logic and renders him speechless, which reflects

McKittrick's discussion of the "surprise" and "wonder" of white people when confronted by long-standing black geographical presences. According to McKittrick, "the element of surprise is contained in the material, political, and social landscape that presumes—and fundamentally requires—that subaltern populations have no relationship to the production of space" (92). The Traveller's material and geographic silence—her demonic grounds—have undermined Livingstone's authorial legacy and reduced his own word, shockingly, to silence. Moreover, the encounter is "surprising" to Livingstone because The Traveller adopts a sexually dominant role, imbuing the exchange with sexualized language and bodily suggestiveness, thus parodying the sexual exploitation underlying the imperialist geographical invasion on "virginal frontiers." Whereas earlier in the text, a fellow explorer named Stanley[4] suggests to Livingstone that "a continent awaits us—like a whore" (25), here the colonizer's gaze is reversed by The Traveller assuming the dominant role of "explorer," invading Livingstone's fixed sense of reason and logic with her very material and alluring silence. The Traveller goes so far as to "violate" Livingstone, as she recalls a recurring dream: "I TAKE HIS WORD—STRONG AND THRUSTING . . . I TAKE IT INTO THE SILENCE OF MY MOUTH—AND IN A CLEARING IN A FOREST HE SITS AND WEEPS" (25).

The Traveller is clearly having a lot of fun with Livingstone—but in her exchange with him, she accomplishes a more serious goal: rewriting history. She counters Livingstone's denial of silence's geographic capability by reasserting it as a material and spatial force—a "sayable" geography, one that is meticulously mapped throughout her journey. By the end of the battle between Livingstone's word and The Traveller's silence, silence prevails as the only thing left "uncontaminated," (65) as it resists appropriation and representation by Livingstone. By means of silence's reinstated agency at the hands of The Traveller, the word/silence dichotomy becomes balanced, and this is figured in the conclusion of the text when she holds Livingstone's hand:

> I touched something warm familiar like my own hand human something I could not see in the SILENCE reaching out through the SILENCE of space the SILENCE of time through the silence of SILENCE I touch it his hand held it his hand *and* the SILENCE.
>
> (75; original emphasis and spacing)

As critic Paul Naylor has noted, Philip has been criticized for ending the text in this "gesture of reconciliation," and he quotes Philip from an interview where she comes to terms with the criticism and reaffirms her choice: "She can reach out and take Livingstone's hand or not take it. She chooses to take his hand, and it all ends in this Silence. Upper case silence speaking to something larger than both of them" (qtd. in Naylor

199). This final act is far from a passive submission; instead, the "something larger" signified by the insistent presence of the capitalized silence in the final passage marks the Traveller's inhabitation of a productive and meaningful (re)imagined geography—a demonic ground—wherein the language and space of both word and silence are balanced.

This final act, then, as Naylor observes, is a displacement of spatial hierarchies between colonizer and colonized, not a replacement of one by the other (199). Earlier in the text, Philip foreshadows this symbiotic relationship between word and silence:

> Word
> and Silence
> balance in contradiction
> Silence and Word
> harmony of opposites
> double planets
> condemned
> to together
>
> (34; original spacing)

McKittrick notes how Wynter's "analysis does not lead her to discuss Man verses other" but that the demonic ground "makes possible a different unfolding, one that does not replace or override or remain subordinate to the vantage point of 'Man' but instead parallels his constitution and his master narratives of humanness" (xxv). This conceptual distinction between replacement and paralleling is crucial to the understanding of Philip's polemic, for The Traveller does not set out to replace dominant discourses; rather, she sets out to reclaim the space and place of silence as a parallel epistemology through which being and history may be expressed.

Philip's work thus answers Edward Said's call for a "fragmenting, dissociating, dislocating and decentering of the experiential terrain covered at present by universalizing historicism" (211). Rather than universalized historical narratives, Said argues for a "plurality of terrains [and] multiple experiences" (214), which involves unsettling the unilateral monoliths of historical record with lived experiences of the ways in which people have always moved through space and place. The project of acknowledging and practicing these human lived geographies is what unites Philip, McKittrick, and Deleuze and Guattari, for their work delineates the spaces and places that seemingly lay outside—but nonetheless prove to be integral to—traditional geographic discourses. As Philip put it elsewhere,

> how does one
> write
> poetry from a place

a place structured
by absence
One doesn't. One learns to read the silence/s.[5]

The Traveller's intensive mapping of the imagined, allegorical landscape establishes a demonic geography that reaffirms the presence of
transgressive, sayable geographies in a hegemonic historiography that
has rendered them unrepresentable and "ungeographic." Moreover, her
eventual practice of the demonic geography of silence corrects the binaries of imperialist discourse by asserting silence's integral (as opposed
to marginal) presence in historical narratives. In this work and others,
Philip highlights the role of literature in reframing spatial production
and reimagining geographic space. Through The Traveller, we can see the
possibility of "more humanly workable" geographies that let our surroundings, our memories, and our herstories speak.

Notes

1. Wynter originally uses the term "demonic" in her analysis of Shakespeare's
   The Tempest. She focuses her discussion on the connection between reproduction and land reclamation. According to Wynter, the absence in the play of
   "Caliban's potential mate through whom the reproduction of his race might
   occur" (McKittrick xxv) prevents the island from being reclaimed by its native
   population. See Wynter, Sylvia. *"Beyond Miranda's* Meanings: Un/Silencing
   the 'Demonic Ground' of Caliban's 'Woman'." *Out of Kumbla: Caribbean
   Women and Literature*. Eds. Carole Boyce Davies and Elaine Savory Fido.
   Trenton: Africa World Press, 1990: 355–67.
2. In contrast to trees, rhizomatic plants (such as the potato) have no central
   root but a series of nodes that spread their roots horizontally and adapt to the
   contours of their environment.
3. It is noteworthy that Philip's collection of poems *She Tries Her Tongue, Her
   Silence Softly Breaks*, and *Looking for Livingstone* originally began as one
   work, but eventually became bifurcated into two separate threads to the same
   fabric. *She Tries* introduces the competing terms of word and silence, and
   Looking for Livingstone is the narrative that stages their confrontation.
4. The "Stanley" alluded to here references Sir Henry Morton Stanley (1841–
   1904), a British explorer who, along with David Livingstone, explored central
   Africa. Stanley was also famous for his commissioned search for Livingstone,
   who was presumed missing in the African continent. Legend has it that upon
   locating Livingstone, Stanley uttered the infamous words ironically reverber-
   ated throughout Philip's text: "Dr. Livingstone, I presume?"
5. Philip, *A Genealogy of Resistance* 121.

Works Cited

Courlander, Harold. *The Drum and the Hoe: Life and Lore of the Haitian People*. Berkeley: U of California P, 1960.
Deleuze, Gilles. *Dialogues II*. New York: Columbia UP, 2002.
Deleuze, Gilles and Felix Guattari. *A Thousand Plateaus: Capitalism and Schizophrenia*. Trans. Brian Massumi. Minneapolis: U of Minnesota P, 1987.

Karpinski, Eva C. *Borrowed Tongues: Life Writing, Migration, and Translation*. Waterloo, ON: Wilfrid Laurier UP, 2012.

McKittrick, Katherine. *Demonic Grounds: Black Women and the Cartographies of Struggle*. Minneapolis: U of Minnesota P, 2006.

Naylor, Paul. *Poetic Investigations: Singing the Holes in History*. Evanston: Northwestern UP, 1999.

Philip, NourbeSe M. "The Absence of Writing or How I Became a Spy." *She Tries Her Tongue, Her Silence Softly Breaks*. Toronto: Ragweed Press, 1989: 10–25.

———. *Frontiers: Essays and Writings on Racism and Culture*. Toronto: The Mercury Press, 1992.

———. *Looking For Livingstone: An Odyssey of Silence*. Toronto: The Mercury Press, 1994.

———. *A Genealogy of Resistance and Other Essays*. Toronto: The Mercury Press, 1997.

Said, Edward. "Orientalism Reconsidered." *Reflections on Exile and Other Essays*. Cambridge, MA: Harvard UP, 2000: 198–215.

7 Rethinking the Beginning

Toni Morrison and the Dramatization of Liminality

Michelle Dreiding

Comme j'aimerais que mes mots,
assurés de leur lieu d'origine et de faire retour, soient des oiseaux
migrateurs!

J.-B. Pontalis

Paradise—A Precarious Space

Beginnings in Toni Morrison's novels enact an uncanny moment of diso-rientation. They are beginnings *in medias res*, and, more importantly, beginnings of spatial deictic uncertainties that leave a reader with the absence of a stable system of reference. A particularly unsettling example is the beginning of *Paradise*, a novel published in 1997:

> They shoot the white girl first. With the rest they can take their time. No need to hurry out here. They are seventeen miles from a town which has ninety miles between it and any other. Hiding places will be plentiful in the Convent, but there is time and the day has just begun.
>
> (3)

The very first two sentences "*They shoot the white girl first. With the rest they can take their time.*" come as a shock; the shock of utter physical violence on the one hand, but also the shock of coming into language out of a moment of silence. This coming into language is unsettling, I would argue, for yet another reason: instead of offering a reliable system of signifiers with an identifiable reference, the deictic uncertainties—that is the "out here", the unidentified town, and the "there" in "there is time"—destabilize the fantasy of a homely and identifiable topography. "*No need to hurry out here. They are seventeen miles from a town which has ninety miles between it and any other.*" Where are we? We must ask ourselves. The mapping of this initial territory is thought in relational terms, that is, the indication of the distances between the "out here", the "town", and "any other [town]". But the mapping of this space that is constituted by its respective distances proves to be ineffective because the vantage point, as it were, the "out here" is a deixis that at this moment of the narrative does not point anywhere at all. We are "here", in the text's immediacy, but we are "out" as well; out of place somehow, at a loss of orientation. Because not only is the place identified in an ironic destabilization of precise indications of distance, but so are the relations between the victims and their perpetrators. The only pivotal point that the narrative does provide and that could give us a sense of the motive for the act of violence is the place of the Convent. But rather than providing a precise spatial indication, the place points to a particular function: the convent is a gendered space, an enclosed space, and a sacred space. The shooting is thus an act of penetration into the Convent if we presume that it is the place where the "white girl" and "the rest" have been residing. In such a reading, the shooting would then at the same time be a sexual violation because the female body is likened to the Convent in a metonymic figuration. However, both spatial relations, distances in this case, and precise interpersonal relations, that is "Why are the girls violated and shot?" and "What is their relation to the shooters?" are as of yet unintelligible and cannot position the reader in a comfortable voyeuristic position. In addition, one will also want to note that the authoritative voice of the narrative is unclear at this point. To whom can it be attributed? Uncannily connected to the perpetrator, and yet disembodied. A voice out of body and out of place.

This is the moment where disorientation is enacted. But it is simultaneously the moment, I would argue, where the imperative for a kind of reorientation, or a new orientation is self-consciously reflected on. The self-conscious absence of context, or rather insecurity of context, positions *Paradise*'s beginning at the other end of the dichotomy that Erich Auerbach in *Mimesis* (1946) establishes between the Homeric epic and *Genesis*. Whereas the former, the Homeric epic, is a text "externalized, a uniformly illuminated phenomena", happening at a "definite time and a definite place" (11), *Genesis*, on the other hand is a text "fraught with background": it is an "externalization of only so much of the phenomena as is necessary for the purpose of the narrative, all else is left in obscurity.... Time and place are undefined and call for interpretation" (11). In analogy to what Auerbach identifies in *Genesis* as the "representation" of the "development of the historically becoming, and the preoccupation with the problematic" (23), *Paradise* in a similar way is a preoccupation with the problematic as a way, and in Morrison's case, an imperative to reflect on a historically becoming—historically becoming that can figure as a viable African American alternative to the dominant discourse of the White American cultural imaginary.

But before the exact nature of the historically becoming in Morrison can be identified, attention needs to be redirected to the geographical insecurities of *Paradise*'s beginning: the mapping of the geography of the "out here" has proven to be unstable in terms of linguistically identifiable signifiers. However, the beginning of *Paradise* establishes an autarkic textual space—a system of textual references that, at this point in the narrative, i.e., at the beginning, substitutes the purely geographical and linguistic insecurities. There is the intertextual relationship to *Genesis* in an Auerbachian sense. But there is also the title of Morrison's novel, *Paradise*, which inscribes it explicitly in the biblical tradition of creation and becoming, the beginning of the world. Revisiting the deictic uncertainties that the "out here" etc. represent in Morrison, then their non-referential deixes have to be considered in the light of this peritext, namely the title. In fact, however, this intertextual relationship does not contribute to a comforting identification with textual familiarity. Instead, the peritextual information is immediately destabilized by the act of violence. Of course, the Garden of Eden, the biblical Paradise, too, is a place of violence. That is a place that can discursively only be thought of in the expulsion to come. Paradise can never be perpetuated. Paradise is always also paradise lost. But it also always dramatizes the utopian fantasy of regression in a psychoanalytical understanding of the term.[1] Safe from harm and phantasmagorically ideal.

In Morrison's *Paradise*, however, the initial fantasy is temporally reversed. Paradise first, in terms of text time, is the place where violence is enacted. Only in the course of the narrative is the phantasmagorical ideal of Paradise developed. Orientation, or rather reorientation in *Paradise*, the novel, is self-reflexive; thought of only as textual becoming. And of course, it is only retroactively, in rereading that the beginning of the novel can become fully intelligible; including its geography as well as its interpersonal relationships. The beginning of Toni Morrison's *Paradise* self-consciously dramatizes a liminal moment, a textual frontier, that needs to be returned to. It is through retrospection only that the deixes, that is the "they" of the shooters, the "out here", the "town", the "Convent", and the relations of distance become fully comprehensible. Returning to the beginning, to the frontier, however, also implies a novel reflection on the starting point; it is a repetition with a difference. In this sense then, the beginning can never be absolute. It cannot function as the absolute origin of the narrative. It is always inscribed in both an inter- and intratextuality and a rereading process. It is thus not *Genesis*, but *Genesis* revisited: *Paradise*. What the beginning of *Paradise* then enacts, I would argue, is the predicament of a beginning that precludes the fantasy of an absolute point of origin.

The inaccessibility of a point of origin in the novel *Paradise* is a condition that cannot be considered in the present text's isolation. It is rather, I would argue, a Modernist condition. At this point, I suggest considering two further intertexts in order to understand *Paradise*'s beginning and the seemingly reference-less deixes that it presents: Freud as a Modernist intertext and Foucault as a commentator of the Modernist condition. Freud, in his essay "Remembering, Repeating and Working-Through" of 1914, defines the concept of what his translator James Strachey has termed *deferred action*, a concept called *Nachträglichkeit* in the German original. It describes the phenomenon of a highly important childhood event that then, that is in childhood, is experienced without understanding, but that retroactively can be endowed with meaning and interpretation. For Freud, the concept of deferred action is a vital process engaged in neurosis formation. Retroactive attribution of meaning is thus, one could claim after Freud, a universal phenomenon in the human being, but it is at the same time also a phenomenon that, according to Foucault, is a particularly Modernist condition:

> In modern thought, such an origin is no longer conceivable: we have seen how labour, life, and language acquired their own historicity, in which they are embedded; they could never, therefore, truly express their origin, even though, from the inside, their whole history is, as it were directed towards it. It is no longer origin that gives rise to historicity; it is historicity that, in its very fabric, makes possible the necessity of an origin which must be both internal and foreign to it.
> (Foucault 1970: 329)

Foucault makes a point about the impossibility of man being contemporaneous with his own origin. "Origin for man," he writes "is much more the way in which man in general, any man, articulates himself upon the already begun of labour, life, and language" (330).

The intertextual references in Morrison, references to this paradox temporality described by Freud as a universal human trait, and by Foucault as a characteristic proper to the Modernist subject position Morrison's text in a historico-cultural continuum that spans from *Genesis* to the turn of the 20th century and beyond. This chronotopical condensation, which the beginning of *Paradise* presents, endows the novel with an epistemological scope that could well be read into the deicitically precarious "out here".[2]

But what is it that makes this beginning not only one that is rooted in the biblical tradition and Modernism, but also one that is rooted in an American discourse? What is it that makes Morrison's text particularly American? Frederick Turner in 1893 identifies the particularly spatial nature of American development and the paramount importance of the frontier, the liminal, and, more importantly, I would argue, the compulsive return to the frontier:

> American development has exhibited not merely advance along a single line, but a return to primitive conditions on a continually advancing frontier line, and a new development for that area. American

social development has been continually beginning over again on the frontier. This perennial rebirth, this fluidity of American life, this expansion westward with its new opportunities, its continuous touch with the simplicity of primitive society, furnish the forces dominating American character.

(Turner 1921, 1996: 1)

The American cultural imaginary, then, is one that is not only characterized by its explicit spatiality, but also one that constantly rethinks itself at the locus of the frontier, the liminal. This fantasy space of perpetual historical and cultural becoming is one that Morrison is inscribed in, but more importantly, one that she undertakes to revise from the perspective of a historically marginalized group; the African American who discursively has been thought of in function of the economic possibility of a westward expansion. A marginalization necessary for the spatial expansion and the unfolding of the colonial settlers, as well as the Modern subject, according to Richard Slotkin:

The original ideological task of the Myth was to explain and justify the establishment of the American colonies; but as the colonies expanded and developed, the Myth was called on to account for our rapid economic growth, our emergence as a powerful nation-state, and our distinctively American approach to the socially and culturally disruptive processes of modernization.

(1992: 10)

The spatial as a particular characteristic of American identity formation is thus a constantly revisited and a particularly pertinent topos of American Modernism. To be noted here shall be Slotkin's use of the inclusive pronoun "our" in "our . . . growth, our emergence", etc. An inclusion and participatory status which Morrison's characters cannot readily assume but instead need to negotiate in a laborious process of narrativization.

Morrison's texts are at once situated in this American cultural imaginary, but always also, and this is the political project, engaged in a revisionist project of the American space; in a reformulation and remapping of a world:

I want to draw a map, so to speak, of a critical geography and use that map to open as much space for discovery, intellectual adventure, and close exploration as did the original charting of the New World—without the mandate for conquest.

(Morrison 1992: 3)

And this is what she does indeed at the beginning of *Paradise*. She draws a map that through its spatial destabilization and imperative to reorientate proposes an alternative return to the frontier, to the beginning, self-consciously enacting a beginning that can never be absolute, and that needs to be returned to. In this the text is analogous to the American spatial discourse of the frontier, but it is also a rewriting in reverse. First comes the infraction, a violent penetration of the paradisiac space, a beginning more historically and culturally congruent with the traumatic history of slavery. And only in a laborious process of renarrativization can utopia be thought about and indeed problematized. Only in a process of renarrativization can the utopian space be conceived of as a therapeutic integral part of a discursive African American rehabilitation.

Jazz—The Pleasure of Epistemological Re-mapping

Less explicit at first sight as far as intertextual references to the American discourse of the frontier are concerned, but nonetheless forcefully present if subjected to close scrutiny, are the opening words of Morrison's novel *Jazz*, published in 1992. More than in *Paradise*, they also enact the *pleasure* and the *desire* that form an integral part of the project of a reconfiguration of a spatial cultural imaginary through the establishment of a spatial poetics: "Sth. I know that woman" (3). As to its deictic insecurities, *Jazz*' beginning is similar to that of *Paradise*: "*That* woman": she is not here, but there. Not yet identified, she is unnamed and distanced. This beginning brings together two poles of a particular geography by establishing their distance in the first place: the two coordinates of this territory are the "I" figure at one end and "that woman" at the other end. "I" is fundamentally close and prototypically subjective. "That woman" is over there, at a distance; she is everything that is not "I". However, this relational geography that stretches between the two figures uncannily hovers over the idea of a more haptic or graspable one, as it were, a more down-to-earth place where people interact. Who is "I" and who is "that woman", and where are they, that is, in what broader context or space is their distance situated? How can we make sense of their distance if there is no information about the two figures' respective immediate vicinity?

In fact, a way out of this disorientation may be found if we pursue the following presupposition: the initial territory of *Jazz* becomes the very aesthetic function which ultimately enables the operation of remapping. The beginning of *Jazz* fails, or rather does not "intend" to provide a mere stage on which the "I" and "that woman" will cooperate to become text. Nor does this space in *Jazz* provide environmental analogies that constitute character: there is no topos to flesh out figures; there is neither "structure of the topos" that, in a Lotmanian understanding, "emerges as the language for expressing other, non-spatial relations in the text" (1977: 231). Instead, this initial territory establishes the possibility of a very particular epistemology that is inextricably tied up with a spatial imaginary. Because in between, that is in between "I" and "that woman", lies the promise of knowledge and familiarity: "I *know* that woman". In fact, however, this knowledge, this epistemology, is not immediately accessible; at the beginning of the text we know nothing as of yet. The "I" is just as unknown to a reader as is "that woman". Having read Roland Barthes and Morrison's *Paradise*, however, we have learned that knowledge will only come about through rereading. Again, it is only retroactively that the characters as well as their relationship to each other become intelligible. In fact, "to know" in *Jazz* becomes the pivotal point of an epistemological orientation, and it can be argued that "to know" contains the entire textual geography that the text will establish in the course of the narrative. In order to find out what this *terra incognita* of "knowing" exactly constitutes, we must ever revisit the boundary, the textual frontier, and come back to the beginning. Because only through the return to that initial territory, which in its essence contains the nomenclature of everything there is to know, only through that return can we really start thinking about what that knowledge is exactly; only through the return to the beginning can we see that "knowing" is that which is at stake. And it is only then that we learn that "knowing" is embedded in a deictically precarious geography and that it is there alone where a new map of the American cultural imaginary can be created. Because not only does the beginning of *Jazz*, just as that of *Paradise*, leave time and space "undefined" (as does *Genesis*) and thus enacts the concern of what Auerbach terms the "historically becoming", but it also situates itself within the American discourse of spatiality, and with this, of course, the negotiation of the locus of the frontier—locus that itself is inherently precarious.

At this point it is important to recognize that "knowledge" in *Jazz* offers an alternative apprehension to what Morrison identifies to be the "validity or vulnerability of a certain set of assumptions conventionally accepted among literary historians and critics . . . circulated as knowledge" (1992: 4). "This knowledge", Morrison argues,

> holds that traditional, canonical American literature is free of, uninformed and unshaped by the four-hundred-year-old presence of, first Africans and then African Americans in the United States. It assumes that this presence . . . has had no significant place of consequence in the origin and development of that culture's literature.
>
> (5)

Indeed, Morrison does create such a "significant place" and retroactively endows the origin of "that culture's literature" with her version of knowledge—knowledge which considers the African American presence to be an integral part of America's cultural imaginary. "To know" in Toni Morrison's *Jazz* is a constant process, ever to be reviewed; not so much a static condition, not so much a finalized and finalizable process, but a dynamic project; imperative, ultimately, for the understanding of her political project of remapping.

In such an understanding, Morrison can be considered epistemologically akin to Nietzsche who, in *The Use and Abuse of History for Life* (1877), poignantly codifies the existential necessity of knowledge remaining ever dynamic: "History, conceived as pure knowledge, once it becomes sovereign, would be a kind of conclusion to living and a final reckoning for humanity" (1998: 7). Through the inauguration of the spatial paradigm, the incipit of *Jazz* could be understood to enact the impossibility of "knowledge" becoming history and thus static and eventually fatal. Also, "knowing" in Morrison must be "territorial", in the sense of being in and of territory. It is only there that an alternative version of knowledge can come into existence and where it can be poetologically established—establishment of both a spatial poetics and a poetics of space that can and must ever be revisited. While "to know" in *Jazz* presents a reader with an intellectual necessity and desire to increase information and to become familiar with interpersonal and geographical relations, "to know" also, in perfect deconstructive manner, constitutes the enigma as to what that knowledge exactly comprises: some thing, some intellectual substance necessary for orientation that is located somewhere between the beginning of the text and its revisiting. It is, in fact, precisely that enigma that perpetuates and ensures the "perennial" return to the beginning in the first place; that is the frontier that is the privileged locus of renewal and rethinking; and it is there that the desire to find closure in the origin is enacted, while at the same time sensing that such closure is ever withheld because it is subject to a circular teleology.

Yet the map that covers the territory between "I" and "that woman", and that sheathes the enigmatic "knowledge", must be further extended into what Toni Morrison (1992: 3) hopes to become a "wider landscape": the very first word, or rather sound, in *Jazz* is a kind of immediate vocal interpellation: "Sth." Not quite identifiable as to its precise meaning, we ask ourselves whether it is an expression of disdain and disrespect, or a demand for silence. This sound disrupts the fantasy of a closed textual space. It in fact unsettles the illusion of textual self-containment; it reaches beyond, wanting to make itself heard, or maybe wanting to silence that "knowledge" which is so problematically exclusive of the African American presence and that does not account for the latter's participation in the conception of the country's origin. The interpellative immediacy of "Sth" offers another vantage point in the form of an address, an invocation almost, that is simultaneously directed inward and outward: inward toward the text that is about to unfold, and outward toward the possibility of readership and intertextuality. In that, "Sth" is the most explicit enactment of the concept of the boundary in *Jazz*, dramatizing the here and beyond simultaneously, while coming into discursive being along the syntagmatic line of words.

The textual boundary in *Jazz* does, however, not only perform the political project of an epistemological rethinking at the liminal. The opening sound, "Sth", and the ensuing affirmation, "I know that woman", also encapsulate the erotic *pleasure* that lies in "knowing" the textual geography between the (problematic because paradoxically unknown) intimacy of "I" and the distance of "that woman". It is, in the first instance, i.e., thematically, the pleasure of the novel's protagonist's adolescent, almost infantile understanding of sexuality, or rather, the discourse of sexuality at the end of the novel. But it is also, and more importantly, the pleasure that comes with rereading, with constantly having to revisit the boundary and the frontier. *Jazz'* beginning in fact condenses both the *imperative* and the *desire* to think and rethink the boundary. At the end of the novel, the protagonist has found her poetic voice and can articulate the pleasure that comes about through the negotiation of what is self and what is other; of what is here and what is beyond:

> It's nice when grown people whisper to each other under the covers. Their ecstasy is more leaf-sigh than bray and the body is the vehicle, not the point. They reach, grown people, for something beyond, way beyond and way, way down underneath tissue. . . . They are under the covers because they don't have to look at themselves anymore; there is no stud's eye, no chippie glance to undo them. They are inward toward the other, bound and joined by carnival dolls and the steamers that sailed from the ports they never saw. That is what is beneath their undercover whispers.
>
> (228)

Reconsidering the initially indeterminable sound "Sth" (Is it an expression of disdain? Is it a demand for silence?) in the light of the novel's ending, a more specific reading can unfold: "Sth" becomes tantamount to the "leaf-sigh" whispers of sexual and textual desire. The entire text, which spans between beginning and end, becomes the whispered discourse of desire: a desire, physical and indeed geographical, that is constituted by the negotiation of what is here and what is "beyond, way beyond". Desire also, textual, that is "way, way down underneath tissue:" underneath the fabrication of textual, textural, and textile tissue.

Love—The Female Body as Liminality

A chiastic inversion of the very two geographical coordinates that, in *Jazz*, delimit the initial territory of the incipit, that is the distance between "I" and "that woman". A chiastic inversion thereof then demarcates the territory established at the beginning of Toni Morrison's novel *Love*, published in 2003: "The Woman's legs are spread wide open, so I hum" (3). Unlike in *Jazz*, "the woman" is situated at the one end of *Love's* territory, while "I" is at the other end. "The woman" here is not only geographically closer, but she is also accorded a more prototypical function than in *Jazz*: she is not "*that* woman" but "*the* woman": the definite affirmation of her gender. She is indeed self-confidently gendered, but she is precariously sexualized too. The pornographic immediacy that a reader is presented with at the beginning of *Love* finds a disconcertingly voyeuristic confirmation in the ensuing lines: "Men grow irritable, but they know it's all for them. They relax. Standing by, unable to do anything but watch, is a trial, but I don't say a word" (3). Instead of the promise of intellectual satisfaction that lies between the opening lines of *Jazz*, *Love* places the female body as the function of male desire between "the woman" and the subjectivity of "I". What is this territory that so disturbingly condenses the woman as the bearer of the beginning? Of biological and textual offspring on the one hand and the woman as the very locus, so to speak, where such a beginning is violated on the other hand? Apart from an immediate ethical concern, I would argue that this beginning problematizes an aspect of the American cultural imaginary that is inextricably bound up with the conception of its territorial beginning. If the frontier is, according to Turner, "the meeting point between savagery and civilization" (1921, 1996: 1), and if that meeting point is the very place where westward advance and development is made possible, then the "savage" is reduced to mere functionality. Fundamentally connected to the notion of the "savage" is, according to Klarer (2013), the latent presence of an eroticized, innocent femininity, which enters the American cultural imaginary through the Pocahontas myth, inaugurated and narrativized by John Smith in his *General History of Virginia, New-England, and the Summer Isles* of 1624 (cf. Klarer 2013: 18). In such a conception of the frontier, namely in that it is an eroticized place, westward expansion also, at least discursively, becomes tantamount to the penetration of the female body, economically justified and expedited. In *Love*'s case, the violently enigmatic beginning ultimately situates itself within the same circular teleology as the other novels, and can thus only fully be comprehended once, after arriving at the text's ending, the beginning is read anew.

The query for an origin, both in its temporal as well as in its spatial understanding, is indeed vital und universally human if we think with Freud. It is also an explicitly Modernist one if we think with Foucault. It is further constitutionally American if we think with Turner and Slotkin. Ruland and Bradbury maintain that the origin of "what we now call American literature" (1992: 3) is a conglomerate of the spatial reality of the settlers and European discursive traditions: it "came from the meeting between the land with its elusive and usually despised 'Indians' and the discoverers and settlers who left the developed, literate cultures of Renaissance Europe" (3). And it is the cogently self-conscious use of the spatial metaphors of the "direction" and the "intersection" with which

Ruland and Bradbury, the authors of *A History of American Literature*, condense their understanding of the country's literary origin:

> the main direction of the recorded American literary imagination . . . was formed from the intersection between the European Renaissance mind and the new and wondrous land in the West the settlers found—between the myths they brought and those they learned or constructed after they came.
>
> (4)

In fact, it is also in Ruland and Bradbury that we learn that the very notion of the origin for American literature is a problematic one, because "[w]e cannot trace its roots directly back into the mists of American antiquity", nor can we "hunt its origins in the remote springs of its language and culture, or follow it through from the oral to the written, then from manuscript to book" (3). Instead, "millenarian and Utopian expectations were already attached to this new land" (5). Thus, the search for the beginnings of American literature is indeed a predicament that precludes the fantasy of an absolute point of origin: the "already there"— the chronotopical antecedence—is always inscribed in the concept of America's discursive genesis.

In Toni Morrison, the search for an origin, both geographical and biographical, is also a constitutive part of African American identity. The textual nature of Morrison's enactment of boundaries, and the epistemological scope that her beginnings of novels contain in their essence, in a condensed form, hold the promise of an autarchy, a discursive identity constitution that can be dissociated from actual geographies of America. In that they have a supra-geographical quality that simultaneously accounts for the very spatiality of the hegemonic discourse in which Morrison's fiction has to situate itself and quite literally find its place, but that at the same time can be dissociated from it, having a discursive force that is indeed trans- and supra-geographical. And yet, it is precisely this rethinking and the establishment of an alternative spatial poetics that makes Morrison's text very clearly American: the condition and indeed the fantasy of being in-the-place and at the same time out-of-place, pivoting around the locus of the boundary, the frontier; that is, the liminal.

Beginnings of Toni Morrison's novels are an unsettlingly beautiful dramatization of the liminal. They advocate a reorientation in an American spatial imaginary by proposing an alternative spatial poetics. African American discursive emancipation must come about through a critical reflection on the frontier myth, a textual destabilization thereof, and a subsequent reformulation of territory. Morrison's poetics is a revision of the American cultural imaginary that distances itself explicitly from the mechanisms which produced slavery as a necessary constituent of its national becoming: that is, conquest of territory through westward expansion and a continual return to the border. Morrison's project is political without subscribing to the economic and violently expansive appropriation of American soil. She draws a textual map, which is an imperative to reorientate in a discursive space—a network of inter- and intratextual trajectories. And it is in her beginnings of novels, I would argue, that this imperative comes about in an aesthetically condensed form. A liminal moment that contains the essence of her subversive mapmaking.

Notes

1. In their handbook, *The Language of Psychoanalysis* (orig. *Le vocabulaire de la psychanalyse* (1967)), Laplanche and Pontalis point to and emphasize the literal meaning of the verb " to regress" for the understanding of the concept of "regression", namely to "walk back, to retrace one's steps—which can be understood as readily in a logical or spatial sense as in a temporal one" (386). The Freudian conception of regression differentiates between a topographical, a temporal, and a formal one. Implicit in each of the categories is a spatio-temporal metaphorization of the psychic apparatus. The term "regression" shall here be understood as "a revision to earlier forms in the development of thought, of object-relationships or of the structure of behaviour" (386). While mainly considered pathological in psychoanalysis and modern psychology, "regression" in the present study's use will also want to emphasize the affirmative, comforting, and ultimately creative aspect that is implied in (and acknowledged by the clinical discourse) retreating to an earlier stage. Earlier stage can here readily be synonymized with the notion of paradise. Regression is thus the harkening back to a textual and discursive past of paradise including its terminological connotation of familiarity and safety.
2. In order to fully comprehend Morrison's embedding in and comment on the Modernist tradition, and the intertextual dialogue she entertains with it in terms of narratological and aesthetic specificities, a comparative reading of Morrison's texts with texts by Virginia Woolf and William Faulkner are imperative—a reading, however, that cannot be pursued here.

Bibliography

Auerbach, Erich. *Mimesis*. 1949. Trans. Willard R. Trask. Princeton: Princeton University Press, 1974.

Bakhtin, Mikhail. *The Dialogic Imaginations: Four Essays*. Ed. and Trans. Caryl Emerson and Michael   Holquist. Austin: University of Texas Press, 1981.

Foucault, Michel. "The Retreat and Return of the Origin." *The Order of Things*. New York: Pantheon Books, 1970. 328–35.

Freud, Sigmund. *Erinnern, Wiederholen und Durcharbeiten*. 1914. Freud Studienausgabe. Frankfurt: Fischer, 1989.

Klarer, Mario. *Literaturgeschichte der USA*. München: C.H. Beck, 2013.

Laplanche, Jean and J.-B. Pontalis. *The Language of Psychoanalysis*. 1967. Trans. Donald Nicholson Smith. New York and London: Norton, 1973.

Lotman. Jurij. *The Structure of the Artistic Text*. 1971. Trans. Gail Lenhoff et al. Ann Arbor: University of Michigan, 1977.

Morrison, Toni. *Playing in the Dark. Whiteness and the Literary Imagination.* New York: Random House, 1992.

———. *Paradise.* 1997. London: Vintage, 1999.

———. *Jazz.* 1992. London: Vintage, 2001.

——. *Love.* 2003. London: Vintage, 2004.

Nietzsche, Friedrich. *On the Use and Abuse of History for Life.* 1837. Trans. Ian Johnston. Calgary: Theophania Publishing, 1998.

Pontalis, J.-B. *L'amour des commencements.* 1986. Paris: Gallimard, 1994.

Ruland, Richard and Malcolm Bradbury. *From Puritanism to Postmodernism. A History of American Literature.* London and New York: Penguin, 1992.

Tally, Robert T. Jr. *Spatiality.* The New Critical Idiom. London and New York: Routledge, 2013.

Turner, Frederick Jackson. *The Frontier in American History.* 1893. New York: Henry Holt, 1921. Online text provided by the University of Virginia, Michael W Kidd (1996). http://xroads.virginia.edu/~HYPER/TURNER/home.html, accessed 16 April 2013.

8 "You've been here before?"

Space and Memory in Stephen Poliakoff's Dramas

Elizabeth Robertson

The relationship between space, place and memory is longstanding. Frances Yates discusses the origins and practice of mnemonics in *The Art of Memory*, where she outlines the establishment of the use of space and place to remember. Following the story of Simonides of Ceos, Yates discusses how the art of memory was formed after Simonides was refused full payment for a victory ode given in honour of his host—a nobleman named Scopas—on account of the number of dedications to the mythical twins Castor and Pollux. Sometime later Simonides was called out of the palace to meet two visitors—later revealed to be Castor and Pollux themselves—and while he was absent the roof of the banqueting hall collapsed, killing all inside. As the only person not killed, Simonides was called upon to name the dead; he did so by recalling where each person was sat in the hall. Thus, the method of loci, or the memory palace, was created (Yates 1–3). The method of loci was used in rhetoric: "as a technique by which the orator could improve his memory, which would enable him to deliver long speeches from memory with unfailing accuracy" (Yates 2). The interest here in the method of loci is in the way in which it uses space and place as a means for remembering. In doing so, it establishes a relationship between space and memory because it creates a means whereby real and imagined spaces might assist us in acts of remembering—whether public or private—when revisiting the past, because the method 'houses' memory.

The work of the British writer-director Stephen Poliakoff has centred upon an examination of memory, history and historical consciousness; space and place have played an important role in the ways in which Poliakoff dramatizes his memory-narratives, particularly in his television dramas. Over the last forty years, he has produced a body of work across the mediums of theatre, film and television, exploring a variety of themes including the post-war urban environment, the lure of extremist politics, technology in contemporary Britain and the recurring themes of family, history and memory. Amongst Poliakoff's most critically successful work has been the television work he made for the BBC between 1999 and 2007—*Shooting the Past* (1999), *Perfect Strangers* (2001), *The Lost*

Prince (2003), *Friends and Crocodiles* (2005), *Gideon's Daughter* (2005), *Joe's Palace* and *Capturing Mary* (2007)—in which Poliakoff developed a distinctive textual and visual style. Poliakoff has advocated the importance of making quality drama for television, whilst maintaining a presence both as writer and director in theatre and film, and occupying an enviable position in which he has artistic control over the work he makes. Using close-reading and theoretical work about space and memory by critics including Gaston Bachelard and Edward S. Casey—themselves building upon Henri Bergson's theories of memory—this chapter will analyze how Poliakoff layers dialogue, voiceovers, flashbacks, still photographs, and visual repetition within spaces to merge past and present. The relationship between space and memory will be explored to consider how memories are 'housed' within space in Poliakoff's work by focusing on scenes from the BBC television dramas *Perfect Strangers* (2001) and *Capturing Mary* (2007), as well as examining the importance of space and memory to dramaturgical structure and use of performance space in the stage dramas *Blinded by the Sun* (1996) and *My City* (2011).

Sarah Cardwell argues that the medium of television has facilitated Poliakoff's development of the "intermedia, cross-temporal, montage" which has become a recognizable feature in his dramas, enabling him to "traverse spatial and temporal boundaries," and forge links "between images and moments" to "emphasise their interconnectedness" (Cardwell 180). Poliakoff uses the montages Cardwell describes in *Perfect Strangers* and *Capturing Mary* when characters revisit a space—in both cases a large London mansion house—after a number of years. The visit in *Perfect Strangers* is instigated at a family reunion weekend when the central character, Daniel Symon (Matthew Macfadyen), is shown a previously unseen photograph of himself as a young boy dressed as a prince and stood on the staircase of the family's London townhouse. Intrigued by the photograph, Daniel attempts to understand why he was dressed in such a way, by whom and for what purpose. Ancestral spaces are an important element of the recovery of elements of Daniel's memory. Poliakoff uses the ancestral homes of the Symon family—places which have been abandoned awaiting sale or already cast off—to function as spaces where events can be reconstructed and the ongoing process of memory restoration can be finalized by the recovery of what has been forgotten.

The process which Daniel undertakes in trying to decipher his photograph is described by Annette Kuhn as 'memory work'; a process that anyone with sufficient interest in making sense of mysterious family artefacts can undertake to do:

> Memory work requires the most minimal resources and the very simplest procedures. Making do with what is to hand—its raw materials are almost universally available—is the hallmark of memory work's pragmatism and democracy. Anyone who has a family

photograph that exerts an enigmatic fascination or arouses an inexplicable depth of emotion could find memory work rewarding.

(Kuhn 6)

The enigmatic photograph—such as the photograph of Daniel—is especially powerful in igniting curiosity because the photograph offers a frozen moment in time which contains traces of the past and of the future. It is the particular moment of the photograph which is unexplained, who took the photograph, when and why? Throughout *Perfect Strangers*, family narratives are woven from memory, but each story is linked to a material object, a family artefact: a photograph, book, coat, house and painting. Family history in Poliakoff's dramas, therefore, combines the three 'pathways' in the practice of family history which Ronald D. Lambert's work on Canadian and Australian genealogy identifies: a descriptive pathway which "relies on factual evidence referencing one's ancestors" (Lambert 318), a narrative pathway which is founded on family stories (Lambert 318) and, finally, an experiential pathway which is "founded in genealogists' interactions with and attachments to ancestral artefacts" (Lambert 319). Daniel's explorations in *Perfect Strangers* offer a combination of different aspects of Lambert's 'experiential pathway' in the practice of family history. The raw materials of the family artefact and the ancestral space converge; the 'big house' occupies *Perfect Strangers* and *Capturing Mary* as a space of memory: a physical and imaginative space where past and present collide. The 'big house' in *Perfect Strangers* is a space which might serve as a Proustian mechanism for the recovery of childhood memories. By examining the relationship between the house and memory, it can be revealed how these memories are 'housed' within this space. Kuhn writes:

> The past is gone for ever. We cannot return to it, nor can we reclaim it now as it was. But that does not mean it is lost to us. The past itself is like the scene of a crime: if the deed itself is irrecoverable, its traces may still remain.
>
> (Kuhn 3–4)

History is gone, the events have taken place and cannot be relived, but they can be reconstructed from traces of memory, material objects, and by experiencing spaces and places within spaces. In her work on family history on British television, Amy Holdsworth argues "what we are left with is the search for presence in absence" (Holdsworth 79). Daniel knows almost nothing about his wider family, or the Symon family history, repeatedly attesting to his ignorance; the reunion he attends comes at the moment when the family patriarch—Ernest (Peter Howell)—is shedding the remaining family properties and along with them the public and measurable image of the family's heritage. The reunion becomes a defining moment in the family's reassessment of itself—both past and present. In light of this reassessment, the crystallisation of the Symon family history moves from a—slightly skewed—focus on the outward characterisation of the family as wealthy and influential, to a more inclusive understanding of the family's breadth and diversity, and along with it, acceptance of oddity and non-conformity within it.

For Daniel, the house functions as an ancestral space where the recovery of lost childhood memories can—at least—be prompted through reconstruction and feats of personal detective work. Lambert's definition of what he calls the 'experiential pathway' includes reference to ancestral landscapes and to experiencing these places kinetically (Lambert 319). The Symon family townhouse is used as an ancestral site of memory and history in *Perfect Strangers* by Daniel not only to connect to the family's past, but also to help him to understand the photograph he is shown by the self-appointed Symon family archivist—Stephen Symon (Anton Lesser). Neither Daniel, nor his parents, can recall him ever being dressed like this, or taking him to visit the 'big' London house. Daniel initially questions whether the photograph is in fact of him; even after being told it is him as a child, by both Stephen and his parents, Daniel asks again if they are sure. Daniel's uncertainty about the photograph is indicative of his inability to recall it being taken or remember why he was dressed in such a way. Daniel's lack of memory of the event is reinforced in the scene which follows his session with Stephen, when he tries to explain the photograph to his cousins Charles (Toby Stephens) and Rebecca (Claire Skinner): "There was this fantastic picture of me as a boy . . . it's just I have no memory of it being taken or how I came to look like that . . ." (Poliakoff, *Perfect Strangers* 36).

While Sue Vice has argued that the narrative of *Perfect Strangers* "rests on a conception of the photograph as more reliable than memory" (Vice 304), it is important to note the memories with which *Perfect Strangers* is concerned are from the principal characters' childhoods. Furthermore, as the plot reveals, the photographs are connected to Daniel's grandfather's ongoing affair with his sister-in-law, something which Daniel—as a five-year-old child—is unlikely to have understood. The photograph does not serve as a memory replacement, and Poliakoff does not rely upon the pictures to fully reveal the memories associated with them; rather the photographs act as a prompt, something akin to the famous madeleine in Proust's *Swann's Way*. Looking at the photographs does not prompt Daniel to remember when the pictures were taken or why he was dressed as a little prince; the photograph serves only as evidence of something having taken place in the house when Daniel was a boy. The images intrigue Daniel and his parents, but they are baffled by what they see. In *Swann's Way* the taste of a madeleine cake allows the narrator to have detailed and powerful recollections from his childhood, which he was not able to voluntarily remember by merely seeing the cakes.

Key to this involuntary memory is a sensory stimulus—in this case, taste: "The sight of the little madeleine had recalled nothing to my mind before I tasted it" (Proust 61). Like the narrator in *Swann's Way*, Daniel needs another sensory stimulus beyond just seeing the photograph of himself as a boy. The stimulus in *Perfect Strangers* comes when his cousins Charles and Rebecca invite Daniel to visit the Grosvenor Place house with them. *Perfect Strangers* reflects that we do not remember, or understand, everything from our pasts. Further to this, the collective nature of family reminiscence through shared conversation is lacking here because his father, Raymond (Michael Gambon), has removed himself, and therefore Daniel, from the wider family. Poliakoff does not offer the photograph as more reliable than personal memory in *Perfect Strangers*, but it is placed in the drama as a raw material of memory work—an object to arouse curiosity. If the photograph is offered by Poliakoff as more reliable than human memory, then it should be taken as a warning about the problem associated with using digital or archival objects to store our memories for us. The photograph can only work as a reliable store of memory if people can actually recall the circumstances of the photograph upon seeing it, or decipher it with other people who do remember. Without this, the photograph remains an unexplained material object which has captured a forgotten moment frozen in time.

When Charles and Rebecca invite Daniel to the house with them in the early hours of the morning, he is given the opportunity to visit the location of his photograph. Memory, Edward S. Casey argues, is "naturally place-orientated or at least place-supported" (Casey 186–87), noting that while we rarely remember the dates of events we usually recall the places where things took place (Casey 214). *Perfect Strangers* demonstrates how memory can be place-orientated. "Thanks to the house", writes Gaston Bachelard in *The Poetics of Space*, "a great many of our memories are housed, and if the house is a bit elaborate, if it is has a cellar and a garret, nooks and corridors, our memories have refuges that are all the more clearly delineated" (Bachelard 8). The London townhouse in *Perfect Strangers* is such a house. The memory 'housed' within it is primarily associated with the grand staircase at the centre of the house, as well as some items which Daniel discovers discarded in a large cupboard in a disused room. On first entering the house, Daniel still does not remember being there as a child, but when Charles shows him the hallway in the shut off, unoccupied, part of the house, Daniel sees the grand central staircase, and begins to recognize it as the staircase on which he is stood in the photograph. At the beginning of this scene, as Charles, Rebecca and Daniel enter the hall in the darkness, the audience glimpses the beginnings of the wrought iron railings of a staircase. In the unlit space the audience's focus is drawn fleetingly to these railings, and the potential usefulness of the house to Daniel, in his attempt to remember, is hinted at; when Charles switches on the lights we are drawn back to the characters. This scene is the first of two occasions when Daniel visits the house in the drama. It lasts just under a minute and contains seventeen different shots which layer past and present, moving image and still photograph, using shifting and repetitive points of view, shadows on walls, flashbacks and sound effects to create a sense of fragmentation, emphasizing how difficult it is for Daniel to remember previously being in the house.

Daniel replicates the photograph of him as a young boy—attempting to use the space to recall the events that took place there, what he was doing there and why he was dressed in such a way. When Daniel first reaches the point on the staircase where he is standing in the photograph, he imitates the pose his five-year-old self has in the photograph. Daniel then sits on a step, making himself approximately the same height as he is in the picture, and peers through the ornate railings in the same way he is looking through the railings in the photograph. The scene constantly cuts between Daniel's point of view looking down the stairs at Charles and Rebecca, to Charles and Rebecca's point of view looking up the stairs at Daniel, mirroring the points of view of the five-year-old Daniel in the photograph and the unseen person holding the camera. These changing points of view are interspersed with close-ups of the black-and-white photograph.

When Rebecca asks Daniel if he can remember what was happening—implying that being sat in the same space as he is stood in the photograph might have helped him to recover his memories of what was happening—the twelfth shot of the scene cuts to Daniel's point of view looking down through the railings, before he turns away to look around the rest of the space; shot thirteen cuts to a close-up of Daniel's face in the grainy black-and-white photograph peering through the railings, with background sounds of children laughing, before the fourteenth shot cuts back to a close-up of Daniel in the present day, again looking through the railings. These repetitive close-ups of Daniel both in the present day and in the photograph, Daniel looking around the space and touching the railings, coupled with Rebecca's question—"Can you remember it now? Can you remember what was happening?" (Poliakoff, *Perfect Strangers* 58)—firmly root the memory of the event at that particular point within the house, implying that Daniel's memory is 'housed' in this space.

Bachelard writes: "Memories are motionless, and the more securely they are fixed in space, the sounder they are" (Bachelard 9). This, however, is a problem for Daniel, because his memory is not securely fixed in this space—as far as he is aware the photograph is evidence of the only time he visited this house, and even returning to the same space only helps Daniel remember a very tiny fraction of what might have taken place. "No—it won't come back" is his response to Rebecca's question (Poliakoff, *Perfect Strangers* 58). In the scenes following the key scene on the staircase, Charles and Rebecca continue to show Daniel the house—which is both impressive and shabby, locked up and waiting to be disposed of; it only contains dust, debris and the ghosts of its past. Rummaging in a large cupboard, Daniel and Rebecca discover one of the shoes Daniel is wearing in the photograph. For Daniel the shoe represents evidence that he *was* in the house, but the shoe itself does not assist any further in Daniel's recovery of his memories of being in the house.

On Daniel's second visit to the house—to see his aunt Alice (Lindsay Duncan) in the third part of the drama—there is another scene on the staircase. This scene is considerably less visually complicated: there are no cuts between past and present, the cuts to and from different shots, and points of view, are less repetitive and less frequent, the scene does not layer past and present or sound over the present-day noises and dialogue, the camera's point of view of Daniel is shot at a wider angle, and the photograph does not make an appearance. A key difference between this scene and the earlier scene is this scene is set during daylight hours when the house is more fully exposed, holding fewer mysteries in the light, fewer possibilities for dreaming. However, the cuts between Alice's point of view and Daniel's mirror—again—that of Daniel as a boy looking down the stairs and the photographer looking up. Daniel's discovery on this visit takes place at the large cupboard where he finds another part of his discarded costume—this time the ruff, which acts as a further prompt, and the scene cuts to a flashback of the five-year-old Daniel watching a group of children dressed as pirates playing a party game. The house, however, holds no further clues for Daniel in uncovering the mystery behind his photograph, and he does not return there.

The plot of Agatha Christie's final Miss Marple novel, *Sleeping Murder*, which was first published posthumously but is likely to have been written during the Blitz between 1940 and 1941, also centres upon a fragmented childhood memory of something witnessed whilst peering through the banisters. The recently married Gwenda Reed returns to England after spending most of her childhood with her mother's family in New Zealand to find a home for Gwenda and her husband Giles. Deciding to settle somewhere on the south coast, Gwenda buys a house in the fictitious Dillmouth, which she instantly feels at home in. Having moved in, there is something, however, which troubles Gwenda about the house: it seems too familiar—she is aware of doors which have been blocked up, recalls the design of the wallpaper in the nursery long since painted over exactly, and on her first viewing of the house Gwenda had a peculiar sensation when walking down the stairs: "They were starting down the stairs when quite suddenly Gwenda felt a wave of irrational terror sweep over her. It was a sickening sensation, and it passed almost as quickly as it came" (Christie 11). After moving in, Gwenda becomes increasingly unnerved by her familiarity with the house and flees to London to visit her husband's cousins, where she meets Miss Marple, and collectively they attend a performance of John Webster's *The Duchess of Malfi*. On hearing the line "Cover her face, mine eyes dazzle, she died young", in Act IV Scene 2 of the play, Gwenda screams, leaps to her feet and runs out of the theatre. The following morning Miss Marple manages to coax Gwenda into explaining what happened, and why she was so frightened:

> "You'll think I'm hysterical or queer or something. It happened quite suddenly, right at the end. I'd enjoyed the play. I'd never thought once about the house. And then it came—out of the blue—when he said those words—."
>
> She repeated in a low quivering voice: "*Cover her face, mine eyes dazzle, she died young.*"
>
> "I was back there—on the stairs, looking down on the hall through the banisters, and I saw her lying there. Sprawled out—dead. Her hair all golden and her face all—all *blue!* She was dead, strangled, and someone was saying those words in that same horrible gloating way—and I saw his hands—grey, wrinkled—not hands—monkey's paws . . . It was horrible, I tell you. She was dead."
>
> (Christie 26)

It transpires that Gwenda as a very young girl lived in the Dillmouth house for a year with her father and stepmother, and from the staircase, whilst peering through the banisters, she witnessed the murder of her stepmother. When Gwenda returns to the house with her husband, Giles, he attempts to get Gwenda to re-enact where she was standing as a child to see if it can help her recall everything which happened, in much the same way Daniel re-enacts his pose in the photograph:

> "Where do you think the body was? About here?" asked Giles.
>
> He and Gwenda were standing in the front hall of Hillside. They had arrived back the night before, and Giles was now in full cry. He was as pleased as a small boy with his new toy.
>
> "Just about," said Gwenda. She retreated up the stairs and peered down critically.
>
> "Yes—I think that is about it."
>
> "Crouch down," said Giles. "You were only about three years old you know."
>
> Gwenda crouched obligingly.
>
> (Christie 42)

While there are some similarities between *Perfect Strangers* and *Sleeping Murder*—the association of memory with space, the main characters inability to voluntarily recall the full details immediately, the need for other people to help interpret the fragments of memory, the re-enactment of where and how they were standing on the staircases—Daniel, unlike Gwenda (with the crucial exception of the identity of the murderer), never fully recalls what took place at the house, and eventually he has to rely upon his father and Stephen Symon to interpret the photographs and piece together events from the past.

It should be noted that the sites revisited in Poliakoff's drama and Christie's novel are the locations of rather different events: Daniel's photograph is eventually revealed to be a symbol of the ongoing love between his grandfather and his grandfather's brother's wife, where Gwenda's experiences are of a traumatic event—the witnessing of a murder. Both stories, however, make a similar use of space. In *Sleeping Murder*, experiencing the space is not enough for Gwenda to recall what she saw, and she requires an external prompt to remember; in *Perfect Strangers*, the photograph alone is not a prompt, but it is sufficiently mysterious as to tempt Daniel to want to decipher it. The photograph and the house together allow Daniel to begin to recall being in the house. Visiting the house and experiencing its interior space provides Daniel with sensory stimuli—visually and physically: sitting on the stairs, touching the railings, the sight and feel of the discarded shoe and ruff, all help Daniel to recall being in the house as a child, but crucially he does not completely remember everything at this point in the drama. Specifically, he cannot recall the photograph being taken, nor by whom. It must be asked, then, if Daniel's memories are 'housed' in this space? Bachelard says in *The Poetics of Space* that the more rooted memories are in a fixed space, the sounder they are. Daniel's memories are clearly not securely fixed in this space; he is not able to voluntarily recall the events there.

There is, however, a clear connection in *Perfect Strangers* between this space, this particular house and its staircase, and Daniel's memories. Once he encounters the space, Daniel is able to recover some involuntary memories of the event. Bachelard refers repeatedly to 'home', and the 'house in which we are born'. Daniel's inability to fully recollect may be a result from his having no emotional relationship with this house—he was not born there, did not grow up there and apparently only visited it once as a child. The relationship between space and memory in *Perfect Strangers* is clear, but in the drama space does not act as a complete and powerful mechanism or stimulus for total memory recall. Instead, Poliakoff uses the space, and the medium he is working in, to create a ghost-like atmosphere of fragmented memories fleetingly remembered. Daniel's search for an explanation of the circumstances of his photograph is, as Holdsworth argues historical and investigative memory narratives on television often are, a search for "presence in absence" (Holdsworth 79).

In revisiting the empty house, Daniel is searching for something which is no longer there. Daniel's search in this space for presence in absence is an attempt to fill a gap in his knowledge of his family history, and in using the house to help discover the story behind his photograph, Daniel creates presence in absence because he re-creates the photograph in a space that has essentially been abandoned. *Perfect Strangers* presents a complicated memory narrative in which space, object, archive, knowledge and fragmented memories come together. Where empty interior domestic space plays a key role in the recuperation of memory in *Perfect Strangers*, such spaces play a more cathartic role in the narrative of *Capturing Mary*. Mary's strong emotional relationship with the house means her memories, unlike Daniel's, are firmly fixed in the space. Like the house in *Perfect Strangers*, the house in *Capturing Mary* is empty, and Mary uses the empty space to find meaning in her past and to confront her memories. *Joe's Palace*—the companion drama to *Capturing Mary*—reveals the reasons for the house lying empty. The house belongs to Elliot Graham (Michael Gambon), having been left to him by his billionaire father. Graham, who has become a recluse, regards his father's mansion with a great deal of suspicion, seeing it as the outward representation of his father's questionable business dealings with the Nazis in the 1930s before the outbreak of the Second World War. Unable to come to terms with how his father made his money, Graham lives in a house on the opposite side of the road, leaving the mansion house empty but immaculately kept. But an 'aura' of something unpleasant associated with the house results in an ever dwindling staff, until the only person left working there is the seventeen-year-old doorman, Joe (Danny Lee-Wynter), whose main task appears to be to keep people out.

The narrative of *Capturing Mary* intersects with the events of *Joe's Palace*, and in Joe's opening voice-over in *Capturing Mary,* the audience is informed that no one is allowed to enter without the express permission of the reclusive owner, but when Mary (Maggie Smith) unexpectedly arrives at the door one day, Joe breaks the rules and lets her in. The interconnecting narratives of *Capturing Mary* and *Joe's Palace* reveal that the house and its contents are not only representative of the intersections between public history and individual lives, but the house is also the space Mary pinpoints has the location where she encounters the mysterious and disturbing Greville White (David Walliams) with devastating personal consequence. *Capturing Mary* offers a narrative which moves temporally in the same space.

The title sequence of *Capturing Mary* begins inside the house, with a shot above the ground floor entrance hall, taking in the staircase and the ornate mosaic flooring below. As the camera slowly turns in an anticlockwise spiral motion the image of the staircase appears to rotate in a clockwise motion as if the viewer were descending the stairs. The sequence then cuts to a close-up panning shot of a number of pairs of old shoes—for all occasions—before the camera pans round to a doorway, which leads to a series of empty rooms which appear static but immaculate, as if in a museum. The sequence then cuts to a close-up of the mosaic flooring of the entrance hall. As the opening narrative voiceover given by Joe begins, the camera follows the line of the central pattern on the floor and then back up the staircase, maintaining the close-up focus as if the viewer were ascending them. As the shot reaches the top of the stairs, Joe comes into view, sitting on the top stair looking down, thinking back on his earlier decision to let Mary into the house, before cutting back in time to a shot of Mary seen through the hatch of the front door from Joe's point of view. Having been let into the house and persuaded by Joe to have some tea, Mary—nervous and awkward—sits in the hallway glancing around the space until the open door of a room off the hall catches her attention and the camera follows Mary's gaze through the space. Simultaneously the scene is overlaid with the sound of a persistent tapping—the hollow tap of a table tennis ball—before the sound of opera singing is introduced.

Within the same space two temporal zones exist in tandem: we have Mary sitting in the hall in the present looking down towards a room which is also in the present, but on screen we see and hear the past in this room. The movement between close-up shots of Mary looking towards the camera and down the corridor whilst remembering a past event which took place in this room and shots which begin as wide-angle shots of the room's doorway in the present, before the camera moves down the corridor and closer to the door as the past then appears on screen, resulting in a sequence which sees Mary looking back directly into her past whilst she sits in and experiences the space. Onscreen, the space of past and present merge and move seamlessly from one to the other. Mary is transfixed, taken right back to her past and the parties she used to attend at the house. This scene shows how a familiar location can evoke events that took place in it; revisiting the house means Mary revisits the past. The tapping of the table tennis ball increases both in sound and speed before the ball itself rolls across the floor, as if it is in the space in the present day rolling past Mary's feet. The sequence lasts approximately forty-five seconds and features fifteen shots moving between Mary in the present and the view of the room in both past and present, and is only interrupted when the loud bang of the table tennis ball coincides with Mary knocking the milk jug off the tea table.

Joe realizes from Mary's behaviour that something must have happened in the house. Mary denies it, but this discussion leads to Mary explaining why she was invited to the extremely select parties held at the house—as a young novelist and culture critic for the newspapers. The story moves from room to room; but it is the first room that is the most significant, because it is the room in which we are first introduced to Greville. The sequence of shots moves from present to past showing the house as it was in the 1950s, and the scenes which accompany Mary's explanation show Greville weaving around the room with ease talking to those gathered there, whilst the younger Mary (Ruth Wilson) observes him from a distance, intrigued, until at one party it seems that Greville might be making his way across the room to speak to her. Mary escapes to the kitchen on the pretence of getting a glass of water only to find that Greville appears in the kitchen doorway; and so began a mysterious, and unnerving, acquaintance between the two. Joe moves off to go down to the kitchen to "see where it happened" (Poliakoff, *Capturing Mary* 133). When they arrive in the room, Mary comments that it has hardly changed, appearing as if it had been preserved (Poliakoff, *Capturing Mary* 134). The house seems as if it has been frozen in time, a still life snapshot of an earlier era, and an air of preservation permeates the whole house, creating an atmosphere of haunting.

By this point in the past, Mary and Greville have moved off to the cellar. In this dark and oppressive space Mary and Greville discuss the significance of the years in which certain wines were bottled—the early 1900s foreshadowing the war to come, the stock market crash of 1929, the continuation of wine making through the Second World War—until Greville unexpectedly reveals a number of horrific secret stories about high-profile members of society. The stories haunt Mary even decades later: "I have never been able to get them out of my head—I find myself thinking about then nearly every week, even now" (Poliakoff, *Capturing Mary* 141). As Mary leaves Greville in the cellar corridors in the past, Mary and Joe arrive there in the present day. From here, the narrative of *Capturing Mary* follows a pattern where Mary tells her story to Joe as they move through the house, with the sequences set in the past taking place almost one place ahead of Mary and Joe's location within the house. Believing Greville now has some hold over her—particularly since she has a sense that he could damage her professional prospects—Mary becomes convinced that she needs to extract herself from Greville's grasp. But when the opportunity arises one night when Mary is staying in the house and Greville arrives at her bedroom door with glasses filled with strawberries, Mary finds herself unable to unsettle him. Instead, Greville offers Mary a key to his house. Despite Greville urging her to not refuse the key, Mary cannot come to terms with the strangeness of the situation and refuses the key, pushing him out of the room and shutting the door in his face. The following morning Mary leaves the house, refusing an invitation from Greville to have dinner with him.

It is at this point that we move outside the house for the first time, into a London park, as Mary walks alone, having returned home from travels abroad, whilst Mary in the present day explains to Joe how her career in journalism collapsed, believing it was systematically destroyed by Greville following her rejection of him. Mary only returns to the house years later when she accompanies her lover, a fashionable artist, to one of Mr Graham's parties. The story then moves into another part of the house, a hideous 1960s conservatory, where again she watches Greville from a distance, surprised that he is there. When Joe and Mary enter the empty conservatory, Joe cannot understand why Mary did not confront Greville there. Mary, however, realizes that she is not at the party in her own right and this realisation is juxtaposed with shots of Greville circulating the room from Mary's point of view, re-emphasizing the connection between Mary's fall from her position as the 'voice of youth' and Greville's undefined powers within the world he moves in. At the party, Mary witnesses a young man tell Greville that his assessment of culture is: "complete crap! Everything you've said is just utter bollocks!" (Poliakoff, *Capturing Mary* 169). Realizing that she was unable reject Greville so absolutely when she refused his house key, and that because of this Greville still has some hold over her, Mary flees the party. Finding herself unable to write without returning to her encounter with Greville in the cellar, she sinks slowly into alcoholism. Walking in the park on the morning of her visit to the house, Mary believes she sees Greville there— whether she does see him or whether she merely imagines him is not clear, but it is this encounter which leads her back to the house that day.

Unlike Daniel, Mary's problem is not that she cannot remember, but that she remembers too well and has allowed her past to destroy her career. The way in which the story moves through the house to instigate a new episode of Mary's memory is not as complicated as the way in which space is used in *Perfect Strangers* to re-enact the past. Where *Perfect Strangers* used space to recuperate memory, *Capturing Mary* uses space to confront memory. Indeed, Mary says this herself:

> And somehow I forced myself here . . . something I've been thinking about for years—to come back here, and confront the place . . . To see if I could get rid of a ghost—which isn't a ghost, of course. Not a proper ghost.
>
> (Poliakoff, *Capturing Mary* 192)

The 'big house' offers a traditional location for haunting. As can be seen in *Perfect Strangers* and *Capturing Mary,* Poliakoff uses empty domestic spaces within urban 'big house' locations in his television dramas as places that are 'haunted' not by paranormal activity, but by the lost, suppressed or overwhelming memories of events from individual characters' pasts. But, as Mary herself notes, "this isn't a ghost story" (Poliakoff, *Capturing Mary* 186).

While *Capturing Mary* takes a more straightforward route to using space to tell a memory-narrative than *Perfect Strangers*, when the dual narratives of *Joe's Palace* and *Capturing Mary* are considered together, the house itself becomes a space which is representative of the memory of public trauma and private anguish. The relationship between the acquisition of wealth—of which the house is a product—and the Third Reich mean that the house is an ancestral space which both houses, and is haunted by, the spectre of the Holocaust. As the site of Mary's quietly destructive encounters with Greville, it is also haunted—as Mary herself is—by her memories of a lost career and a wasted life. Furthermore, the house itself is a space which haunts Mary; she enters tentatively, and resists Joe's first attempts to show her around, but through her behaviour it becomes clear to the audience that not only has Mary been there before, but the house represents some sort of internalized horror from her past. Where Daniel's memories were not sufficiently fixed in space, Mary's are locked in and attached securely to the house. Mary's resistance to the house is not a resistance to recuperating a memory of what took place there (Mary clearly remembers what took place there), but is instead a resistance to confronting it. Nonetheless, as soon as she enters the space Mary's memories rise up and as she and Joe walk around the house each room prompts the telling of an episode of a significant encounter with Greville and builds Mary's memory-narrative. Where in *Joe's Palace*, Mr Graham's distrust of the social and economic circumstances that enabled his father's acquisition of the house is influenced by his own sense of historical consciousness of an event from public history, Mary's story is predicated upon a sense of place consciousness. Re-entering the location of her encounters with Greville is a process Mary needed to go through so that she could attempt to cast off the ghost of Greville—a ghost which has been looming over her for most of her adult life.

While the televisual medium means, as Cardwell has noted, Poliakoff can achieve visual effects on screen which transcend temporal boundaries because the time zones of past and present can exist simultaneously on screen, it is important to remember these sequences—which are characteristic of Poliakoff's dramas and can be seen in *Perfect Strangers* and *Capturing Mary*—take place within spaces, and that the spatial boundaries in these houses offer a structure within which past and present can be melded and scrutinized through Poliakoff's cross-temporal, intermedia montages. It is space in both these dramas which both enables and necessitates these layered montages. Poliakoff's use of space in these montages allows him to overcome issues with temporal boundaries on screen. While television offers the dramatist opportunities to work with visual media, Poliakoff has also successfully used performance space in some of his stage plays to contain multiple time zones. By using a technique in which past and present exist within the same narrative and performative space, Poliakoff opens up the possibilities for narrating memory on stage. As Patrice Pavis has noted, the difficulty of understanding time, space and action in live performance lies not in describing these terms separately, but in observing how time, space and action interact in performance. In the theatre time, space and action are interdependent— one cannot exist without the other two. Time and space are both fixed—the physical theatre space and the time of the performance; and intangible— the fictional time and place on stage. Action adds yet more layers to this; both action which is performed and action which is imagined (Pavis 148). Time, space and action are not merely about what appears or takes place on stage. Theatre space is shared space. The performance, the performers and the audience occupy the same physical space; the time and space of the events unfolding onstage and the 'real' time and space co-exists with the theatrical time and space beyond the world created inside the auditorium by the audience and the performance. Plays such as *Blinded by the Sun* (1996), where Poliakoff makes use of a retrospective character-narrator structure, complicate this still further, creating a dual temporality within the performance: the time of the narration and the time of the action, where events which have already taken place in time and space in the time of the narration, and are recalled in the present, all of which takes place in the same space both onstage and in the drama's narrative.

During a scene towards the end of the play, one character—Elinor—is on one side of the stage where she is located in the narrative of the past—which is the time of the action—and the character-narrator, Al, is located in another part of the space, having stepped out of the time of the action to enter the present—the time of narration—to narrate Elinor's future (an event which has already taken place in Al's past, but has not taken place in the time of the action). The play occupies past (Al's past and the past which is the time of the action), present (Al's present) and future (Elinor's future) simultaneously in this moment within the same performance space. In the staging of Al's final monologue in *Blinded by the Sun,* the ways in which the time of the narration and the time of the action co-exist create layers of time, action and narration within the same space. In a key scene in Poliakoff's 2011 play *My City*, a teacher, Mr Minken, tells the story of his father's escape from Nazi Germany. The scene provides a significant illustration of how Poliakoff uses the stage space to be simultaneously occupied by past and present. In the production at London's Almeida theatre in autumn 2011, directed by Poliakoff himself, this scene was staged simply with no scenery except a projected backdrop of a large railway clock, and no props aside from a leather suitcase and a small model aeroplane. The importance—and complications—of time in this scene loom large. Time is layered in space: there is the present time of the performance and the present time of the main narrative strand of the play, within which the time of Minken's story takes place in the past, with finally the historical time of the story Minken is telling. For the duration of the monologue, four temporal strands occupy the same space, the passing and the pressures of time amplified by the large clock on the back wall of the stage. In television or cinema, attempts to create multiple time and space, on screen simultaneously, typically result in the use of split screen, flashbacks or multiple cuts between scenes and locations. Poliakoff uses the intermedia montage for the same purpose, mirroring his use of performance space in the theatre, creating a more detailed and visually complex way of visualizing and dramatizing memory. In theatre, multiple times and action can occupy the same space simultaneously, and in these scenes from his plays, Poliakoff explores the ways in which time, space and action in the theatre can be used to create memory-narratives.

Both *Perfect Strangers* and *Capturing Mary* create memory-narratives where memory is mapped onto space. By revisiting the empty houses, Daniel and Mary remember—each to a different extent—what took place there. Without space the memory-narrative cannot be told. To show what these memories are, and some of the processes of memory relating to certain physical senses—sight, touch and hearing—Poliakoff uses montages of layered media and sound to visually and aurally evoke the characters' memories within space. In his examination of memory, Casey analyzes 'body memory' as how we are in the world and 'place memory' as where we are in the world. Daniel and Mary's return to the spaces of memory mean that they experience them physically—kinetically—as well as emotionally, bringing performative body memory and place memory together on screen. Daniel's re-enactment of the photograph in the space in which it was taken is a process of what Casey calls "performative" remembering (Casey 148), whereas Mary's return to the house to confront the place, and her memories, shows an understanding that space/ place is "a container of experiences" as well as being where "the past can revive and survive" (Casey 186–87). Poliakoff makes use of the big house setting in both dramas to construct memory-narratives where the house acts as both memory trigger and memory location. By exploring the relationship between memory, space and place, Poliakoff's dramas echo—with a focus on private history and memory—Philip J. Ethington's argument that "historical interpretation" might be reconceived "as the act of reading places, or *topi*" (Ethington 466). Poliakoff's dramas on stage and screen make sophisticated use of space and place to present multiple narrative strands and memory-narratives in which space becomes a container for past experiences. Through the fragmentary lens of personal experience in character-driven narratives, Poliakoff explores individual microhistories which are embedded in characters' memories and strongly associated with their relationship with place and space as sites of memory. The static, empty spaces in *Perfect Strangers* and *Capturing Mary* offer the characters the opportunity to revisit and reread the past through place and space. For memory to be sustained, retrieved and passed on, space and place must be experienced and re-experienced; without the physical experience of a given space, or place within space, both the survival and the retrieval of memory are put in jeopardy.

Works cited

Bachelard, Gaston. *The Poetics of Space*. Trans. Maria Jolas. Boston: Beacon Press, 1994. Print.

Cardwell, Sarah. "'Television Aesthetics' and Close Analysis: Style, Mood and Engagement in Perfect Strangers (Stephen Poliakoff, 2001)." *Style and Meaning: Studies in the Detailed Analysis of Film*. Eds. John Gibbs and Douglas Pye. Manchester: Manchester UP, 2005. 179–94. Print.

Casey, Edward S. *Remembering: A Phenomenological Study.* 2nd ed. Blooming-ton: Indiana UP, 2000. Print. Studies in Continental Thought.

Christie, Agatha. *Sleeping Murder.* Glasgow: Fontana, 1978. Print.

Ethington, Philip J. "Placing the Past: Groundwork for a Spatial Theory of History." *Rethinking History* 11.4 (2007): 465–94. Print.

Holdsworth, Amy. *Television, Memory, and Nostalgia.* Basingstoke: Palgrave Macmillan, 2011. Print. Palgrave Macmillan Memory Studies.

Kuhn, Annette. *Family Secrets: Acts of Memory and Imagination.* London: Verso, 1995. Print.

Lambert, Ronald D. "Descriptive, Narrative, and Experiential Pathways to Symbolic Ancestors." *Mortality* 11.4 (2006): 317–35. Print.

Pavis, Patrice. *Analyzing Performance: Theater, Dance, and Film.* Ann Arbor: U of Michigan P, 2003. Print.

Poliakoff, Stephen. "Blinded by the Sun." *Blinded by the Sun & Sweet Panic.* London: Methuen Drama, 1996. 1–122. Print.

———. *Perfect Strangers.* London: Methuen Drama, 2001. Print.

———. *Perfect Strangers.* BBC, 2001. Film.

———. *Capturing Mary.* BBC, 2007. Film.

———. *Joe's Palace and Capturing Mary.* London: Methuen Drama, 2007. Print.

———. *My City.* London: Methuen Drama, 2011. Print.

Proust, Marcel. *Swann's Way.* London: Chatto and Windus, 1951. Print.

Vice, Sue. "Yellowing Snapshots: Photography and Memory in Holocaust Literature." *Journal for Cultural Research* 8.3 (2004): 293–316. Print.

Yates, Frances Amelia. *The Art of Memory.* Chicago: U of Chicago P, 1966. Print.

Part III
Geography in the Text

9 Caves as Anti-Places

Robert Penn Warren's *The Cave* and Cormac McCarthy's *Child of God*

Ralph Crane and Lisa Fletcher

According to the standard scientific definition, a cave is a natural hollow beneath the surface of the earth that is large enough for humans to enter, but in broader cultural terms caves are rarely understood or depicted as spaces where humans belong or fit. Instead, from the human/aboveground perspective, caves are *other* spaces—settings within which we can only dwell uncomfortably and temporarily. Edward Relph begins *Place and Placelessness* by insisting on the primary significance of place to human life: "To be human is to live in a world that is filled with places: to be human is to have and to know *your* place" (1). Yi-Fu Tuan makes a similar claim on the first page of his seminal book *Space and Place: The Perspective of Experience* when he yokes "a sense of place" to the human need for home: "Space and place are basic components of the lived world; we take them for granted" (3). Relph's and Tuan's books were published within a year of each other—in 1976 and 1977, respectively—and, while others have interrogated some of the nuances of their arguments, their central claims remain current and influential, and continue to warrant further unpacking. For these key figures in late twentieth-century humanistic geography, place is an ontological necessity that merits serious and ongoing theorization. In this paper, we look to fictions set partly in deep caves to ask: what can we learn about the concepts of space and place—and, in particular, their relevance and value for literary studies—by thinking about locations beyond what Tuan terms "the lived world"?

It has become a critical commonplace for scholars of space and place to point to the imprecision of these foundational terms and the consequent lack of certainty about their relationship. Phil Hubbard begins his entry "Space/Place" in *Cultural Geography: A Critical Dictionary of Key Ideas* by pointing to the ongoing challenge these terms pose in cultural geography and cognate fields: "Though the concepts of space and place may appear self-explanatory, they have been (and remain) two of the most diffuse, ill-defined and inchoate concepts in the social sciences and humanities" (41). Place, Tim Cresswell writes, "is a word that seems to speak for itself" (1), whereas "[s]pace is a more abstract concept" (8). Cresswell offers "a meaningful location" as "the most straightforward and common definition of place" (7) and, in broad terms, this simple definition holds sway in the theoretical discourse informing geocriticism as it develops and refines its critical vocabulary. How, for instance, does the term "setting" operate in relation to the space-place dyad? Is setting an under-theorized concept in literary studies because, as Creswell writes of place, it too "is a word wrapped in common sense," "a word that seems to speak for itself" (1)?

The distinction and the relationship between "space" and "place" is, fairly obviously, a key question for geocriticism as it seeks to build flexible and resilient theoretical frameworks for analyzing the meaning and significance of literary settings. In Robert T. Tally Jr.'s words, "geocriticism attempts to understand the real and fictional spaces that we inhabit, cross through, imagine, survey, modify, celebrate, disparage and on and on in infinite variety" ("Translator's Preface" x). The still-evolving geocritical brief asks more of researchers than the close analysis of settings in literary texts, but this work is clearly one of its primary hermeneutic challenges. This article responds to this challenge by attempting a geocritical analysis of the subterranean settings in Robert Penn Warren's *The Cave* (1959) and Cormac McCarthy's *Child of God* (1973), and argues that the baseline terms "space" and place" are inadequate conceptual tools for thinking about caves—real or imagined.

Tuan's pithy explanation of the relationship between space and place is well-known and resonates with both authors' approaches to setting: "What begins as undifferentiated space becomes place as we get to know it better and endow it with value" (6). Once the caves in these novels are entered and inhabited by humans they cease to be *spaces*, but to designate them *places* would be to miss the important subtleties of their authors' fictional (and theoretical) projects. The exploration of the spatial continuum in these novels—with undifferentiated space at one extreme and home at the other—suggests a third term: the caves are *anti-places*. They are locations that seem to mirror the personal and communal places through which characters traverse and within which they dwell on the surface, but that never become their equivalents. We use the prefix anti- here for a number of reasons: to denote opposition, reversal, rivalry, and difference. Both novels, although to different degrees, depict caves and surface environments in a relation of opposition, most notably with reference to the absence of light. The caves are portrayed as antithetical to the normative places of everyday life; in each novel they attract male central characters that are anachoristic figures in the domestic and social spaces of East Tennessee. Further, the absence of diurnal rhythms deep underground fuels both novels' fascination with the capacity of cave settings to reverse or undo the spatial logics that are the basis of the "lived world." One of the goals of geocriticism is to challenge the assumed supremacy of character over setting in most literary criticism, but, unsurprisingly, achieving this goal is hindered by the lack of a rich and nuanced critical vocabulary to rival that available for analyzing the roles and functions of human actors in fiction. The idea of "anti-place" is therefore a somewhat speculative one, a response to what we perceive as a need for an equivalent spatial term to "anti-hero." The caves in these novels exploit and expose conventions of spatial representation in fiction (and, we would argue, beyond the pages of novels) and thus shed new light on the assumptions which govern the depiction of more mundane settings.

In his recent book, Eric Prieto explains, place is a "*human* relation. There is no set of immanent ontological features adhering to a given site that would allow us to define it as a place" (xx). This article focuses on the spatial identities of two characters who, unable to find their place in the aboveground world, albeit for different reasons, search for a place in the labyrinths under Tennessee: Jasper Herrick, the "poor cave-crawling hillbilly" (25) from Warren's *The Cave*, and Lester Ballard, the "misplaced and loveless simian" (21) who retreats underground in McCarthy's *Child of God* (1973). For James H. Justus, *The Cave* is both Warren's "most experimental novel" ("Introduction" viii) and, when judged as a realist novel, a "mimetic failure" (ix) for its depiction of both people and place. The novel is set in 1955 in a fictional East Tennessee town, Johntown, "located somewhere between Knoxville and Chattanooga" (Justus, "Introduction" ix), but, for Justus, the setting is "curiously generalized and only perfunctorily anchored to geography" (x). Justus reads *The Cave*, which is loosely based on the death of cave explorer Floyd Collins in Sand Cave, Kentucky in 1924, as a "subterranean drama of the self" (xi) in which setting's main function is symbolic. Warren visited and made notes about Sand Cave in preparation for writing the novel (Justus, "Introduction" vii), but the description of place itself, for Justus, remains subordinate to characterization, which, he claims, draws "almost compulsively . . . on metaphors of *inside, within, beneath, underneath,* and similar spatial images" (xiv). *Child of God*, in contrast, is deeply anchored in the geography and history of Sevier County, where McCarthy lived in the 1960s (Luce 172). Dianne C. Luce explains that the caves "which form a locus for much of the significant action of the novel, are verifiable in all their mineral and organic details" (172) and compares the historical records of floods in Sevierville with the plot of the novel to suggest that novel's main action takes place in 1957.[1] Whilst *The Cave* may not be deeply anchored in the geography of Tennessee in the way McCarthy's novel clearly is, setting is nevertheless foregrounded throughout the novel, securely locating it in spatial if not strictly geographic terms.

Jay Ellis, in the first chapter of his book *No Place for Home: Spatial Constraint and Character Flight in the Novels of Cormac McCarthy*, offers a brief, but useful, definition of his key terms, space and place:

I will employ the terms [*sic.*] *place* in opposition to *space* to distinguish between constraints on character movement (both indoor and

outdoor) and the void of the natural world without human construction. Briefly, a *place* is a construction of the possibilities of *space* into
a fixed set of circumstances. Place is ontological, space existential.

(17)

There are two issues raised by Ellis's approach to space and place as key
concepts for literary analysis, which suggest the need for more nuanced
ways of accounting for the continuum of spatial possibilities describable
as "place." First, to describe space as "the void of the natural world without human construction" is to designate it as utterly abstract and beyond
human perception. Space, according to this view, is the empty and null
zone which exists prior to place, but which can never be apprehended
as such. The upshot of this approach is that space is, in itself, unrepresentable from the viewpoint of characters, except as an abstracted and
imaginary site of possibility; "space" is thus not a synonym for "setting."
Second, for Ellis, place transforms "the possibilities of *space* into a fixed
set of circumstances," but—as dramatized by the novels discussed in
this article—place-making does not negate the potential for change Ellis
attaches to the concept of space. Not only can a place be reconstructed
and re-mapped, but the same "space" can be seen and experienced as
multiple, even opposed, "places" by different people, both individually
and collectively. Ellis argues that McCarthy's fiction is built on an awareness of the complex dynamics of space and place and points in particular
to the frequency with which his novels depict characters constrained by
the "gravity of houses" and caught up in "the pull of unnatural graves"
(17). He writes that "McCarthy relies more on setting than on plot, or
even character" (1); this claim rings as true for Warren, who, as Ellis says
of McCarthy, "lavishes words on space and place" (2).

As Justus notes, "Warren was drawn to caves" (vii). His 1978 autobiographical poem "Speleology" recalls his boyhood adventures exploring
a cave near his home in the Kentucky karst. According to the poem, he
"first found the cave-mouth" when he was six years old and returned
every summer to peer in to its "inner dark" and to creep gradually
deeper, but was not bold enough to venture into its true depths until he
was twelve and "now had me a flashlight." Deep in the cave, the boy "cut
off the light" and "Knew darkness and depth and no Time." He crawled
further and lay still, "Light out, unmoving":

> Lulled as by song in a dream, knowing
>   I dared not move in darkness so absolute.
>   I thought: *This is me.* Thought: *Me—who am I?* Felt
>   Heart beating as though to a pulse of darkness and earth, and
> thought
>   How would it be to be here forever,

(382)

The physical dimensions of the cave restrict the boy's movement the deeper he goes—the roof becomes "lower and lower"—but it is the absolute darkness that immobilizes him. Laying still deep in the cave, the boy both experiences his body as the container of self (*"This is me"*) and is prompted to question where the coordinates of his self begin and end (*"Me—Who am I?"*). In a scene of existential reverie, the boy and the cave become almost coextensive phenomena as he feels his "Heart beating as though to a pulse of darkness and earth" (382). Relph, in *Place and Placelessness*, mentions caves as one of a variety of places that can "constitute the basis for the discovery of self" in childhood: "caves or trees or even a corner of the house" exemplify the kinds of "childhood places" which "frequently take on great significance and are remembered with reverence" (11). Relph's inclusion of caves in this short list seems counter-intuitive. Unlike the nooks and crannies of childhood houses and gardens, for most of us, caves are not part of our everyday environment, but extraordinary settings of wonder and adventure, or fear. The psychological significance and power of the cave in Warren's poem comes not from a sense that it became a "private place" to which he could retreat—the depths of caves resist such domestication—but its status beyond the boundaries of everyday life. Simply, the boy is changed by his encounter with the cave, but he does not belong there.

The lure of the cave continues to exert its pull on Warren's narrator into adulthood. "Years later, past dreams" the poem's narrator/Warren has "lain in darkness and heard the depth of that unending song" (382) and wondered, "What would it be like to be, in the end, part of all" (383). The poem's next and final line presents the narrator's imaginative return to the cave of his boyhood as an existential habit: "And in darkness have even asked: *Is this all? What is all?*" (383). This poem, like so many other literary representations of subterranean spaces, pictures the cave as a tomb—the boy lies still as a corpse beneath the ground. Importantly, however, the cave is more than a symbolic space in "Speleology." It is a series of hollows carved in limestone by water over millennia where "chambers of darkness rose and stalactites down-stabbed" and cannot be defined or co-opted by the human processes which impose meaning on the spaces of the Earth.

To an extent, Warren's poem depicts a process of personal place-making which transforms a cave from undifferentiated "space" into meaningful "place" for one individual, but we argue that these terms are inadequate to the task of analyzing literary (and, indeed, non-literary) representations of caves. Thinking about "cavescapes" reveals blind spots in the lexicon of literary and cultural geography that, for obvious reasons, has been developed to describe and analyze natural and built environments on the planet's surface.

The aboveground bias in theories of space and place is not surprising (and may even be necessary), but it does merit consideration, not least because turning our attention to caves involves asking what is taken for granted in the definition and use of key spatial concepts across the social sciences and humanities. For instance, Tuan explains that the "organization of human space is uniquely dependent on sight" (16). This means that, as Tim Cresswell writes, "Landscape is an intensely visual idea" (10). The panoramic perspective that "landscape" implies is impossible deep underground, not just because there is no natural light, but because—even with the aid of a flashlight—there is no horizon. From the perspective of phenomenology, the "vocabularies of spatial organization and value have certain common terms," which are "ultimately derived from the structure and value of the human body" (Tuan 37): upright/prone, high/low, front/back, right/left. However, entering deep caves recalibrates perceptions of circumambient space when underground and then invites reflection on experiences of space on the surface. The Norwegian archaeologist Hein Bjartmann Bjerck argues that, in phenomenological terms, caves present us with the "opposite of the living world": "caves are silent and static— the chaotic complexity of movements and sensory impressions in the day life outside is absent" (58–59). For humans, Bjerck writes, "being in a cave is like being dead or unborn." He therefore wonders whether the "most profound embodied experience" of spending time in a cave occurs not underground, but at the moment when

> you re-enter life and the light outside: your reset senses are suddenly bombarded by all the ordinary things that filled them and your brain to a degree that borders on invisibility prior to the time spent in the dark void.
>
> (59)

Warren's *The Cave* and McCarthy's *Child of God* show that thinking about caves puts pressure on key concepts for describing and understanding the Earth and our place on (or in) it. Both novels reveal the potential of caves to confound assumptions about the roles people play in assigning meaning to the Earth's spaces and to approach fuller responses to the question, "Where are we?"

The plot of Warren's *The Cave* revolves around the fate of Jasper Harrick, the cave-crawler who is trapped underground for the entire novel. Justus refers to him as a "kind of non-character who appears only in flashbacks" (viii). Similarly, Randolph Runyon suggests that he is "the absent center around which the plot unfolds" (45), but it is more apposite to suggest that while he is undoubtedly the absent *character* around which the plot unfolds, a geocentric reading of the novel favors the cave itself as the *space* around which the plot of the novel revolves. This is true metaphorically in so much as Jasper's entrapment and death in the cave is at the center of the novel, but also literally as all the major characters of the novel—Jo-Lea Bingham, Monty Harrick, Jack and Celia Harrick,

MacCarland Sumpter, Isaac Sumpter, and Nick Papadoupalous—as well as a number of minor ones are drawn to the cave mouth. Indeed, the gathering of Warren's congeries of searchers at the cave mouth is central to the action of the novel, and provides its structural climax (Justus, "The Uses of Gesture" 451). In this novel, *setting* occupies the central position that is normally filled by the protagonist. Further, the working title of the novel, *The Man Below*, which, as Allen Shepherd notes, "would have better suggested the centrality and mystery of Jasper Harrick's fate" (47), was dropped in favor of *The Cave*, which better suggests the centrality of spatiality, and recognizes the way cave images shape every aspect of the novel.

Isaac Sumpter, who had hoped to gain from Jasper's discovery of a new cave on land owned by his family, sees new potential for profit in the caver's disappearance and pretends to have found him trapped and alive. Isaac calls the editor of the Nashville *Press-Clarion* to report that a Korean War veteran is lost in his cave: "There is a guy caught in a cave up here. He is a sort of romantic and colorful guy, half-ass war hero etcetera" (195). The journalist is not persuaded that Jasper's entrapment is a "big" story: "I don't care—and the whole bleeding world waiting for the sunrise does not care—if half the hillbillies in East Tennessee get stuck in caves" (184). The name Sumpter is doubly ironic: sumpter is a now rare word for a pack-animal or beast of burden, and, in caving parlance, a sump is a water-filled section of cave passage, impassable without submergence. Isaac carries food, water, and a heat pad underground but is lying when he tells the press and the community that he has reached the dying boy: "I am the guy went in. I am the guy found him. I am the guy with the face-to-face" (236). Still determined to cast Jasper as a new Floyd Collins (195), Isaac makes tape recordings for Nashville radio, speaking into his recorder at the cave mouth, " 'A man is in the ground,' he began to speak to the tape":

> A man is in the ground. He is a young man. He is a brave man. He has been decorated for valor, in the Korean War. Wounded, he rallied a platoon, and hung to a shell-swept, hell-swept hill-side. This afternoon, he looked into my face, deep underground, trapped in the crawlway of a cave, a stone on his leg, and said, "This is tougher than Korea. But I'm going to make it," he said.
>
> (236–37)

"A man is in the ground"—Isaac's brief opening sentence is a distillation of one of the key ideas raised by the novel; Jasper's identity is determined by his spatial condition. Setting is the bedrock for character here and throughout the novel.

In keeping with our geocentric reading, Jasper can be seen as an anti-character (hardly an anti-hero), anachoristic or out of place, who seeks to escape the identity imposed on him by his father (perhaps an anti-hero) and a community that persists in casting him as Jack Herrick's son, "a chip off the old block" (14). This explains in part why the deep cave in which he is entombed is never more than an anti-place. Moreover, the reader rarely enters the cave, few characters enter the cave (and only one character actually reaches Jasper), but every major character in the novel, as well as a number of minor ones, congregates in the clearing around the cave mouth—what Madison Jones labels "a center-stage in the novel" (54)—a liminal space that during the course of the novel is transformed into an anthropomorphized place. Ironically, by getting stuck in the cave, Jasper draws toward him the very community he is trying to escape, and in the process, the hitherto undifferentiated space of the cave mouth is transformed into differentiated human place.

The first paragraph of *The Cave*, which describes a pair of boots, concludes with a sentence which highlights Jasper's absence in the novel in spatial terms: "But the man was not there" (3). The chapter as a whole introduces the spatial tensions which are central to the novel: between here and there; home and away; inside and outside; open and closed; and, of course, above and below. It goes on to describe a karst landscape, a guitar, and the mouth of a cave:

> a longitudinal opening in the rocks, a vestibule, a jutting overhang of mossy limestone, and farther in, another opening, not nearly as big, a couple of feet high, three across. The opening of the vestibule, dark green with moss, fern hanging lacily over it, trefoil to one side, is very pretty.
>
> (6)

This early description begins the process of articulating the cave mouth as place. The word "vestibule," which carries with it a metaphor of home, replaces the more abstract "longitudinal opening" with a sense of security, which is reinforced by the words "lacily," "trefoil," and "pretty."

And just as we encounter the cave mouth through anthropomorphic and architectural metaphorics, so the reader is constantly invited to see human bodies and the interiors of houses in the novel through cave metaphorics. Thus, for example, in a passage which recalls the transition through the darkening zones of a cave, Monty imagines Jo-Lea going into her house, "moving into the gloom of the front hall . . . into the deeper gloom of the back hall and body of the house . . . into an even more mysterious and shadowy region" (11). There are references to "the dark of the hall" (385) in the Harrick house, the other site that along with the cave mouth draws all the major characters of the novel. Similarly, self and cave metaphors are ubiquitous: Jo-Lea "drowned darkly inward into herself" (12); "in that deep, dark, angry secret center of [Nick Pappy's] being tears fell without ceasing" (42); and Monty's chest "seemed as big and deep as a cave" (343). These are, as Richard A. Davidson rightly observes, "the dark inner recesses . . . that must be explored just as the actual cave in which Jasper is trapped must be explored" (352). In this the novel draws a comparison between the processes of identity formation and place making, not least because both processes (apprehensible only in retrospect) are at once deeply personal and inescapably social and cultural.

Jasper has taken refuge in caves, which for him, as he crawled through them, were transformed from undifferentiated spaces to places of retreat, places where he could breathe. According to his mother, Celia, "That's why he crawled in the ground. To get away from everything" (298). When Celia asked him what lured him underground he answered:

> It's not what you'd expect down there . . . It's not like what above-ground folks would expect . . . It's a nice temperature down there . . . It is not summer and it is not winter. There aren't any seasons to bother about down there.
>
> (239–40)

The incommensurability of human time and geological time Jasper identifies here reinforces our idea of the dark recesses of the cave as anti-place. For most of the characters in the novel, caves are spaces of darkness, separate from the places where they dwell, and with Jasper trapped underground Celia imagines him among the eyeless cave creatures: "They hopped on your face in the dark, and, oh God, can you breathe darkness instead of air?" (203). For Celia, the absolute darkness of the cave makes it a space to be feared; but for Jasper, the subterranean passages are transformed into a secure, albeit solitary, place. Jasper, alone, could breathe the darkness, because his knowledge of the deep cave, and the value with which he endows it, has transformed it, *for him*, from space to place, while for the other characters in the novel it remains, in Tuan's terms, undifferentiated space.

The human proximity to caves, here as in Warren's poem "Speleology," prompts existential questions about identity. "Who am I?" is a key question that each of the major characters must confront during the course of this novel, and the cave proves to be the key metaphor used by Warren for the exploration of the inner self of his characters. Jasper, quite literally, searches for his identity in the subterranean karst caverns below East Tennessee. His metaphorical search, plainly manifested in his cave-crawling, leads him away from place into space or what turns out to be anti-place, where he dies. Jasper's quest for self-discovery leads to darkness and silence; it is an anti-bildungsroman, simultaneously an exploration and a burial, through which other characters do achieve growth as they perform their roles in the drama of the trapped caver. Or, as Davison puts it: "Jasper's figurative search is implicit in his cave-crawling. He alone is sacrificed. And it is through his physical entombment and eventual death that others achieve insights into themselves" (356). Thus, as Jasper is trapped in the actual cave, so each of the other major characters is trapped in the dark recesses of the caves of their inner selves. Jasper will not emerge again into the daylight, but others, through his plight, are given that opportunity.

Andre Keller Estes identifies space/place as one of a set of interrelated binaries that are especially relevant to reading MacCarthy's fiction, which, he argues, "shift[s] the emphasis of the narration from people to the environments which surround them" (43).[2] In the opening scene of *Child of God* the titular character, Lester Ballard, watches from the sidelines as his family property is sold at auction, but he is not the focalizer here or at any point during the novel. In the novel's first paragraph, people approach the auction site "like a caravan of carnival folk up through the swales of broomstraw and across the hill in the morning sun" (5) to stop before "an aged clapboard house that stood in blue shade under the wall of the mountain" (5). The first description of Ballard depicts him as an already displaced figure, a witness to the oddly festive auction, but on its periphery: "To watch these things issuing from the otherwise mute pastoral morning is a man at the barn door" (5). Ballard watches from a distance—as he does on numerous occasions throughout the novel, sometimes through the sights of his rifle—but he is a voyeur without authority. Like Jasper Herrick, Ballard does not fit comfortably in the social economy and geography of East Tennessee, even though the community and environment of Sevierville is ill defined in comparison to Warren's Johntown. Whereas Jasper retreats into caves voluntarily (even happily), Ballard is forcefully rejected and ejected, and so is driven first to the outskirts of the community and then underground.

As the auction gets underway, Ballard stands beyond the house at the barn door, "small, unclean, unshaven," his investment in the event indicated by "a constrained truculence" (5). Importantly, Ballard's distance from the narrative viewpoint is signaled by the same sentence that asks readers to consider their own proximity to him. The narrator proposes that this man in the shadows is, "A child of God much like yourself perhaps" (6). Standing in the "laddered light from the barnslats" (6) Ballard is symbolically caged: "he moves along the barn wall, himself fiddlebacked with light, a petty annoyance flickering across the wallward eye" (6). Three perspectives overlap in the phrase "wallward eye"—the abstracted third-person narrator, the people filling up the yard, and the reader—a conflation which positions the reader as both audience to and complicit in Ballard's eviction. When Ballard challenges the auctioneer— "I want you to get your godamn ass off my property" (8)—he is struck in the head with the bit of an axe, after which he "never could hold his head right" (10). Jay Ellis argues that "every subsequent action" (68) of Ballard, from murder to necrophilia to troglodytism, follows from this double "unhousing" (69), which both sees him without a home and leaves him with an acquired brain injury. In these terms, Ballard is a disturbing (even sickening) figure of devolution or degeneracy, but the key to understanding his actions is not deciphering his personal motivations, but appreciating the grave consequences of violent social exclusion.

Ballard seeks shelter first in an abandoned two-room cabin, where, through somewhat heavy-handed symbolism, he is compared to a prehistoric cave dweller and his descent into the caves foreshadowed. On his first night in the house, he gathers his meager belongings around him, puts a lamp on the floor in the middle of the "barren room" and sits, "crosslegged" before it, roasting pieces of potato on a coat-hanger (15–16). Later scenes expand on this cruel (or crude) parody of the life of a Stone Age cave dweller. Rejected by the dumpkeeper's daughters— "gangling progeny with black hair hanging from their armpits" (27)— Ballard finds a "lady sleeping under the trees in a white gown" (40) on Frog Mountain and watches to see if she is dead. When she wakes, "slack mouth twisted" and emitting "a sweet ferment of whiskey and rot" (40), the ensuing struggle between the half-drunk, staggering woman armed with a rock and brain-addled Ballard emphasizes the latter's extreme isolation. At a local fair, he wins two bears and a tiger at the shooting gallery before the "pitchman" takes the rifle away from him, hissing, "That's it for you, buddy" (61), effectively banishing him from the social space of the fairground. The stuffed animals "watch from the wall" (64) of his cabin as he eats his cornbread mush, like spoils of the hunt, "their plastic eyes shining in the firelight and their red flannel tongues out" (64). Ballard, crouching alone in his hovel-cum-cave on the fringes of town, is good with a gun, but the townspeople fail to recognize that his decline into degeneracy presages abject violence.

The characterization of Ballard as a regressive figure is reinforced by the strong parallel the text draws between him and the child Billy, a "huge-headed bald and slobbering primate that inhabit[s] the lower reaches" (74) of his neighbor's house. Like Ballard, Billy (the off-rhyme of their names seems deliberate) is an "idiot child" (113) who occupies "the lower reaches," watching those who look down on him through "dull eyes" (74). Ballard's strange alignment with this "gross tottertoy" (85) and his view from beneath, is strengthened by his association with the dump, the quarry, and the turnaround on Frog Mountain, all environments of detritus, rubble, and waste.

Ballard's degeneration gains momentum when he stumbles upon a dead couple in a car, suspended mid-coitus by carbon monoxide poisoning, and drags the woman from the vehicle. He becomes an opportunistic necrophile: "A crazy gymnast laboring over a cold corpse. He poured into that waxen ear everything he'd ever thought of saying to a woman" (84). After he loses his first "dead girlfriend" (Sullivan), Ballard shoots Billy's mother and carries her away into the night, and, as is revealed later in the novel, toward the "constant night" of the dripping caves beneath the mountain (125). Despite the subtle link drawn between the women's bodies and the "damp stone corridors down inside the mountain" (126)—his first victim's "waxen ear" is recalled by the cave walls' "waxed or lacquered" (126) appearance—the caves in this novel are more back passage than they are birth canal. Billy's mother's dismissal of Ballard as "shit crazy" (110)—moments before he murders her—turns out to be more insightful than it first seems.

In the scene immediately following the horrific death of Billy's mother, Ballard is interrogated by the sheriff about the fire that destroyed the abandoned cabin, now identified as "Mr Waldrop's house" (115). The lawman's advice to Ballard is portentous: "you are either going to have to find some other way to live or some other place in the world to do it in" (115). The "other place" Ballard finds is, of course, the caves:

> Here the walls with their softlooking convolutions, slavered over as they were with wet and bloodred mud, had an organic look to them, like the innards of some great beast. Here in the bowels of the mountain Ballard turned his light on ledges or pallets of stone where dead people lay like saints.
>
> (126–27)

In the mythology of many and diverse cultures, Tuan writes, "The earth is the human body writ large" (89). Caves are routinely imagined in literature and art as the cavities and inner passages of the human body (Crane and Fletcher). In *Child of God*, they are the bowels. Later, when Ballard walks outside, his tracks come "from the cave bloodred with cave-mud" (132–33), joining the patterns on the snow already made by the tracks of a fox "intaglio like little mushrooms and berrystains where birds shat crimson mutes upon the snow like blood" (130). Ballard does not emerge from the earth reborn but as human waste; in figurative terms, he is not coated in vernix caseosa, but in excrement.

According to the dark geopoetics of *Child of God*, the binary hierarchies and structures of power that exclude some people and sustain others follow spatial logics. Ballard fails in his attempt to create his home in caves because place-making cannot be an eccentric process, but must be socially, culturally, and economically endorsed. The caves are thus rendered anti-place and function as a literary device to force readers to take heed of the consequence of failing to attend to the expelled and to the zones of exclusion. When Sevierville floods, Ballard attempts to salvage his belongings—"a crate of odd miscellany" (146)—and wades into the surging creekbed. A log spins "broadside to him": "It came bobbing and bearing in its perimeter a meniscus of pale brown froth in which floated walnuts, twigs, a slender bottle neck erect and titling like a metronome" (146–47). The imagery here explicitly recalls the description of the "darker pool" of Ballard's urine when he relieves himself against the barn wall in the opening scene, a pool "wherein swirls a pale foam with bits of straw" (6). As in this early scene—when the reader is asked to consider that this pathetic figure is "A child of God like yourself perhaps" (6)—the narrator exhorts readers to acknowledge that Ballard's depravity is not his alone:

> You could say that he's sustained by his fellow man, like you. Has peopled the shore with them calling to him. A race that gives suck to the maimed and the crazed, that wants their wrong blood in its history and will have it.
>
> (147)

Ballard is emblematic of the dispossessed and the disowned, but the reader is continually reminded that this "crazed mountain troll" (143) who "passe[s] beneath" (145) the townsfolk was produced and sustained by them.

After Ballard is captured and imprisoned following a failed attempt to murder John Greer—who shoots the crazed caveman's arm off—he guides a vigilante mob underground and becomes lost after evading his captors. The metaphoric register used to picture the caves in the novel's final pages expands and they become brain hollows and birth canal. Trapped for more than three days in the dark and the damp, Ballard imagines mice nesting in the "lobed caverns where his brains had been" and has "cause to wish for some brute midwife to spald him from his rocky keep" (180). After digging his way to the surface, Ballard returns to the hospital: "His eyes were caved and smoking. I'm supposed to be here, he said" (182).

In the end, Ballard cannot exist elsewhere, and so—with pathetic insight—returns to the only *place* he can survive. In contrast, in Warren's *The Cave*, Jasper Herrick is trapped in an *anti-place* where he cannot survive.

Though it is tempting for the literary scholar to take space and place for granted—to accept that they are components that *seem* to speak for themselves—the spatial otherness of the subterranean settings in both these novels cannot readily be understood through a straightforward space/place binary. Moreover, our understanding of the two central protagonists, Jasper Harrick and Lester Ballard, is limited by the extent of our understanding of setting in these novels. Thus the term anti-place has been a key concept in our reading of Warren's *The Cave* and McCarthy's *Child of God*. It is no longer space, but nor is it humanized place. Importantly, anti-place is not an inflexible neologism, a convenient term for our discussion of these two admittedly unusual novels, but a concept that, by extending our understanding of space and place—"the lived world"— may prove useful to researchers wishing to approach settings (real or imagined) in literary texts from a more nuanced and flexible geocritical perspective.

Notes

1. See Luce's essay for a detailed discussion of McCarthy's historical and scientific sources for *Child of God*, especially in relation to the history and geography of Tennessee and the psychology of necrophilia.
2. The other pairs of terms suggested by Estes are environmental criticism/ ecocriticism, machine/garden, nature/culture, biocentrism/anthropocentrism, and wilderness/civilization, all of which would be relevant to a fuller study of the literary representation of caves.

Works Cited

Bjerck, Hein Bjartmann. "On the Outer Fringe of the Human World: Phenomenological Perspectives on Anthropomorphic Cave Paintings in Norway." *Caves in Context: The Cultural Significance of Caves and Rockshelters in Europe.* Eds. Knut Andreas Bergsvik and Robin Skeates. Oxford: Oxbow, 2012. 48–64. Print.

Crane, Ralph, and Lisa Fletcher. *Cave: Nature and Culture.* London: Reaktion, 2015.

Cresswell, Tim. *Place: A Short Introduction.* Malden: Blackwell, 2004. Print.

Davison, Richard A. "Robert Penn Warren's 'Dialectical Configuration' and *The Cave.*" *College Language Association Journal* 10 (1967): 349–57. Print.

Ellis, Jay. *No Place for Home: Spatial Constraint and Character Flight in the Novels of Cormac McCarthy.* New York: Routledge, 2006. Print.

Estes, Andrew Keller. *Cormac McCarthy and the Writing of American Spaces.* Amsterdam: Rodopi, 2013.

Hubbard, Phil. "Space/Place." *Cultural Geography: A Critical Dictionary of Key Ideas.* Eds. David Atkinson, Peter Jackson, David Sibley, and Neil Washbourne. London: I.B. Tauris, 2005. 41–48.

Jones, Madison. "Robert Penn Warren as Novelist." *A Southern Renascence Man: Views of Robert Penn Warren.* Ed. Walter B. Edgar. Baton Rouge: Louisiana State UP, 1984. 39–57. Print.

Justus, James H. "The Use of Gesture in Warren's *The Cave.*" *Modern Language Quarterly* 26.3 (1965): 448–61. Print.

———. "Introduction." *The Cave.* Ed. Robert Penn Warren. Lexington: UP of Kentucky, 2006. vii–xvi. Print.

Luce, Dianne C. "The Cave of Oblivion: Platonic Mythology in *Child of God.*" *Cormac McCarthy: New Directions.* Ed. James D. Lilley. Albuquerque: U of New Mexico P, 2002. 171–98. Print.

McCarthy, Cormac. *Child of God.* 1973. London: Picador, 2010. Print.

Prieto, Eric. *Literature, Geography, and the Postmodern Poetics of Place.* London: Palgrave Macmillan, 2013. Print.

Relph, E. *Place and Placelessness.* London: Pion, 1976. Print.

Runyon, Randolph. "The Fictive Fetus in *The Cave.*" *Time's Glory: Original Essays on Robert Penn Warren.* Ed. James A. Grimshaw. Conway: U of Central Arkansas P, 1986. 45–63. Print.

Shepherd, Allen. "The Case for Robert Penn Warren's Second Best Novel." *Cimarron Review* 20 (1972): 44–51. Print.

Sullivan, Nell. "The Evolution of the Dead Girlfriend Motif in *Outer Dark* and *Child of God*." *Myth, Legend, Dust: Critical Responses to Cormac McCarthy*. Ed. Rick Wallach. Manchester: Manchester UP, 2000. 68–77. Print.

Tally, Robert T., Jr. "Translator's Preface: The Timely Emergence of Geocriticism." *Geocriticism*. Ed. Bertrand Westphal and Trans. Robert T. Tally Jr. New York: Palgrave Macmillan, 2011. ix–xiii. Print.

Tuan, Yi-Fu. *Space and Place: The Perspective of Experience*. Minneapolis: U of Minnesota P, 1977. Print.

Warren, Robert Penn. "Speleology." *The Collected Poems of Robert Penn Warren*. Ed. John Burt. Baton Rouge: Louisiana State UP, 1998. 382–83. Print.

———. *The Cave*. 1959. Introd. James H. Justus. Lexington: UP of Kentucky, 2006. Print.

10 A Geocritical Approach to the Role of the Desert in Penelope Lively's *Moon Tiger* and Michael Ondaatje's *The English Patient*

Sarah Ager

Much has been written concerning the role of history in Penelope Lively's *Moon Tiger* (1987) and Michael Ondaatje's *The English Patient* (1992). A geocritical approach incorporates the history of the spaces depicted in literature by focusing on the stratification of time on a space, but also by addressing the complex relationships between characters and the spaces they occupy. Written between the late 1980s and the early 1990s, both novels look retrospectively at events of World War Two in the Western Sahara, how the desert space changes over time and how it is perceived during the lifetimes of the protagonists. The desert space plays a central role for protagonists Almásy and Claudia, who are, in many ways defined by their relationship with the desert. There are several parallels between them as they both find and lose their lovers in the desert and in later life, re-create the space in their imaginations as a means of returning to the desert. Comparisons can also be drawn between Almásy's transformation in the desert and T.E. Lawrence's autobiographical account of his adaptation process in *Seven Pillars of Wisdom: A Triumph* (1922). Marc Augé's concept of "non-places" can be applied to these novels as a means of exploring whether the physical desert is represented as a transitory space that does not incite a sense of belonging in the characters.[1] The depiction of the desert as a "non-place" may then be contrasted with Gaston Bachelard's geocritical concept of "home" as a mental space if we consider that the imagined desert imbues characters with a sense of identity and belonging.[2]

As a setting, the chronological juxtapositions of the Egyptian landscape encapsulate the geocritical concept of the stratification of time on a place. In *Moon Tiger*, the experience of Cairo is described as being able to step, "from fields to desert in one pace; in which a crumbling monument might be Greek, Roman, Pharaonic, Medieval, Christian, Muslim."[3] In Egypt, the progression of history and its effect on the desert space are conspicuously evident. Both protagonists are concerned with the stratification of time upon this space. As a historian, Claudia observes the effect of time on ancient civilisations while Almásy, a cartographer, maps the shifting margins of the desert during World War Two. Ondaatje and Lively's non-linear narratives place the reader in the position of archaeologist during the novels' unearthing of the desert's history and the characters' pasts. The characters are represented as self-aware and they re-evaluate their pasts utilising their professional capacities as historian and cartographer, respectively. Although Claudia is a historian by profession, she is interested in archaeology and investigates her personal history like an archaeological site, acknowledging that her "strata are less easily perceived than those of Warwickshire rock" (*Moon Tiger* 14). In a broader sense, Lively and Ondaatje are linked by their interest in archaeology and its application to their novels.[4] Ondaatje stated that, "as a writer, one is busy with archaeology . . . on one level you're moving forward, but in the other, you're revealing the past."[5] The import placed upon archaeology in the characters' and authors' careers can be extended to the psychological landscapes of Claudia and Almásy. The stratification of time on the desert space echoes the superimposition of the characters' personal histories onto the landscape. The desert space becomes a museum of intimate stratified memories contained within the characters' psyches.[6]

There are two parallel landscapes: physical and psychological, connected by the protagonists' imaginations: the physical desert landscape with its associated memories and an imagined desert which houses the characters' memories. The grafting of intimate associations upon the desert, the backdrop for the meetings of both sets of lovers, alters the space. The subsequent emotions that Claudia and Almásy inscribe upon the desert due to their relationships transform it from an empty *space* into a meaningful *place*. Bachelard argues that "space considered in isolation is an empty abstraction," and in relation to these novels, it is clear that in the absence of a lover, the *space* is an empty void, and it only becomes a *place* when the lovers are together.[7] It can be argued therefore that the desert is defined by and intimately related to the presence (or absence) of lovers within that space.

In Claudia's mind the space is intrinsically linked to the presence of Tom as she "saw it through him and with him. Now, he and that place are one . . . his touch, those sights and those smells" (*Moon Tiger* 175). Lively's exploration of the relationship between space and the senses correlates to Westphal's geocritical concept of "polysensoriality" whereby space is not only perceived by vision but by all senses.[8] Henri Lefebvre proposes in *The Production of Space* that smell, desire and nostalgia are linked within a space.[9] The relationship between smell, space and Tom in Claudia's mind is such that the smells within a space act as signifiers for Tom. The odours of "Moon Tiger, kerosene, dung and dust," inversely act as signifiers for his absence (*Moon Tiger* 50). The smells assign the space to specific time-locked memories that evoke the identical sensations in Claudia several years later even though "the place didn't look the same but it felt the same," when she revisits the desert (68).

In comparison, the absence of Katherine, rather than prompting nostalgia in Almásy, affects his sense of identity. As a cartographer, he defines himself by his ability to demarcate the desert *space* into a *place* that can be located on a map. Almásy says "I am a man who can recognise an unnamed town by its skeletal shape on a map."[10] In this way, maps give him a sense of identity. If he knows *where* he is, he knows *who* he is. When Katherine is absent from the space, however, and "he lies in the room surrounded by the pale maps" and "he is without Katherine," the physical absence supersedes the value of the maps (*English Patient* 156). Indeed "when he is without her" he can no longer identify himself as a man "who has never felt alone in the miles of longitude between desert towns" (165). Once Katherine deserts, so to speak, the desert is defined by the void, imbuing Almásy with a sense of loneliness. This leads to Almásy's rejection of maps when he exclaims "all I desired was to walk upon an earth that had no maps" and instead he creates a mental map by delineating in narrative the spaces of his life (277).

Just as Almásy defines himself by his ability to map spaces, he also recognises that the desert changes his identity. Marc Augé claims that the question of identity lies "at the heart of all the spatial arrangements."[11] The relationship between identity and the desert can be related to Augé's concept of the "non-place," the spaces which incite no sense of belonging in a person. They create "neither singular identity nor relations; only solitude, and similitude." The spaces Augé classifies as "non-places" are frequently associated with transport: airports and motorways for instance; transitional spaces that one crosses without settling. While the desert is not singled out as a "non-place" by Augé, he states that "the traveller's space may thus be the archetype of 'non-place.'"[12] The desert can thus be regarded as an archetype of a traveller's space due to its nature as a temporary abode and as a space that is to be crossed rather than lived in.

The transitional quality of *desert* is reinforced if considered in relation to the etymologically related transitive verb *desert* which means "to abandon" or "to depart from (a place or position)." The desert is a transitional space that requires an absence created by something departing from it. When Claudia remains in the desert, she claims "there are moments, out here in this place and at this time, when she feels that she is untethered . . . adrift in the cosmos." The words "untethered" and "adrift" emphasise the idea that one cannot settle in the desert and one's ability to form a sense of identity is affected. If "home" is "a place, region, or state to which one properly belongs," then a desert seems to be diametrically opposed to the concept of "home" as you cannot have a true sense of "properly" belonging to that space. The subsequent phrase in this definition of "home," however, is as a place "in which one's affections centre." This description suggests that the only way in which the protagonists can have a sense of belonging to the desert is if they inhabit the space with a loved one.

The protagonists' inability to settle within the desert space is magnified by the fact that they are "displaced persons" in Egypt and Libya. While a displaced person is generally forced to leave their birth country, Almásy has a conscious objective to "get away from his homeland" and lose his identity (*English Patient* 188). He states, "I wanted to erase my name and the place I had come from" (147). This distinction can be related to the words of the poet Edmond Jabes who wrote, "you do not go into the desert to find identity but to lose it, to lose your personality, to become anonymous. You make yourself void."[13] Almásy reveals a similar desire for anonymity in the desert when he claims, "[We] wished to remove the clothing of our countries. . . . We disappeared into landscape" (147). The metaphorical stripping of national clothing corresponds to Salman Rushdie's claim that the crossing the frontier strips the migrant of identity.[14] Almásy's words go further than simply saying the migrant loses his identity by suggesting a process of absorption by the desert. Thus, the body and space become indistinguishable from one another, allowing Almásy to disappear. Indeed, absorption is a characteristic of the desert city in *Moon Tiger* as Cairo "both absorbed and ignored" the British army which imposed itself upon the landscape (*Moon Tiger* 75). The desert is depicted as both active and passive in Lively's descriptions. This active representation is further demonstrated when Claudia describes the desert sands as "starting to digest the broken vehicles." Ondaatje's representation, however, suggests that absorption by the desert is protective rather than destructive for Almásy. The desert shields Almásy from recognition by enemies. Almásy achieves this desired anonymity and declares that "by the time the war arrived, after ten years in the desert, it was easy for me to slip across borders, not to belong to anyone, to any nation" (*English Patient* 147). Therefore, detachment from his roots is a positive means of survival for Almásy.

During the process of shedding his ethnic and cultural identities, Almásy develops a desert mentality. This is evident in his rejection of concepts of ancestry, ethnicity and permanence. The requirement to think like a desert native as a means of assimilation is suggested by T. E. Lawrence who wrote "the effort for these years to live in the dress of Arabs, and to imitate their mental foundation, quitted me of my English self."[15] Lawrence suggests that it is not sufficient to dress superficially as a native; one has to emulate their psychological essence. By understanding their way of thinking, one can begin to behave like a native. Similarly, Almásy rejects his own ancestry as a result of his psychological interaction with the desert space. It is implied by Ondaatje that Almásy is attempting to cast off the weight of ancestry associated with being a Count when he declares "erase the family name!" Almásy's claim that he "was taught such things by the desert" suggests that the space has taken on an educative role (*English Patient* 147). Similarly, Lawrence describes how the Bedouins "lost material ties . . . and other complications to achieve a personal liberty," indicating that the desert can be a liberating space where you are freed from cultural obligations (*Seven Pillars* 31).[16]

Not only does Almásy reject his own ancestry, Ondaatje also portrays him as anti-nationalist. He states, "we were German, English, Hungarian, African—all of us insignificant to them. Gradually we became nationless. I came to hate nations" (*English Patient* 147). On the surface, Almásy appears to be referring to his fellow cartographers, but this could be interpreted a subtle reference by Ondaatje to Almásy's multiple ethnic identities. The nationalities indicated are those Almásy has been mistaken for or comes to identify with: Hungarian by birth, German by trade, English by accent and African by geographical location in the desert. Ondaatje's use of first-person plural, while being inclusive of multiple ethnicities, demonstrates Almásy's evasion of being limited to one fixed identity. Here lies the predicament of *going native*. The traveller loses his original identity but can never be truly native. This complexity is described by Lawrence as having "dropped one form and not taken on the other" (*Seven Pillars* 31). In the same way, Almásy no longer identifies himself as Hungarian but neither does he classify himself as native.

The only identity available to Almásy is anonymity. As such he can, in the words of Lawrence, go "unnoticed" thereby avoiding "frictions" (*Seven Pillars* 30). Although Almásy adopts ethnic anonymity in an attempt to liberate himself, it is actually the crucial factor in his capture. This contradiction can be related to Augé's concept of non-places because although they do not instil a sense of identity, Augé argues that it requisite to show a document of identification to enter or leave a non-place.[16] When the British discover Almásy in the desert, he has no identification because Bedouins stole his personal documents. Therefore, Almásy's anonymity marks him as "other" and so he is labelled as a spy.

More generally, the protagonists' outlooks on life are affected by observations made of the desert, specifically the concept of permanence. They both observe the effect of time on the desert space that was once ocean is now barren and arid. After discovering a fossilised starfish, Claudia reflects "here in the desert, which had been an old sea, where nothing was strapped down or permanent, everything drifted" (*English Patient* 244). The stratification of time on the desert functions as evidence of the inescapable evolution of spaces which man cannot control. The "fragility of places," as described by Claudia, is epitomised by Lively's description of Memphis as "a series barely discernible irregularities" on the landscape (*Moon Tiger* 113). Ondaatje depicts Almásy adopting a similar attitude towards permanence in his emotional outlook on love as Almásy says, "I don't believe in permanence, in relationships that last ages." Claudia, rather than being defeatist, seeks refuge in the permanence of language to preserve her relationship with Tom. She believes in "the power of language. Preserving the ephemeral; giving form to dreams, permanence to sparks of sunlight" (9). Claudia realises that the physical desert cannot fully act as a signifier for Tom because it changes over time. The sands shift. Claudia counters the instability of spaces using language and narrative to secure her memories by re-creating the desert as a psychological space.

Through the use of narrative, Claudia maps an imaginary space that both she and Tom can occupy. The relationship between narrative and space is described by Robert T. Tally Jr., who argues that "in a sense, all writing partakes in a form of cartography, since even the most realistic map does not truly depict the space."[17] According to this logic, an imaginary depiction is just as valid as a supposedly factual depiction because a space can only be partially perceived rather than completely captured in words. This corresponds to a key concept of geocriticism: the idea that imaginary spaces should be studied in the same way as real spaces. Bachelard expressed the idea that "spaces exist because they are perceived."[18] In order to map an imagined desert space, there are several spatial boundaries Claudia has to overcome. She is doubly separated from Tom. Not only are they spatially divided, but they also occupy different temporal spaces after Tom's death. He is "left behind, in another place and another time" (*Moon Tiger* 206). Lively depicts time as a physical barrier as Tom is "shut away behind a glass screen of time." Claudia reflects, however, that, "death is total absence, you said. Yes and no. You are not absent so long as you are in my head" (206). Claudia attempts to cope with Tom's death and subsequent absence by transposing the physical desert in which they co-inhabited for a short time onto the mental landscape of an imagined desert. Claudia states, "the mirror world, the vanishing oasis, is in my head now, not in his, and he is with it," demonstrating that Claudia and Tom are united in her memories (104).

Lively's image of the desert oasis brings to mind the psychological phenomenon of the mirage, a displaced image, reinforced by the preceding word "mirror," which shares the same etymological root as *mirage*. Earlier in the novel, Tom is described observing that for every mirage, somewhere there is the "mirror place going on about its business" (102). While in the "real" world of the frame narrative Claudia and Tom are separated; in the realm of Claudia's imagination, the lovers are reunited in a mirror world of memory. Lively reveals through the previous extract, however, the complexities and potential flaws of relying on memory as a permanent means of containment. The word "mirror" illustrates the fact that Claudia's mental landscape is a mere reflection of the desert that she experienced. By extension, her relationship with Tom within this space is an abstract reflection rather than something tangible. The phrase "vanishing oasis" is a metaphor for the fact that Claudia's mental desert construction will fade because memories deteriorate over time. Claudia's awareness of vanishing memories is exacerbated by her knowledge that she is dying. Memories can only be held in Claudia's mind for as long as she has consciousness. Lively poignantly highlights the loss of memories after death in the latter part of Claudia's statement, "I preserve you, as others will preserve me. For a while," which demonstrates Claudia's acceptance that memories are not permanent (206).

Within the novels' framing narratives, Claudia and Almásy are on the verge of dying in hospital and if considered in terms of non-places, neither author portrays the hospitals as imbuing any sense of belonging in either protagonist. Augé categorises hospitals as non-places because they are transitional places that you do not dwell in for long periods.[19] Claudia loses her identity as she is patronised by nurses who treat her as a generic elderly non-entity. A nurse enquires "was she someone?" to which a doctor replies, "probably." Similarly, Almásy is an invalid in hospital. The desert provides Claudia and Almásy with a greater sense of identity than their current surroundings, as they are not "at home" in their respective hospital beds. Not only does the desert provide them with a stronger sense of identity than the hospital, but it also acts as an imaginary refuge from their present circumstances. Their psychological wanderings in the desert are presented as a form of escapism from their physical pain. Claudia, dying of cancer, finds comfort in nostalgia about her relationship with Tom. For her, the fictional desert is "more enduring than [the] reality" of the sterile hospital (*Moon Tiger* 6).

Similarly, Almásy seeks refuge in an imagined desert as he lies in hospital dying as a result of physical injuries. The narrative desert space he maps is a form of escapism from his pain. Almásy's re-imagining of the desert can also be related to Lively's view that although events in life are often arbitrary, "we re-write and edit the narrative of our life" to make it "seem like there was a plan."[20] It could be argued, therefore, that Almásy's nostalgia is an attempt to comprehend how he arrived at his current location by re-examining his past.

If Claudia and Almásy are able to find refuge in the idea of the desert, this detail implies that the desert cannot be a non-place but it should instead be considered in terms of "home," a place of refuge. "Within this context, "home" is a mental state with the desert being the visual manifestation." This representation demonstrates Gaston Bachelard's concept of "home" as an intimate mental space. Bachelard says "the house protects the dreamer, the house allows one to dream in peace," emphasising the importance of protection and shelter within that space. Bachelard continues, "the sheltered being gives limits to his shelter," which implies "home" can offer protagonists the possibility of control.[21] As architects of their imagination, Claudia and Almásy condense the indefinable sprawling desert into the constructed confines of an imagined desert. In theory, the protagonists can control their created deserts. In reality, the process is more complex. Both authors portray the protagonists experiencing difficulty in controlling their imagined spaces due to their declining health and the effect of drugs.

Claudia's general state of mind is more stable than Almásy, whose mental capability is impaired by morphine. The crucial factor in Claudia's relative stability, however, is the fact that the central core of her life is Tom rather than the desert. Although the desert represents many things for Claudia, such as transience and spatial instability, the presence of Tom within a space overrides the value of the space itself. For instance, Claudia says "it had seemed, for the year or so in which I had been there, merely a backcloth," revealing that the desert space is an arbitrary setting to their love affair. This coincidence does not diminish, however, the vital role that the desert assumes for Claudia in later life. It is not so much the desert itself but the process of re3-creating it in her mind which enables Claudia to access memories of Tom. Lively depicts the desert as the medium through which Claudia can address Tom directly, as demonstrated by Claudia's reflection, "you are also, now, a part of me, as immediate and as close as my own other selves" (*Moon Tiger* 206). The imagined desert is a catalyst through which Tom becomes an integral part of Claudia's identity, thereby uniting the otherwise divided lovers.

Before considering Almásy's psychological return to the desert, one has to take into account that Almásy's relationship with the desert is more complex than that of Claudia's. An important factor is the greater time Almásy spent in the desert. He had already shed his European identity in the years before meeting Katherine. Therefore, Almásy's desert identity cannot simply be considered in terms of his romantic relationship. Certainly, Ondaatje presents Almásy's love of Katherine and her presence or absence within the space as significant to Almásy's desert experience. He states that he has "translated her strangely into my text of the desert," showing that Katherine has been interwoven into Almásy's desert narrative, just as Tom is interwoven into Claudia's psychological desert (*English Patient* 250). Although acknowledging her importance, Ondaatje does not portray Katherine as the fundamental reason for Almásy's desire to return to the desert. Unlike Claudia, Almásy does not require a lover to belong to the desert. Almásy wants to be in the desert physically even after Katherine's death. The core of Almásy's life is the desert, not Katherine. Therefore, Ondaatje's description of Almásy's duration in hospital can be seen as a personal struggle to deal with his geographical displacement.

Almásy's relationship with the desert should be considered in terms of his professional capacity as a cartographer. As such, he has an innate need to be somewhere that is uncharted. Therefore, the unmapped desert afforded him a professional identity as a cartographer which the mapped Tuscan landscape cannot provide. Imagining the desert does not satisfy Almásy's inherent need to be there physically. The desert gives him his sense of belonging, and in that sense it is his home. Bachelard's concept, "without it [home], man would be a dispersed being," can be applied to Almásy when he is removed from the desert. He becomes a dispersed being, without an ethnic or physical identity, in the hospital.[22] Even more significant is the fact that Almásy's "essence" remains in the desert. It is the place to which he is led back in his imagination even though he remains physically in the hospital. Ondaatje demonstrates the idea of Almásy's essence being divided from his physical body when Hana observes that his "sleeping body is probably miles away in the desert" (37). Similarly, Claudia's essence remains in the desert, but she does not become a divided being. Claudia finds unity from being with Tom on an emotional rather than physical level within her own psyche.

While Claudia's imagination provides her with stability, Almásy's relationship with his imagined desert demonstrates the hazards of mental wandering. Augé states that, "dream journeys become dangerous when they venture too far from the body conceived as a centre."[23] Almásy attempts to return to the desert in his mind but he confuses reality and imagination and loses the ability to locate where he is. Caravaggio observes that Almásy "doesn't know where the fuck he is" (*English Patient* 129). This is particularly destabilising for someone who relies on an awareness of geographical position for their sense of identity. Almásy's inability to perceive his location comes, in part, from increasing drug dependence. The desert and "its architecture of morphine" (129) is a world constructed by drugs which implode "time and geography the way maps compress the world onto a two-dimensional sheet of paper" (161). His confusion is exacerbated by his psychological wanderings which position him in two spaces simultaneously: both the physical hospital bed and the psychological desert. Although Almásy attempts to use the imagined desert as a means of getting home, he instead loses himself further because he is increasingly unable to distinguish between real and imagined spaces, and the chronology of events which occurred within them. Likewise, Claudia occupies two spaces: the real hospital and her imagined desert. The key difference being that Claudia's memories, which are scattered across diverse locations, are united in the mental concept of "home" (represented by the desert) which she carries in her mind. Claudia's desert home stabilises her even when she is unsure whether she is occupying a real or imagined world.

From a geocritical perspective, the role of the desert in *Moon Tiger* and *The English Patient* corresponds to Bachelard's concept of "home," particularly if considered in conjunction with Anshuman Mondel's assertion that ""home" is where the " 'self" is located."[24] The desert is the space where the protagonists are able to define themselves, providing them with an awareness of who they are. It is the desert which gives them an identity. For Claudia, she defines herself in relation to Tom. Subsequently, her identity comes from being emotionally united with him in the space of a psychological desert. Hence, the imagined desert provides her with a sense of wholeness despite Tom's physical absence. Almásy is able to locate, and therefore identify himself, in the Saharan desert. Almásy's imagined desert therefore remains a non-place for him because it is the physical act of being in the desert which gives him his sense of identity. Indeed, Almásy adapted himself to the desert so effectively that he became unable to identify himself outside the desert space. He becomes reliant on the desert, more so than his dependence on morphine, which Ondaatje's descriptions suggest is a desperate attempt to return to the desert. Ondaatje's portrayal of Almásy's struggle in hospital show that rather than feeling "detachment" and "isolation" in the desert, emotions described by Lawrence as inevitable products of adapting to the desert, Almásy experiences these negative feelings in the Tuscan space because he is removed from the physical desert, his "home" (*Seven Pillars* 32). Without being able to identify himself, Almásy cannot feel at "home" and thus he dies a dispersed and divided being.

Notes

1. Marc Augé, *Non-places: Introduction to an Anthropology of Supermodernity*, translated by John Howe (London: Verso, 1995, 2000 edition).
2. Gaston Bachelard, *The Poetics of Space*, translated Maria Jolas (Boston: Beacon Press, 1969).
3. Penelope Lively, *Moon Tiger* (London: Penguin Books Ltd, 2006), 89.
4. Penelope Lively, 'An Evening with Penelope Lively' Interview at 'The Arthur Miller Centre Literary Festival Autumn 2010' (Norwich: University of East Anglia, 17 November 2010).
5. Ellen Kanner, "New Discoveries from the Author of The English Patient", in *Bookpage Interview* (Miami: 2000). www.bookpage.com/0005bp/michael_ondaatje.html, Accessed 10 November 2010.
6. Silvia Albertazzi, *Lecture: 'Introduzione alla Geocritica'* (Bologna: Sala Convegni, 10 October 2009).
7. Bachelard, *The Poetics of Space*, 12.
8. See Albertazzi, *Introduzione alla Geocritica*.
9. Henri Lefebvre, *The Production of Space* (Oxford: Blackwell, 1992), 197.
10. Michael Ondaatje, *The English Patient* (London: Picador, 1993).
11. Augé, *Non-places*, 58.
12. Ibid., 103, 85–86.
13. See David Jaspar, *The Sacred Desert: Religion, Literature, Art and Culture* (Oxford: Blackwell Publishing Ltd, 2008).
14. Salman Rushdie, *Step Across This Line: Collected Nonfiction, 1992–2002* (New York, NY: Random House, 2002).
15. T. E. Lawrence, *Seven Pillars of Wisdom: A Triumph* (Oxford: Alden Press, privately printed 1926 edition), 31.
16. Augé, *Non-places*, 102.
17. Robert T. Tally Jr., "Review of Bertrand Westphal's La Géocritique: Réel, Fiction, Espace", *L"Esprit Créateur: The International Quarterly of French and Francophone Studies* 49.3 (Fall 2009): 134.
18. Bachelard, *The Poetics of Space*, 12.
19. Augé, *Non-places*, 78.
20. Lively, *An Evening with Penelope Lively*.

21. Bachelard, *The Poetics of Space*, 5.
22. Bachelard, *The Poetics of Space*, 7.
23. Augé, *Non-Places*, 58.
24. Anshuman A. Mondel, "The Ground Beneath Her Feet and Fury", in *The Cambridge Companion to Salman Rushdie*, edited by Abdulrazak Gurnah (Cambridge: Cambridge University Press, 2007), 179.

Bibliography

Albertazzi, Silvia. "Geolinguistica", in *Abbecedario Postcoloniale*, edited by R. Vecchi (Macerata: Quodlibet, 2003).

Albertazzi, Silvia. *Lecture: 'Introduzione alla Geolinguistica'* (Bologna: Universitá di Bologna, 11 November 2009).

Augé, Marc. *Non-places: Introduction to an Anthropology of Supermodernity*, translated by John Howe (London: Verso, 1995).

Bachelard, Gaston. *The Poetics of Space*, translated by Maria Jolas (Boston: Beacon Press, 1969).

Jasper, David. *The Sacred Desert: Religion, Literature, Art, and Culture* (Oxford: Blackwell Publishing Ltd, 2008).

Kanner, Ellen. "New discoveries from the author of *The English Patient*", in *Bookpage* (Interview) (Miami: 2000), www.bookpage.com/0005bp/michael_ondaatje.html, Accessed 10 November 2010.

Lawrence, T. E. *Seven Pillars of Wisdom* (Oxford: Alden Press, privately printed 1926 edition).

Lefebvre, Henri. *The Production of Space* (Oxford: Blackwell, 1992).

Lively, Penelope. *Moon Tiger* (London: Penguin Books Ltd, 1989).

Lively, Penelope. *Interview: 'An Evening with Penelope Lively' as Part of 'The Arthur Miller Centre Literary Festival Autumn 2010'* (Norwich: University of East Anglia, 17 November 2010).

Mondel, Anshuman A. "The Ground Beneath Her Feet and Fury", in *The Cambridge Companion to Salman Rushdie*, edited by Abdulrazak Gurnah (Cambridge: Cambridge UP, 2007).

Ondaatje, Michael. *The English Patient* (London: Picador, 1993).

Rushdie, Salman. *Imaginary Homelands* (London: Granta Books, 1992).

Rushdie, Salman. *Step Across This Line: Collected Nonfiction 1992–2002* (New York: Random House, 2002).

Soja, Edward W. *Postmodern Geographies: The Reassertion of Space in Critical Social Theory* (London: Verso, 1989).

Tally, Robert T. Jr. "Review of Bertrand Westphal's La Géocritique: Réel, fiction, espace", *L"Esprit Créateur: The International Quarterly of French and Francophone Studies* 49.3 (Fall 2009): 134.

11 Isolated Spaces, Fragmented Places

Caryl Phillips's Ghettos in *The Nature of Blood* and *The European Tribe*

I. Murat Öner

Caryl Phillips's exploration of human condition in *The Nature of Blood* stretches through different parts of history offering the readers a complex spatiotemporal, chronologically nonlinear and fragmented narration. Phillips builds his narration on two undeniable European enterprises: racism and the Holocaust. He further merges these concepts with the spatial dimensions of isolation. His choice of locales—such as ghettos—is even more significant for the narration of *The Nature of Blood*. Ledent suggests that each space in *The Nature of Blood* is "suggestive of the characters' experience," and, to be more precise, each space echoes "characters' isolation" (2002, 150). As Westphal suggests that literature and the mimetic arts reveal the unseen potential of space-time somewhere between reality and fiction, which he calls 'third space' (2011, 73), Phillips, in *The Nature of Blood*, creates "ghettoized spaces" as examples of this third space. Phillips further personifies the isolation, if not segregation, of these ghettoized spaces in the characters of Eva Stern; a Jewish character who survived the Holocaust; Malka, a black Jew who migrated to Israel from Ethiopia; the commandant of the Venetian army; and a black African, or Othello, as we infer from Phillips's direct references to Shakespeare's *Othello*. Phillips, as a writer, has also acknowledged using pastiche as a narrative technique in his narratives to "send [the reader] back to the original source to find out more" (qtd. in Eckstein, 2001). Phillips's Othello, however, recounts his arrival in Venice, his explorations of Venice, Venetians, Venetian language and customs, and his marriage to Desdemona, and finalizes his story with his arrival in Cyprus. We should also note that the Shakespearean Jew, Shylock, also lingers in the ghettoized spaces in *The Nature of Blood* as well as Venice and Othello's recounts. Phillips also supports this argument by creating Jewish characters (Eva, Stephen and Malka) in *The Nature of Blood* as Jews have been primarily considered archetypical for the ghettoized existence. Shylock's existence, like Othello's, is that of a deviance in the striated space of Venice, hence, very much relevant in our argument. Phillips weaves the fragmented narration of *The Nature of Blood* between these deviant characters' individual stories in spatiotemporal oscillations, articulating the communal experiences of a people in these characters' persons, and creating a discourse of "a multi-spatial collective memory." He makes his statement about the post-effects of these collective and historical experiences through Eva Stern's inner speech with a spatiotemporal undertone: "A human river of shattered lives. Passing houses that had become our prisons and our tombs" (1997, 198).

In this study, we will only be focusing on Phillips's Othello and his transformation and perception of and in the ghettoized space of Venice in a geocritical scope. Geocriticism provides us with genuinely unique approaches to explore the real-and-fictional space of Venice in *The Nature of Blood* and other literary and non-literary materials. Interdisciplinary methods of geocriticism also help us analyze the cartographies and continuously changing spatial relations and discover unseen power correlations by using various cultural discourses such as architecture, philosophy, sociology and geography (Tally, 2013, 113–14, 140).

Westphal erects the theoretical foundations of geocriticism on three concepts: firstly, 'spatiotemporality,' which emphasizes that places have to be recognized "in a temporal depth in order to uncover or discover multilayered identities," and stresses, "the temporal variability of heterogeneous spaces" as "globality implies polychrony" (Westphal, *Geocritical Explorations*, 2011, xiv). Secondly, 'transgressivity,' which includes "all aspects of border crossings" which come with movement; one may not transgress if he conforms to "the traditional definition of a code, a compendium of norms and benchmarks" (Westphal, *Geocriticism*, 2011, 45). Westphal further notes on the inevitability of transgression at an individual level: "Transgression is somehow the result of an oscillation, little attributable to a singular, individual responsibility but more like continental drift, the shock of geological plates" (46) and "as in Deleuze's deterritorialization process, permanent fluidity is the characteristic of representations and consequently, of identities" (*Geocritical Explorations*, 2011, xv). Thirdly, 'referentiality,' which notes that all textual spaces intertexually relate to other spaces in literature and reality (Westphal, *Geocritical Explorations*, 2011, xv; *Geocriticism*, 2011, 75–84).

Geocriticism also renders three approaches to the text; firstly 'multifocalization,' which emphasizes that creating the literary space requires many different points of view in order to avoid "individual bias or stereotyping," and, therefore, in this study, various resources ranging from tourist guides to historical accounts are used to investigate the literary space of Venice; secondly, 'polysensoriality,' which states that space may not be perceived only by vision. Other senses provide important input to evaluate different spaces, thus, it is significant to indicate how a space appeals to different characters and their sensory impressions of a given space in a convergent form. And, finally, 'stratigraphic vision,' in which the topos is understood to contain several meaning levels, and is deterritorialized and reterritorialized (Tally, 2013, 142). Therefore, the literary space of Venice contains many levels of interpretation. For instance, the Rialto bridge contains various images and connotations as a striated space. Westphal also promotes the usage of non-literary texts including tourist guides and the advertising rhetoric of travel brochures for geocritical analysis (*Geocriticism*, 2011, 121).

The word 'ghetto' was presumably first used in 1562 by Pius IV as a generic term for the settlements where Jews throughout Italy were separated from the rest of the population until the middle of the nineteenth century, and initially it did not hold a negative connotation (Debenedetti-Stow, 1992; Wirth, 1927; Michman, 2011, 20–22; McGregor, 2006, 208). The foundation of the first ghetto in Venice was based on the zeal for the hatred of Jews and pragmatic economic reality of Venice (Finlay, 1982, 141; McGregor, 2006, 276). Holderness adds that the ghetto, providing the protection Jews needed, also played a spatial role for Jews to flourish their cultural identity within their community (2010, 41). Bassi, on the other hand, maintains that, even though the ghetto isolated them in Venice in its structural framework, Jews in the Venetian ghetto enjoyed some sort of autonomy and self-governance, and the ghetto provided them with the dynamism which the Jewish identity has always been evaluated with. Roth states that Shakespeare fictionalized a known reality in Shylock's character in *The Merchant of Venice* (1933, 148–56). Shylock, confirming the constant repression against Jews in Venice, delivers his famous speech in 3.1 in *The Merchant of Venice*: "He hath disgraced me, and hindered me half a million, laughed at my losses, mocked at my gains, scorned my nation, thwarted my bargains, cooled my friends, heated mine enemies—and what's his reason? I am a Jew" (43–46).

Even though ghettos used to refer to the spatial isolation of Jews in Venice and Nazi Germany, today we may associate the term with any space where isolation and segregation occurs. Hence, if a group of people is considered 'deviant' due to their racial, social or religious backgrounds, and is segregated from the community in sundry ways in a place, that place may be viewed as ghettoized. Ghettos, which were previously imposed on people, might also be shaped deliberately either by a class of people because of their fear of unacceptance or exploitation by others, or by an elitist group who wish to segregate themselves from the average members of the society (Madaj, 1968, 65). A primary feature of a ghetto is the spatial segregation of a group of people, which also appeals to Foucault's concept of the heterotopias of deviation. Foucault's heterotopias of deviation are places such as rest homes, psychiatric hospitals and prisons that cage the deviants of the society. Foucault, placing the elderly between the heterotopia of crisis and the heterotopia of deviation, points to the their deviant characteristic as old age and idleness (2008, 18).

In *The European Tribe*, Phillips points to the tall structures of the Venetian ghetto along with its synagogue, bakery, kosher shops and tiny streets surrounding a large square (52–53). In the same work, Phillips's description shows that his contemporary ghetto features "predominantly white working-class areas" with "red disposal pipes, yellow-stripped façade," "skylines broken up by twenty-four-storey blocks of flats" and "dog shit all over the play grounds so parents can't send the kids out to play, and within a month someone has been stabbed" (Phillips, 1987, 3). Such a polysensorial description by Phillips incorporates three features of a ghetto space: *crowd*, considering the size of the blocks, *filth* and *crime*. All these three ghetto traits, one way or another, are applicable to any isolative space in *The Nature of Blood* whether it be Venice, Venetian ghetto, ghettoized cities, Cyprus, concentration camps or Israel.

In *The Nature of Blood*, Othello's observation of the ghetto includes the windowless structures of the buildings, and how Christian guards protect the gates leading into the ghetto and two boats patrol the island in the surrounding canals (Phillips, 1997, 129). Othello also notices how the ghetto lacks the Christian elements that Venice has in abundance: "the complete absence of shrines, madonnas, carved crosses, or images of saints" (130). Other features of the ghetto, in Othello's words, include "filthier alleyways," "oppressive tall hovels," "damp staining walls" and "poverty" (130). Katz confirms that the architectural structure of the Jewish quarters in the Venetian Ghetto with small windows and bolted doors would protect the rights of Christians "from the unwanted views of the Other," and that the Venetian authorities even "legislated fenestration constrictions for religious outsiders" (133). Thus, window closure was required in the Jewish Ghetto. However, these restrictions or precautions were not considered as hardship by the Jews of the Ghetto, as these provided them with the security they needed. Even Spanish and Portuguese Jews considered the Venetian Ghetto as a heaven where they could practice their religion with relative ease (Phillips, 1997, 129; McGregor, 2006, 277).

Ghettoized spaces manifest an intrinsic transgressive quality. Transgression, in Westphal's definition, occurs when "a code or rite" is contravened (2011, 43). He further suggests that transgression necessitates a closed and striated space and a will to penetrate, which the state apparatus assumes as a crime; or in other words, transgression requires those who contravene and those who attest to the contravention. Hence the state apparatus determines how these rules are to be "applied, disregarded, or violated." These rules may include "the code of hospitality" and "the contact zone between social actors," and they are regulated by explicit rules and feature "a shared rhythm, a spatiotemporal correlation" (Westphal, 2011, 42–43). Westphal also suggests that transgression is supposed to be defined by "a minimum set of defining criteria [as] there can be no transgression without the contravention of a code or rite" (2011, 43). He states: "In the absence of a common rhythm, transgression is inevitable. In certain cases, transgression is massive, becoming a deliberate intrusion—hence war, a vast state transgression. Transgression is disparate, perhaps by definition" (43).

Westphal also uses "epistrata"—a term he borrows from Deleuze and Guattari—to identify the borders of the tolerance for transgressions. In other words, epistrata is the narrow gap between the action and the transgression, or "the margin of tolerated deviance" (2011, 42). This margin in Venice on a vast and spatial scale is the ghetto. The Venetian ghetto functioned as an epistrata through which the Jews were allowed to live in Venice. The ghetto was an in-between space where deviants within their tolerated limits could dwell within the encompassing striated space of Venice. However, diverse social institutions possess "different thresholds of tolerance for deviation from a norm" (Bonta and Protevi, 2004, 82). Thus, the Venetian Ghetto stands out as having a different level of tolerance toward its so-called deviants or others than the isolative space of Israel and the ghettos of Nazi Germany or Nazi concentration camps, which we may consider as some of the most radical isolative and ghettoized spaces ever, as shown in *The Nature of Blood*.

In the case of Venice, Jewishness was the transgression. McGregor asserts that while Jews were confined and forced to live in the ghetto, the key to full acceptance into the society for Jews was solely through conversion into Catholicism and a total break-up with Jewish community, which indicates a different transgression or border crossing through deterritorialization into a new faith. Converts could fully assimilate into Venetian social and economic life; however, this also carried certain hazards if they attempted to contact their old cycles or return to their old faith. Reverting to the old faith could be punishable by death (McGregor, 2006, 216). As depicted in *The Merchant of Venice* in 4.1, Shylock was forced to convert into Christianity—as proposed by Antonio in return of his property that was confiscated by the state of Venice, as a form of repentance for his transgression:

> So please my lord the Duke and all the court
> To quit the fine for one half of his goods,
> I am content, so he will let me have
> The other half in use, to render it
> Upon his death unto the gentleman
> That lately stole his daughter.
> Two things provided more: that for this favour
> He presently become a Christian
>
> (*The Merchant of Venice* 4.1.376–83)

At this point, concentrating on Othello and how Phillips uses the referentiality of the text will be of much use for the development of our argument. As Westphal notes, "fiction has a mimetic relationship to the world [and] the representation fictionalizes the source from which it emanates"

(2011, 75). The intertexual retelling of Othello's story, as Whitehead notes, is important in that it has premonitional effects of how the story ends for the reader of *The Nature of Blood* (2004, 91). Intertextual text, Whitehead further suggests, assumes that the reader has onset knowledge of the destiny of the characters the text refers to, and it can widen the view of critical researches with possible new meanings and can also suggest alternative outcomes for the original text (2004, 91).

Westphal states that representation is "re-presentation" and revises "the source in a new context" (2011, 75). The reader knows Othello's eventual doom; thus, in *The Nature of Blood*, Phillips fictionalizes what paves the way to his eventual demise, using, in Whitehead's terms, "intertextual resistance [to] racism" (2004, 91). Whitehead believes that the determining factor of Othello's downfall is the Venetian society and latent racism within the society (91–92). This assumption does not undermine but strengthens the traumatic role of transgressive space that drives Othello to isolation in *The Nature of Blood*. Eventually, the experience of isolation in the ghettoized spaces leads Othello into a social and psychological transgression or border crossing. In other words, Othello physically moves from "the smooth space" of his African homeland into "the striated space" of Venice, and this movement leads him into a transgression, as Tally observes in Deleuze's concept of nomads:

> Deleuze's nomads continually map and remap, altering spaces even as they traverse them. They are in Deleuze's language, forces of deterritorialization, unsettling to a greater or lesser extent the metric ordering of space that is subject to the power of the state.
>
> (2013, 136)

Smooth space, as Deleuze and Guattari notes, is 'the nomad space' where the war machine develops—bearing in mind that Othello is a general in the Venetian army—and striated space is 'the sedentary space' where the space is instituted by the state apparatus; thus, they are not of the same nature and they do not communicate with each other in the same way (2005, 474–75). Othello initially defines himself with the smooth space, which produces "the war machine" (Deleuze and Guattari, 2005, 355), with the undertone of transformation he goes through: "I, a man of born royal blood, *a mighty warrior*, yet a man who, at one time, *could view himself only as a poor slave*" (Phillips, 1997, 107, emphasis added).

Holderness states that the Venetians hired foreign mercenaries for their army to avoid military dominance of any leader over the city-state (2010, 90). Venice, in McGregor's term, was a company town; the system the Venetians developed guarded the city against any dynastic ambition and the city was based on trade. All administrative and military personnel served Venice part-time (2006, 87). In *The Nature of Blood*, Othello also confirms that "the republic preferred to employ the services of great foreign commanders in order that they might prevent the development of Venetian-born military dictatorships" (Phillips, 1997, 116). Venice and Othello fit the concepts that Deleuze and Guattari propose in *A Thousand Plateaus*:

> The State has no war machine of its own; it can only appropriate one in the form of a military institution, one that will continually cause it problems. This explains the mistrust States have toward their military institutions, in that the military institution inherits an extrinsic war machine.
>
> (2005, 355)

The principles of the mixture of smooth and striated spaces are not symmetrical, and cause a passage from one to the other according to entirely different movements (Deleuze & Guattari, 2005, 474). Venice as a place of continual passages of 'smoothness' and 'striation' causes continual transgression for the deviants and nomads of the society, as we see in the characters of Othello and Shylock. Deleuze and Guattari strengthen this theory: "The maximum deterritorialization appears in the tendency of maritime and commercial towns to separate off from the backcountry, from the countryside (Athens, Carthage, Venice)" (2005, 432).

In Othello's observations of the city, we may assume he is captivated by the sheer force of this striation which Venice produces: "Nothing in my native country had prepared me for the splendor of the canals . . . The magnificence of the buildings that lined the canals overwhelmed my senses" (Phillips, 1997, 107). The transition from the nomad space to the sedentary space intensely affects him, and he first reacts to this passage in the trajectory of Eurocentric cartographic segregation between the center and the periphery: "I had moved from the edge of the world to the centre. From the dark margins to a place where even the weakest rays of the evening sun were caught and thrown back in a blaze of glory" (Phillips, 1997, 107). Interestingly, Amin in *Eurocentrism* points to the period of Renaissance when Eurocentric consciousness in the European mind began to take its current form that emphasizes European superiority (2009, 154). Othello monitors the contradictory cues of striation, which Venice presents itself, and wishes "to hold these various images close [to his] dark bosom," and disregards the spatial hints given by the labyrinth of Venice: "I soon came to understand that, behind gaudy façade, much of Venice was quite different from the pretty city of the watercolour. But this caused me little concern" (Phillips, 1997, 109). More, Othello decides to dress in Venetian fashion, which indicates that he strengthens the transgression through cultural adaption, as well. He confirms that even though the exotic displays of other cultures are tolerated in Venice, "such stubbornness [is] unlikely to aid one's *passage* through society" (Phillips, 1997, 120, emphasis added). Othello willingness to be accepted into the Venetian society is manifest, although he feels that this passage is not feasible.

> My complexion was a feature that was unlikely to aid me in my attempts to attract admiration.
>
> (Phillips, 1997, 143)

> I wondered if my new costume might convince some among Venetians to look upon me with a kinder eye.
>
> (122)

> And now to be married, and to the heart of the society. I wondered how such a change could be wrought in a man's life, and in so short a period.
>
> (144)

With his marriage to Desdemona, however, he irrationally assumes that the conditions are different.

Deleuze and Guattari, defining striated spaces with fabrics they produce, present a certain number of characteristics: intertwining and intersecting vertical and horizontal, mobile and fixed elements; and delimited shapes closed on at least one side, such as circular or cylindrical figures implying closed spaces, with a top and a bottom (2005, 475). They further assert that smooth space is not homogeneous and it is the space of the smallest deviation (371). Thus, we may assume that transgression occurs on a smaller scale. The description of Deleuze and Guattari on the striated and smooth spaces is created on a metaphor; they state that

> the needles produce a striated space; one of them plays the role of the warp, the other of the woof, but by turns. Crochet, on the other hand, draws an open space in all directions, a space that is prolongable in all directions—but still has a center. A more significant distinction would be between embroidery, with its central theme or motif, and patchwork, with its piece-by-piece construction, its infinite, successive additions of fabric.
>
> (2005, 476)

Similarly, Venice as a striated space produces continual transgression within her own architectural fabric of "water" "canals"—two words used together also indicate the continual passages and movements of smooth and striated spaces, as Deleuze and Guattari note (2005, 334), and the transgressive and deterritorializing nature of Venice with her vertical and horizontal bridges controlled by the state apparatus. Deleuze and Guattari state that bridges and roadways are directly related to striation and the control mechanism of the state apparatus (2005, 365).

McGregor states that the Venetian bridges were multi-functional; for instance, the Rialto Bridge, dividing the Grand Canal into two parts, obstructed the ocean vessels to pass further into the lagoon; thus, goods had to be transferred to smaller ships and the Rialto market was located exactly at this point (2006, 217–18). Beard draws attention to the similarities of Pompeii and Venice; both cities are similar in the sense that, while Venetian bridges pragmatically served the merchants of the city, "stepping stones" in the streets of Pompeii did not just provide pedestrians with safe crossing from one pavement to the other one, but it also enabled the owners of the carts, which had standard axle sizes, to run the monopoly in Pompeii by leaving the carts of the visitors, which had different axle sizes, outside the city gates (Beard, 2009, 53–54; McGregor, 2006, 217–18). Venetian bridges similarly provided the spatial controlling of the flow of the goods through the canals that also exemplify the transgressive cycles of striated and smooth spaces:

> If canals were the emblems of the city's *openness* to commerce, bridges were the valves that *controlled* the flow of goods. Land-based people think of bridges in just the opposite way—as links between places separated by water. For the water-minded Venetians, however, bridges were erected as obstacles.
>
> (McGregor, 2006, 217, emphasis added)

It is worth quoting Deleuze and Guattari once again to show how eighteenth-century bridges were erected under the control of the state apparatus, and how the striation the bridges imposed was strengthened by the same control mechanism:

> Is Anne Querrien right to find yet another echo of the same story in the case of bridges in the eighteenth century? Doubtless, the conditions were very different, for the division of labor according to State norms was by then an accomplished fact. But the fact remains that in the government agency in charge of bridges and roadways, roadways were under a well-centralized administration while bridges were still the object of active, dynamic, and collective experimentation. Trudaine organized unusual, open "general assemblies" in his home. Perronet took as his inspiration a supple model originating in the Orient: *The bridge should not choke or obstruct the river.* To the heaviness of the bridge, to the striated space of thick and regular piles, he opposed a thinning and discontinuity of the piles, surbase, and vault, a lightness and continuous variation of the whole. But his attempt soon ran up against principled opposition; the State, in naming Perronet director of the school, followed a frequently used procedure that inhibited experimentation more than crowning its achievements.
>
> (2005, 365, emphasis added)

Othello's observation of the Rialto Bridge in *The Nature of Blood* shows the transgressivity and striation in the very fabric of Venice. As he observes the surrounding area from the bridge's vantage point, his description takes a polysensorial turn that also reflects his own isolation along with the spatial control mechanism of the state apparatus.

In *Italian Hours,* Henry James also describes the Rialto Bridge as a place where one's polysensorial perception would function all at once: "All one's senses indeed are vigorously attacked; the whole place is violently *hot* and *bright,* all *odorous* and *noisy*" (2004, 118, emphasis added). As Westphal puts it, "seeing and hearing work in concert helps to discover meaning in the text" (*Geocriticism,* 2011, 131). Othello's observations help us analyze the mental isolation he feels along with the physical isolation which Venice imposes upon him. In the following quotation, the italic words manifest how Phillips uses sensorial references to create narrative fluency in the transitions or concurrent border crossings of smooth and striated spaces:

> I dressed quickly and soon found myself on the *wintry* Rialto *bridge,* from whose *vantage-point* I was able to watch a *lean* cat *scurry noiselessly* into a *blind alley.* I had grown extremely fond of the *city* under the *moon,* for it was at such moments that I truly appreciated the full grandeur of her *silent* majesty. Only the occasional *tolling of bells* trespassed upon the *night,* but their *song,* together with the sister *sound* of water *swirling* and *sighing,* created the most wondrous accompaniment to the *silence.* And then, of course, there was the *moonlight,* which produced spellbinding *patterns* as it struck the *water, illuminating buildings* here, and withholding its *light* there.
>
> (Phillips, 1997, 121, emphasis added)

As Deleuze and Guattari categorize the air, the sea and the earth as smooth spaces (2005, 362–64), we conclude that all concepts related to smooth and striated spaces also show such qualities. Thus, as the Rialto Bridge itself is striated "by the fall of bodies, the verticals of gravity, the distribution of matter into parallel layers, the lamellar and laminar movement of flows" (Deleuze and Guattari, 2005, 370). All the structural components of the bridge and all concepts related to the bridge are also striated, such as the control mechanism, the flow of the goods and the connection of the lands. Similarly in the extract, all the words related to the air, the sea and the earth such as "moon," "moonlight," "light" and "illuminating" indicate smoothness, while other words such as "alley," "the city" and "buildings" point to the striated structure of Venice. While "vantage-point" echoes the controlled structure of the city by the state apparatus, "tolling of bells" resonates the rhythmical movements of the boats, just as "boat" represents striation on water's smooth body. "Patterns," "alley" and "buildings" that limit the flow by their intertwining and intersecting vertical and horizontal elements are striated (Deleuze and Guattari, 2005, 475). These transitional cycles of striation and smoothness also reflect Venice in the trajectory of deterritorializing and reterritorializing forces; the same forces by which Othello is compelled to transform himself.

Urban structure of Venice can also be compared to the human body that, as Frichot notes, being both fluid and hard, is smooth and striated in the cycles of deterritorialization and reterritorialization as it enters the power relations; when the relations of power are manifested in an oppressive character, striating the body, the body tends to act inharmoniously (2007, 173–74). Hence, on the micro level, the very fabric of Venice leads Othello into a deterritorialization through mimesis, and then it is accompanied by compensatory reterritorialization. Bonta and Protevi state that humans, being rule-followers as well as free agents, break codes and reform new patterns that are new codes for others (2006, 34). Similarly, Othello considers certain passages in a society where Jews are ghettoized due to their 'deviance':

> I had often wondered if a marriage of the finest of my customs with their Venetian refinements might not, in due course, produce a more sophisticated man. Or, if not this, perhaps such a conjunction of traditions might at least subdue the portion of the ill-feeling to which my natural state seemed to give rise.
>
> (Phillips, 1997, 120)

Delueze and Guattari exemplify the process of deterritorialization and reterritorialization with the relationship of an orchid with a wasp:

> The orchid deterritorializes by forming an image, a tracing of a wasp; but the wasp reterritorializes on that image. The wasp is nevertheless deterritorialized, becoming a piece in the orchid's reproductive apparatus. But it reterritorializes the orchid by transporting its pollen. Wasp and orchid, as heterogeneous elements, form a rhizome. It could be said that the orchid imitates the wasp, reproducing its image in a signifying fashion.
>
> (mimesis, mimicry, lure, etc.) (2005, 10)

Similarly, as also indicated in the original text by Shakespeare, Othello lures Desdemona with his stories of valiance, exotic lands and slavery; hence, he deterritorializes by reshaping himself in a form that appeals to Desdemona. The exotic stories are used in the same way the orchid forms an image as "a tracing of a wasp" which attracts the wasp:

> Her father loved me, oft invited me,
> Still questioned me the story of my life,

> From year to year—the battles, sieges, fortunes,
> That I have passed
>
> (*Othello* 3.1.128–31)

In *The Nature of Blood*, Othello also declares that these stories are really appealing to Desdemona: "she wished to know principally of my adventures as a soldier and of many dangers to which my life had been subjected. She listened intently, and I spun some truthful tales" (Phillips, 1997, 133). Consequently, Desdemona reterritorializes herself on the image Othello has created for her, as indicated in Shakespeare's *Othello*:

> These things to hear
> Would Desdemona seriously incline.
> But still the house affairs would draw her hence.
> Which ever as she could with haste dispatch,
> She'd come again, and with a greedy ear
> Devour up my discourse
>
> (*Othello* 1.3.145–50)

Desdemona is deterritorialized, becoming "a piece" in Othello's "reproductive apparatus," and they form "a rhizome" with their marriage—Deleuze and Guattari use this botanic term to point out the rootlessness and unpredictable expansion of rhizomes. May further states:

> It can shoot out roots from any point, leaves and stems from any point. It has no beginning: no roots. It has no middle: no trunk. And it has no end: no leaves. It is always in the middle, always in process. There is no particular shape it has to take and no particular territory to which it is bound. It can connect from any part of itself to a tree, to the ground, to a fence, to other plants, to itself.
>
> (May, 2005, 133–34)

Othello mimics the image of a Venetian, and is becoming, as Phillips puts it, "a figment of a Venetian imagination" (1997, 182). We assume that the term "rhizome" befits the transformation Othello has gone through; Othello and Desdemona form a rhizome with "no roots," "no particular shape" and "no particular territory" they are bound to. We should also remember the original text by Shakespeare and Brabantio's foreshadowing warning to Othello that also points to deterritorializing and reterritorializing transformative characteristics of Othello/Desdemona relationship: "Look to her, Moor, if thou hast eyes to see./She has deceived her father, and may thee" (*Othello* 1.3.293–94).

Furthermore, in one case in *The Nature of Blood*, Othello confesses his inability to fully comprehend the real nature of Venice and Venetians; he thinks to himself about his awkward situation, at the same time observing his sleeping wife in the "wintry reflections" and the "whispered echoes" of the city:

> In her chastity, loyalty and honour, she is the most un-Venetian of women, yet is there some sport to this lady's actions? I am familiar with the renowned deceit of the Venetian courtesan, yet I have taken a Venetian for a wife. Has some plot been hatched about me? I am a foreigner. I do not know.
>
> (Phillips, 1997, 106)

In Othello's narration, Phillips uses the polysensorial images to reveal the true nature of Venice. Tuan confirms in *Topophilia* that our responses to visual inputs are different from other sensorial inputs in that seeing makes the world around us more objective than other senses (1990, 9–11). However, olfactory sense triggers memories in the cortical vastness of the human brain. Hence, in describing a space, Phillips also uses olfactory cues of isolative spaces along with visual ones to plant certain images along with the visual ones in the readers' perception. Othello comes to Venice in a spring day, and his polysensorial description of the city-state changes as he approaches to the port, uncovering her façade:

> I approached by water and found myself *propelled* by the swift tides across the lonely empty spaces of the forbidding lagoon. I stepped out and observed the *grey choppy* seas, the high arch of the sky, and low horizons to the monasteries, forts and fishing villages for the surrounding islands. Above me, the sails and flags *snapped* in the *damp* Venetian wind, and then, to our side, I spied a boatman hurrying back to the city ahead of the oncoming storm, with swallows flying low and skimming the water to either side of his unsteady vessel. As we neared the city, the air became *warm* and *moist*, and its smell somewhat *like the breath of an animal.*
>
> (Phillips, 1997, 106–07)

This description explicitly confirms that Othello moves from his smooth space into the striated space of Venice, and allows a voluntary reterritorialization and transgression into the ghettoized space of Venice. Othello's movement on the sea is also indicative and foreshadowing of the striation he faces in Venice, as Deleuze and Guattari note: "the sea is a smooth excellence, and yet it [is] the first to encounter the demands of increasingly strict striation" (2005, 479). Similarly, this extract is mixed with words indicating smoothness such as "water," "tides," "seas," "high," "sky," "horizons," "winds" and "lagoon," and striation, such as "monasteries," "forts," "villages," "islands" and "vessel." Hence, their mixture creates a transgression in the text as well. As noted before about

Phillips's description of a ghetto, Othello also describes Venice with olfactory references to filth and bad smell with some undertones to the real characteristics of this place, such as "whose sluggish canals were choked with refuse" (Phillips, 1997, 115), "the canal about this place smelt putrid, and I clasped a handkerchief to my nose and mouth" (146) and rumored crimes by "braves [who are] armed with a coat of mail, a gauntlet upon their right hand and a short dagger, were known to lurk by the waterside and attack passing strangers" (133).

Othello achieves his utmost tactile sense of Venice through his marriage to Desdemona: "She proved, as I had hoped, an eager, if somewhat naïve partner, but what she lacked in knowledge she made up for in the softness of her touch" (Phillips, 1997, 147). This passage indicates that Othello has felt Venice in the most tactile way possible, which also reveals that the true nature of Venice is not its soft touch, keeping in mind Phillips's intertexual use of Shakespeare's Othello as a pastiche, and Othello's imminent downfall in the original text.

To conclude, Othello, as Ledent suggests, disregarding the warnings of the Jewish ghetto as the spatial monument of how Venice, and Europe, deals with 'others' like him (2002, 142), condemns himself to his own demise through spatial transgression or border crossing that leads him into a further social isolation and makes him more vulnerable for Iago's deceitful plots as the original text proposes. Phillips creates a warning passage in *The Nature of Blood* for Othello by combining the smooth space of "an African river" with the striated space of "a Venetian canal" to indicate the very nature of Othello's downfall, and the passage suggests that he has not only transgressed against himself through this border crossing, but also his nomad land, his African wife and his son:

> My friend, *an African river* bears no resemblance to *a Venetian canal.* Only the strongest spirit can hold both together. . . . Did you truly ever think of *your wife's soft kiss?* Or *your son's eyes?* Brother *you are weak. A figment of a Venetian imagination.* While you still have time, jump from her bed and *fly away home.* Peel your rusty body from hers and *go home.* No good can come from your *foreign adventure.*
> (1997, 182, emphasis added)

Works Cited

Amin, Samir. (2009). *Eurocentrism* (2nd ed.). Translated by Russell Moore and James Membrez. Monthly Review Press. New York.

Bassi, S. (2002). The Venetian Ghetto and Modern Jewish Identity. *Judaism, 51(4)*, 468.

Beard, Mary. (2009). *Pompeii: The Life of a Roman Town. London.* GBR: Profile Books. London.

Bonta, M., and Protevi, J. (2004). *Deleuze and Geophilosophy: A Guide and Glossary.* Edinburgh University Press Ltd. Edinburgh.

Debenedetti-Stow, S. (1992). The Etymology of "Ghetto": New Evidence from Rome. *Jewish History, 6(1/2),* 79–85. doi:10.2307/20101121

Deleuze, Gilles, and Guattari, Felix. (2005). *A Thousand Plateaus: Capitalism and Schizophrenia.* Translation and Foreword by Brian Massumi. The University of Minnesota Press. Minneapolis.

Eckstein, L. (2001). Dialogism in Caryl Phillips's Cambridge, or the Democratisation of Cultural Memory. *World Literature Written in English, 39(1),* 54–74. doi:10.1080/17449850108589345

Finlay, R. (1982). The Foundation of the Ghetto: Venice, the Jews, and the War of the League of Cambrai. *Proceedings of the American Philosophical Society, 126(2),* 140–54. doi:10.2307/986357

Foucault, M. (2008). Of Other Spaces. *Heterotopia and the City: Public Space in a Postcivil Society.* Eds. M. Dehaene and L.D. Cauter. Routledge. New York.

Frichot, Helene. (2007). Holey Space and the Smooth and Striated Body of the Refugee. *Deleuzian Encounters: Studies in Contemporary Social Issues.* Eds. Anna Hickey-Moody and Peta Malins. Palgrave Macmillan. New York.

Holderness, Graham. (2010). *Anglo-Italian Renaissance Studies: Shakespeare and Venice.* GBR: Ashgate Publishing Grou. Farnham, Surrey.

James, Henry. (2004). *Italian Hours.* E-book. Project Gutenberg. www.gutenberg.org/ebooks/6354

Katz, Dana E. (2010). "Clamber not you up to the Casements": On Ghetto Views and Viewing. *Jewish History, 24(2),* 127–53. doi:10.1007/s10835–010–9105-z

Ledent, Benedicte. (2002). *Caryl Phillips.* Manchester University Press. Manchester and New York.

Madaj, M. J. (1968). The Polish Community: A Ghetto? *Polish American Studies, 25(2),* 65–125. doi:10.2307/20147784

May, Todd. (2005). *Gilles Deleuze: An Introduction.* Cambridge University Press. Cambridge.

McGregor, James H. S. (2006). *Venice from the Ground.* Harvard University Press. Cambridge.

Michman, Dan. (2011). *The Emergence of Jewish Ghettos During the Holocaust.* Translated by Lenn J. Schramm. Cambridge University Press. New York.

Phillips, Caryl. (1987). *The European Tribe.* Vintage Books. New York.

Phillips, Caryl. (1997). *The Nature of Blood.* Vintage Books. New York.

Roth, C. (1933). The Background of Shylock. *The Review of English Studies, 9(34),* 148–56. doi:10.2307/507864

Shakespeare, William. (2003). *The Merchant of Venice.* Edited by M.M. Mahood. Cambridge University Press. Cambridge.

Shakespeare, William. (2005). *Othello.* Annotated by Burton Raffel. Yale University Press. New Haven and London.

Soja E. W. (2009). Taking Space Personally. *The Spatial Turn: Interdisciplinary Perspectives.* Eds. B. Warf and S. Arias. Routledge. New York.

Tally. R. T. (2013). *Spatiality.* Routledge. New York.

Tuan, Y.-F. (1990). *Topophilia: A Study of Environmental Perception, Attitudes, and Values.* Columbia University Press. New York.

Warf, B., and Arias, S. (Eds.). (2008). Introduction: The Reinsertion of Space in the Humanities and Social Sciences. *The Spatial Turn: Interdisciplinary Perspectives* (1st ed.). Routledge. New York.

Westphal, Bertrand. (2011). Foreword. *Geocritical Explorations: Space, Place, and Mapping in Literary and Cultural Studies*. Ed. Robert T. Tally Jr. Palgrave Macmillan. New York.

Westphal, Bertrand. (2011). *Geocriticism: Real and Fictional Spaces*. Translated by Robert T. Tally Jr. Palgrave Macmillan. New York.

Whitehead, A. (2004). *Trauma Fiction*. Edinburgh University Press. Edinburgh.

Winkler, K., Seifert, K., and Detering, H. (2012). Literary Studies and the Spatial Turn. *JLT Articles*, *6(1)*. Retrieved from www.jltonline.de/index.php/articles/article/view/482

Wirth, L. (1927). The Ghetto. *American Journal of Sociology*, *33(1)*, 57–71. doi:10.2307/2765040

12 The Eternal Return and the Country/City Dynamic in Milan Kundera's *The Unbearable Lightness of Being*

Adam R. McKee

The concept of the division between country and city has been of interest to cultural critics since the beginning of urban experience. Perhaps the most complete history of this binary is the landmark work *The Country and the City* (1973) by Raymond Williams. In this work, Williams attempts to thoroughly document this dynamic split throughout the history of British literature. Williams traces the way in which the country and the city have been portrayed as existing across a radical cleavage and the influence of industrial capitalism on the ideological binary at play in this deployment. Remarking on the divide, Williams writes,

> On the country has gathered the idea of a natural way of life: of peace, innocence, and simple virtue. On the city has gathered the idea of an achieved centre: of learning, communication, light. Powerful hostile associations have also developed: on the city as a place of noise, worldliness and ambition; on the country as a place of backwardness, ignorance, limitation.
>
> (1)

Williams examines this myth almost from the origins of English literary output up through the twentieth century, showing the way in which the pastoral and a displaced form of life are almost constantly ideologically reflected upon at any given moment in British literary history.

Yet, these concerns can, as Williams notes, also be seen throughout the literary output of many other countries. One author in the twentieth century outside of Williams's critical apparatus who examines the country and the city as opposing forces is the Czech-French writer Milan Kundera. Kundera's novel *The Unbearable Lightness of Being* (1984), while displaying a profound preoccupation with binaries, reflects upon the split between the country and the city. However, this novel confronts the split from the standpoint of a Central European nation bound up in totalitarian, Soviet-communist rule, rather than through the capitalist standpoint of Williams's England. Williams's study provides us with a blueprint to understanding the way in which the country/city split has operated in

English literature, a blueprint that is helpful in navigating both how and why Kundera engages and inverts this binary. This essay will examine Kundera's novel through the ideological country/city split, Friedrich Nietzsche's theorization of eternal return (or recurrence), and the privileged binary system of Parmenides that Kundera utilizes in the novel's opening, and what these philosophical underpinnings subsequently provide for an understanding of the ideologies placed on the country and the city in *The Unbearable Lightness of Being* through the experiences of the characters of Tomas and Tereza. While many critics have responded to Kundera's somewhat flawed engagement with philosophical issues in the text, none have addressed the way in which the philosophical discourses he adopts for the novel contributes to the specific deployment of the country/city binary in the novel, describing the ideologically saturated geographies of the Czech countryside and Soviet Prague.

This examination will illustrate that any critical engagement with Kundera's novel and the central philosophical notion of Nietzsche's eternal return must be read through the ideological divide between the Czech countryside and the city of Prague, as Kundera utilizes Nietzschean concepts applied to the geographical and ideological divisions described by Williams. This argument expands upon conversations such as Petra von Morstein's on the importance of the Nietzschean concept by filtering it through the country/city divide. Additionally, this essay will establish the ways in which Kundera contributes to the theoretical conversations on the ideological split between the country and the city by grounding the binary in a specific historical moment in Czech political struggle. This historical conjuncture allows Kundera to do something unexpected with the country/city discourse by deconstructing the narrative.

In order to understand the philosophical structure of *The Unbearable Lightness of Being* and how it alters the perception of Prague and the Czech countryside, it is necessary to first understand the concept of eternal return (or recurrence) developed in the late-nineteenth century by Nietzsche. The concept of eternal return has major ramifications on the entirety of the novel, and it also provides important background for the discussion of the country and the city in the characters of Tomas and Tereza. Petra von Morstein has demonstrated the importance of the concept to the novel when she writes that, "To read *The Unbearable Lightness of Being* is to witness the birth of a novel from the spirit of eternal return" (70). This is evident from the beginning of the text, as Kundera opens with a brief description of the Nietzschean concept. He writes, "The idea of eternal return is a mysterious one, and Nietzsche has often perplexed other philosophers with it: to think that everything recurs as we once experienced it, and that the recurrence itself recurs ad infinitum!" (*ULB* 3). In his subsequent critical work, *The Art of the Novel* (1986), Kundera links this opening with the character of Tomas and his way of experiencing the world. Kundera states, "That reflection introduces directly, from the very first line of the novel, the fundamental situation of a character—Tomas; it sets out his problem: the lightness of existence in a world where there is no eternal return" (*The Art of the Novel* 29). Kundera labels this issue Tomas's "central problem", one that he will struggle with throughout the text. However, the implications of Nietzsche's concept on the ideological differences of the country and the city in the text have largely been overlooked, perhaps even by Kundera.

The issue of Tomas's struggle through a world with no eternal return also relates to the second important philosophical issue within the text: lightness versus heaviness. The second paragraph of the novel sets forth this dilemma as Kundera writes,

> Putting it negatively, the myth of eternal return states that a life which disappears once and for all, which does not return, is like a shadow, without weight, dead in advance, and whether it was horrible, beautiful, or sublime, its horror, sublimity, and beauty mean nothing,

> (*ULB* 3)

an implicit statement on the weightlessness of Tomas's existence at the beginning of the text which relates to Nietzsche's initial discussion of the concept of eternal return in *The Gay Science* (1882). In section 341 of *The Gay Science*, titled "The greatest weight", Nietzsche provides the reader with the hypothetical situation of a demon appearing to proclaim the concept of eternal return: "The eternal hourglass of existence is turned upside down again and again, and you with it, speck of dust!" (273). This section contains the first explicit mention of eternal return in the oeuvre of Nietzsche, and the end of this section provides Kundera with the important reference to heaviness and lightness through eternal return. The demon states,

> If this thought gained possession of you, it would change you as you are or perhaps crush you. The question in each and every thing, "Do you desire this once more and innumerable times more?" would lie upon your actions as the *greatest weight*.

> (274)

For Nietzsche, the concept of eternal return proposed that each time a decision is made, it is not only made once but for all time, perpetually, ceaselessly repeating in the same manner. Hence, a person's actions bear the "greatest weight" or heaviness; they are not simply one-time actions without consequence, but decisions made for all time, making the weight of them so heavy that they risk crushing an individual.

Eternal return appears as a crucial concept in Nietzsche's work *Thus Spoke Zarathustra* (1883–92). In the section "On the Vision and the

Riddle", the central character of the text, Zarathustra, tells a riddle about attempting to ascend a mountain while a dwarf, labeled the spirit of gravity, rests upon his shoulders. As Zarathustra reaches the top of the summit he confronts the dwarf with a vision of linear time, stating that there are two paths that converge at a gate labeled "Moment", one stretching eternally into the past, one eternally into the future, to which the dwarf replies "All that is straight lies . . . All truth is crooked; time itself is a circle" (158). The proposition of eternal return, the heaviness of this concept, frightens Zarathustra, who states that: "Thus I spoke, more and more softly; for I was afraid of my own thoughts and the thoughts behind my thoughts" (158). This thought weighs on Zarathustra who wishes to perfect himself shortly after the discussion. Man's greatest weight, Nietzsche's concept of eternal return, threatens to crush Zarathustra, just as it does the hypothetical reader in *The Gay Science*.

Nietzsche's concept of eternal return produces a sense of heaviness that invests the actions of an individual with meaning and significance. However, in *The Unbearable Lightness of Being*, as Kundera himself previously acknowledged, the character of Tomas lives in a world where there is no eternal return, and no heaviness placed upon his actions. The question in *The Unbearable Lightness of Being* is not whether or not the concept of eternal return is present; the real question in the text revolves around whether or not a lack of weight applied to existence is an essentially positive or negative aspect, and whether the concepts of eternal return and repetition are preferable to experiences that are one-time decisions. Here, Kundera brings in the philosophy of Parmenides and his reading of the system of privileged binaries discussed at the beginning of the novel. In Kundera's reading of Parmenides's philosophy, there are a series of binaries, such as good and evil, of which Parmenides labels one side positive and the other side negative. For Kundera, it is easy to understand why good would be positive and evil negative, or being positive and non-being negative, yet the concept of heaviness and lightness provides a more problematic equation for Kundera. He writes; "Parmenides responded: lightness is positive, weight negative. Was he correct or not? That is the question. The only certainty is: the lightness/weight opposition is the most mysterious, most ambiguous of all" (*ULB* 5–6). Kundera's chief dilemma (and the novel's primary philosophical question) then rests not on the problem of whether eternal return exists or not (since Tomas exists in a world where it does not) but whether or not it is preferable to live in a world of heaviness or lightness. Kundera asks whether his characters desire the heaviness of eternal return or the lightness of living in a world where decisions do not reverberate for all time but rather happen only once. At this point, Kundera merges the philosophical systems of Nietzsche and Parmenides, but the exchange with a third concept makes Kundera's conversation unique.

Here the concepts of eternal return and the privileged binary come into contact in one important way: the characters' perceptions of the opposition between the city of Prague and the Czech countryside. While the character of Tomas demonstrates the dilemma of a character living in a world without the concept of eternal return, his wife Tereza develops from a different perspective. As Petra von Morstein notes; "Tereza's life perspective is one implied by the idea of eternal return. What is must be. What must be precludes alternatives" (74). However, the notion of eternal return does not represent how Tereza's existence is, but rather the notion of eternal return indicates the way in which Tereza desires to exist. Indeed, several moments in the text amplify Tereza's attitude toward the perspective of eternal return compared to the lightness of being Tomas experiences. These key sections appear at the very end of Part Five ("Lightness and Weight") and throughout Part Seven ("Karenin's Smile") in dialogue and Tereza's interior monologue. These moments address the duality of country versus city in the novel, as well as the debate over whether lightness or heaviness should be on the positive end of Parmenides's binary.

The first mention of this conversation appears in Section 21 of "Lightness and Weight" when Tomas and Tereza are discussing what to do now that Prague has "grown so ugly". Tereza proceeds to suggest that they move to the country because, "We'd be alone there. You wouldn't meet that editor or your old colleagues. The people there are different. And we'd be getting back to nature. Nature is the same as it always was" (*ULB* 233). This is an important statement for several reasons. The first of which is the way in which this plays into Williams's observations regarding the construction of the country as more peaceful and natural compared to the city as a place of lightness and achievement. Further exhibiting this split between the natural countryside and the achieved city, Petr Bilek observes that,

> The city in the actual world is an artificial, man-made structure. It is based on radical reconstruction of the natural world that brings into existence certain spatial settings and arbitrary rules that model the behavior of its inhabitants and visitors.
>
> (249)

The third important element of this statement is that it brings the idea of eternal return into the conversation of the country and nature as a place of repetition and sameness compared to the fluidity and flux of the city. This is the first mention of this issue in the text, but both Tomas and Tereza expand on this idea in the final section of the novel: "Karenin's Smile".

The opposition in ideologies of the country and the city reveals an aspect of the problem of eternal recurrence that has been largely overlooked in Kundera's novel. Shortly after the couple's move from Prague to the countryside, the conversation surrounding the country/city dynamic takes center stage once more. Initially, the countryside is positioned as in a sense "outside" of the control of the Soviet controlled state: "Perhaps it was the fact that no one wished to settle there that caused the state to lose its power over the countryside" (*ULB* 283). Hence, the countryside is unquestionably separated from the life of the city in Prague, which was highly controlled and highly influenced by the Soviet occupation, yet the countryside remains separate. As Bilek notes, this separation from the city is a crucial element in the novel,

> The word *Prague* enters the fictional world of the novel almost seventy times; usually with a spatial preposition: *in, to, from, over, out of*. Such a general reference expressed by just one unspecified word also implies another spatial relation: Prague versus non-Prague.
>
> (252)

The separation of Prague versus non-Prague represents the binary split here; there is Prague and the negation of Prague, here exemplified by the countryside. This is certainly evident in the passage referencing the state's loss of power in the countryside, and is on display in the two separate settings for the characters of Tomas and Tereza at this point in the novel. With the state's "loss of control" in the area, it is much more likely to remain, in Tereza's words, "the same as it always was".

Clearly, Tomas and Tereza are the central human characters in this section of the novel, but it is also quite apparent that Karenin, their dog, acts as a vehicle for philosophical reflection, especially for Tereza. Earlier in the novel Kundera writes of the difference between dog time and human time in a reflection that sounds very similar to the dwarf's statement in *Thus Spoke Zarathustra*;

> Dog time cannot be plotted along a straight line; it does not move on and on, from one thing to the next. It moves in a circle like the hands of a clock, which—they, too, unwilling to dash madly ahead—turn round and round the face, day in and day out following the same path.
>
> (*ULB* 74)

Karenin lives in a world where the concept of eternal return does exist. His time, linked to the circularity of the clock and the rhythms of nature, becomes the time of Tomas and Tereza only after they leave Prague; "Never before had his (Karenin's) position as keeper of the clock been so respected. The country was no place for improvisation; the time in which Tereza and Tomas lived was growing closer to the regularity of his time" (*ULB* 284). The country, where the couple is now living with unchanging nature, undoubtedly changes the couple's perception of both time and "return". Indeed, for the first time in his life, Karenin wakes Tomas and Tereza because, "he felt compelled to share his overwhelming joy, a joy of return and rebirth" (*ULB* 285). This was Karenin's conception of time while the group lived in Prague, but only now, in the country, can Tomas and Tereza view time in the same fashion.

Here, it is important to note the text's explanation of why it is that Karenin has a different conception of time than Tomas and Tereza; here, Kundera links the concept of the fall from Paradise with man's attainment of linear rather than circular time. Kundera develops this issue thoroughly in Section 4 of "Karenin's Smile" with a sustained discussion of the idyllic image of Paradise. He writes;

> life in Paradise was not like following a straight line to the unknown; it was not an adventure. It moved in a circle among known objects. Its monotony bred happiness, not boredom. As long as people lived in the country, in nature, surrounded by domestic animals, in the bosom of regularly recurring seasons, they retained at least a glimmer of the paradisiac idyll.
>
> (*ULB* 295–96)

Williams thoroughly demonstrates throughout *The Country and the City* that the countryside has been commonly portrayed not only as an innocent Edenic way of life, but has also become synonymous with recurrent cycles such as seasons, an essential connection that allows Kundera to reintroduce Nietzsche in this context. Here, the structure of Paradise was a place of eternal recurrence for man, a place that we no longer have access to, but animals like Karenin do because; "only animals were not expelled from Paradise" (*ULB* 298). It is clear that by linking the concept of eternal return to Paradise, Kundera is embedding Tereza in the point of view that life in nature is preferable to the city.

Perhaps the key passage in this discussion occurs in Tereza's interior monologue after her contemplation of animals as figures still existing within the eternal return of Paradise. Tereza thinks,

> And therein lies the whole of man's plight. Human time does not turn in a circle; it runs ahead in a straight line. That is why man cannot be happy: happiness is the longing for repetition. Yes, happiness is the longing for repetition, Tereza said to herself.
>
> (*ULB* 298)

If happiness is the longing for repetition, then a world with eternal return, and therefore heaviness, is preferable for Tereza. While Kundera, as previously mentioned, places Tomas from the beginning of the novel in world where eternal return is absent, his perspective undergoes a dramatic shift toward that of Tereza once outside Prague. As Morstein notes; "At the end of their life which fulfills his (Tomas's) initial vision of the common death, the perspective implied by eternal return supersedes his perspective from transience and fleetingness" (76). After escape from the city life of Prague, Tomas is able to live a life of repetition, and by the end of the novel he is able to seek happiness in isolation with Tereza. It is at this point that the struggle with Parmenides's binary system becomes important. Tomas finds his life in the country with Tereza preferable to his life in the city. The change in Tomas is noticeable in his conversation with Tereza at the very end of the novel. Kundera writes,

> "That's a silly comparison to make," said Tereza. "Your work meant everything to you; I don't care what I do, I can do anything. I haven't lost a thing; you've lost everything."
> "Haven't you noticed I've been happy here, Tereza?" Tomas said.
> "Surgery was your mission," she said.
> "Missions are stupid, Tereza. I have no mission. No one has. And it's a terrific relief to realize you're free, free of all missions."
> (*ULB* 313)

Tomas transitions to celebrating the country life that he and Tereza now have and he also counters the "quests" he has had throughout the novel. The "unbearably light" life of Prague, where Tomas endlessly pursues women and refuses to sign the statement prepared by the Ministry, leads to his fall from surgeon to window washer. Kundera explains that he "descended voluntarily to the lowest rung of the social ladder" (*ULB* 192), because,

> Once he had reached the lowest rung on the ladder, they would no longer be able to publish a statement in his name, for the simple reason that no one would accept it as genuine. Humiliating public statements are associated exclusively with the signatories' rise, not fall.
> (*ULB* 192)

Tomas abandons his missions in the countryside, instead referring to them as "stupid".

It is obvious throughout Kundera's deployment of the country/city split that this is not simply a geographical distinction, but also part of the ideological divisions highlighted in Williams's work. In addition to the inside/outside narrative of Prague and the countryside, the novel also illustrates the way in which each of these spaces carries with it an ideological structure. The city of Prague has been labeled with the "noise, worldliness, and ambition" that Williams examines, while the Czech countryside has been deployed as a "natural way of life: of peace, innocence, and simple virtue" (1). In *The Unbearable Lightness of Being*, this ideological construct plays out most obviously in Tomas's shift to fidelity upon the couple's move to the countryside. However, Kundera seemingly fits into the classical notion of this ideological opposition of the country and the city in several ways.

The aforementioned implication of Tereza's equation of the countryside with repetition and therefore Paradise is part of a much longer story surrounding the ideological construction of the country and the city. As Williams writes, "in a conventional association of Christian and classical myth, the provident land is seen as Eden" (24). However, Tereza's equation of the countryside with Paradise/Eden rests, perhaps, more on the sense of repetition and less on the countryside as a place for man's interaction with fertile and "provident land". Tereza's equation comes from seeing the country as the opposite of the city; or, in Williams's words, "The 'timekept City' is implicitly contrasted with the natural rhythms of blood, day and night, and the seasons; a rural past is conflated with faith or with innocence: a new version of pastoral, by the emphasis of *urban negations*" (240–41, emphasis added). This sense of "urban negation" is evident in Tereza's motivations for moving into the countryside. As Kundera writes, she desires to escape, "her jealousy and his infidelities" (*ULB* 234). In "Karenin's Smile", Kundera writes that,

Tereza was happy to abandon the city, the drunken barflies molesting her, and the anonymous women leaving the smell of their groins in Tomas's hair. The police stopped pestering them, and the incident with the engineer so merged with the scene on Petrin Hill that she was hard put to tell which was a dream and which the truth. . . . In any case, Tereza was happy and felt that she had at last reached her goal: she and Tomas were together and alone.

(*ULB* 234)

Tereza's explicit desire to escape the chaos of Prague, including her own sexual encounter with the engineer and not simply Tomas's infidelity, reinforces the ideological construction of the countryside as the "negation" of the urban. Williams argues of this desire to escape the confines of the city that, "The individual was the person who must escape, or try to escape, from the repulsive and degrading mass" (222). Indeed, the conceptualization of the countryside that Tereza carries with her is emblematic of this ideological tendency observed by Williams. This marks a distinct transformation from the urban crowd and alienation to a sense of community and privacy.

However, Tereza's way of thinking is not unique to her position in the novel. Williams notes that this construct of the countryside is part of another long-standing and much commented upon ideological split. In addition to the Edenic and natural countryside split with the man-made city, the divergent ways in which time is experienced also appear. Williams explains, in a development of this binary through D. H. Lawrence,

> A working country, that is to say, was becoming, yet again but in a new way, a place of physical and spiritual regeneration. It was now the teeming life of an isolated nature, or the seasonal rhythm of the fundamental life processes. Neither of these feelings was new in itself. What was new was their fusion into a structure of feeling in which the earth and its creatures—animals and peasants almost alike—were an affirmation of vitality and of the possibility of rest in conscious contrast with the mechanical order, the artificial routines, of the cities
>
> (252)

Once again we see the negation of the urban in the pastoral, and this appears analogous to the conception of Karenin's "time" compared to that of Tomas and Tereza. An earlier statement by Williams in *The Country and the City* furthers this notion. He explains that, "a country community, most typically a village, is an epitome of direct relationships: of face-to-face contacts within which we can find and value the real substance of personal relationships" (165). This is evident in Kundera through the change in Tomas and Tereza's relationship after the move to the countryside. The ideological construction of Prague and the countryside is not simply one of human interactions, but rumination on the political ramifications of Prague's occupation. Aside from to the countryside as a place of innocence and natural rhythms, it also stands in opposition to Prague as a place of peace and distance from the totalitarian government, bringing Kundera's construction of the binary into the realm of ideological apparatus. As Williams illustrates, "in times of war and civil disturbance . . . the peace of country life could be contrasted with the disturbance of war and civil war and the political chaos of the cities" (17). Williams expands on this notion by stating that, "country life, as traditionally, is an innocent alternative to ambition, disturbance and war" (24).

The ideological constructs expanded on by Williams here find correlations in the philosophy of Nietzsche. Nietzsche's original conception of eternal return/recurrence does not take this ideological form in the same way that Williams's country/city division does; yet in Kundera's text, the issue of eternal return mixes with the light/heavy binary and the country/city binary to produce an ideological construct by filtering Williams's dynamics through the philosophy of Nietzsche. In Kundera's novel, the country becomes not just a place of innocence, peace and tranquility, but it also becomes a place of repetition and heaviness. These two concepts, repetition and heaviness, become preferable ideas for the couple by the end of the novel. This ideological construct is perhaps most evident in the lives of the characters before and after their move from Prague to the countryside.

The most obvious result of Tomas's move to the countryside is the aforementioned change in his relationship with women. After the regime demotes him to window washer in Prague, Tomas sets out on an almost never-ending stream of affairs with various women. The affairs continue throughout his marriage to Tereza in a pseudo-mission for Tomas. Kundera writes, "He was not obsessed with women; he was obsessed with what in each of them is unimaginable, obsessed, in other words, with the one-millionth part that makes a woman dissimilar to others of her sex" (*ULB* 200). The search for dissimilarity allows Tomas to live in a world without repetition where each woman he engages in a sexual encounter with represents a linear progression in a sense through a new experience. In his sexual encounters it is evident that Tomas's lack of eternal return is exhibited in the fact that his decisions carry with them a sense of lightness rather than heaviness. Only after his encounter with the stork-like woman does Tomas feel rattled because of the unusual nature of their sexual encounter. Rather than a parade of encounters where the women are indistinguishable, "one-millionth part" gives Tomas the lightness of being where his actions do not return upon themselves. Once in the countryside, however, his fidelity to Tereza results in the heaviness of repetition. Once the couple moves, Tomas becomes faithful to Tereza when he incorporates Tereza's perspective of eternal return into his own life, seeking heaviness in a place of repetition.

The move to the countryside draws attention to the concluding and perhaps most important issue within the novel (given the title): the privileging of lightness or heaviness in the philosophical framework of Parmenides. Kundera himself asks which one should be more preferable, lightness or heaviness. In a sense, this is the primary question the novel itself sets out to answer. Tomas certainly lives in a world with "unbearable lightness of being" throughout. In a world without eternal return, Tomas makes no decisions that will resonate for all time, only decisions that do not persist; equating lightness not weight: his life, "whether it was horrible, beautiful, or sublime, its horror, sublimity, and beauty mean(s) nothing" (*ULB* 3). However, once he and Tereza move to the countryside they are able to find happiness in the repetition of nature, a repetition that provides "the greatest weight" of Nietzsche's eternal return. By the end of the novel, which ironically concludes before Tomas and Tereza's death even though the reader has been privilege to that information for some time, it is clear that this weight of eternal return is positive. Without this weight we live in a world with an "unbearable lightness of being", the weight and the repetition at the end become positive, lightness the negative in their binary opposition.

Even in the totalitarian government of the novel, Tomas and Tereza are able to find this ideological relief in the countryside. Kundera illustrates that, "Under Communism, however, village life no longer fit the age-old pattern" (*ULB* 282), yet there is a certain amount of distancing and negation that still exists in the Czech countryside for the couple. Kundera's conceptualization of the collective farming community envisions a space with more freedom than the totalitarian regime of Prague (represented in Tomas's fall from grace and Tereza's suspicion of the engineer as a regime spy), but also a more democratic space where leaders are elected and allowed to maintain autonomy from the state. While Kundera's development of the countryside here takes away the common ideological element of the countryside as a place of communion with the land (the farmer "forms no allegiance to either region or work"), he still places the countryside as a negation of the city, here in the difference between totalitarian and democratic leadership.

At this point in the novel, Kundera does something both and new and unexpected with the deployment of the ideologies of the country and the city experienced by Tomas and Tereza. In Tereza's conceptualization of the countryside, she

> discovered in herself a picture of country life originating in memories of books she read or in her ancestors. It was a harmonious world; everyone came together in one big happy family with common interests and routines: church service on Sundays, a tavern where the men could get away from their womenfolk, and a hall in the tavern where a band played on Saturdays and the villagers danced.
>
> (*ULB* 282)

This conceptualization of the countryside that Tereza carries with her into the Czech countryside was extremely common, as Williams notes, this dates back to "Christian and classical myth" where "the provident land is seen as Eden" and the "recurrent myth of a happier and more natural past." Tereza's preconceived notion of the countryside finds agreement in this pastoral, communal and more socialist notion of the countryside that Williams observes in *The Country and the City*.

However, this *a priori* notion of the countryside that Tereza carries with her is undermined by the political position of the actual Czech countryside. As previously noted, Kundera writes that the pattern of village life has been changed under communism. The belief, conceived under the pressures of Capitalism in Williams, of the communal and socialist countryside collapses under Communist control of the Czech countryside. The countryside, rather than a socialist space of communal relations becomes a democratic sphere of relationships devoid of connection to a pastoral and idealized past. Furthering this notion, Kundera portrays the countryside as a place of individualism. He writes that,

> at the end of a day's work filled with boisterous shouting and relaxed chatter, they would all shut themselves up within their four walls

and, surrounded by contemporary furniture emanating bad taste like a cold draft, stare at the refulgent television screen,

(*ULB* 283)

and that, "The country offered them nothing in the way of even a minimally interesting life" (*ULB* 283). In the novel, the Czech countryside has lost the communal relations that were so idealized in the pastoral conception of the times past.

In addition to the loss of communalism associated with the Czech countryside, the pastoral implications of a natural way of life tied "to the seasonal rhythm of the fundamental life processes" (Williams 252) of the land also remain elusive for Kundera's characters in *The Unbearable Lightness of Being*. Kundera writes,

A farmer who no longer owns his own land and is merely a laborer tilling the soil forms no allegiance to either region or work; he has nothing to lose, nothing to fear for. As a result of such apathy, the countryside had maintained more than a modicum of autonomy and freedom.

(*ULB* 283)

In fact, Kundera's countryside under communism is a reversal of the system typically vilified under Capitalism. The political ramifications alienate the farmers from their production on the collective farm because they are no longer granted access and control over the land and the items that come from it. Tereza comes to the countryside with the notion of a communal connection to the land; a connection that has disappeared, for Kundera, through communism.

In a further modification to the typical narrative of the country/city split, the countryside also becomes the only democratically run space in Czechoslovakia throughout the text, because it is run by elected leadership. Once again, Tereza's conception of a communal countryside deconstructs itself in Kundera's novel. He notes, "The chairman of the collective farm was not brought in from outside (as were all high-level managers in the city); he was elected by the villagers from among themselves" (*ULB* 283). Under the totalitarian Communist rule of Prague, officials are chosen for the people. Yet, the countryside provides the citizens with the agency denied to them in the city through a democratic election of leadership. Once again, the traditional associations of the countryside are altered in Kundera's novel.

Williams's insights help to explain these modifications to the ideologies of the country and the city in the novel. In *The Country and the City*, Williams mentions Friedrich Engels's hope in his discussion of Manchester in *The Condition of the Working Class in England* that socialism could destroy the split between the country and the city. Yet, while Engels envisioned the removal of the structural devices employed to hide the working-class from the middle-class in Manchester, Kundera's novel complicates this binary by destroying the stable categories that many, such as Tereza, bring with them upon entering the countryside. Williams himself observes that "the common image of the country is now an image of the past, and the common image of the city an image of the future. That leaves, if we isolate them, an undefined present," before declaring that, "we use the contrast of country and city to ratify an unresolved division and conflict of impulses, which it might be better to face in its own terms" (297). In the end, both Kundera and Williams begin to deconstruct this country/city binary by showing the inherent instability in both categories and their most common conceptualizations.

This essay has shown the way in which Nietzsche's concept of eternal return, Parmenides's notion of binary oppositions, and the conflict between the country and the city collide within *The Unbearable Lightness of Being*. This also displays the way in which Kundera approaches the ideological split of the country and the city through the lens of Nietzschean philosophy and continues on to modify this binary under the specific conditions of Prague and the Czech countryside. By the end of the novel, Kundera has examined the way in which the concept of eternal return, complete with Nietzsche's "greatest weight" is preferable to becoming "only half real, [with] movements as free as they are insignificant" (*ULB* 5). As Morstein states:

> In a world without eternal return we would have to live with a terrifying sense of weightlessness. If we believe in eternal return we transform the weightlessness of fleeting appearances into the greatest weight. It is just this terrifying sense of weightlessness that Tomas experiences and struggles with.
>
> (67)

It is clear in the novel that while weightlessness is terrifying, heaviness and burden are man's path to happiness and meaning, and these characteristics are met only when Tomas and Tereza move to the countryside.

Works Cited

Banerjee, Maria Nemcova. *Terminal Paradox: The Novels of Milan Kundera*. New York: Grove Weidenfeld, 1990.

Bedient, Calvin. "On Milan Kundera." *Salmagundi* 73 (1987): 93–108.

Bilek, Petr A. "Reading Prague: Narrative Domains of the Image of the City in Fiction." *Style* 40.3 (2006): 249–57. Print.

Kundera, Milan. *The Art of the Novel*. Trans. Linda Asher. New York: Grove Press, Inc., 1988. Print.

———. *The Unbearable Lightness of Being*. Trans. Michael Henry Heim. New York: Perennial Classics, 1999. Print.

Morstein, Petra von. "The Eternal Return and *The Unbearable Lightness of Being*." *The Review of Contemporary Fiction* 9.2 (1989): 65–78. Print.

Nietzsche, Friedrich. *The Gay Science*. Trans. Walter Kaufmann. New York: Random House, Inc., 1974. Print.

———. *Thus Spoke Zarathustra: A Book for All and None*. Trans. Walter Kaufmann. New York: Penguin Books, 1978. Print.

Williams, Raymond. *The Country and the City*. New York: Oxford UP, 1973. Print.

13 Transgression, Boundaries, and Power

Rethinking the Space of Postcolonial Literature

Dustin Crowley

Space, Henri Lefebvre tells us, is a tool for thought and action. Space enables and space constrains. Alongside history and metrics like race, class, and gender, space demands our attention as a foundational feature of social production and struggle. In the decades following Lefebvre's provocatively suggestive text *The Production of Space*, interest in spatial studies has burgeoned across academia, and literary studies are no exception. Though still relatively nascent, spatial literary studies has already been established on firm ground by works like Robert Tally's *Spatiality* and Bertrand Westphal's *Geocriticism: Real and Fictional Spaces*. These and other writers have already made a strong case for the necessity and usefulness of spatially or geographically focused criticism as a way to enunciate "the dialectical nature of the relations between texts and their real-world referents" (Prieto). Yet, as Tally suggests, geocriticism is a heterogeneous field, and even as Westphal's groundbreaking text lays out a detailed analytical method, it also "invites others to engage in a debate" about the nature and practices of spatial literary studies (Tally 2–3). By way of further developing the methods and conceptual tools of geocriticism, I intend here to supplement the predominately postmodernist assumptions that have provided the basis for much geocriticism, notably Westphal's formative work. In particular, I want to challenge the tendency in such frameworks to dichotomize types of space in ways that privilege transgressive uncertainty over bounded emplacement. Refracted through the work of cultural geography and political ecology, transgression and boundedness become relational and dynamic concepts that are themselves not inherently liberatory or repressive, but are (as Lefebvre famously insisted) social products, equally subject to cooption and shaping by forces of power and resistance.

Using this alternate understanding of space and borders, I hope to move geocriticism beyond categorical and essentializing assumptions about particular kinds of space, instead opening up possibilities for analyzing with more nuance the often ambiguous and complex geographical representations of postcolonial writers like Nigerian author Chris Abani and Kenyan author Ngũgĩ wa Thiong'o. I have chosen to focus on postcolonial literature for two reasons: first, postcolonial literature in general (and African literature in particular) has not been much explored in geocritical analyses to date. This, despite the second reason: that Westphal and others point directly to postcolonial theory as a body of thought informing their own work on the oppressive or resistive nature of space. It would seem to beg the question, then, whether the literature itself bears out the claims that have been drawn from the theory.

The gesture toward postcolonialism is hardly surprising, given that field's pronounced concern for issues of geography and the relations between places under the auspices of imperialism. Edward Said, for example, has argued that "Imperialism and the culture associated with it affirm both the primacy of geography and an ideology about the control of territory" (qtd. in *Seeking Spatial Justice* 36). As the means of that control, European colonialism adopted "powerful spatial strategies of territorial dispossession, military occupation, cultural domination, [and] economic exploitation," practices of intrusive colonial organization that produced and reproduce spatial conditions of "exclusion, domination, disciplinary control" (*Seeking Spatial Justice* 37). Westphal extends this notion to include imperialism's attempt to stifle the inherent heterogeneity of space with "the old empire of that totalizing space, of positivism, of colonialism, of the always absolute and inhuman constriction" (Westphal 38). From this basis in postcolonialism, it is not a long leap to generalizing about the repressive nature of state power in general, manifested in and executed through strict borders and controlled, controlling boundaries of all sorts. We can find support for this critique of managed spatiality from Lefebvre himself: the state, he argues, "plans and organizes space 'rationally' with the help of knowledge and technology, imposing analogous, if not homologous, measures" on space through which the state "promotes and imposes itself as the stable center" (Lefebvre 23). Premised on a certain kind of postmodernist postcolonialism, then, Westphal and others have tended to formulate geocriticism on the basic assumption that borders (and attendant notions of stable, concrete, or bounded place) are inherently problematic, typically operating as a mode of domination imposed from above.

Following the work of Gilles Deleuze and Félix Guattari, Westphal frames this problematic as "striated space." As the space of "sedentary" and restrictive city life, this space is "striated by walls, enclosures, and roads between enclosures" (Deleuze and Guattari, qtd in Westphal 39); it is the space "occupied by the state apparatus. This is the space of the polis, politics, the policed, and the police" (Westphal 39). Necessarily and binarily opposed to striated space is "smooth space," nomadic space, the space of "bedouinism" that is "virtually open to infinity" (39). In Westphal's description, smooth space bears many similarities to Foucault's heterotopia, the convergence "in a single real place [of] several spaces, several sites that are themselves incompatible," symbolized by a ship, "a floating piece of space, a place without a place" (Foucault 6, 9). It also parallels Edward Soja's thirdspace, *"a space of radical openness, a vast territory of infinite possibilities and perils"* that lay "beyond" any structured or bounded formulation of centers and peripheries (*Thirdspace* 33). There is a common postmodernist thread here—a desire to define a space that escapes definition or strict delineation and that can be opposed to the constricting tendencies of established boundaries.

Yet there is also a crucial difference in the conceptions of these thinkers: for Soja, thirdspace is precisely the space that gets "beyond" binaries, that acts as "a critical 'other-than' choice that speaks and critiques through its otherness" (*Thirdspace* 61). The smooth/striated construction of Westphal, Deleuze, and Guattari, however, enacts a clear dichotomy between these kinds of space. Though Westphal notes that these spaces are naturally "mixed" and that "the striated can become smooth, just as smooth space is exposed to striation" (Westphal 40), his reference to American military intervention in Iraq as a striating effort in the "smooth" Iraqi desert (40) strongly implies the inimical and conflictual nature of their relationship, with smooth space unambiguously the more virtuous of the two. After all, smooth space is by definition more in line with the oft-repeated claim that space itself is (and ought to be) "a heterogeneous (and socially open)" phenomenon; more smoothing, more openness, more indeterminacy of borders, then, would seem to be the privileged position of those who seek a space that "consistently escapes political control" (38).

Indeed, if strictly demarcated spatial relations are the basic geocritical problem, then it follows logically that smoothing the striations of political control would be the principal solution. This is a more or less natural dynamic in Lefebvre's estimation, as "state-imposed normality makes permanent transgression inevitable" (Lefebvre 23). Westphal makes this notion of transgression a central part of his own geocritical model, claiming that "Transgression corresponds to the crossing of a boundary beyond which stretches a marginal space of freedom. When it becomes a permanent principle, it turns into transgressivity" (Westphal 47). In the dichotomous formulation of smooth and striated, where one represents the possibility for freedom and alterity in a world of global mobility and mixity, and the other represents oppressive restriction and homogeneity, transgressivity by necessity "provides the best model for spatial thinking in the postmodern era" (Prieto), an era in which we are making "the transition from a reading of the world still fully guided by residual grand narratives to an erratic reading arising from a full-fledged postmodernity" (Westphal 37). Under the sign of postmodern transgression, any borders or stable, "striated" places are shunned, penetrated, or exploded in favor of digression, indeterminacy, "borderlands, interstitial zones, and hybrid identities" (Prieto), all animated by "the principle of mobility" (Westphal 49).

To an extent, this model for understanding spatial relationships aligns nicely with its postcolonial antecedents, and we might easily find similar claims being made about postcolonial literature. Critics of Chris Abani's work, for instance, have regularly argued that the urban and globalized spaces of his literature represent a fluid and liberating cosmopolitanism. Abani sets most of his narratives in the heart of heterogeneous urbanity, developing in detail each city's dynamic and multivalent character as the concrete expression of, and medium for, the converging relations and overlapping populations that palimpsest and blend there. In the novella *Becoming Abigail*, he draws attention to London's long history as a place both colonized and colonizing, with "tired crumbling walls built by Caesar" (ch. 12) and "Cleopatra's needle . . . an Egyptian souvenir" with two "sphinxes [facing] the wrong way, gazing inward contemplatively . . . rather than outward, protectively" (ch. 2), standing as perhaps awkward reminders of the city's imperial past. In *The Virgin of Flames*, he recalls the Spanish influence of Los Angeles with a description of the old Mission, "once the center of civilized Los Angeles" (154), which gave way to increasingly eclectic influences like "migrant Jews from the East" who built "two-, sometimes three-story brick buildings that leaned on rusty metal fire escapes that would have been more at home in New York" (153). As such passages suggest, Abani is keenly aware of the way urban particularities crystallize out of often far-flung movements and relations of people, ideas, and material, consciously or unconsciously taking on a global character that perhaps escapes clear definitions and betrays the porosity of its borders. We can readily see the global character of Los Angeles' population reflected in its flora: "palm trees from the Canary Islands, eucalyptus from Australia, bougainvillea from Brazil, birds of paradise from South Africa. Nearly everything now native to Los Angeles came from somewhere else" (177). By narrating the overdetermined development of cities like these, Abani writes globalization and urbanization as entwined, mutually enabling processes that mirror the smoothing and striating dynamic.

The shared dynamics of global migration that shape Abani's cities also dominate the experiences of the characters that populate them. In all of Abani's narratives, characters come to cities from elsewhere, often across national borders. In *GraceLand*, Elvis and his father Sunday come to Lagos from a small town looking for work, and by the end of the novel Elvis is set to leave Nigeria for the United States. The title character in *Becoming Abigail* is sent from Nigeria to London because her father believes "London will give you a higher standard of education and living" (ch. 8). Black, the protagonist of *The Virgin of Flames*, is the son of a Nigerian father and a Salvadoran mother who makes his way to Los Angeles after years of wandering across America. Though all these characters have strong ties with Africa (only Black is not directly from there), they all end up outside the continent, global Bedouins of a sort, dispersed to the global cities of Britain and the US (not unlike Abani himself). The result is a diasporic engagement with Africa that resists seeing its people and places confined to the continent. Rather, Abani seems often at pains to demonstrate Africa's connections with global forces that manifest within and link together places like Lagos and London. These migrations suggest the way Africa's urbanity is relationally constituted through its exchanges with the rest of the world, just as people and materials from Africa contribute to the globalization of other places.

The mutual articulation of the global within the urban makes Abani's cityscapes tempting to analyze through a framework of postmodernism or postcolonial hybridity and indeterminacy. Certainly, the postmodernism of Los Angeles has been the subject of any number of studies that need not be rehashed here; suffice it to say that *The Virgin of Flames* in many ways adopts this familiar characterization of the city. With its "confusion of Art Deco, Hacienda, Lloyd-Wright and ugly 60s modernist architecture" and its mélange of cultures, Los Angeles is "a segregated city" with "several cities within it" that nonetheless "still managed to work as a single canvas of color and voices" (*Virgin* 73, 86, 177). Through this coalescing variety, the city reveals "the trick of its becoming; a city constantly digesting its past and recycling itself into something new" (153), something that can only be defined by its indefiniteness.

Perhaps more interesting, however, is whether or not Abani attributes this sort of postmodernist subjectivity to all global cities; whether, say, his depiction of Lagos shares this capacity for cosmopolitan mixity and flow as part of the common urban experience. For Chielozona Eze, the answer is clearly, yes: in fact, he argues, this globalized hybridity acts as the salient feature of the city in *GraceLand*. He contends that the "multidimensional cultural hybridity" of the city (106) offers a space "Where people lose their primary attachment to blood in its closed, ethnic sense" (108) and instead adopt "a more open-minded or global approach to reality" (99). Assuming a natural and necessary equivalence between urbanization, globalization, and a postmodern cosmopolitan ethic, Eze writes of *GraceLand*'s Lagos: "This is, indeed, the state of things: the postmodern, global and the transcultural condition in which ideas, people, and commodities move to and fro" (105), embodying the "idea of freedom, of the struggle to transcend boundaries" (103). In this world city, Elvis is freed from Afikpo, "one of the Igbo towns"; when he "lands in Lagos . . . he instantly links up with the larger world" (102), including a Yoruba step-family and Western books, commodities, ideas, and tourists. Because his mother and one of his teachers had taught him to appreciate other cultures through American rock music and Western dance, Eze argues, Elvis's emergence into the global sphere of Lagos "is no problem for him" (107), and even facilitates his exploration of his own complex identity.

Obi Nwakanma takes the productive interplay of mobility, hybridity, and freedom even further, claiming that by having Elvis leave Nigeria at the end of the novel, Abani questions "the value of nation and national belonging" (13), instead privileging the "highly mobile, literate, increasingly transnational . . . Igbo traveling identity" that resists the homogenizing strictures of nationalism in favor of "migration, exile, displacement, marginalization" expressed in "the urban centers of postmodern culture" (13). In such readings, cities—as global and transgressive spaces—allow Abani's characters to doff restrictive subjectivities and relations (presumably centered in places like Afikpo) and more productively syncretize their heritage with other cultures in a transcultural, postmodern indeterminacy that allows the free expression of self.

Setting aside for a moment the many reasons to be extremely dubious about such a rosy picture of Elvis's encounter with globalization and urbanization in Lagos (where he experiences abject poverty, gets entangled with crime, is jailed and tortured, and eventually exiled), Abani's whole body of literature does bear out his wariness regarding rigid divisions, especially ethnic and cultural ones. His narratives consistently (if not always directly) suggest the possibility of cities to forge or enable more flexible subjectivities, set against more traditional and divisive identities. In *GraceLand*, older characters like Sunday and the revolutionary leader the King of the Beggars represent problematic attachment to strict Igbo ethnicity that proves inimical to the needs and interests of Elvis and the people of Lagos generally. Frustrated by his loss of status in the new military government, Sunday clings violently to masculinist Igbo beliefs and practices, lashing out at Elvis for wearing makeup and wanting to be a dancer. Worse, he protects his brother from accusations of rape (both of Elvis and his cousin Efua), and he has his misfit nephew killed "because he was a threat to all we had . . . he was killed for honor" (187). For his part, the King does not espouse the same hypermasculinity when appealing to "the beauty of the indigenous culture," but his rhetoric of protest is itself "essentialist, maybe even prejudiced, because the culture he spoke of was that of the Igbo, one of nearly three hundred indigenous peoples in this populous country" (155). Elvis is unconvinced by such thinking, noting that it "didn't account for the inherent complications he knew were native to this culture" and wondering "why the King didn't speak about how to cope with these new and confusing times" (155). By equating resistance to "the evils of capitalism" with a simple and total "return to the traditional values and ways of being" defined in narrowly ethnocentric terms (155), the King excludes the variety and diverse positionalities of the community he claims to represent.

It should be noted, however, that Abani does not relegate Igbo culture to the "hitherto monolithic identities" Eze speaks of; rather, he counters the King and Sunday's rigid understanding of Igbo ethnicity in the depictions of the kola nut ceremony that precede each chapter. In one of the final excerpts regarding the ceremony, he writes,

> For the Igbo, tradition is fluid, growing . . . changing with every occurrence. So, too, the kola ritual has changed. Christian prayers have been added, and Jesus has replaced Obasi as the central deity. But its fluid aspects resist the empiricism that is the Western way . . . The Igbo are not reducible to a system of codes, and of meaning.
>
> (291)

Still, this understanding of Igbo cultural flexibility only lends credence to Nwakanma's assertion that Abani privileges the global, cosmopolitan, urban setting as a place where that dynamism might come to fuller fruition.

In that regard, Abani represents Los Angeles as a place especially amenable to complex identities and cultural crossover. It is the city where the Mexican transsexual Sweet Girl comes to escape her family that "betrayed me . . . because I was different" (*Virgin* 270). Like so many others, Sweet Girl comes to Los Angeles to rebel and find herself in a city where "there is no common mythology. . . . There is just you and what you see and imagine this place and your life in it to be, moment by moment" (206). Here, she finds acceptance and camaraderie with people like Iggy, "a lapsed white Jew from East LA" who has become "a fakir-psychic" with metal rings in her back from which she "suspended her body in midair from meat hooks in order to induce a trance" (30). Iggy owns a café called the Ugly Store, cluttered with "broken toys, voodoo dolls, fetishes from Java, Africa, New Zealand, Australia and Papua New Guinea" (30), as well as "an eight-foot-tall evil-looking statue of Anubis, the Egyptian god of the dead" (29). The Ugly Store occupies a central place in *The Virgin of Flames*, a metonym for the eclectic embrace of the city and a refuge for cultural and sexual in-betweens like Black and Sweet Girl.

Emplaced in the Ugly Store and East LA generally, Black resists his Rwandan friend Bomboy's assertion that "Your father was African, and so therefore, you are African" (195). Instead, he attempts to chart out and negotiate a more complicated and elusive identity as a "shape-shifter . . . taking on different ethnic and national affiliations as though they were seasonal changes in wardrobe" (36). The relative "freedom" of the city and its cosmopolitan ethos empower Black to act out a complex sexuality in his relationship with Sweet Girl and to express himself artistically through public murals painted surreptitiously on the concrete channel of the Los Angeles River. Overall, the "expansiveness" of the city gives him "the feeling that he could become the person he always wanted to be" (53), a person that does not conform with the ethnic classification of Bomboy, the gender demands of his father, or the Catholic strictures of his mother, even as he tries to find ways to incorporate all three. It is perhaps worth noting that Abani himself, writing in London and Los Angeles, finds similar expressive empowerment within these global urban spaces. In exile from Nigeria, he gains "courage and freedom" to delve into issues especially of gender and sexuality otherwise circumscribed within an Igbo or Nigerian context (Ojaide 46). For both Black and Abani, Los Angeles might be seen as the thirdspace of Soja's characterization of that city, opening space for radical difference and empathy over the strictures of essentializing or universalizing identity politics.

From these examples, we can understand and perhaps expand on Eze's characterization of Abani's global urban aesthetic and ethos as a liberating, open, connective space of transgression. The trouble here is that Abani's representation of postmodern mobility and cosmopolitanism are not nearly so directly or simplistically positive. The experiences of these characters reflect a deep ambivalence about the possibilities and sources of transgression, especially given the multiform metrics of power and control that inflect each character's entry into and position within the transgressions of global diaspora. Abani's narratives make clear that the causes and conditions of becoming inculcated into the processes of migration that bring people to these global cities are often far from benign. Paralleling Abani's own political exile from Nigeria, many of these characters lack autonomy over the dynamics of "mobility" that shuttle them to and from these cities and around the world, stemming instead from some measure of forced or coerced displacement. Elvis and his father are pushed from Afrikpo after Sunday loses a corrupt election, leaving him jobless and in debt, and leaving Elvis bewildered: "How did they come to this?" he asks himself. "Just two years ago they lived in a small town and his father had a good job and was on the cusp of winning an election. Now they lived in a slum in Lagos" (*GraceLand* 6). Similarly, Black and his mother are pushed to East LA "After his father didn't come back from Vietnam. After they lost the small house in Pasadena when the bank foreclosed on it" (*Virgin* 50). And though Abigail's father consents to send her to London under the auspices of a better life, he has been deceived by a relative who wants her as part of the sex slave trade. These examples make clear Abani's understanding that while mobility is a key component of both globalization and urbanization (and whatever benefits may arise from them), movement itself is highly subject to "social differentiation" as a process that "both reflects and reinforces power" (Massey 318). As Tim Cresswell points out, theorists and writers have "alternately coded mobility as dysfunctional, as inauthentic and rootless and, more recently as liberating, antifoundational and transgressive" (Cresswell 161). Depending on one's position vis-à-vis the "power geometries" of global flows, mobility may be something chosen or something imposed, making simple evaluations unsatisfactory.

Because the mobility in these texts lacks the clear autonomy and liberatory effect presumed by Eze and Nwakanma, the urban experience in Abani's fiction often involves more struggle and a sense of dislocation in the shifting, disruptive spaces of the global city than they give voice to. Black, Elvis, and others cannot simply revel in the globalized multiculturalism of Lagos and Los Angeles; rather, they often display an anxiety and desire to connect with familial and cultural heritage from which they are cut off in the city. Elvis obsessively carries his dead mother's bible and journal, which includes Igbo recipes, botanical knowledge, and snippets of the kola nut ritual. Black is "obsessed with origins" (*Virgin* 123), confused by and groping after cultural links he can largely only read about after his father's death in Vietnam (205). And Abigail burns names and memories onto her skin in an attempt to inscribe and solidify an identity and a past that are otherwise tenuous and unstable due to her mother's death. In each case, the feeling of disconnection from larger collective identity is exacerbated by their position in a city in which they do not always feel at home. Elvis had been "miserable and unable to fit into school" in Lagos, "where his small-town thinking and accent marked him" (*GraceLand* 8). Abigail, too, feels conspicuous in London, where people "would forgive you anything except a foreign accent" (*Abigail* ch. 14). And Black is desperate "to get out of this town" (206) where "you have no people, without people you have no lineage, without a lineage you have no ancestors, without ancestors you have no dead and without the dead you can never know anything about life" (255). These characters find themselves uprooted in the urban space, in some ways freed from repressive or abusive subjectivities and relations, but also struggling in places where "any idea of a solid past, as an anchor, is soon lost" (*Virgin* 206). In an apt image for the way these characters struggle to ground themselves in the "confusing plurality of cultures" in these world cities, we see Abigail astride the Prime Meridian:

> She stood on the line that cut the earth into two time zones, feet inches apart, marveling at how true to life it all was. That once could be only a step away from another world, another time, and yet caught firmly in one or the other, or in her case, trapped forever between two.

In such instances, being in the cosmopolitan transculturality of the city is of little help in their search for stable collective identity and connection. That all these main characters end up either fleeing or committing suicide seems evidence enough to challenge any simplistically positive view of their experiences in global cities, which clearly engender at least some measure of troubling displacement in their lives.

According to Eze, these "moments of alienation" are in fact "moments of transcendence" (108) in which characters ostensibly make the (perhaps difficult) transition from attachment to "blood" identities to a more cosmopolitan hybridity. Yet one could also argue the mobility and indeterminacy expressed here resembles the postmodern condition as famously articulated by Frederic Jameson: a "hyperspace" that "has finally succeeded in transcending the capacities of the individual body to locate itself, to organize its immediate surroundings perceptually, and cognitively to map its position in a mappable external world" (Jameson 44). Characters like Black, Elvis, and Abigail struggle (and generally fail) to ground themselves in the postmodern deracination of the urban space, casting doubt on the possibilities for transgression alone to be a liberating or resistant force in these novels.

In fact, Jameson's work implies that, beyond failing to simplistically provide a productive sense of resistance to centralized power, the indeterminacies and transgressions of postmodernism (and postcolonialism) may in many ways be the *products* of power, manifested by an imperialism and neoliberalism that operates under a similar logic of deterritorialization, border-crossing, openness, fluidity, and difference. Though Lefebvre argues that "the trend toward fragmentation, separation and disintegration is" is the result of "centralized power" (Lefebvre 9), others have noted a trend toward the dissolution of separations and boundaries as a crucial strategy of power. Though power may "originate in political and economic command centers," it is also "unequally . . . clustered at centers, or dispersed across peripheries," and achieves hegemony "by extending coercion and power over spatial fields" that often extend beyond its self-established boundaries (Peet and Watts xiv). This complex geographic structure of power can and does utilize various, sometimes seemingly contradictory, methods to extend its reach. Speaking specifically about environmental governance and control, Michael Watts, Paul Robbins, and Richard Peet claim that environmental policy has become a sort of "governance through markets" that seeks to mitigate ecological costs not through state regulations but a more "open" and "hybrid" system of financial incentives and self-regulation, coordinated under transnational institutions like the World Bank (Peet et al 7). The result of this "upward" displacement of power is a simultaneous breakdown of state control, which "provides the thin regulatory context for the *smooth operation of global capital*" (Peet and Watts xv, emphasis added). The parallels to the language and metaphors of smooth space here should not be missed or undersold. Where Westphal and others seem to presume transgression and smooth space to be inimical to the strict and repressive structurations of state power, these political ecologists highlight its potential usefulness to an increasingly globalized capitalism that also desires the lessening of state control through freedom of movement, border-crossing flows, and hybridized relations—though now in the service of capital accumulation and exploitation.

Indeed, though Westphal claims that "Globalization assumes the homogeneity of space" (Westphal 41), Arif Dirlik counters that globalization "is not to be confounded with . . . universalization of economic, political, social, and, especially, cultural forms" (Dirlik 27). In large part, this is due to the fact that global capitalism must still "take place" in distinct localities, must still transact its exchanges and accumulations within a varied geography of difference. So,

> the very process of globalization results in a situation where place-based differences, which must be addressed to make globalization possible and feasible, are incorporated into the very process of globalization, abolishing the boundary between the external and internal, bringing differences into the interior of the process of globalization.
>
> (26)

In other words, neoliberal global capitalism itself enacts a form of hybridity as "[t]he corporation, seeking domestication, strives for an abolition of the boundary between corporation and community" (30). The processes of globalization and imperialism are themselves "glocal" phenomena which at once engage the particularities of place and hybridize those differences so they can be mobilized within "free-flowing" and "open" markets that transgress the confines of place and borders. In fact, as David Harvey suggests, the processes of "integration and differentiation" are contradictory yet dialectically related pressures within postmodern capitalism (Harvey 305). He sums up the issue this way:

> The less important the spatial barriers, the greater the sensitivity of capital to the variations of place within space, and the greater the incentive for places to be differentiated in ways attractive to capital. The result has been the production of fragmentation, insecurity, and ephemeral uneven development within a highly unified global space economy of capital flows.
>
> (296)

What I hope to elucidate here is the complicated nature of the "geographical and temporal flexibility of capital accumulation" (194), a flexibility that makes the alignment of transgression and borders with liberation and oppression respectively a tenuous proposition at best. Where postmodernist spatial studies tend to privilege transgression and hybridity as "third space . . . that does not eliminate the other two spaces but enriches and complicates choice," Dirlik poses the question:

> But what if the hybrid were to lead to the extinction of the originals out of which it was produced? . . . Hybridity suggests merely

a proliferation of alternatives, but in real life may also lead to the extinction of alternatives,

as hybridity itself becomes a strategy of power and as the transgressions of imperialist capital lead to new divisions and restrictions (Dirlik 29).

Here, we might turn again to Abani's narratives as a representation of this contradictory dynamic, particularly with regard to the fate of Maroko, the Lagos slum where Elvis finds himself after his father's political displacement from the interior town of Afikpo. The cosmopolitan character of the city praised by Eze and Nwakanma might be attributed largely to a kind of global mobility and cultural exchange as the world and the city become mutually penetrable and penetrating. Yet, to the extent that this exchange is driven primarily by the interests of capital, the hybrid parts of Lagos are clustered around the wealthiest sectors of the city, the segregated beneficiaries of globalization and transnational exchange. This sort of "hybridity," then, marks Lagos as "a site of entrenched social, political, and economic divisions" (Harrison 96), boundaries that both stem from and reproduce the city's uneven engagement with the global relations of material culture.

Indeed, as Elvis discovers, most Lagosians have very little contact with these global luxuries. Just outside the affluent confines of Lagos's wealthy quarters, the underside of the global-urban dynamic sprawls out in informal settlements like Maroko. In this part of the city, Elvis experiences starkly different conditions from those of the cosmopolitan center: much of the shantytown is suspended over a swamp, built on stilts over "green swampy water" teeming with sewage and disease (*GraceLand* 14). Plank roads wind through a sludge of dirt, excrement, offal, and waste "whipped into a muddy brown froth" (6). At best, Elvis wakes to "the smell of garbage from refuse dumps, unflushed toilets and stale bodies" (4); at worst, to rats swimming in his oft-flooded room (32). This, too, is Lagos; this, too, Abani seems to suggest, in the nature of the urban, the "common companion of every city's luminescence—darkness ("Las Vegas" 90). By setting his narratives primarily in places like Maroko, Abani portrays the way globalization and urbanization seem to breed opulence alongside deprivation, inequality alongside access, seriously complicating the sense of liberation and progressive cultural exchange Eze and Nwakanma attribute to these phenomena and suggesting the way certain forms of transgressive smoothing might make way for new striations and divisions.

In many ways, the de- and reterritorialization of Lagos/Maroko reenact the processes of colonialism that shaped the peculiar ways the region was brought into globalized urbanity in the first place. To further their economic and administrative interests, imperial powers tended to reterritorialize colonies around cities, capitals, and ports, especially for the purposes of raw material export. The development of cities like Lagos represents a "commercial notion" left over after independence (Fanon 187), disproportionately drawing people and resources from the rest of the country and funneling them to Western markets (Imoagene 60). After independence, the new era of neoliberalism "has left little or no place for Africa outside of its old colonial role as a provider of raw materials" (Ferguson 8), a role prone to creating inequality and corruption within a nation. Clashing with Eze's vision of globalization as a process helping people like Elvis "link up with the larger world" culturally, James Ferguson argues it is more divisive than connective economically: through Nigeria's petro economy, Lagos "is indeed 'globally connected,' but such 'global' links connect in a selective, discontinuous, and point-to-point fashion" that "leaves most Africans with only a tenuous and indirect connection to 'the global economy'" (Ferguson 14). Abani echoes this notion of disconnection in an evocative metaphor for the city: "If Lagos is a body, and the oil pipelines crisscrossing it are veins, then the inhabitants are vampires" ("Lagos" 4). Cut off from access to the national oil (and oil profits) flowing through their own city, poor Lagosians tap the lines and steal oil, for which the "body" treats them like a "virus" or "parasites," violently killed off by the thousands each year (4).

It is this dynamic that primarily accounts for the huge disparities in Lagos, as export dollars are concentrated in the hands of a very few to the exclusion of the national and urban poor, all enabled by neoliberal emphasis on "free markets." Elvis remembers reading an editorial boasting that Nigeria had one of the highest percentages of millionaires in the world, but that neglected to mention that "their wealth had been made over the years with the help of crooked politicians, criminal soldiers, bent contractors, and greedy oil-company executives," an economic exploitation that also led to Nigeria having "a higher percentage of poor people than nearly any other country in the world" (*GraceLand* 8). The neocolonial system allows Nigeria's government and urban elites to horde the nation's wealth for themselves, "in no way [allowing the people] to enjoy any of the dues that are paid to it by the big foreign companies" (Fanon 165). In trying to help Elvis better understand the mechanisms of injustice behind Lagos and Nigeria's dichotomous conditions, the King of the Beggars tells him, "Someone does not become a beggar; we are made beggars" (31), in part by the globalization that pairs highly selective development and connection with "widespread disconnection and exclusion" (Ferguson 14).

That is not to say that the people of Maroko are entirely cut off from the exchanges of globalization in the urban sphere—for better or worse, even the most degraded and deprived areas of the city are awash in the trappings of American culture, as people throughout Nigeria are made consumers of Western products. Hardly an engagement with benign cosmopolitanism, we see the way these products exacerbate the marginalized economic position of many Lagosians within the structures of globalization. For instance, the movies Elvis enjoys as a child are shown free, "courtesy of an American tobacco company, which passed out packets of free cigarettes to everybody in the audience, irrespective of age" (*GraceLand* 146). Elvis proceeds to smoke throughout the novel, spending what little money he has on American cigarettes. We might also consider the (lack of) food pervasive in the narrative. The recipes from his mother's journal that preface each chapter constantly remind readers of indigenous foods and Igbo knowledge regarding the place and environment; yet these foods and practices are absent in Elvis's "transcultural" city life. Instead, Elvis fills his belly with Coke, Bazooka gum, and so on.

Elvis's lack of access to Nigerian food mirrors the situation in the country generally, according to Bolanle Awe, where Nigeria was encouraged to grow cash crops for export in lieu of food and "to become a consumer nation importing chocolate and beverages," even to the point of needing to import staples like "rice and sugar, which were obtainable at prices cheaper than that of traditional crops produced locally" (Awe 9, 11). Through processes of disruption and substitution in global markets, the poor of Nigeria are made beggars *for* the products and relations they are disadvantaged *by* in the first place. Abani uses commodities throughout *GraceLand* as evidence of the uneven and exploitative potential in globalization, especially as it pertains to Africa, where the exchange is as often empty and disillusioning as it is gratifying and world-expanding. Thus, we see Elvis at one point in the novel desperately "seeking words of wisdom" from Bazooka gum wrappers, only to find meaningless, culturally irrelevant platitudes like "A stitch in time saves nine" (240), signifying an utter lack of benefit from Western commodity culture. By the end of the novel, readers are fully disabused of faith in global exchange to redeem Nigeria's poor with Marlboros or rock and roll.

From this understanding of globalization as a process proliferating inequalities, Abani represents urbanization also as a process made unequal through its transnational relations. Pushed from rural areas to urban centers by an export economy focused on plantation cash cropping and an oil boom, thousands yearly join what Fanon calls "the incoherent rush towards the cities" (157), drawn by the appearance of opportunity. Most, like Elvis, "hadn't known about the poverty and violence of Lagos" until they arrive (*GraceLand* 7), and like Sunday, they find no quality work in the city. The economically displaced become marginalized once more, pushed out of the formal urban center and made refugees of a sort in the informal periphery. Settlements like Maroko spring up to absorb the influx, hastily constructed on undesirable land, lacking services, drainage, and sewage. The global economy and state policies work in tandem "to produce informality" of this kind (Myers 73), an uneven urbanization that concentrates wealth in some areas while it simultaneously "denies people jobs in their home areas and denies them homes in the areas they have gone to get jobs" (Neuwirth 12). Echoing the King's sentiment that people are "made beggars," Garth Myers insists that the presence of informal settlements like Maroko does not reflect the intentions of its inhabitants to circumvent formal rules, spaces, and economies; instead, "the system threw them down and out to a place where that is their only choice" (Myers 82). Through his education by the King, Elvis comes to understand the selective, uneven, exploitative, and often corrupt character of the global economy in Nigeria as the answer to the riddle of Lagos's schizophrenic geography of opulence and degradation. Not only do people suffer from the wrongdoing of "dose army bastards" running the state, the King tells him, but also from "dose tiefs in the IMF, de World Bank, and de U.S." (280) pushing free-market policies that enable "the smooth operation of global capital" to exploit resources without the limitations of state intervention.

The deep irony of *GraceLand*, however, is that once the operations of imperialism and capitalist power have "smoothed" the precolonial structures and relations to make space for their own interests, once places like Lagos/Maroko have subsequently been "striated" with inequalities and divisions, the process begins again under the mantle of "development." Labeling Maroko an unsavory, unproductive place, Nigerian authorities declare "Operation Clean de Nation," framed as an "attack on de centers of poverty and crime" and an attempt to remove "a pus-ridden eyesore on de face of de nation's capital" (247). But as with most everything else in *GraceLand*, the costs and consequences of "improvement" are differentially distributed, primarily benefitting the already wealthy. Elvis's friend Redemption hints at the interests of the state and urban elites fueling the demolition when he points out the closeness of the wealthy to Maroko: "though dey hate us," he says, "de rich still have to look at us" (*GraceLand* 137). This uncomfortable proximity provides plenty of motivation to be rid of the slum, as the state employs a battery of discursive attacks on Maroko in order to legitimate its destruction. Following Nigeria's history of shunning rehabilitation in favor of "outright demolition, after forced eviction and forced population relocation" (Agbola 271), Maroko is bulldozed and its inhabitants dispersed to other slums, creating space for a "beachside millionaire's paradise" (*GraceLand* 248). The former residents are worse off for their "mobility," having lost what housing, jobs, resources, and communal support they had managed to develop there, and instead evicted to even worse areas.

The fate of Maroko (and all too many places like it) can be cast as part of capitalism's own "transgressivity": as the built environment of striated space becomes a hindrance to capital flows, there is a constant need to deterritorialize the divisions of its own making in order to "colonize space for the affluent" (Harvey, qtd. in *Seeking Spatial Justice* 95) by dispossessing the poor, undoing the boundaries of their emplacement, and propelling them into a forced migration. Given the experience of

Elvis and the people of Maroko, the notions of movement and nomad-ism in Westphal's geocriticism take on a markedly different tenor. Where he argues "postcolonial space is certainly nomadic," we might be hard-pressed to disagree; yet when he claims its nomadic character stems from "constant deterritorialization and reterritorialization according to a logic that is not neocolonial, or at least that should not be" (Westphal 54), it begs the question of what ensures that it is "not neocolonial." Transgres-sivity itself, I would argue, provides no such assurance.

Informed by Abani's narratives, we would be better off understand-ing the forces of territorialization and deterritorialization, movement and fixity, transgression and boundary-making not as strictly oppositional, but as complementary sides of the same spatial coin, which might be put to service by the forces of power or of resistance, or both. By the same token, then, established borders and a more concrete and stable sense of emplacement need not be relegated to the purview of domination. Though certain spatial "striation" may be erected as "a means of con-trol, and hence of domination, of power," Lefebvre tells us, it necessarily "escapes in part from those who would make use of it" (Lefebvre 26) and opens opportunities for that bounded space to not simply be exploded or eroded, but transformed or appropriated.

Perhaps no geospatial formation provides a more appropriate example than the nation-state itself, which has garnered enormous attention in postcolonialism. Much of that theoretical attention has been critical of the nation, especially in postcolonial contexts, as a homogenizing force imposed on heterogeneous peoples, both arbitrary and abstract in ways that repress the multiple and dynamic realities of a hybrid world. Predict-ably, the postmodern response echoes Westphal's nomadic transgression, calling for "the progressive dissolution of the nation, with its colonial and neocolonial legacies, regarding the very idea of the state as oppres-sive" (Lovesey 156) and instead enabling the freer play of borderlands identities and relations. Yet Laura Chrisman suggests that, in the context of exploitation by transnational corporations and financial institutions like the World Bank, the disbanding of the nation creates "a crisis of political authority" in these places that ultimately works "to block the realization of liberatory, socialist nationalism" (Chrisman 196). This seems to be the case in Ngũgĩ's *Wizard of the Crow*, where the fictional nation of Aburĩria suffers incredible deprivations at the hands of both a dictatorial Ruler and the Global Bank, which produces "all the laws and regulations governing the economic and monetary policies of the nations of the earth" (Ngũgĩ 503).

For most of the novel, the nation-state figures as the instrument of the Ruler's dictatorship; he usurps its sovereignty by claiming no distinction between himself and the country (Ngũgĩ 136) and uses the police, the army, and the government to serve his own selfish ends at the expense of the people. He also adopts the discourse of nationalism to insulate himself from foreign intervention or calls for democratic reform. As an independent nation, he claims,

> we cannot allow ourselves to take orders from the West all the time. . . . I want to remind you that we are in Africa, and we, too, have our *African forms of governance*. The democracy that is suitable for America and Europe is not necessarily suitable for Africa.
>
> (583)

Instead of "Western" democracy, he imposes a nativist ideology, equating nationalism with the "march backward to the roots of an authentic unchanging past" (622) and claiming that "the real threat to Aburīria's future lay in people's abandoning their traditions" like polygamy, wife beating, and "unquestioning obedience" (621–22). Here, nationalism and the nation-state act as the very sort of striated control bemoaned by Westphal and others, enabling the Ruler's tyranny and defending it from external political pressures. The world media in particular is a "pest" for the Ruler (611), checking his open abuses of the population and spurring "questions about the missing minister" Machokali, whom the Ruler has had killed (612).

At the same time, the "new global order" of media transparency and democratization carries its own threats to the people of Aburīria. As the US envoy from the Global Bank explains,

> the history of capitalism can be summed up in one phrase: *in search of freedom*. Freedom to expand, and now it has a chance at the entire globe for its theatre. It needs a democratic space to move as its own logic demands.
>
> (Ngũgĩ 580)

The pressure for Aburīria to reform, then, stems not from concern for the people themselves, but for "a free and stable world where our money can move across borders without barriers erected by the misguided nationalism of the outmoded nation-state" (580). The dissolution and privatization of the nation-state equates to a form of "corporonialism" (760), in which the resources of the nation are "freed" for exploitation by transnational corporations and "the neoimperial class imports en masse the cheapest [goods] from abroad and undermines the efforts from within" (760).

Against the machinations of neoliberalism, the nation reemerges as an instrument of the Movement for the Voice of the People, a claim to "political and economic sovereignty over a finite landmass" that allows them to counter the exploitative claims of global capital (Chrisman 187). The Movement's main goal is "to imagine a different future for Aburīria after people united take power from these ogres" (Ngũgĩ 758). Unlike the Ruler's egomaniacal and nativist nationalism, however, this "New Aburĩria" is premised on "a coalition of interests all united by one desire to recover their voice in running the affairs of the land" (676). The goals and strategies of the Movement at times fit with a sort of transgressive push toward smoothing out some of the exploitative and oppressive constrictions of the Ruler's tyranny, but they are equally engaged in establishing unified bulwarks against the disruptive transgressions of the Global Bank. Here Ngũgĩ seems engaged in an effort to "reinvent the nation-state radically to serve the needs of its own people" (Chrisman 184), one that can wield its sovereignty "to protect laws for social justice" (Ngũgĩ 759) based on the specific interests and conditions of the nation.

Measured against that effort to appropriate the authority of the nation to ground a unifying resistance to the large-scale disruptions and manipulations of global capital, the contention that for postcolonial minorities "instability is the distinctive feature of a unity formerly taken for granted" becomes less useful, if not troubling (Westphal 45). To the extent that such instability prevents the creation of new unities (linked together by an alternative set of boundaries and sense of emplacement), it may well serve alongside precisely the kind of divisiveness and fragmentation presumed to be the work of repressive striation, resulting in a *de facto* dissolution of resistance itself. According to Dirlik,

> Contrary to the logic of theory, which calls for the erasure of boundaries, the inequality of power calls in practice for the delineation of those same boundaries, for without them, spaces must invade places, and an 'off-ground' economy must put an end to the groundedness of everyday life.
>
> (Dirlik 30)

Faced with "a geography of power to which places are . . . inconveniences" (30), bounded place itself may well at times provide the most productive forms of resistance. A trenchant postmodernism that uncritically privileges the transgression of such boundaries, then, may well serve as "an efficient way, under the circumstances, to defuse . . . claims to alternative possibilities" (Dirlik 40).

The critique offered here should not be taken for an outright rejection of transgressivity or its attendant motifs of mobility, heterogeneity, indeterminacy, and so on. Nor am I arguing that we replace the postmodernist understandings with a privileging of bounded place or the erasure of difference. I am urging instead that spatial literary studies take another lesson from postcolonialism—the necessity to account for the particular conditions and histories that variously shape the relations between space and place, rather than relying on dichotomous categories with preset evaluations. Abani and Ngũgĩ's narratives provide an embodiment of Dirlik's assertion, "The question then is not the confrontation of the global and the local, but of different configurations of 'glocality'" that serve different interests (Dirlik 29); we could easily substitute *smooth* and *striated* or *transgression* and *boundaries* for global and local and arrive at a fair summation of the argument I am after here. Drawing from Abani and Ngũgĩ's refusal to simply privilege or disregard either the forces of boundedness or openness, geocriticism should develop methods to examine with more nuance the multivalent relations between these spatial forms and more critically evaluate their dynamic potential for domination or resistance.

Works Cited

Abani, Chris. *GraceLand*. New York: Picador, 2004. Print.
———. *Becoming Abigail*. New York: Akashic Books, 2006. Kindle file.
———. *The Virgin of Flames*. New York: Penguin Books, 2007. Kindle file.
———. "Lagos: A Pilgrimage in Notations." *African Cities Reader* 1 (2008/9): 1–8. Web. 19 September 2012.
———. "Las Vegas: The Last African City." *African Cities Reader* II (2011): 89–91. Web. 19 September 2012.
Agbola, Tunde and A. M. Jinadu. "Forced Eviction and Forced Relocation in Nigeria: The Experiences of Those Evicted From Maroko in 1990." *Environment and Urbanization* 9.2 (October 1997): 271–88. *JSTOR*. Web. 23 April 2008.
Awe, Bolanle. "Conflict and Divergence: Government and Society in Nigeria." *African Studies Review* 42.3 (December 1999): 1–20. *JSTOR*. Web. 23 April 2008.
Chrisman, Laura. "Nationalism and Postcolonial Studies." *The Cambridge Companion to Postcolonial Literary Studies*, edited by Neil Lazarus. New York: Cambridge UP, 2004: 183–98. Print.
Cresswell, Tim. "Towards a Politics of Mobility." *African Cities Reader* II (2011): 159–71. Web. 19 September 2012.
Dirlik, Arif. "Place-Based Imagination: Globalism and the Politics of Place." *Places and Politics in an Age of Globalization*, edited by Roxann Prazniak and Arif Dirlik. New York: Rowman and Littlefield Publishers, Inc, 2001: 15–51.
Eze, Chielozona. "Cosmopolitan Solidarity: Negotiating Transculturality in Contemporary Nigerian Novels." *English in Africa* 32.1 (May 2005): 99–112. *JSTOR*. Web. 3 January 2013.
Fanon, Frantz. *The Wretched of the Earth*. New York: Grove Press, 1963.
Ferguson, James. *Global Shadows: Africa in the Neoliberal World Order*. Durham, NC: Duke UP, 2006. Print.
Foucault, Michel. "Of Other Spaces." *MIT.edu*. Massachusetts Institute of Technology, n.d. Web. 2 February 2014.
Harrison, Sarah. "'Suspended City': Personal, Urban, and National Development in Chris Abani's *Graceland*." *Research in African Literatures* 43.2 (Summer 2012): 95–114. *Expanded Academic ASAP*. Web. 3 January 2013.
Harvey, David. *The Condition of Postmodernity: An Enquiry into the Origins of Cultural Change*. New York: Blackwell, 1989. Print.

Imoagene, Onoso. "Migrating Into Unemployment and Poverty: Some Consequences of the Urban Revolution in Nigeria." *Africa Development* 3.1 (January–March 1978): 51–64. *JSOTR*. Web. 3 March 2008.

Jameson, Frederic. *Postmodernism, or, The Cultural Logic of Late Capitalism.* Durham, NC: Duke UP, 1991. Print.

Lefebvre, Henri. *The Production of Space.* Cambridge: Blackwell, 1991. Print.

Lovesey, Oliver. "Ngugi wa Thiong'o's Postnation: The Cultural Geographies of Colonial, Neocolonial, and Postcolonial Space." *Modern Fiction Studies* 48.1 (Spring 2002): 139–68. *Expanded Academic ASAP.* The University of Kansa Libraries, Lawrence KS. 23 November 2009. www.galegroup.com.

Massey, Doreen. "A Global Sense of Place." *Reading Human Geography*, edited by Trevor Barnes and Derek Gregory. New York: Arnold, 1997: 315–23. Print.

Myers, Garth. *African Cities: Alternative Vision of Urban Theory and Practice.* New York: Zed Books, 2011. Print.

Neuwirth, Robert. *Shadow Cities: A Billion Squatters, a New Urban World.* New York: Routledge, 2004. Print.

Ngũgĩ wa Thiong'o. *Wizard of the Crow.* New York: Pantheon Books, 2006. Print.

Nwakanma, Obi. "Metonymic Eruptions: Igbo Novelists, the Narrative of the Nation, and New Developments in the Contemporary Nigerian Novel." *Research in African Literatures* 39.2 (Summer 2008): 1–14. *JSTOR.* Web. 3 January 2013.

Ojaide, Tenure. "Migration, Globalization, and Recent African Literature." *World Literature Today* 82.2 (March–April 2008): 43–46. *JSTOR.* Web. 3 January 2013.

Peet, Richard, Paul Robbins, and Michael Watts, eds. *Global Political Ecology.* New York: Routledge, 2011. Print.

Peet, Richard and Michael Watts, eds. *Liberation Ecologies: Environment, Development, Social Movements.* New York: Routledge, 2004. Print.

Prieto, Eric. "Geocriticism Meets Ecocriticism: Bertrand Westphal and Environmental Thinking." *Épistémocritique: Littérature et Savoirs* IX (Autumn 2011). Web. 12 February 2014.

Soja, Edward. *Thirdspace: Journeys to Los Angeles and Other Real-and-Imagines Places.* Cambridge: Blackwell, 1996. Print.

———. *Seeking Spatial Justice.* Minneapolis, MN: U of Minnesota P, 2010. Print.

Tally, Robert T., ed. *Geocritical Explorations: Space, Place, and Mapping in Literary and Cultural Studies.* New York: Palgrave Macmillan, 2011. Print.

Westphal, Bertrand. *Geocriticism: Real and Fictional Spaces.* New York: Palgrave Macmillan, 2011. Print.

Part IV
The Problematics of Place

14 "Oh, man, I'm nowhere"

Ralph Ellison and the Psychospatial Terrain of Mid-Century Harlem

Walter Bosse

In 1946, the Lafargue Psychiatric Clinic opened in Harlem. Staffed by both black and white volunteers, the clinic was headed by Doctors Hilde Mosse and Frederic Wertham, socially motivated practitioners committed to providing psychotherapy to the underprivileged, regardless of race. The first integrated institution of its kind, the clinic's mission derived from the emergent field of practical social psychiatry; Wertham and Mosse saw in the slum-like conditions of post-war Harlem an urban space especially antagonistic to the psychological health of the city's residents (Doyle 752).[1] Upon its opening, left-leaning thinkers based in New York City championed the clinic's cause. Among them was Ralph Ellison, who in 1948 wrote a profoundly significant piece detailing Lafargue's mission in Harlem, its service to the city's residents, and its impact on the broader cultural milieu. Ellison titled his essay "Harlem Is Nowhere."[2]

In his recent and comprehensive biography on Ellison, Arnold Rampersad suggests that "Harlem Is Nowhere"—though unpublished until its inclusion in *Shadow and Act* (1964)—served a very practical purpose for Ellison's craft. Specifically, the essay allowed him to explore and develop ideas, themes, and motifs that he would return to in his most famous novel, *Invisible Man* (1952). Rampersad claims that "[n]o single task honed more sharply Ralph's ability to depict Invisible's experience in Harlem and New York City" (219). To be sure, there are palpable aesthetic traces of the essay within *Invisible Man*, and many of these traces can be observed in the novel's probing portrayal of the urban scene. Like the essay, the novel explores the cracks and crevices of Harlem, and its exposure of the city's literal and figurative underworlds constitutes a major component of Ellison's commentary on race. In what follows, however, I proceed from my contention that "Harlem Is Nowhere" deserves exclusive critical attention because it voices radical sociopolitical arguments in its own right. In other words, the essay has significance beyond its utility as a warm up for *Invisible Man*.

I argue that "Harlem Is Nowhere" deploys a radical theorization of space, and engages a politics of resistance that identifies and pushes against the constraints of urban black modernity. Navigating the subterranean halls of the Lafargue clinic, Ellison leads us through "the only center in the city wherein both Negroes and whites may receive extended psychiatric care" (295). He thus situates racial politics within a specific institution, where he writes in the manner of an ethnographer. Inside Lafargue, Ellison identifies that the phrase "I'm nowhere" was common amongst the patients. Offered as a response to the cordial question "How are you?", the phrase attempts to represent an overdetermined agency. The individual interprets a question of condition as a matter of *place*. The respondent actively reroutes an ontological query into the realms of geography and phenomenology: "How are you?"/"Oh, man, I'm nowhere" (297). In spite of the crushing desperation that the utterance appears to convey, it is nonetheless possible to see redemptive value in the words by viewing "nowhere" as a matter of strategic positionality. By claiming "nowhere" as a category of lived experience, the Harlemites circumvent the center/periphery binary that perpetuates social marginality. In doing so, they construct an alternative space filled with potential, and demonstrate "how fragmentation, ruptures, deviation, displacements, and discontinuities can be politically transformed from liability and weakness to a potential source of opportunity and strength" (Soja 117). In Ellison's study of Harlem and Lafargue, the concept of being "nowhere" provides a new way of articulating displacement as a central moment in the history of the black Atlantic.

In many ways, the intellectual trajectory of "Harlem Is Nowhere" follows a logic familiar to specific threads within the fabric of postcolonial thought. Ellison illustrates a heightened awareness of geopolitics, he provides institutional contexts when discussing racial identity, and he ultimately critiques a national "democracy" that upholds segregation. All of this works toward an understanding of social marginality which is in tune with the likes of Frantz Fanon, Edward Said, and Homi Bhabha, among others.

Ellison's ethnographic work employs a spatial analysis to access the otherwise impenetrable universe of the ghetto, and the essay strives to empower those who inhabit that space. In "Harlem Is Nowhere," Ellison writes about institutional and geographical spaces in a way that unveils the power structures and sociopolitical contradictions that exist at their core. He explores the enunciation "I'm nowhere" as an expression that strategically circumvents the structures constraining urban black subjects. In this way, "Harlem Is Nowhere" identifies that an alternative and potentially revolutionary space might exist within the margins, and Ellison situates this potential for resistance squarely within the black vernacular.

Spaces of Contradiction

Drawing heavily on the work of Henri Lefebvre, Edward Soja establishes the ideological implications of physical and conceptual space: "Power is ontologically embedded in the center-periphery relation" (31). For Soja, "power—and the specifically cultural politics that arise from its work-ings—is contextualized and made concrete, like all social relations, in the (social) production of (social) space" (87). Such spatial constructions of power can oppress or enable, can sustain the political status quo or generate the possibility for resistance and emancipatory change. Indeed, "Harlem Is Nowhere" illustrates Ellison's prescient awareness of the complex constitution of power in its spatial forms. Much earlier than 1948, Harlem had achieved a fame that had transformed the locale into a highly racialized space; Harlem constituted both a material and a concep-tual center that concentrated the phenomenal reality of black America in the twentieth century. The popular imagination conceived of Harlem as an urban locale marked by blackness. In a sense, the place had been con-flated with a race. Thus, when Ellison claims that "Harlem Is Nowhere" in his title, he also suggests that there is a crisis in locating blackness in the US. Of course, this also points to the longer history of displacement that he writes about in the pages that follow. The seemingly cryptic title is thus highly strategic, in that it allows Ellison to lay bare the lived experi-ence of the city's ghettoization, and at the same time recognize concrete potential in its marginality, its "nowhere"-ness.

As critics and historians have noted time and time again, early twentieth-century Harlem was a magnet for the socially, geographically, and politically displaced. From 1920 to 1930, its population increased from 84,000 to more than 200,000, becoming—as one historian puts it—"the biggest black city in the world" (Gill 282). To be sure, Harlem was not the only metropolis to experience such an influx. Chicago, Detroit, Los Angeles, and many other locations sustained huge numbers as well; such numbers facilitated local "renaissances" in these other places, though the near-mythical stature of Harlem has tended to eclipse them. Of course, the uptick in cultural and artistic innovation was only one consequence of the unprecedented surge in numbers. Crime, violence, poverty, and all manner of social exploitations proceeded from the mounting urban con-gestion. The economic, political, and racial histories specific to Harlem are incredibly complex, as evidenced by the veritable and multidiscipli-nary industry of scholarship that continues to unpack the city's cultural baggage. In "Harlem Is Nowhere," Ellison, too, wrestles with this com-plexity. In just a few pages, he telescopes into view the long histories and aftermaths of the Great Migration, Great Depression, and Second World War, and he localizes his study to show the African-American Mecca as addled by racism, riots, poor health, and addiction (Gill 334).[3]

Focusing its racial and cultural analysis in the basement spaces of the Lafargue Clinic, "Harlem Is Nowhere" achieves a depth that accom-plishes far more than journalistic reportage on the city's state of affairs. As its later rejection by *Harper's* suggests, which "thought it too impres-sionistic," the essay observes a stylistic and philosophical complexity that may have seemed overwrought to the editors there (Rampersad 222). Lawrence Jackson rightly points out that "Ellison thought of black life as a maze," and the essay develops this Kafkaesque metaphor to describe the physical and psychological constitution of the city in the late 1940s (373).

The reader gets a sense of this from the start, as Ellison invokes the mythical descent of Orpheus or perhaps Dante, guiding his readers below St. Philip's Protestant Episcopal Church on 215 West 133rd Street, the home of the Lafargue Clinic (Doyle 752). Ellison describes the process of entry: "One must descend to the basement and move along a confusing mazelike hall to reach it. Twice the passage seems to lead against a blank wall; then at last one enters the brightly lighted auditorium" (294). In Ellison's estimation, accessing the clinic is not for the faint of heart. The entryways are "confusing" and labyrinthine, illusory dead ends distort one's navigation, and the stark differentials in light further disorient the traveler. Yet Ellison carefully works with contrasts from the onset of the essay, as he counterbalances the oppressive, institutional ambience with the "friendly smiles and low-pitched voices of the expert workers" (294). He proceeds to describe the clinic as "one of Harlem's most important institutions" (295). Ellison touts its value as a clinic that advocates for mental health, and he champions its sociopolitical mission as a racially integrated facility. He calls it "an underground extension of democracy" (295).

Ellison thus begins by establishing Lafargue as a unique space within Harlem and, by extension, within the larger context of the US. Indeed, he uses this initial discussion of the racially integrated clinic as a kind of spatial counterpoint to the surrounding geopolitical landscapes. As "an underground extension of democracy," the interracial space of Lafargue allows Ellison to leverage his primary argument that institutional segregation perpetuates a pervasive racism that in turn compromises the psychology of all black Americans. In short, a national "democracy" that adheres to segregation is no democracy at all. The essay illustrates that this glaring political contradiction had wrought untold injury upon the mental constitution of African Americans, who experienced "perpetual alienation in the land of [their] birth":

> Hence the most surreal fantasies are acted out upon the streets of Harlem; a man ducks in and out of traffic shouting and throwing imaginary grenades that actually exploded during World War I; a boy participates in the rape-robbery of his mother; a man beating his wife in a park uses boxing 'science' and observes Marquess of Queensberry rules (no rabbit punching, no blows beneath the belt).
> (Ellison 296–97)

This observational montage of insane and obscene acts intends to characterize Harlem's day-to-day activity in the late 1940s. The residents' chaotic, irrational, and illegal behavior plays out on the city's streets in broad daylight, and Ellison explicitly faults the prevailing political contradiction by which the State professes democracy while at the same time sustaining inequality: "Not quite citizens and yet Americans, full of the tensions of modern man but regarded as primitives, Negro Americans are in desperate search for identity" (297). He sets up the initial relation between the clinic and Harlem-at-large to explore the ideological dimensions of space, showing the conflicted psychology of the urban black subject to be a direct upshot of his physical surroundings and the power relations inscribed there.

Thus, the discrete and subterranean space of the Lafargue clinic can be seen in Ellison's essay to constitute what Soja calls a "real-and-imagined place" (11). In Ellison's description of it, the clinic proactively redresses the racial dualism between white and black, as well as the homologous spatial dualism between center and periphery, "but extends well beyond them in scope, substance, and meaning" (Soja 11). The Lafargue ethos not only imagines but also puts into practice a sociopolitical paradigm that overcomes the rigid and politicized dichotomies that hold sway outside its walls.

Critic Shelly Eversley discusses Ellison's use of contradiction within his aesthetic project, which is exemplified in the previously quoted passage when he describes African Americans as *both* non-citizens *and* Americans, *both* modern *and* "regarded as primitive" (Ellison 297). Eversley links his vision to that of Richard Wright, and suggests that their work actively performs according to specific poststructuralist priorities:

> Their epistemology engages contradiction and posits the interplay of terms deemed mutually exclusive: black and white, the universal and the particular, public and private, the political and the aesthetic. Their perspective . . . amounts to an assault on the cultural status quo. . . [A]s black men and as intellectuals, Ellison and Wright relish contradiction.
>
> (455)

Concerned with the psychosocial character of the city space, Ellison considers contradiction as a defining feature of its residents, who occupy a liminal position between "urban slum conditions and folk sensibilities":

> Historically, American Negroes are caught in a vast process of change that has swept them from slavery to the condition of industrial man in the space of time so telescoped (a bare eighty-five years) that it is possible literally for them to step from feudalism into the vortex of industrialism simply by moving across the Mason-Dixon line.
>
> (296)

This concise description quickly concentrates deeply complex histori-cal phenomena. Ellison stylistically condenses industrial developments and the subsequent migrations of human beings so as to convey the unprecedented forces—both temporal and geographical—that impact black consciousness. He goes on to explain the consequences of such an abrupt transition, maintaining that "the resulting clash of cultures within Negro personality account for some of the extreme contrasts found in Harlem, for *both* its negative *and* positive characteristics" (296, empha-sis added). Again, building from conflict and contradiction, Ellison here exposes the instability of binary divisions, and opts instead for a "both/and" approach to cultural identity and analysis. It is within this approach that the social margins begin to exhibit their potential. As Ellison phrases it, "if Harlem is the scene of the folk-Negro's death agony, it is *also* the setting of his transcendence" (296, emphasis added). In this formulation, we can see "the 'also' reverberating back to disrupt the categorical clo-sures implicit in the either/or logic" (Soja 7); Ellison thus intervenes in the binary structure and opens it up to new possibilities.

Indeed, Ellison does describe qualitative differences between the cul-tures of the rural South and the labyrinth of the urban ghetto. However, in doing so, he collapses the two terms into each other in order to expose the instability of a modern/primitive dichotomy. Metropolitan cultural activity plays side by side with human remnants from a distant southern geography:

> Here it is possible for talented youths to leap through the develop-ment of decades in a brief twenty years, while beside them white-haired adults crawl in the feudal darkness of their childhood. Here a former cotton picker develops the sensitive hands of a surgeon, and men whose grandparents still believe in magic prepare optimistically to become atomic scientists. Here the grandchildren of those who possessed no written literature examine their lives through the eyes of Freud and Marx, Kierkegaard and Kafka, Malraux and Sartre.
> (296–97)

Within Ellison's treatise on the urban sphere of Harlem, the represen-tational space of the South emerges and imparts the sense that multiple alternative geographies and temporalities can exist simultaneously. This idea complicates the terms of national "progress." As such, it is crucial to Ellison's critique of inequality and segregation. Because multiple con-tiguous temporalities give the lie to a unified, linear movement through time, the metanarrative of "progress"—and the concept of "the mod-ern" which derives from it—undergoes a reconstruction: "It explains the nature of a world so fluid and shifting that often within the mind *the real and the unreal merge*, and the marvelous beckons from behind the same sordid reality that denies its existence" (Ellison 297, emphasis added).

Modernist scholar Leigh Anne Duck clarifies how the spatial proximity of different temporal frameworks impacted the national psychology in the years leading up to Ellison's artistic emergence: "The idea that people living in contiguous space might inhabit different times emerged also from developments in psychological theory, which had become particularly interested in the temporal displacements of the individual mind" (152). Because he recognizes that black consciousness in Harlem is predicated on conflict and contradiction—indeed, he describes it as a kind of geographical schizophrenia—Ellison must move beyond the modern/primitive, center/periphery dichotomies to approximate a viable subjectivity within the urban condition. He accomplishes this by turning to the unique linguistic reservoir of Harlem's black vernacular.

Nowhere Man: Enunciating an Alternative Space

Ellison sees the black residents of Harlem as existing under a contradictory political system. The irresolvable tension between a democratic ethos and sustained racial inequalities produce internal, psychic disruptions within America's marginalized subjects. However, in perhaps the essay's most powerful moment, Ellison sounds a redemptive note. He gives a voice to the city's residents, and he shows how a particular turn of phrase not only resists conditions of oppression, but also creates a new domain that exists beyond the hierarchical dialectics of centers and margins. He writes,

> Rejecting the second-class status assigned them, [the Harlemites] feel alienated and their whole lives have become a search for answers to the questions: Who am I, What am I, Why am I, and Where? Significantly, in Harlem, the reply to the greeting, "How are you?" is very often, "Oh, man, I'm *nowhere*"—a phrase revealing an attitude so common that it has been reduced to a gesture, a seemingly trivial word. Negroes are not unaware that the conditions of their lives demand new definitions of terms like *primitive* and *modern, ethical* and *unethical, moral* and *immoral, patriotism* and *treason, tragedy* and *comedy, sanity* and *insanity.*
>
> (297–98, emphases in original)

Clearly, this catalogue of opposites illustrates the need for a new epistemology—an alternative, third term that circumvents the divisive and alienating constraints of an "either/or" categorical imperative. The condition of *being nowhere* in Harlem provides the impetus for just such a rearrangement of the center/periphery spatial dichotomy. Indeed, "the conditions of their lives *demand* new definitions of terms," and with such a demand comes opportunity. Since he identifies that the phrase was commonly used, "nowhere" in Ellison's essay thus functions as a rhetorical "space of collective resistance" (Soja 35). The utterance carves out new territory and makes a claim to what Soja calls

> a *Thirdspace of political choice* that is also a meeting place for all peripheralized or marginalized "subjects" wherever they may be located. In this politically charged space, a radically new and different form of *citizenship* (*citoyenneté*) can be defined and realized.
>
> (35, emphases in original)

Of course, it should be acknowledged that the phrase "I'm nowhere" is, on the surface, far from an outspoken and explicit cry for sociopolitical resistance. In fact, it sounds remarkably like a blues lyric. However, as Houston Baker has shown, the blues "represents a *force* not unlike electricity" (6, emphasis in original). It is a symbolic response to racism and its material effects. Despite its desolate sound, its vernacular rhetoric has the ability to expose and subvert the discursive forces of white hegemony, which it does from the margins of lived experience. Donald J. Shaffer discusses the musical genre as Ellison employs it in *Invisible Man*: "The performance of the blues functions as a signifier for collective experience and as a symbolic means of establishing a sense of place and belonging in the city" (8). Given the communal use of the phrase "I'm nowhere" in Harlem and Lafargue, it attests to a shared reality in much the same way that the blues articulates a sense of collective struggle. The phrase, though, accomplishes far more than "establishing a sense of place and belonging in the city"; it also calls into question the very terms that dictate *who* belongs in *what* places in cities.

When Ellison lists such terms as "modern and primitive" and "sanity and insanity," his attention to hierarchical oppositions "expose[s] to debate the institutional arrangements that rely on the hierarchies and thus open[s] possibilities of change" (Culler 179). Given the emphasis on spatial, geographical markers in the essay, Ellison's critique of specific power structures has direct relevance to postcolonial theory. Indeed, contemporary critics such as John Callahan have identified Ellison as an "ambidextrous" writer, and I would argue that his multiple dexterities manifest in his prescient application of critical-theoretical discourse (qtd. in Blair 113). Frantz Fanon, writing at the same time as Ellison in a different cultural context, provides a perspective worth noting here. Indeed, his work as a psychiatrist and as a postcolonial theorist and activist necessitates his inclusion. Analyzing the psychology of the colonized black subject, Fanon shows how the center/periphery, metropole/colony spatial binaries have an extensive affective impact on the psyche of the colonized black subject. First published in French in 1952—the same year as Ellison's *Invisible Man*—Fanon's *Black Skin, White Masks* provides an early intellectual testimony on global politics and race. However, where Fanon draws clear distinctions between the powerful center of the metropole and the repressed margins of the colonies, Ellison complicates the binary by recognizing that third-world conditions persist *within* the context of the so-called First World.

In a sense, the Harlem residents in the essay occupy what Chela Sandoval recognizes as an "internally colonized community" (76). "Harlem Is Nowhere" thus collapses the spatial dichotomy between center and periphery, First World and Third. "Nowhere" serves as a strategic alternative. Neither "here" nor "there," the position confounds the epistemology that engenders fixed hierarchical spaces. The phrase enables the speaking subject to slip beyond the logical impasse that stymies, isolates, and others his subjectivity.

Significantly, alongside its fascinating analysis of urban space, the essay also maintains a realistic outlook of the Harlem scene as it appeared under the conditions of the political status quo at midcentury. According to Ellison, the system of contradictions that surrounds and constrains the black subject can potentially cause a different quality of transcendence than that provided by the thirdspace of "nowhere," "what Dr. Frederick Wertham, Director of the Lafargue Clinic, terms 'free-floating hostility,' a hostility that bombards the individual from so many directions that he is often unable to identify it with any specific object" (Ellison 301). Ellison distinguishes that this specific psychological state is qualitatively different than that of being "nowhere." Indeed, both constitute reactions to social marginality. However, the individual who concedes to being "nowhere" orally performs a social deconstruction that strategically moves beyond the hierarchical opposition of center/periphery. In contrast, "free-floating hostility" comprises an unreflective psychic consequence of institutional racism, and is perhaps best exemplified by Ellison's description of the man lobbing imaginary grenades in the street.

Without undermining the ingenuity of its reflections on urban space and minority discourse, the essay is careful to observe an ambivalence toward the contradictions of living in black America. Near the conclusion, Ellison contemplates the impact that being nowhere exerts on one's personal identity and concept of one's self: "[o]ne's identity drifts in a capricious reality in which even the most commonly held assumptions are questionable. One 'is' literally, but one is nowhere; one wanders dazed in a ghetto maze, a 'displaced person' of American democracy" (300). In her long essay on abjection, Julia Kristeva articulates a sense of this drift in a way so closely resembling Ellison's that one wonders if she had "Harlem Is Nowhere" in hand as she worked:

> Instead of sounding himself as to his 'being,' [the overdetermined subject] does so concerning his place: '*Where* am I?' instead of '*Who* am I?' For the space that engrosses the deject, the excluded, is never *one* . . . but essentially divisible, foldable, catastrophic. A deviser of territories, languages, works, the *deject* never stops demarcating his

universe whose fluid confines . . . constantly question his solidity and impel him to start afresh.

(8, emphases in original)

There is indeed critical potential in embracing the thirdspace of "nowhere"; nonetheless, like Kristeva, Ellison reminds us that radical subjectivity is serious business. Saying "I'm nowhere" can unhinge the structures that constrain and marginalize, yet there remains the need to rebuild new and more empowering spaces, in both theory *and* practice.

Ellison ultimately remains cautious of embracing wholesale a condition of radical subjectivity, of fluid and endless reinvention. This indicates a practical awareness on his part that conditions of displacement and inequality are very real and incredibly harsh. His discerning view on this matter anticipates that of bell hooks, who, in "Postmodern Blackness," issues a caveat regarding the poststructuralist tendency to eschew all forms of stability and structure at a time when historically dominated subjects are coming to voice for the first time (2482). In my emphasis on spatial discourse, however, I hope to show how questions about *positionality*— questions that produce such puzzling responses as "Oh, man, I'm nowhere"—can provide an alternative way of theorizing sociopolitical agency. Sounding from the internally constituted margin of the American ghetto, such voices are intimately aware of the ideology of their urban maze. Within such an awareness of place lie strategies of negotiation, the power of which Homi Bhabha describes best: "the exercise of power may be both politically effective and psychically *affective* because the discursive liminality through which it is signified may provide greater scope for strategic maneuver and negotiation" (208). Operating as a kind of urban geographer at mid-century, Ellison navigates the Harlem maze with an eye toward its cultural wreckage and the sociopolitical potential therein. To be sure, his analysis of Harlem bears a utility for us today as we continue, perhaps more than ever, to struggle with these dynamic processes in our American cityscapes, processes that continue to involve racial conflict, urban displacement, and ghettoization.

Notes

1. For more on the mission, history, and operations of the Lafargue Clinic, see Dennis Doyle, " 'Where the Need is Greatest': Social Psychiatry and Race-Blind Universalism in Harlem's Lafargue Clinic, 1946–1958," *Bulletin of the History of Medicine*, 83.4 (Winter 2009): 746–74. For further information about Lafargue, including records of patients' personal experiences there, see Dennis Doyle, " 'A Fine New Child': The Lafargue Mental Hygiene Clinic and Harlem's African American Communities, 1946–1958," *Journal of the History of Medicine and Allied Sciences*, 64.2 (April 2009): 173–212.
2. *48* magazine originally commissioned Ellison to write the essay about Lafargue. While developing the project, he worked closely with the photographer

Gordon Parks. Ellison felt that the genre of the photo essay would be the most suitable for the subject because it would "transform his theories about Harlem's schizophrenia and day-to-day psychoses into visual images" (Jackson 372). However, *48* declared bankruptcy in June of that year, and Ellison was unable to give "Harlem Is Nowhere" a public audience until 1964—and even then without the photographs. The photographs are housed in the Ellison Archives at the Library of Congress, Prints and Photographs Division.

3. Many viewed the Harlem Riots of 1935 and 1943 as sure signs that the city was experiencing its death agonies, and these events most definitely contributed to the overall form and force of the essay. For more on the history of the riots, see Gill.

Works Cited

Baker, Houston, Jr. *Blues, Ideology, and Afro-American Literature: A Vernacular Theory*. Chicago: U of Chicago P, 1984. Print.

Bhabha, Homi. *The Location of Culture*. New York: Routledge, 1994. Print.

Blair, Sara. *Harlem Crossroads: Black Writers and the Photograph in the Twentieth Century*. Princeton: Princeton UP, 2007. Print.

Culler, Jonathan. *On Deconstruction: Theory and Criticism after Structuralism*. Ithaca: Cornell UP, 1982. Print.

Doyle, Dennis. " 'Where the Need is Greatest': Social Psychiatry and Race-Blind Universalism in Harlem's Lafargue Clinic, 1946–1958." *Bulletin of the History of Medicine* 83.4 (Winter 2009): 746–74. Print.

Ellison, Ralph. "Harlem Is Nowhere." 1948. *Shadow and Act*. New York: Random House, 1964. Print.

Eversley, Shelly. "The Lunatic's Fancy and the Work of Art." *American Literary History* 13.3 (Fall 2001): 445–68. Print.

Gill, Jonathan. *Harlem: The Four Hundred Year History from Dutch Village to Capital of Black America*. New York: Grove Press, 2011. Print.

hooks, bell. "Postmodern Blackness." 1990. *The Norton Anthology of Theory and Criticism*. Ed. Vincent B. Leitch. New York: W.W. Norton & Company, 2001. 2478–84. Print.

Jackson, Lawrence. *Ralph Ellison: Emergence of Genius*. New York: John Wiley & Sons, Inc., 2002. Print.

Kristeva, Julia. *Powers of Horror: An Essay on Abjection*. Trans. Leon S. Roudiez. New York: Columbia UP, 1982. Print.

Rampersad, Arnold. *Ralph Ellison: A Biography*. New York: Alfred A. Knopf, 2007. Print.

Sandoval, Chela. "U.S. Third World Feminism: The Theory and Method of Oppositional Consciousness in the Postmodern World." *Feminist Postcolonial Theory: A Reader*. New York: Routledge, 2003. 75–102. Print.

Shaffer, Donald J. " 'Harlem Is Nowhere': Blues Spaces in Ralph Ellison's *Invisible Man*." *The Griot: The Journal of African American Studies* 31.2 (Fall 2012): 1–13. Print.

Soja, Edward. *Thirdspace: Journeys to Los Angeles and Other Real-and-Imagined Places*. Malden, MA: Blackwell Publishing, 1996. Print.

15 Covington Is the Non-Place for Me

Walker Percy's Topophilia in the Deserts of Theory and Consumption

Chris Margrave

In a short, seemingly one-off essay, "Why I Live Where I Live," Walker Percy writes that particular cities can either aid or restrict a writer's ability to make sense of one's existence in the tumultuous twentieth century. For Percy, the ghosts of the past can inundate a place. He advised writers, especially Southern ones, to "avoid the horrors of total placement." In citing Charleston, South Carolina, and Mobile, Alabama, as places where a Southern writer's family has lived for 200 years, Percy remarks that such cities are prone to be haunted places where "ancestors perch on your shoulder" (3).

In a letter to Shelby Foote in 1970, Walker Percy admonished his good friend, an equally well-known writer, about settling down in Memphis, Tennessee: "I told you before you bought a house to buy it in New Orleans. No reason why any writing man should want to live in Memphis" (*Correspondence* 141). Percy then suggests that he and Foote purchase a couple of houses—two each, why not?—along Gulf Shores, Alabama. Percy confesses that, ever after living for over twenty years in Covington, a town of fewer than 10,000 on the shores of Lake Pontchartrain, twenty-five miles from New Orleans, he felt himself more of an outsider than when he first moved there in 1947. Percy concludes the letter with a final thought on writers and place:

> It is interesting how a writer lives in a place. I was reading about John Fowles living in this little Covington-like seaside place in England and not knowing a soul there, being flatly ignored by the locals and ignoring them and liking it. At that, I like living here better than NYC—or Memphis—or Lake Washington.
>
> (142)

Although nowhere was really "home" for Percy, he was not without roots. Above all, he was a Southerner, born in Birmingham, Alabama, raised in Greenville, Mississippi, and later a temporary resident of New

York City and upstate New York; Santa Fe, New Mexico; New Orleans; and finally Covington, Louisiana. Ten years after the letter to Foote, Percy was still living in Covington when he published the short piece, "Why I Live Where I Live."

Writing from his practically anonymous Covington life, Percy expresses that for writers, place is a special problem because they never fit in in the first place. For artists, the weight of personal history and the anxiety of latent future creativity can press the chronological present into a space in time in which the artist experiences what Milan Kundera famously termed the "unbearable lightness of being." Percy's city-centric theory of place reveals how an artist's physical residence further complicates the already-complicated quest for creative stability. Percy believes the writer's artistic goal should then be to choose a place of residence where "one's native terror is not completely neutralized but rendered barely tolerable" ("Why I Live Where I Live" 6).

Percy admits that some kind of escape from one's familiar territory is probably necessary. A writer should "escape the place of one's origins and the ghosts of one's ancestors but not too far. You wouldn't want to move to Tucumcari" (3). Percy defines the idea of *total non-placement* as the Southern writer in Waterbury, Connecticut, or the writer-in-residence at Purdue University in Indiana. He concedes that for some writers, such an *extra-regional escape* might be necessary. By his own lights however, and as he shows in an essay like "New Orleans Mon Amour," he would miss the South too much. Total *misplacement*, for himself, would then be:

> to live in another place, usually an exotic place, which is so strongly informed by its exoticness that the writer, who has fled his haunted place or his vacant non-place and who feels somewhat ghostly himself, somehow expects to become informed by the exotic identity of the new place.
> ("Where I Live Where I Live" 4)

This is Hemingway in Paris and Madrid. This is the stereotypical artist's flight to New York, the actor's pilgrimage to Los Angeles. Percy writes of New Orleans as a similarly seductive place of which a wise writer should be weary:

> The occupational hazard of the writer in New Orleans is a variety of the French flu, which might also be called the Vieux Carree syndrome. One is apt to turn fey, potter about a patio, and write feuilletons and vignettes or catty romans a clef, a pleasant enough life but for me too seductive.
>
> (9)

Percy claims that Americans engage in a "species of Consumption" in which people use up spaces. The more inviting the place, the quicker the inhabitants ingest it. Santa Fe, for instance, became used up for Percy. In his essay, "The Loss of the Creature," Percy discusses how this process of consumption has affected perceptions of the *Grand Canyon*. According to Percy, the sightseer does not appreciate the Grand Canyon on its own merits; he or she appreciates it based on how well or poorly it conforms to the preexisting image of the Grand Canyon formed by the *mythology* surrounding it. In Percy's estimation, cities are no different. "Free people have a serious problem with place," he says, "being in a place, using up a place, deciding which new place to rotate to. Americans ricochet around the United States like billiard balls" (5).

Percy credits Covington, Louisiana as possessing two redeeming traits: nearness to New Orleans and a relative lack of identity and placeness. From his wooded perch across Lake Pontchartrain, he is in the South but not be of the South. Remarking on twentieth-century existence in light of the Chinese curse of living in "interesting and eventful times," Percy refers to his life in Covington as being "in a certain sense out of place and time but not too far out and therefore just the place for a Chinese scholar who asks nothing more than being left alone" (9). What Covington ultimately offers Percy is a shelter of anonymous solitude in which he can heed his vocational calling and ride out the storms of personal and national history.

In his book of geospatial literary criticism, *Spatiality*, Robert Tally addresses the so-called existentialist writers' response to the anxiety of being. In speaking of Sartre's aims in particular, Tally claims that the French writer responds to the disorientation of being by projecting a "schematic representation" onto the world that makes sense of existence. Tally calls this schematic representation a kind of figurative cartography that helps give form to the experience of what Heidegger calls human being's *not-at-home-ness* in the world. In the way Percy applies the ideas of placement, non-placement, and misplacement to his choice of residence, Percy engages in a similar act of existential mapmaking that affords him a home base from which he can, in his own words, "feel as good as it is possible to feel in this awfully interesting century" (9).

Critics often refer to Percy as an existential novelist, an offshoot of Camus and Sartre, and his novels and essays reflect those French writers' emphasis on the use of philosophical inquiry as a means of making sense of human existence. All of Percy's novels reveal an author less interested in proscribing solutions to human's crisis of being than in articulating the ideal conditions under which an artist searches to ameliorate the ache of a seemingly contingent existence. The opening essay in his collection, *Message in the Bottle: How Queer Man Is, How Queer Language Is, And What One Has to Do with the Other*, embodies this theme and gets right to the existential point:

> Why does man feel so sad in the twentieth century? Why does man feel so bad in the very age when, more than in any other age, he

has succeeded in satisfying his needs and making over the world for his own use? Why has man entered on any orgy of war, murder, torture, and self-destruction unparalleled in history and in the very century when he had hoped to see the dawn of universal peace and brotherhood?

(*Message* 1)

Percy once identified his novels as falling somewhere between Kurt Vonnegut and Saul Bellow. While Percy's writing does possess a playfully inquisitive tone similar to Vonnegut's, and while Percy's protagonists might as well be fictional descendants of Bellow's larger-than-life searcher in *Henderson the Rain King* (a novel Percy once remarked was his favorite of Bellow's), Percy differs from Vonnegut and Bellow in his ultimate embrace of religious belief. Still, Percy employs similar spatial stratagems in providing the best possible environment for his protagonists (as well as himself) to pursue the existential search for meaning. Vonnegut's *Galapagos* reveals its author's distrust of the power abuses brought about by humanity's big brain. In *Mr. Sammler's Planet*, Bellow presents the eponymous character as a "registrar of madness," a compiler of the ways humanity gone to rot. Each of these three novelists are diagnosticians who situate their protagonists as observers of society gone to hell. Percy, a trained doctor and firm believe in the appropriate use of the scientific method, believed that humanity cannot understand its place in the world through scientific methods alone, i.e., by examining the human being as an organism—such as a frog or polar bear—within a given environment. To even begin to understand and analyze himself, man must take the posture of a wayfarer. In Vonnegutian terms, this would be the Billy Pilgrim character "unstuck in time." In Bellow's world, this is Henderson alighting for Africa.

As a trained physician, Percy addressed the dislocation of twentieth-century man in a diagnostic manner. But since human beings cannot objectively observe themselves as a scientist observes a non-thinking, non-language-bearing creature, Percy suggests a spatial reorienting is necessary to discovering significant existential truth:

The truth is that man's capacity for symbol-mongering in general and language in particular is so intimately part and parcel of his being human, of his perceiving and knowing, of his very consciousness itself, that it is all but impossible for him to focus on the magic prism through which he sees everything else. In order to see it, one must be either a Martian, or, if an earthling, sufficiently detached, marooned, bemused, wounded, crazy, one-eyed, and lucky enough to become a Martian for a second and catch a glimpse of it.

(*Message* 29)

Percy again resonates with Vonnegut's protagonists by emphasizing the outsider's perspective. In 1975, having already written *Love in the Ruins*, his own quasi-apocalyptic novel, Percy was not satisfied with the questions his book raised. So he wrote an essay called "Notes for a Novel on the End of the World" (which also appears in *The Message in the Bottle*), in which he echoes Vonnegut when he says that "the novelist is . . . like the canary that coal miners used to take down into the shaft to test the air" (*Message* 100). Percy remarks further that

> when the novelist writes of a man "coming to himself" through some such catalyst as catastrophe or ordeal, he may be offering obscure testimony to a gross disorder of consciousness and to the need of recovering oneself as neither angel nor organism but as a wayfaring creature somewhere between.
>
> (113)

It is in the "somewhere between" where Percy conducts his and his characters' search for existential meaning. Many of Percy's fictional characters are homeless, homesick, or do not know where home is. Pilgrim is looking for a foothold. Sojourner is in search of stasis, in fear of stasis. The self with such a worldview is precariously nomadic and in need of stability. Gaston Bachelard, in his book *Poetics of Space*, explores the ways common spaces, enriched with reveries and daydreams, foster our sense of self. When speaking of spaces as potential refuge from nature's elements, Bachelard claims that "reminders of winter strengthens the happiness of inhabiting" (39). From Baudelaire and Poe to Rilke, Bachelard claims these dreamers "trust in the wisdom of the storm" to define their place in the world (42). In the preface to 1994 edition of *The Poetics of Space*, John Stilgoe writes that "storm makes sense of shelter, and if the shelter is sound, the shelter makes the surrounding storm good" (viii). This sentiment resonates with Percy's thoughts on why people feel happier in a hurricane, winds whipping against a shuttered house, than on an ordinary Wednesday afternoon, exposed before the raw and seemingly meaningless light of existence.

Tally has suggested that the vocation of literature lies in producing "imaginary solutions to real contradictions" (*Spatiality* 72), and this dovetails nicely with Percy's aims to imaginatively theorize certain cities, which also resonates with Bachelard's poetics of space. Bachelard goes on to define spaces as shelters that protect the dreamer or artist. "The house shelters day-dreaming," Bachelard contends, "the house protects the dreamer, the house allows one to dream in peace" (6). Bachelard's interpretation of the relationship between comforting space and wild elements, in which "everything comes alive when contradictions accumulate," allows us to view Percy's pleasant non-place as a kind of contradictory place of refuge: Covington is the non-place adjacent to the exotic locale of New Orleans (39).

Many writers crave solitude. Some conceal themselves in pseudonyms, like Kierkegaard. Yet Percy warns that too much solitude can be negative. The desert near Santa Fe was too vacuous for Percy, too emptied out for him of culture and history. Solitude in a city fully aware of itself, in a city that is a *place*, however, is as difficult to foster in the urban environment as it is easy to find in the desert. With a mindset that would resonate with that of Binx Bolling from *The Moviegoer*, Thomas Merton writes in *New Seeds of Contemplation* that "there is no more dangerous solitude than that of a man who is lost in a crowd, who does not know he is alone and who does not function as a person in a community either" (54). Covington is the perfect non-place for Percy because it allowed him to pursue a both/and life (in the South but not of it) instead of an either/or existence in which one must escape history or be drowned by it. This theoretical framework of the sustaining non-place that defines the artist as an observer/seeker on the margins not only offered Percy creative stability but informed the lives of his fictional characters as well. We might read Covington as Percy's perfect non-place as being both his source of artistic shelter as well as his locational muse: the non-place sustains as it inspires.

Percy's most famous protagonist, Binx Bolling, is an early representative mouthpiece of Percy's spatial theories. Binx plays out his search for existential meaning, a fictionalized working out of Percy's theories on place, under the auspices of what Binx calls his Little Way, a simply anonymous life that mirrors the life Percy celebrates in "Why I Live Where I Live." "It is not a bad thing to settle for the Little Way," Binx remarks halfway through the novel, "not the big search for the big happiness but the sad little happiness of drinks and kisses, a good little car and a warm deep thigh" (*The Moviegoer* 135). Binx lives on the outskirts of downtown New Orleans and the French Quarter. He is content at first to live his life as an observer from afar: watching movies, interacting with people from an emotional distance. He finds solace in his Little Way on the margins by making money and courting women. The Little Way is most likely a reference to St. Therese of Lisieux, or the Little Flower, who is famous for desiring to live a simple unknown life. That Binx's half-sister, with whom he is not particularly close, is named Theresa is no accidental moniker. Such names demonstrate how Percy saturates Binx's search in inherited religious terms that Binx either rejects or inverts.

Binx is the most complex of Percy's protagonists because he is at once aware of his desire to live more deeply even as he seeks the comforts of a shallow unattached life. His gradually awakening desire for a deeper life beyond the solace offered by his counterfeit Little Way provides the fuel for the existential search that begins with the book.

While Binx consciously pursues the carnal happiness found in a "good little car and a warm deep thigh," an observation he relates after a tryst to the coast with his secretary, he is becoming aware of the futility of such an existence. He is vehement in his rejection of religion, but also does not desire to become sunk in the everydayness of twentieth-century existence. Binx is aware of his pursuit of the flesh as an empty endeavor, but expresses reluctance in finding hope or answers in any one creed or object. In his eventual choice of his cousin Kate as a mate over his voluptuous secretary Linda, Binx chooses the search over resignation to pleasing the body as the panacea to an ailing spirit. Binx would rather be a pilgrim—or in Percy's own terms, a wayfarer—aware of the search than settling for becoming sunk in everydayness.

Binx's perceptions on place are not symptoms of being sunk in everydayness. They are evidence first of his having already marginalized himself from society to the status of observer. Yet he is aware of his need for grounding. Before entering a theater and watching a movie, Binx must "learn something" about the theater's history or its employees.

> If I did not talk to the theater owner or the ticket seller, I should be lost, cut loose metaphysically speaking. I should be seeing copy of a film which might be shown anywhere and at any time. There is a danger of slipping clean out of space and time. It is possible to become a ghost and not know whether one is in downtown Loews in Denver or suburban Bijou in Jacksonville. so it was with me.
>
> (75)

His desire to not simply slip "clean out of space" demonstrates Binx's intuition of the need for human community. Yet his strategic enactment of such community-forming gestures reveals Binx's inability to fully embody, as in a non-self-conscious state, the precepts he espouses. This of course partly stems from his stance toward religion—he claims that God is not religious (*The Moviegoer* 197). Though Binx cannot embrace the religion of his familial roots—Catholicism and Presbyterianism, respectively—he does treat religion, as seen in his relationship with his hyper religious half-brother, Lonnie, as a mysteriously vital source of meaning. Binx thus finds himself betwixt the flesh's pleasures that he feels less guilty about than aware of its shallowness, and the blind acceptance of religious faith, which while it offers a potentially sustaining narrative meaning, is a source of Truth that Binx is deeply skeptical toward. Binx ultimately chooses the unattached pilgrim's search rather than becoming a member of any one faction, be it fleshly or spiritual.

Caught in this Cartesian split existence, Binx articulates Percy's theory of place through the theorizing of everydayness and in the claim that cities possess a genie soul. Binx intimates that everydayness is a state of unawareness of the conditions and forces acting upon one's existence. Being sunk in everydayness leads one to not being aware that the examined life—regardless whether it's worth living—is not even remotely on 98% of American citizens' existential radar screen. Binx alights cautiously for he knows he has used up his old places and that his newly awakened search is now placing his "Little Way" in Gentilly under the introspective microscope. Of the place where he grew up, Binx says, "my old place is used up (places get used up by rotary and repetitive use) and when I awake, I awake in the grip of everydayness" (*The Moviegoer* 145). Binx concludes his definition of everydayness by categorizing the condition as a kind of entrenched existential ailment, the relief from which he experienced only once, in the Korean War:

> Everydayness is the enemy. No search is possible. Perhaps there was a time when everydayness was not too strong and one could break its grip by brute strength. Now nothing breaks it—but disaster. Only once in my life was the grip of everydayness broken: when I lay bleeding in a ditch.
>
> (145)

Part of Percy's purpose vis-à-vis Binx is to illustrate the interior workings of a mind suddenly discovering how his happily detached life has been a posturing of opting out of the Cartesian conundrum. Binx is gradually realizing that his Little Way of a good car and a warm thigh is nothing but a pleasant distraction from the pursuit of life's deeper meaning.

The Moviegoer is Percy's least-proscriptive novel because its narrative focuses more on one man's awakening to the search than the abstract concepts or material objects that might provide existential solace. Where Binx does not find solace reveals the main point of Percy's diagnostic rather than proscriptive novelistic aim. On the prospect of traveling to Chicago, Binx refers to that city as "a great beast lying in wait." Binx relates further that it is his

> fortune and misfortune to know how the spirit-presence of a strange place can enrich a man or rob a man but never leave him alone, how if a man travels lightly to a hundred strange cities and cares nothing for the risk he takes, he may find himself No on and Nowhere. Great day in the morning. What will it mean to go moseying down Michigan Avenue in the neighborhood of five million strangers, each shooting out his own personal rays? How can I deal with five million personal rays?
>
> (*The Moviegoer* 99)

This is Sartrean angst urbanized in the American Midwest, and it is important to note Binx's worry of a person's possibly becoming "No one and nowhere," terms that Percy employs in his Covington essay.

For Binx, Chicago represents an idea that obliterates individuality in its subsumption, or flattening, of the self into one among many strangers. It is not that Chicago is particularly ghostly, but that the large city is not Binx's proximate ghostly place. Even in New Orleans, Binx must ground himself in the story of his most proximate places: the movie theaters he regularly visits. Chicago to Binx is an overwhelming place that could easily render him without a released self. Binx's "secret existence among the happy shades of Elysian Fields" is actually a carnal inversion of St. Therese of Lisieux's spiritually rooted anonymity (*The Moviegoer* 99). Such a life is possible only insofar as Binx can remain an observer—a moviegoer—of his rooted Southern existence.

When Binx finally arrives in Chicago, his fears of place come to fruition. Binx longs for grounding and expresses a comical idea for an existential tour both:

> if only somebody could tell me who built the damn station, the circumstances of the building, details of the wrangling between city officials and the railroad, so that I would not fall victim to it, the station, the very first crack off the bat. Every place of arrival should have a booth set up and manned by an ordinary person whose task it is to greet strangers and give them a little trophy of local space-time stuff—tell them of his difficulties in high school and put a pinch of soil in their pockets—in order to insure that the stranger shall not become an Anyone.
>
> (*The Moviegoer* 201–02)

Binx positions Chicago as a vacuous place full of five-million strangers against the known haunted places of the American South. "Nobody but a Southerner," Binx argues, "knows the wrenching rinsing sadness of the cities of the North" (202). Where Chicago possesses a genie soul with a singularly oppressive, industrially fabricated spirit, the South's cities are "places populated with ghosts more real than people." To Binx, the Southerner knows all "about the genie-souls and living in haunted places like Shiloh and the Wilderness and Vicksburg and Atlanta where the ghosts of heroes walk abroad by day and are more real than people" (202).

Percy expresses this same opinion in his Covington essay when he writes that while he "prefers to live in the South," he does so on "his own terms. . . . It takes some doing to insert oneself in such a way as not to succumb to the ghosts of the Old South or the happy hustlers of the new Sunbelt South" ("Why I Live Where I Live" 4). Though Binx is not as far along in his search as Percy his creator, Binx serves as his author's canary in the coal mine of the twentieth century. Binx's observation on place and cities, and his flight back to the pleasantly haunted South in Gentilly, indeed mirrors Percy's choice to live in the pleasant non-place of Covington, LA. Instead of placing Binx in a kind of Promised Land, however, Percy leaves his character with the itch of the search, which has "spoiled the pleasure of [his] tidy and ingenious life in Gentilly" (*The Moviegoer* 191).

Binx and Percy also share a desire to reside in a safe place in which to search as well as ride out their existential storm. Here Bachelard is helpful in applying the phenomenology of inhabited spaces to Binx's and Percy's plight. Of the various spaces Bachelard psychoanalyzes in *The Poetics of Space*, he generally deals with what he calls the house and the universe. Specifically, he illustrates the way certain writers pit nature against houses. For Baudelaire, a writer who Bachelard calls "a great dreamer of curtains," houses offer protection against the harsh cold of winter (39). Dreamers, Bachelard says, love a severe winter. Dreamers, or searchers in the mode of Binx and Percy, like a good storm or war injury to wake one from their spiritual apathy. At the beginning of *The Moviegoer*, Binx remarks on being shot and lying in a ditch in the Korean War. For Binx, "what [was] generally to be the best times are for me the worst times, and that worst times was one of the best" (*The Moviegoer* 10). A "disaster" such as being shot is actually the agent, such as a thunderstorm or heavy snow storm, that breaks the everydayness and wakes individuals from existential torpor.

For Binx, the South is an inhabited space, and Gentilly is to Binx what Covington is for Percy—a house that shelters the dreaming, or process of awakening, that shapes the mode of existential search. Bachelard ultimately postures a house as a form of defense against the forces of the universe, an analogy that mirrors Percy's and Binx's commitment to the sustaining fruits of a Little Way. Here, Bachelard expounds on the ways a house, set against the threat of a storm, also functions as the bastion against the chaos of living in a contingent universe:

> And so faced with the bestial hostility of the storm and the hurricane, the house's virtues of protection and resistance are transposed into human values. The house acquires the physical and moral energy of a human body. It braces itself to receive the downpour, it girds its loins. When forced to do so, it bends with the blast, confident that it will right itself again in time, while continuing to deny any temporary defeats. Such a house as this invites mankind to heroism of cosmic proportions. It is an instrument with which to confront the cosmos.
>
> (Bachelard 46)

By appreciating how Binx finds comfort in his familiar haunted Southern places, we can claim that his inhabited life in Gentilly possesses the same generative benefits as Bachelard's house, which once "experienced is not an inert box." Bachelard's claim that "inhabited space transcends geometrical space" resonates with Binx's desire to ground himself in a known place (Bachelard 47).

Still, Binx and Percy both are aware of the need for keeping one's distance from one's chosen place—i.e., not becoming stuck or sunk in everydayness. Binx's response is to engage in the search toward meaning, even if the object is ambiguous. Part of his search entails him reflecting on his identity in response to external clues he observes in the world, and one such clue is his acute awareness of Jews. Binx senses there is import in his awareness but is not sure what the clue portends. Reflecting on one of his theosophist relative's claim that Binx is a reincarnated Jew, Binx remarks:

> Perhaps that is it. Anyhow it is true that I am Jewish by instinct. We share the shame exile. The fact is however I am more Jewish than the Jews I know. They are more at home than I am. I accept my exile.
>
> (The Moviegoer 89)

According to Binx, "when a man awakens to the possibility of a search and when such a man passes a Jew in the street for the first time, he is like Robinson Crusoe seeing the footprint on the beach" (89). For Crusoe, the footprint provides concrete evidence that he is not alone. For Binx, the Jew on the street is evidence that a member of God's chosen tribe still remains. This brief mentioning of the Jews alongside Dafoe's stranded hero represents Percy's attempt to position Binx in a newly articulated space with respect to the historically symbol-laden people. That Binx feels at home in his exile demonstrates how Percy's theory of place serves as a creative survival strategy for a character like Binx caught between the Cartesian divide.

Bachelard also employs Crusoe when describing the ways artists attempt to reinvigorate the muse of their creative pursuit. After quoting Van Gogh's brother, in which the brother admonished Van Gogh to retain something of the original character of a Robinson Crusoe, Bachelard claims that when a "dreamer can reconstruct the world from an object that he transforms magically through his care of it, we become convinced that everything in the life of a poet is germinal" (69–70). Borrowing from Bachelard's language, we can view Binx's penchant to Kierkegaardian feats of repetition and rotation (visiting the same theater again, experiencing a blow to his war-injured shoulder), and Percy's theorizing of Covington as a pleasant non-place, as attempts to magically transform through artistic theoretical care their chosen places of residence. Binx is ultimately unable to incorporate the tug of his physical desire into his Godless framework. He is astute, however, to note that his only hope is to remain on the search from within his ghost haunted suburb and city.

Percy appears to have succeeded in his search, by his own lights, because unlike Binx, he has articulated a space (Covington, Louisiana) that is not haunted by the South's ghosts but is proximate to the sustaining particulars of a Southern city. For both Binx and Percy, place is a space in which to ride out the storm of history and the insane present.

A city is a house that inspires in its anonymity even as it shelters with its familiarity.

New Orleans, San Francisco, New York City, Chicago, and Paris are cities saturated by history and, insofar as cities possess sentience, are fully self-aware of their singular identity. A writer living in one of these cities would have to take care not to let the city define him or her according to the pre-conceived notions attached. Recall Percy's Vieux Carre Syndrome. Elsewhere in *New Seeds,* Thomas Merton defines solitude as a type of kenosis, a self-emptying that has its correlation in Percy's idea of the ex-suicide. Merton writes:

> the man who has found solitude is empty, as if he had been emptied by death. He has advanced beyond all horizons. There are no directions left in which he can travel. This is a country whose center is everywhere and whose circumference is nowhere. You do not find it by traveling but by standing still.
>
> (81)

Times change, of course. And late in his life, Percy jokes that he can hear the grass growing outside his Covington home. He confesses that he is tired of cutting his grass, perhaps a symbol of suburban servitude. And so New Orleans finally sounds nice to him. Place for Percy is not an end but a means to achieving a perspective: that the human condition is an unrooted experience. Home for Percy is a mindset that frames wherever he happens to be. Covington is the non-place for him *for a time.* He was aware that his in his Covington existence he could become *mis-placed.* New Orleans then would become a non-place, if the tourists ruined it, which would be for Percy a delightful outcome.

The non-place is the place for Percy because it is a place where he could imagine, dream, diagnose, and forecast unencumbered, left alone, in a cottage near the post-lapsarian garden of New Orleans. A non-place like Covington allows Percy anonymity and proximity. The former: to speak freely; the second: the audience to whom he can freely speak. For someone aware of the doldrums of an ordinary Wednesday afternoon, when a few inches of bourbon offer temporary escape, one does not look to place as the source of inspiration (i.e., an end in itself) but rather as a conduit through which to filter the message. It is within the locus of his "pleasant backwater" life, composed of an intentionally distanced but still involved relationship to his community, that Percy was able to now and then drive

> across the lake to New Orleans, still an entrancing city, eat trout amandine at Galatoires, drive home to my pleasant, uninteresting place, try to figure out how the world got into such a fix, take a drink, and listen to the frogs tune up.
>
> ("Why I Live Where I Live" 9)

In both his fiction and non-fiction, Percy applied his schematic of place to the Cartesian conundrum. He believed individuals must take care to not become entrapped or lost in the deserts of *theory* (an intellectually abstracted life spent in the mind) and *consumption* (a carnal life in which experiences fill the void). Kierkegaard defined three main stages of life that people experience: the aesthetic, the ethical, and the religious. Percy embraced instead a kind surrendering to the despair, or ache, of being by becoming a pilgrim-citizen of a pleasant non-place. His choice of Covington represents a willfully marginal existence that allows him the perspective of proximate observer. That his fictional characters share the same marginal positioning in their fictive worlds illustrates how Percy's choice to live in Covington influenced the way he imaginatively plotted his characters' search for meaning as taking place on the margins. Here, Frank Kermode, in *The Sense of an Ending*, articulates why Western civilization has played with plots throughout history:

> It is our insatiable interest in the future (towards which we are biologically orientated) that makes it necessary for us to relate to the past, and to the moment in the middle, by plots; by which I mean not only concordant imaginary incidents, but all the other, perhaps subtler, concords that can be arranged in a narrative.
>
> (52)

When we view Binx Bolling as a figure who constructs his own spatial experiences, regardless of whether he's satisfied with his results, we see him engaging in spatial theorizing as an existential sustaining enterprise. "It is not that we are connoisseurs of chaos," writes Kermode, "but that we are surrounded by it, and equipped for co-existence with it only by our fictive powers" (64). Just as borders are imaginary lines projected from maps onto geographical reality, theories of cities as non-places or haunted spaces represent fictional frameworks overlaid onto a chaotic reality. And by situating oneself on the margins of imagined spatial constructs, a character like Binx Bolling and a writer like Walker Percy create environments in which they are "sufficiently detached, marooned, bemused," like a Robinson Crusoe, in order to "catch a glimpse" of the meaning of life.

Percy's choice to live in Covington ultimately represents a kind of personal death, a renunciation of his former life in Alabama and Mississippi, where his reluctance as a college student to accompany Shelby Foote to meet William Faulkner foreshadowed his reluctance to embrace the living ghosts of his home region. For Percy, people are places too, and Faulkner was an iconic a place as any famous city. And so Percy sought solitude on his own terms. Covington provides Percy a shelter of retreat, an artistic hermitage, in a sleeper suburb just down the road from America's ghost town of history. In its proximity to New Orleans, Percy maintained contact with a place entrenched in the past. In its separateness, Covington afforded him a life of anonymous retreat. But, to use an analogy that underscores the difference between religious intent and vocational function, this movement is not so much a retreat *from the world* as it is a monastic effort to pray *for the world* through writing.

The writer and fellow-doctor Robert Coles, with whom Percy developed a close friendship, writes that the Percys purposefully eschewed a life in New Orleans, a city which, though only twenty-five miles away, was

> a little too much for them—too charming, attractive, tempting. They wanted quiet rather than diversion—and maybe, to draw on Kierkegaard's way of putting things, they wanted a certain freedom from the "aesthetic stage" in order to pursue life "on the plane of the ethical." . . . Even in Covington they sought seclusion, though by no means were they hermits. They went to church regularly, sometimes on weekdays as well as Sunday.
>
> (Coles 73)

Though Percy was social in his life in Covington—he dined at local sea food diners and spoke at regional schools and colleges—we deepen our understanding of his literary vocation by seeing him, if not as a societal recluse, then as an artistic hermit. And in speaking of a hermit's hut, Bachelard claims that such a space "possesses the felicity of intense poverty; as destitution increases it gives us access to absolute refuge" (32).

By interpreting Percy's choice to live in Covington as a manifestation of his artistic need to live adjacent to an exotic place (the ghost haunted garden of history that is New Orleans) but remain free of such a place's attachments and expectations, we can view Percy's life in Covington as a willful contradiction of place in which his imagination "comes alive." In a non-place like Covington, he creates a solitude from which he observes the dislocated South and the dislocated twentieth-century modern human being. There he embraced his Catholic faith, and like Thomas Merton, and went into his own desert, "not to escape other men but in order to find them in God" (Merton 53). Covington, then, is Percy's desert of solitude where, happily for him, everyone ignores the cranky old writer.

Of his life in Covington, Percy writes in "The Questions They Never Asked Me" that though he had lived in Covington for thirty years, he was less well-known than the Budweiser distributor. The only famous person in town was a linebacker for the Rams and Percy liked it that way. Percy reveled in the freedom of being thought an idler, as opposed to a writer in Sartre's France for whom expectations could enliven or suffocate. One day near the end of Percy's life a fellow Covington citizen asked Percy:

"What do you do, Doc?"

"Well, I write books."
"I know that, Doc, but what do you really do?"
"Nothing."
He nodded. He was pleased and I was pleased.

(401)

Works Cited

Bachelard, Gaston. *The Poetics of Space*. Translated by Maria Jolas. Boston: Beacon Press, 1994.

Coles, Robert. *Walker Percy: An American Search*. Boston: Little, Brown & Co., 1978.

Kermode, Frank. *The Sense of An Ending*. New York: Oxford UP, 2000.

Merton, Thomas. *New Seeds of Contemplation*. New York: New Directions, 1972.

Percy, Walker. *The Message in the Bottle: How Queer Man Is, How Queer Language Is, and What One Has to Do with the Other*. New York: Picador, 1975.

———. *The Moviegoer*. New York: Vintage, 1989.

———. "The Questions They Never Asked Me." *Signposts in a Strange Land*. New York: Farrar, Straus, and Giroux, 1991.

———. "Why I Live Where I Live." *Signposts in a Strange Land*. New York: Farrar, Straus, and Giroux, 1991.

———. *The Correspondence of Shelby Foote and Walker Percy*. Edited by Jay Tolson. New York: W.W. Norton & Co., 1997.

Tally, Robert T. *Kurt Vonnegut and the American Novel: A Postmodern Iconography*. New York: Continuum, 2011.

———. *Spatiality*. London: Routledge, 2013.

16 Alfred Hitchcock's *Rear Window*

Cold War, Spatiality, and the Paranoid Subject

Beatrice Kohler

"That's a secret, private world you're looking into out there," Detective Doyle (Wendell Corey) warns the protagonist of the movie, L.B. 'Jeff' Jefferies (James Stewart). Handicapped after a severe accident in a car race, Jeff has been wheelchair-bound for weeks and left to observe his neighbors across an almost enclosed Greenwich Village courtyard. He ignores his friend's objections and, together with his girlfriend, Lisa Fremont (Grace Kelly), continues spying on one of his neighbors: Ms. Lonelyhearts, who is returning home with a young man. The promising scene is soon interrupted as he forces himself onto her and she subsequently throws him out. Ashamed by their witnessing this private episode, Lisa closes the blinds and announces that the "Show's over for tonight" and presents a "Preview of coming attractions" in the form of an elegant nightgown. As she returns to the room in her new garment, a woman's cry pierces through the night. Lisa hastily opens one of the blinds and, for the first time in the movie—after more than eighty minutes have elapsed—the camera is located outside of Jeff's apartment and frames the two in the window.

The description of this short scene points to two decisive issues at stake in Alfred Hitchcock's *Rear Window* (1954): spectatorship and surveillance. Indeed, the spatial givens as well as the close alignment of the camera to the protagonist create a world that narrates and visualizes that of a voyeur observing his neighbors in excess. As has been suggested by a large body of research on Hitchcock and this particular film, the audience is heavily implicated in the protagonist's illicit spying. The complicity in the voyeuristic peeping, however, goes far beyond a self-reflexive gesture that equates the spectator with Jeff and the cinematic screen with the neighbor's windows. For many critics fail to take into account the significance of the very moment in which the camera, for the first time in the movie, is positioned in a location markedly outside the visual field of the protagonist. On the diegetic level, a neighbor's dog has been murdered, which is why the entire neighborhood has been brought to their balconies—with the exception of Lars Thorwald (Raymond Burr), Jeff's nemesis and propeller of the main narrative, the murder plot. On a meta-level, however, the protagonist has lost his privileged position and the issue of spectatorship to be discussed is rendered considerably more complicated.

This chapter discusses issues of spectatorship and surveillance in the context of the Cold War and its cultural implications. First, the question of invading and observing private spheres is highly contemporary in that the film takes place at a historical moment where American-Soviet tensions have fostered a climate of intense suspicion and anxiety about individuals' and the nation's identity. Furthermore, the figure of Jeff will be read as a wounded veteran that serves as a vivid reminder of the millions of soldiers who returned to the United States after World War II and the nervousness about their reintegration this homecoming entailed. Jeff's intense occupation with his neighbors seems to be a substituting act for something that he remains unaware of but that the narrative—both in terms of story and images—declares as a traumatic memory of the war. By trying to solve an alleged murder case, the protagonist attempts to reinstate his agency, which he fears to lose. His anxiety is closely connected to his girlfriend Lisa; her mobility and autonomy contrast starkly with his stasis and incapacity. Both narrative strands, the murder and the love plot, are governed by the theoretical token of paranoia. A means to render highly complex relations coherent as well as to affirm a subject's autonomy in the face of great danger, paranoia is a fruitful tool to theorize the issues previously outlined in the context of post-war America.

The analysis of *Rear Window* that is proposed here largely rests on the notion of *Cold War culture*. As the humanities took a 'cultural turn' in the mid-1980s to take a closer look at the Cold War, more and more critics became interested in how propaganda and psychological warfare affected the home fronts both in America and the Soviet Union, and how cultural output influenced the perception of ideology and national characteristics (Johnston, 291). Robert Corber was one of the earliest cultural analysts to draw an extensive connection between post-war American politics—"liberal intellectualism," to use his phrase (127)—and the cultural production of ideology. He argues that the hegemony of the social welfare state, that is to say the legacy of the New Deal, could not easily be upheld after the economic recuperation from the depression following World War II, which is why the influence of the ruling liberal elite had to be applied not only in defense against conservatives and the more radical Left, but also in fields other than politics. As a consequence, he continues,

> they [liberal intellectuals] also had to gain control over the way in which Americans thought and lived their relations to the world. The postwar settlement needed to occur on a cultural, as well as a political, level to win the free and spontaneous consent of the American people.
>
> (127)

Building on this analysis, Gordon Johnston presents a useful study describing the mechanisms that posed a broader set of questions about patterns of behavior, attitudes and structures of thought and meaning associated with the Cold War—what he describes as Cold War culture (294). This theoretical token signals a shift from a predominantly instrumental understanding of culture to an active one, focusing on culture as a sphere that both produces and negotiates meaning. Therefore, instead of conceiving of the Cold War as a mere given that intrudes on the cinematic screen, it is more productive to conceive of it as a cultural site that provides a space for the imaginary resolution of conflicts. This site displaces the principal conflict by transcoding socio-political reality into narratives that play out this conflict as the tension and resolution between fictional characters. Rather than providing a direct, mimetic representation of given conflicts, fictions rework and refigure them. Therefore, the premise of this article is that *Rear Window* is a prime example of a cultural product that negotiates socio-political concerns of the 1950s by means of displacing the actual conflict onto the cinematic screen that in turn features a narrative that repeatedly redeploys thematic issues to substitute sites.

The elements of observation/spectatorship belong to the most well-researched aspects of *Rear Window*. As early as 1960, Jean Douchet proposes in "Hitch et son public" to conceive of Jeff as a projector producing its own cinema onto the opposite wall by observing his neighbors (cited from Stam and Pearson, 236). Ocular vocabulary and cinematic analogies run through the history of critical analysis. Robert Stam and Roberta Pearson note:

> The title "Rear Window," apart from the literalness of its denotation, evokes the diverse "windows" of the cinema: the cinema/lens of camera and projector, the window in the projection booth, the eye as window, and film as "window on the world."
>
> (238)

Milan Bozovic equates Jeff's darkened living room with a "*camera obscura*" (162). As for Jeff's function in this highly cinematic diegesis, critics note with a fair amount of consistency that he is closely aligned with and thus implicates the "traditional film spectator" with his illicit peeping on others (Belton, 82). Moreover, since he is so active in constructing various narratives underlying his neighbors' doings, for Stam and Pearson he "clearly functions as substitute director/auteur" (239). Bozovic's image of a camera obscura is particularly useful to describe one of the central mechanisms in the movie that connect the various subsidiary strands with Jeff's primal occupation. As he points out: "What unfolds in the room on this side of the window is precisely the inverted image of what unfolds beyond the window of the flat on the opposite side of the courtyard—the Thorwalds' flat" (162).

The insistence on *Rear Window* as a prime example of scopophilia and cinema's self-reflexivity thereof is certainly valid, as the movie abounds in visual metaphors and symbols. However, much criticism has failed to interpret these givens in a context other than the perpetuation of cinematic self-referentiality. I want to argue that, given the intense culture of suspicion and nervousness out of which *Rear Window* emerges, the visual and narrative strategies of the movies must be interpreted in political terms.

The film's preoccupation with surveillance is only befitting for a period in which anxieties about foreign infiltration and subversion abounded. On the political level, 'McCarthyism' constitutes the key term illustrating the nervousness about the rise of Communism in the Soviet Union and Eastern Europe in the 1950s, and the repercussions at home. As chairman of the House Un-American Activities Committee (HUAC), Senator Joseph R. McCarthy became the figurehead of the anti-communist movement proclaiming infiltration and treason almost indiscriminately. His fiery witch-hunt culminated in a mediatized appearance where he promulgated unsubstantiated accusations against alleged Communists in the US State Department (Carruthers, 82). What the events surrounding the Wisconsin senator illustrated is that the war against an outward enemy also had an impact on domestic affairs. As the committee was entitled to call any citizen to testify in matters concerning alleged un-American activities, a climate of suspicion and betrayal was fostered. Moreover, the surveillance and interrogation techniques constituted a massive infringement of private rights. Thus, ironically, the Cold War conflict produced a climate at home that was said to be threatening the nation from outside.

It is important to remember that as much as private individuals were subject to attack by McCarthyite hysteria, so too were public figures in Hollywood. Indeed, in the late 1940s and early 1950s, the FBI and the House Un-American Activities Committee (HUAC) invested enormous resources to trace and unveil alleged Communist infiltration in the motion pictures industry. Director of the FBI, J. Edgar Hoover, testified before the HUAC on March 26, 1947:

> The Communists have developed one of the greatest propaganda machines the world has ever known. They have been able to penetrate and infiltrate many respectable and reputable public opinion mediums . . . Communist activity in Hollywood is effective and is furthered by Communists and sympathizers using the prestige of prominent persons to serve, often unwittingly, the Communist cause. . . . What can we do? And what should be our course of action? The best antidote to Communism is vigorous, intelligent, old-fashioned Americanism with eternal vigilance.
>
> (Quoted in Shaw, 42)

When Hoover asserted the imminent threat of foreign infiltration, cinema was still at the peak of its drawing power in the United States with over 80 million tickets sold per week. As a consequence, as Shaw notes, "those working in the film industry in the United States in the late 1940s were put under unprecedented political pressure to act in 'the national interest'" (45). Before the commercial advent of television in the early 1950s, the number of moviegoers was still exceptionally high, thus governmental bodies went to great lengths to ensure Hollywood's output was in line with official Washington policies. The role of the FBI was particularly extensive at the time. It installed a broad surveillance network aimed at unveiling communist subversion in the industry and identifying movies that were subverting American ideals. Furthermore, together with the HUAC, the Bureau pressurized the industry into establishing a blacklist and thus purging 'devious' members from Hollywood (Shaw, 53).

Rear Window does not explicitly discuss this issue; however, the movie does engage with the political implications of the interference on the part of the intelligence agencies insofar as a member of this constitutional body obstructs a "filmmaker's" efforts to produce a movie. In concrete terms, Detective Doyle (who, admittedly is not a member of the CIA or FBI, but as a detective is semantically connected to activities of information gathering) actively tries to dissuade Jeff from pursuing the alleged murder across the yard by presenting—or citing, that is—evidence against Jeff's observations and conclusions thereof. Indeed, taking into account the plurality of criticism that describes him as a director or cinematographer, as well as his ostensible use of visual aids to create narrative coherence of the discrete episodes he witnesses, Jeff is a filmmaker. As a consequence, the constellation of an intelligence agent obstructing a filmmaker is established, at least in symbolic terms.

The detective's position, however, is ambivalent. On the one hand, he appears as one of the voices of reason that does not want to jump to conclusions merely because of his friend's fragmented and subjective observations. When Jeff demands that he uses his authority to search Thorwald's apartment, Doyle reminds him that it is forbidden to walk into an apartment and simply search it. Jeff, however, retorts that the end in this case must justify the means. "At the risk of sounding stuffy", Doyle responds, "I'd like to remind you of the constitution and the phrase 'a search warrant issued by a judge' who knows his Bill of Rights verbatim. He must ask for evidence". Here, Doyle functions as a defender of civil rights, dismissing calls for private infringement on the basis of speculations. On the other hand, his reluctance to investigate in the alleged case raises some suspicion. When Jeff insists that Thorwald left his apartment in the middle of the night with a woman other than his wife, Doyle counters with two witnesses' accounts. When the former insists that the couple's appearance at a railway station was a mere deception manoeuver, the detective is quick to cite a wire by Mrs. Thorwald stating that she had arrived at a resort. Doyle seems to have a rebutting counter argument for every observation of Jeff's fairly quickly. However, within the diegesis, it never becomes apparent how he obtains his evidence. In terms of the spatial strategy of the movie, it is only consistent that the camera never follows the detective into the outside world. Nevertheless, Doyle's appearance is not beyond doubt, an intuition that is poignantly fueled by a curious moment toward the end of the movie.

Doyle arrives at the apartment and receives a phone call on Jeff's phone. An anonymous man asks for him and, when Doyle picks up the receiver, he hears a voice ask "Lieutenant Doyle, sir?" and answers, "Yeah, speaking." The conversation continues; however, on the soundtrack, the caller's voice is muted while we hear Doyle giving short answers and comments. This peculiar incident renders his position even more ambivalent than before. Indeed, it seems as if a member of the intelligence agency is entitled to secrecy while everyone else is not. As the contents of the conversation are never revealed, it also becomes apparent that the intelligence body operates on levels that elude the other players within the diegesis. Uncannily, this short scene reminds the extradiegetic audience that it moves in a sphere in which the private is subject to heavy surveillance, often in the name of national security—a catchword that subsumed a variety of highly delicate measures to fend off or counter threats which were often based on latent fears and exaggerated political propaganda.

What is most interesting about Hitchcock's movie is that it presents a suggestive combination of extradiegetic politics and intradiegetic aesthetics. Therefore, it is necessary to discuss the spatial givens of the movie and how they implicate the narrative construction of both the film's protagonists as well as the audience. In the credit scene, vivid jazz music sets in while the Paramount Studio logo fades away. The credits start to fade in and out. A tripartite, open window fills the screen. While the first two names appear and disappear on the screen, one of the three blinds starts to roll upward without a visible operator, thereby revealing a backyard between four brick houses. The camera remains immobile while the rest of the credits appear on the screen and the remaining blinds reveal more of the aforementioned yard. A few select movements can be discerned in the background—a car, a pedestrian on the street and one of the neighbors in an open window. With the final credits fading out of the screen, the camera immediately starts to track toward the window. It halts for a brief moment when it reaches the sill.

Then, the first cut. What follows is a high-angle shot and slight tilt. The camera pursues a cat in counter-clockwise order and subsequently pans through the yard, exhibiting various neighbors on their balcony and opposite windows. As the camera returns to the sill of the open window, it shows the forehead of our protagonist bathed in perspiration as he sleeps in a wheelchair. The camera cuts again and shows a thermometer at 95° F, only to start a second tour through the yard back to Jeff's leg. Subsequently, the camera roams around again, this time through his apartment. The two cyclical movements of the camera raise two important issues: firstly, the camera is outstandingly mobile and is capable of moving through space without narrative motivation. As it starts its tours after the credits, it is not attributed to a character's gaze, and, as the quick framing of the protagonist reiterates, it is also not done so retrospectively. Therefore, the very first scene already puts emphasis on the importance of the spatial arrangement of this fictional world. Though limited in terms of spatial complexity, the narrative space stands in opposition and thus contrasts Jeff's immobility. Secondly, the tour through the living room hints at the temporal dimension of the narrative. What is foregrounded, on the one hand, is Jeff's profession and his equipment—metonymic references of his function within the diegesis. On the other hand, his military past is unequivocally stressed through the images on the walls that bear military affiliation.

There are three photographs on the wall showing firemen fleeing from a fire, a man with a rifle presumably in a war zone and three soldiers in front of a large smoke column that is reminiscent of a mushroom cloud, respectively. The images make it clear that he is not only willing to remember this time but that he actively wants to linger on his memories. Though Jeff's service in the Army is never explicitly addressed except for a brief comment of his to Doyle, the images constitute the visual preface to the main narrative and thus provide a significant backdrop for the story that also bears extradiegetic connotation. Furthermore, the military frame is also reinforced by the other two items that are of particular importance: there is a shattered camera that precedes the images on the wall, which, thus the obvious conclusion, has been damaged during the race that Jeff photographed and that caused his injury. Together with the war images, the broken camera and the image of the race imply that Jeff has chosen a hazardous profession in order to retain the military way of life—continuous reassignment, danger and self-reliance.

These tokens also function as a reminder that the early 1950s, and many of the prevalent discourses, were heavily influenced by the domestic aftermath of World War II. The visual reminders of the war also immediately indicate that Jeff functions as a latent memento of a wounded veteran. As Colleen Glenn notes, the connection between Jimmy Stewart's postwar roles and the heightened anxieties regarding soldiers' homecoming after the war has been discussed astonishingly rarely. Her interest lies in the "considerable number of roles after WWII in which he [Stewart] portrayed men who were increasingly disturbed or neurotic"; she claims that in Hitchcock's *Vertigo* (1958), Stewart's personification of a veteran suffering from post-traumatic stress disorder finds its culmination (28). Glenn's deliberations take a distinctly autobiographical turn, because she draws parallels between Stewart's service as Army Air Corps pilot and his alleged traumatization and the actor's role as Scottie in *Vertigo* (32).

However, in light of the prominence of military material in the movie, I would argue that the figure of Jeff stands in for a broader phenomenon of the post-war era, namely the reintegration of the millions of war veterans into society.

Although Jeff perceives his forced absence from his profession as a break from his ordinary daily routine, it is justified, with the focus on his status as a veteran in mind, to argue that the injury constitutes the opposite. His photojournalism, with its adrenalin-oriented tasks and the obvious threat for life and limb, bears resemblance to Jeff's position taking aerial reconnaissance photos during the war. The six-week rehabilitation phase, therefore, is the beginning of his reintegration into society. Despite the tranquil, urban setting he finds himself in now, the beginning of the movie still recalls his former occupation. As the camera pans through the courtyard for the first time, it captures a hovering helicopter over the yard, dangerously close to two young women. Other critics have described it as a "perfect 'vehicle' for the spectatorial desire to enjoy a fantasy omniscience, to go everywhere and see everything. . . . The helicopter evokes the technological resources available to the cinema and enlistable in the service of the scopic drive" (Stam and Pearson, 241). The aspect of visual pleasure is valid in this episode, but it ignores the decidedly military slant. In fact, as Michel Chion shrewdly points out, when the camera returns from its first pan, Jeff's back is turned to the courtyard while he is asleep; therefore, it seems as if the yard were "a sort of extension of his dream-filled cranium" (156). The image of the helicopter floating above the yard can thus be read as a spatial and contextual conflation of Jeff's military past with his civilian presence.

The diegetic world is thus marked as a heterogeneous site where different levels of signification coincide. The notion of multiple meanings of the surface images also holds what various critics describe as the reciprocal relationship between the primary narrative that Jeff belongs to and the sub-narratives played out in the windows. As Glenn correctly points out, one of the traits of trauma—a condition that Jeff might well suffer from—is its displacement from the original event (34). Jeff's troubled memory of the war and his remaining aggressive potential are displaced into the other windows. As John Fawell notes,

> Perhaps no Hitchcock film is so packed with doubles as *Rear Window* with its dozen or so miniature reflections of Jeff and Lisa. Hitchcock was at his cleverest in the games he played in these apartments, which represent a colorful play filled of hidden parallels and symbols.
> (12)

In fact, Fawell devotes two chapters of his book to deciphering the significance of every window in relation to the main narrative (72–109). For him, and a majority of critics alike, the most significant connections are to be drawn between the 'love plot' of Jeff and Lisa and the 'murder plot' of the Thorwalds.

The first connection of the two plots is produced by interchanging images of the Thorwalds quarrelling with reverse shots of Jeff as well as a dialogue between the protagonist and his editor on the audio level. The editor wants to assign Jeff to a job in Kashmir because he mistakenly believes that his photographer has already rid himself of the cast. "The place is about the get up in smoke", he says and Jeff retorts: "What did I tell you? Didn't I tell you that was the next place to watch?" Disappointed at the missed opportunity to go on a new mission, Jeff implores his editor: "If you don't pull me out of this swamp of boredom I'm gonna do something drastic". Quite comically, the drastic gesture for Jeff would be to marry his girlfriend. During the conversation, he observes his neighbors as they confront each other in disapproval and emotional coldness. The overlapping of the visual impression and the auditory announcement of the 'drastic' act of getting married already foreshadows what the events to follow will make abundantly clear: marriage—as is often the case in Hitchcock's films—is a type of war zone.

There is, however, an additional implication in the window narratives that goes beyond their self-reflexive function as *mise-en-abime* of Jeff's cinematic screen. As discussed earlier, his status as a spy always also carries an extradiegetic connotation referring to the intelligence services. For the audience that participates in the ambivalent observation of others in their private sphere, then, the windows also recall the hundreds of thousands of television sets that enabled Americans to follow the HUAC's televised investigations and hearings. The issue of spectatorship is thus far more complicated than a simple equation between the audience watching a movie and Jeff watching his neighbors. The viewer is complicit in peeping in on the cinematic dwellers and the concomitant enjoyment along with the protagonist; at the same time, however, the audience is not passively identifying with everything the protagonist undertakes (though the film makes sure that parts of our sympathy always remain with the character, who, after all, is Jimmy Stewart) but is capable of formulating its own criticism toward the actions of the diegetic figures. To add a third layer of complexity, the visual allusion to television sets lends a decidedly political dimension to the film because it reminds the audience of current happenings and its participation in this cultural sphere.

To return to the main plot and its military undercurrent, apart from a visual memento of the war, the hovering helicopter also prefigures the new battlefield opened in the courtyard, that is to say the struggle between Jeff and Lisa. On a basic level, their fight revolves around the questions of matrimony and domesticity—interestingly, two consequences that the female protagonist tries to force upon the male lead. Here, too, however, an additional level of meaning connected to the extradiegetic world feeds into the cinematic text. If Jeff is an example of the wounded veteran having returned from the war, then Lisa is a specimen of a woman at the home front having exited the war as an entrepreneurial subject.

It is essential to recall the fact that America's involvement in World War II entailed unprecedented changes in demographics and economics. In order to be able to sustain the enormous need of material and labor, women had entered the workforce in vast numbers. After the end of the war, and in spite of propagandistic efforts to persuade women to return to their domestic spheres, many had proven unwilling to relinquish their newly won freedom (Grant, 324f.). Though there is no direct or implicit allusion to Lisa's position during the war, she is a successful entrepreneur in the fashion industry and, despite her resolution to convince Jeff of settling down with her, markedly opposed to vacating her profession. On the contrary, she assures her lover that she possesses the relevant network to support him in opening a studio in the city in order to work in a steadier surrounding. Jeff, however, responds with spite. "Can't you just see me", he asks "driving down to the fashion salon in a jeep wearing combat boots and a three-day beard?" His dismissal is expressed with military language because he obviously still adheres to a perception of himself as a soldier.

Jeff's inability to adapt to his new situation points to the broader issue of individual agency that is at stake for him. Physically confined to his living room, he tries to substitute his inability to act with the mental potency to solve a crime. There are no boundaries to his fantasy, which he proves, for example, when he dwells on the details of how the alleged dismemberment of Thorwald's wife must have taken place. While paranoid narratives in American cinema only reach their peak fifteen years later, I would argue that the figure of Jeff constitutes the precursor of the paranoid subject populating the screen. Although Richard Hofstadter only writes in 1965 on the paranoid style in American politics, his observations seem quite befitting of Jeff's behavior. He speaks of a 'paranoid style' "simply because no other word adequately evokes the qualities of heated exaggeration, suspiciousness, and conspiratorial fantasy that I have in mind" (3). Indeed, Jeff's severe accusations against Thorwald, his unyielding insistence on finding proof of the murder in the neighbor's apartment and his accusations that Doyle's passiveness in the case seem a particularly suspicious fit to Hofstadter's pattern. The combination of Jeff's anxiety regarding his incapacitation as well as his heated insistence on the murder case confirms the notion of paranoia.

Paranoia in this cultural context serves as a metaphor to denote a form of misguided perception of the world, its machinations and an individual's relation to the former. It is—to use Timothy Melley's allusion to the term's origin in clinical psychology—an "interpretive disorder" (16). Indeed, Jeff is intensely invested in trying to read the various pieces of the murder puzzle, as it were. Ironically, however, Jeff misinterprets two seminal aspects of the story. First, he is at fault as to his position to the world, i.e., the diegetic world. Due to his narcissistic disposition he fails to notice the surveillance he himself is under. Second, and most importantly, while he busies himself with solving the alleged crime he fails to notice the real conspiracy in the story—namely the fact that Lisa deviously tries to attempt to trap him by using his own weapons.

Jeff's inability to depart from his fixed position becomes manifest both in narrative as well as spatial terms. Despite the discouraging evidence that Doyle presents to him, he retains his conviction that something 'is the matter' with Thorwald. Although he receives support from Lisa and his nurse Stella (Thelma Ritter) in his investigations, the alleged case remains a deeply personal enterprise for him. As both Hofstadter and Melley note, the paranoid mind functions in a deeply egocentric way, either predicated on the assumption that a conspiracy is directed at the paranoid himself or unable to see oneself in the bigger picture, as it were. Indeed, although his magnifying lens and visual aids allow Jeff to penetrate others' private spheres, he remains unable to see himself as either a voyeur or in a function other than the principal viewer/director of the events. It is true that Jeff, at one point, muses about the fact that he could become the victim of the same visual attacks that he brings to bear on his neighbors. "Of course, they can do the same thing to me, watch me like a bug under a glass, if they want to", he says to Lisa. On the visual level, however, he does not appear to sustain any suspicion as to whether he himself is observed until his adversary looks directly at him (and the audience) toward the end of the film, which clearly emphasizes that he can be seen.

Though the protagonist remains largely ignorant of the fact that he, too, is the object of a gaze, the film is more nuanced on the subject. The scene described in the opening paragraph when the camera frames Jeff for the first time from outside his apartment is not merely an instance where the spatial strategy of the film is broken. Various critics list this episode as one of two moments (together with Jeff's defenestration) where Jeff's subjectivity is overtly undercut. The significance of this shot, however, goes far beyond the visual rendition of a character's subjective position. When the neighborhood, except for Thorwald, gathers on their windows and balconies because of the dog's death, Jeff and Lisa are briefly framed from outside the yard twice. As the lamenting owner of the dog finishes her speech about the dwellers' indifference toward everyone, the two discuss the fact that only Thorwald has not appeared at this window, again framed from outside. As the camera cuts back to the window of the missing Thorwald, he himself is not discernible, though the flickering of a cigarette discloses his presence. The camera is for the last time positioned in the yard as it cuts back to the couple. At this very moment, the focalization of the narrative shifts subtly. Although the focus in narrative terms lies on the investigating couple, visually, their looking at the dark window with the smoldering cigarette can be interpreted as a reverse-shot. The first framing of the two, then, equals the initial shot from Thorwald's point of view (the frontal framing on the same eye level underline this notion), though interestingly, the visual motivation, that is to say Thorwald emitting a gaze, is missing.

The lack of subjective motivation to the initial shot, however, indicates that the issue of spectatorship is much more ambivalent and indeed more uncanny than usually recognized by critics. In structural terms, this short episode ties in with one of the core traits of paranoid narratives, namely that the principal subject is observed (and often controlled) by invisible yet powerful sources. On the diegetic level the protagonist remains unaware of the possibility of being observed, however, the paranoid gesture, I would argue, is directed at the audience. It is a reminder of the sobering fact that surveillance is by its nature a mechanism operating in and from the dark.

The second threat that Jeff overlooks is his girlfriend. Certainly, the entire love plot revolves around his attempts to hold her at a distance. As Stam and Pearson note "His involvement with people exists in inverse proportion to their distance from him; such is his code of perspective" (241). In a passive-aggressive way he lets her know that to settle down and marry would mean to lose his autonomy. Lisa's initial overbearingness finds its visual parallel in her first appearance, which is in the form of a shadow. The camera stays on the sleeping Jeff in a close-up, as a shadow creeps up his upper body until his mouth is covered—a first hint at Lisa suffocating him metaphorically. The intersecting frame shows Lisa with a glowing face; next, her shadow eclipses Jeff entirely. The image is symptomatic for their entire relationship. Jeff's argument is that Lisa is far too sophisticated and frail to accompany him on his journalistic tours. Given her career and appearance in high fashion this might be valid. However, it is more likely that Jeff entertains fantasies of reentering his militaristic occupation again alone. Thus, Jeff initially succeeds in driving her off, but he eventually succumbs to her.

Lisa's position does not discernably change in the course of the film. However, she adapts her strategy to reach her goal. Because she realizes that Jeff is entirely absorbed by the fiction he entertains, she decides to become his partner in crime, so to speak. Not only does she share his opinions against Detective Doyle's skepticism, she actively supports him in solving the case. In order to satisfy Jeff, she functions as his extension at times. While he is immobilized in his apartment, reduced to an observational function, she enters the relevant space in order to find evidence for Thorwald's crime. It is only through her adventurous intervention that she can compete for Jeff's attention. "Though still object of spectacle for Jeff, Lisa has inserted herself, as spectacle, within the space of the murder plot, i.e., Thorwald's apartment, where she herself is in danger" as Belton concedes (79). Indeed, his increased interest in Lisa after she has been attacked by Thorwald only confirms his narcissism. Because she, as a type of proxy, has performed for him what he can no longer do, she has kept alive his fantasy of an adventurous, dangerous life.

The impression that Jeff is no longer in power is reinforced in the film's climactic scene as he and his adversary finally meet in person. Lisa has been arrested for her intrusion in Thorwald's apartment and Stella has left to deliver the bail money. Thorwald enters Jeff's apartment, remains for a moment in the dark—only his eyes are temporarily illuminated by an unknown source—and inquires as to why Jeff has observed him. With his back to the courtyard, Jeff also remains in the dark without moving. In his hand he holds a flashlight and various bulbs, with which he wanted to warn Lisa earlier should Thorwald return to his apartment. As his neighbor approaches, Jeff fires three flashes in order to blind Thorwald. After every flash, the camera takes the subjective position of Thorwald and illustrates his impaired vision with a red-orange ring exploding from the center of the image toward the frame to evaporate again. The implied point of view shot described earlier has now reached completion in that Thorwald's point of view is directly associated with his eyes.

Jeff, on the other hand, has to avert his gaze from his opponent for the first time, on the diegetic level because he has to protect his eyes from the flash, on the metaphorical level because he has lost the ability to use his chief weapon—the camera—in the face of a threat that presents itself in flesh and blood. He is no longer the director of images but finds himself powerless. His greatly diminished agency is most strikingly illustrated when recomparing the image of the car accident with his position in this seminal scene. One of the two crashing cars, which is considerably more in focus, carries the number 87; the driver is shaken uncontrollably and his right arm, out of control due to the forces at work, covers his face. This is that last image that Jeff must have seen before the diegetic narrative sets in. As has been illustrated, the mechanism of inversion is crucial to *Rear Window*, and it has been argued that the plots (both murder and love) function as displaced substitutes for Jeff's traumatic war experience. Therefore, what follows from these observations is that the inverted car image reveals the number 87 to be the letters LB—that is to say, Jeff's initials as exhibited on his cast—and that the car driver covers his face with his left arm, a gesture that Jeff repeats when he shields his eyes from the flashes attacking Thorwald. Along the lines of our argumentation that Jeff wishes to reenter the war, the image that documents his hazardous encounter on the racetrack is inverted so as to express the fact that his fantasies have become dangerously real in the face of Thorwald as an actual attacker.

Lisa and Doyle arrive right in time to overwhelm Thorwald as he attempts to murder Jeff. He does, however, succeed in pushing Jeff out of the window. This is the final act in disrupting Jeff's fantasy setting by removing him from the previously secure space of his living room. His privileged position as unobstructed voyeur does not exist anymore and he consequently loses control of the fantasy narrative. When he hits the bottom, Lisa readily receives him. Their relationship has markedly changed as he beams at her radiantly. "If anything had happened to you . . . Gee, I'm proud of you", he says as she caresses his face. The choice of Lisa's dress—which surrounds Jeff's head and fills the entire frame—is very suggestive. For a great part of the story, Jeff, Lisa and Stella have entertained the thought that Thorwald might have buried his wife's head in the flowerbed in the courtyard. Though no evidence was found of this, Jeff's head encompassed by an array of flowers implies that the fantasy has now been inverted and that he is trapped and, at least figuratively, dead.

On the narrative level, the film has found a solution in the classical sense: a specific problem has presented itself, various destabilizing positions have been played out in order to solve the problem and a changed but conventional state of order has been reestablished. On the visual level, however, the ending is not only ambivalent but also critical of the idyll that many commentators see as the successful reintegration of Jeff into society by entering a heterosexual, conservative bond. If we take the analogy between the main plot and the murder plot seriously, then we must notice that Thorwald is arrested by the police and faces possible incarceration. Consequently, Jeff's double injury and the absolute incapacitation that results of it is a symbolic incarceration brought about by Lisa. Ironically—and also symptomatic for paranoid narratives—Jeff was too invested in solving the principal mystery of his neighbor's murder, so devoted to convincing his immediate entourage and himself of his capability to solve a problem, that he retained a blind spot on the real conspiracy: Lisa's attempt to entrap him.

In a circular closure, the final sequence shows the courtyard in a counterclockwise pan once again. On the surface, the images seem to support the newly established peace between Jeff and Lisa: Ms. Lonelyhearts flirts with the singer (another neighbor), the Thorwald apartment is repainted, a new dog has been bought by the childless couple and Ms. Torso welcomes her soldier boyfriend back home after a long absence. Only the newlyweds are bickering. Jeff lies asleep with his two legs in casts. The last shot is of Lisa reading a book entitled *Beyond the High Himalayas* as the camera pans over her entire body starting from the feet to her head. "The temperature has dropped about twenty degrees and so, we assume, has the corresponding tension between Jeff and Lisa" (Fawell, 50). However, glancing over to Jeff controllingly, she switches the book for a copy of *Harper's Bazaar*. The final image of her asserts her autonomy and power and once again contrasts her agency with his stasis. As if to underline her control in a double sense, the front cover shows a fashionable young model—the cover that Lisa used to blind Jeff on her ulterior motives as well—while the back cover, slightly blurred, shows a car driving through rough, rocky terrain, signaling that she is willing to go on this detour in order get her way. All the while, on the soundtrack a song has been playing that ends with a male bass singing "but dream forever in your arms, Lisa"—which is what Jeff will probably keep on doing.

To return to the initial claim, the cinematic screen has functioned as a site of cultural construction of a given conflict without explicitly referring to it. Though the Cold War is primarily remembered as a political conflict between the United States and the Soviet Union, the impact on the cultural sphere, in particular in terms of domestic discord, is not to be underestimated. The issues of surveillance and infringement on civil rights permeated a large part of public discourse and private action. As has been suggested, the figure of Jeff as a veteran who has returned from the war doubles the film's emphasis on domestic repercussions of the Cold War. *Rear Window* continuously cycles around his repressed discontent of having lost his battlefield, which he tries to substitute with, and the movie subsequently displaces unto, a proxy conflict. In a paranoid attempt to defend his agency, however, Jeff falls victim to an opponent that he did not discern as one. The paranoia he embodies is a means for him to render coherent what he cannot understand anymore. After the war, the idiosyncrasies of civil life present an illegible text for him that he tries to render legible by entertaining a fantasy of his intact agency. Because Jeff stands in for a type of the American subject, then, the movie's paranoia comes to represent a mechanism that combines extradiegetic politics with intradiegetic aesthetics, two parameters that mutually exchanged energies within a highly complex Cold War culture.

Works Cited

Belton, John. "The Space of *Rear Window*." In: Walter Raubicheck and Walter Srebnick (eds.). *Hitchcock's Rereleased Films. From Rope to Vertigo.* Detroit: Wayne State UP, 1991: 76–94.

Carruthers, Susan L. "*The Manchurian Candidate* (1962) and the Cold War Brainwashing Scare." *Historical Journal of Film, Radio and Television*, Vol. 18/01, (1998): 75–94.

Chion, Michel. "The Fourth Side." In: Slavoj Žižek (ed.) [1992]. *Everything You Always Wanted to Know about Lacan (but were Afraid to Ask Hitchcock).* London and New York: Verso, 2002: 155–60.

Corber, Robert J. "Resisting History: Rear Window and the Limits of the Post-war Settlement." *Boundary 2*, Vol. 19 (1992): 121–48.

Fawell, John. *Hitchcock's Rear Window: The Well-made Film.* Carbondale: Southern Illinois UP, 2001.

Grant, Susan-Mary. *A Concise History of the United States of America.* New York: Cambridge UP, 2012.

Hofstadter, Richard [1965]. *The Paranoid Style in American Politics and Other Essays.* New York: Random House, 2008.

Johnston, Gordon. "Revisiting the Cultural Cold War." *Social History*, Vol. 35 (2010): 290–307.

Melley, Timothy. "Agency Panic and the Culture of Conspiracy." In: Peter Knight (ed.). *Conspiracy Nation: The Politics of Paranoia in Postwar America.* London: Routledge, 2000: 57–81.

Rear Window [1954]. Dir. Alfred Hitchcock. Perf. James Stewart, Grace Kelly, Raymond Burr. Universal Pictures, 2006. DVD.

Shaw, Tony. *Hollywood's Cold War.* Edinburgh: Edinburgh UP, 2007.

Stam, Robert and Roberta Pearson [1983]. "Hitchcock's *Rear Window*: Reflexivity and the Critique of Voyeurism." In: *Alfred Hitchcock. Critical Evaluations of Leading Film-Makers*, Vol. I. London: Routledge, 2014: 236–50.

17 Locating the Clearing

Contested Boundaries in *Beloved* and *Song of Solomon*

Will Cunningham

Borders and Boundaries

Halfway through Toni Morrison's *Song of Solomon*, as Milkman lies in Guitar's bed waiting for a potentially murderous Hagar to return, he recalls a recent conversation he'd had with his friend. This conversation was one installment of an extended, heated argument spread out over several days. The chief concern of the dispute was whether Milkman more belonged in "Honore," a place Guitar refers to as a "Nigger heaven" (103), or Montgomery, Alabama. Midway through the conversation, as Guitar begins to return to an old and somewhat worn line of reasoning, Milkman exclaims "Gimme the tea, Guitar. Just the tea. No geography." Guitar responds:

> No geography? Okay, no geography. What about some history in your tea? Or some sociopolitico— No. That's still geography. Goddam, Milk, I do believe my whole life's geography. . . . For example, I live in the North now. So the first questions come to mind is north of what? Why, north of the South. So North exists because South does. But does that mean North is different from South? No way! South is just south of North.
>
> (114)

The context for Guitar's exasperation is Milkman's repeatedly jaded, veiled, and limited geographic knowledge. Guitar's exclamation that his *entire* life "is geography" is especially relevant to his concluding summation of Milkman's personal geographic associations: "You don't live nowhere. Not Not Doctor Street *or* Southside" (103). Milkman is the spatial opposite of Guitar: the only definitive geographic component to his life is simply where he cannot live; he is a "man that refuses to live in Montgomery, Alabama" (104). He is defined geographically only by his limitations.

Guitar (and Morrison) establishes clear geographic zones that certain characters confront, exist in, and move between. But where we see specific places continually set up as oppositional referents, they are usually accompanied by a third, less pronounced locale that interacts and often destabilizes these oppositional places. For example, Guitar points to at least three spatial, politically and socially charged locations as possible sites for Milkman's existence: a thoroughly suburbanized, gentrified black place (Honore) and a thoroughly marginalized and potentially violent place (Montgomery, Alabama). But if Milkman is in neither of those, then he must be in a third locale that exists in relation to the first two places. What is that third, unnamed place? What does it mean to exist in the place? What other places are like this? Macon Dead, Milkman's father and a successful real estate businessman, exclaims as he walks down 15th Street that the houses looked like "squat ghosts with hooded eyes . . . he felt as if the houses were in league with one another to make him feel like the outsider, the propertyless, landless wanderer" (27). Even with documented ownership, Macon is made to feel as if he is somehow out of place.

And the novel also opens on a similar note:

> The North Carolina Mutual Life Insurance agent promised to fly from Mercy to the other side of Lake Superior at three o'clock. Two days before . . . he tacked a note on the door of his little yellow house: "I will take off from Mercy and fly away on my own wings."
>
> (3)

Morrison has stated that this opening line "contains the information that the novel both centers on and radiates from" (*Unspeakable Things* 155). Morrison discloses that the sentence moves from North Carolina to Lake Superior, "with the sly implication that the move from North Carolina (the south) to Lake Superior (the north) might not actually involve progress to some 'superior state'—which of course it does not." (27). Morrison argues that the binaries of the north and south have already lost their associative qualities of economic, social, or political upward mobility—or oppression. She concludes of the flight of the agent that "although it carries the possibility of failure and the certainty of danger, is toward change, an alternative way, a cessation of things-as-they-are." This is the penultimate flight of the novel, a nod to Milkman's final leap, whose lifelong geography lesson leads him certainly toward change, and the option to choose an alternative way.

Guitar is not alone in his appreciation of geography. The lived embodiment of Guitar's geography lesson is Pilate, Milkman's aunt. Pilate spends nearly her entire life carrying on her person a fourth grade geography textbook, referencing its contents repeatedly. One could easily argue that, like Guitar, her "whole life" is also about geography. Unlike Ruth, Milkman's mother, who was "well-read but ill traveled," Pilate "had read only a geography book, but had been from one end of the country to another" (139). In fact, "it was as if her geography book had marked her to roam the country, planting her feet in each pink, yellow, blue, or green state" (148). Before the acquisition of her geography book, Pilate "just walked around and lived in them woods" (40) without aim. For Pilate, the acquisition of the geography book opened up avenues of self-actualization: it set her in flight. But Pilate's geography is remarkably grounded in the material world, and unlike the other characters in the novel, as Morrison elucidates in the Foreword, Pilate's movements were a "conundrum" to Milkman because "without ever leaving the ground she could fly" (xiv). Geographic knowledge preempted Pilate's spatial movement and subsequently unique historical-cultural perspective; it both revealed and diminished borders and boundaries.[1] Her book revealed to her a spatial reality that was heretofore unknown to her: geographic difference, represented by different colored states. This image foregrounds how the two spatially aware geographers in this novel—Guitar and Pilate—each become keenly aware of the relationship between geographic difference and personal identity.

There exists great continuity between Guitar and Pilate's geography lesson and Morrison's other novels, *Beloved* in particular. Morrison dedicates *Beloved* to the "Sixty Million and more" captured, displaced, and murdered Africans whose physical lives and cultural identity were terminated by the transatlantic slave trade. Morrison's invocation of the transatlantic slave trade frames the story of *Beloved* within the context of spatialized violence—a complex industrial and capitalistic endeavor that specifically targeted black identity. The belly of the slave ship, an image invoked in *Beloved*'s monologue, is a place that occupies the liminal space betwixt and between opposing binaries: this space is the borderland, the indefinable, a temporary and fluctuating zone governed by both regulatory and lawless forces. The slave ship was the first in a long line of spaces that the sixty million and more occupied. The plantation, the big house, the slave quarters, and the auction block were all locations where to varying degrees, as Katherine McKittrick notes, white hegemonic systems "situate black people and places outside modernity" (949). These were the locales where enslaved blacks were kept "in place" by virtue of legal and cultural placelessness.

Morrison's acute attention to spatial construction in *Beloved* and *Song of Solomon* follows the general outline offered by Brooke Neely and Michelle Samura in "Social Geographies of Race: Connecting Race and Space" of the connections between place-making and race. Neely and Samura note that specifically racialized moments involved in identity and subject formation also actively create and re-create the spaces inhabited by singular and collective identities. By drawing on both the fields of spatial and critical race theory, Neely and Samura articulate a theory whereby the social constructedness of space overlaps in key areas with the production of racial identities. This overlap is characterized by four tenets that signify the ways in which racial difference and struggles of inequality are spatially organized and enacted. A summary of these four tenets are as follows: (1) Space and race are contested places where conflict, confrontation, and subversion are enacted in a struggle for both resources and subjective identity formation; (2) Space and race are not essentialized units; rather, they are fluid, historical, and performative; (3) Space and race are interactional and relational in such a way that individuals, groups, and institutions create and disrupt spatial processes; and (4) Space and race are defined by inequality and difference, with dominant interest groups regulating and defining both spaces and racial constructions.

This overlap between theoretical models allows critics a more precise way of understanding the implications of racial formation within and through spatial constructs. Especially within the context of the urbanization and industrialization of late nineteenth- and early twentieth-century America, during which Morrison's novels are set, spaces are often naturalized through constant economic and social forces, creating an illusion of spatial stability and coherence—stability not unlike the transparent boundaries that comprise Morrison's fishbowl-as-whiteness metaphor from *Playing in the Dark*. The key to understand the link between race and space is locating the point of meeting between the seemingly naturalized, exclusionary forces of whiteness and that which it intends to regulate (in this case, "othered" races; these borders are also imminently visible along sexual and gender lines). At this point of meeting, a border space acts as a palimpsestic archive[2] of social and political processes which have composed the formation of racial identity—an archive often characterized by oppressive, hegemonic forces of whiteness and an erasure of blackness. It is in these spaces that racial processes stake claims and create an organized social order.

This kind of space is the geographic center-mass of Morrison's *oeuvre*. In particular, the Mason-Dixon line is a preeminent physical locale and ideological anchor in her fiction. She draws attention to it not because so many black Americans have crossed over it, but because it is a place that is also existed in, situated between oppositional currents. It is not a line that divides, but rather a place that reckons with and confronts division. It is a contested site where the very act of contestation becomes a defining characteristic. This and other such spaces often take the form of a boundary and, during the moment(s) of contestation, become hybrid places with permeable borders. It is when this binary is obfuscated, blurred, or otherwise transgressed that we see the implications of a spatialized reading of race.

Contending and Contesting

When Sethe encounters the Ohio River as she flees Sweet Home plantation, she finds herself amidst a space of national contestation as well as local subversion. The hybridity of this space reflects on both an oppressive whiteness and the act of re-visioning and remembering—the narrative of the oppressed—which is the home of counter-hegemonic practices and their spatial manifestation. In the following paragraphs, I will demonstrate the associative thickness of this border space by drawing out the various boundaries that Sethe contests, and this analysis will begin with an important textual and spatial orientation of the physical, topographical geography of the border between Ohio and Kentucky. Twice Sethe remembers significant changes of elevation as she approaches the river, once when Denver insists that they "get off this here hill. Come on. I'll take you *down to the river*" (emphasis added, 88), and later as a "ridge of pine near the Ohio River" (127). Additionally, after being poled across the river by the old man and boy, they "helped her up the steep bank . . . to a brush-covered hutch" (91). Later in the narrative, shortly after her move into 124 Bluestone, we learn that Paul D walked from there "six miles to the riverbank; did a slide-run-slide down into a ravine made almost inaccessible by brush." These small details provide significant geographic data points in that they affirm Sethe was forced to navigate the most topographically difficult portion of the border, unlike a conventional traveler who would cross the river on a bridge in the low-lying floodplains.[3] The 1899 Standard Topographical map produced by the U.S. Geological Survey reveals a great deal about this space. Tightly compacted red-orange contour lines indicated major changes in elevation that form a ring around the city, with a narrow gap to the north that allows for the flow of the major canals (which, consequently, lead to the likely location of 124 Bluestone north of the city limits). This topographical shape, which bows out on both sides of the river, provides an excellent topographical visual of a border space. The natural shape indicates a bubble concentrated around the dividing line. Cincinnati is situated in the one place along this border without significant topographical interference. The physical shape is, as Guitar seems to indicate in *Song of Solomon*, neither North or South, but a little bit of both as it extends across the river.

The text gives no indication that Sethe used the relatively famous "freedom stairway"[4] located just forty miles south and west of Cincinnati when Stamp Paid led her up the ravine and off the riverbank; however, this stairway does provide a compelling visual of the extreme topographical definition of this border, and points to the need for organization and community to overcome it. While it is textually unclear whether Sethe crossed to the east or west of Cincinnati, her brief boat journey with Stamp Paid and his boy seems to indicate that she approached from the west. She notes that they poled "upriver" for a while, which would indicate movement from west to east. Because she became afraid that she was being led back into slavery, one might infer that the move east and up the river was a move toward the port of Cincinnati, but only for a momentary spell. This is significant to the end that the old man's intimate knowledge of the physical geography of the border space, against the grain of intuitive wisdom, leads her to freedom. This is vitally important because it demonstrates, on one level, a highly individualized, specifically local knowledge of topography, and at the same time, on a larger scale, a subversive organization that is capable of controlling and dictating the terms of the topography and by association, the border space.

But before this crossing and her encounter with Stamp Paid, when Sethe stands on the edge of the hill, she sees the physical, topographical borders meant to keep her out, but also begins to sense the proliferation of other boundaries she must also cross, even if only in her subconscious. For example, Sethe notes that she looks out over "one mile of dark water" (83). But at no point within a 100-mile radius of Cincinnati does the Ohio River even begin to approach that width—in fact, it averages less than a quarter of that distance, between .2 and .3 miles in width. Perhaps Sethe visualizes such a great distance because she also realizes that she must cross more than a single physical barrier. Her mind begins stretching out the physical shape of the border, opening up the inside to allow more space for her presence—and literally, for the presence of her newborn child. This moment begins to reveal the multiplicity of boundaries, as social and cultural flows become increasingly noticeable within the geographic space laid out before her eyes.

This increasingly complex border is further developed later in the narrative when Paul D contemplates the ethical quandary of removing Beloved from 124 Bluestone, where he thinks of the "territory infected by the Klan. Desperately thirsty for black blood, without which it could not live, *the dragon swam the Ohio at will*" (66, emphasis added). In the same moment that Sethe was "looking at one mile of dark water" that wasn't actually a mile, the narrator also observes that the "current [was] dedicated to the Mississippi hundreds of miles away" (83), echoing Paul D's sentiments and adding a second, definable layer of fear to the border space. The Ohio River, even as it creates the physical boundary between self-actualization and enslavement, is imbued with the fears of the oppressed and the signs of the oppressors, which are interpolated and conflated by the characters with natural movements in the water. Paul D invokes the immediate fear of the Ku Klux Klan, yet the importance of a current dedicated to the Mississippi promises perhaps even greater fear— the fear of being sold "down the river" to the deep south, a place both physically further away from freedom as well as notorious for housing the utter extremities of horrific slavery practices (if such a distinction can even be made). It is in this moment, however, when Sethe stands facing this doubling of fear, that we most explicitly see the signs of a national space of racial identity and uplift, because to Sethe, this view "looked like home" (83). Sethe stands at a bifurcated precipice: on one side is a home, a place of belonging; on the other side is the uncanny—an *unheimlich* horror of closed spaces and unrequited trauma, and immediately before her is the space of the river which is neither of these, though it borrows and embodies flows from both.

When Sethe engages in the act of crossing the river, she enters into the borderland. After Amy leaves her on the riverbank, she encounters two boys and an older man, Stamp Paid, and "begged him for water and he gave her some of the Ohio in a jar. Sethe drank it all and begged more" (90). In this moment, Sethe ingests all that the river connotes: she takes the fear of the Klan as a part of her being, willfully entering a space that is marked by contestation and fluidity. That Sethe vigorously ingests water from a place so marked by hybridity immediately before crossing that water, only to enter a city *defined* by water, demonstrates the fluid, historical, and performative nature of the confluence of space and race. Katherine McKittrick expands this idea in her article "On Plantations, Prisons, and a Black Sense of Place" by defining a black sense of place "as the process of materially and imaginatively situating historical and contemporary struggles against practices of domination and the difficult entanglements of racial encounter" (949). One such way that Sethe performs this process of struggle is first through her engagement with Stamp Paid as they cross the river, as he takes a route "contrary to what she expected." Later, a woman sent to find her proclaims that she "saw the sign a while ago . . . Stamp leaves the old sty open when there's a crossing. Knots a white rag on the post if it's a child too" (91). Sethe benefits directly from practices that had developed outside the official tenets of mainstream cartography. McKittrick notes that "fugitive and maroon maps, literacy maps, food-nourishment maps, family maps, [and] music maps" signified an alternative way of demarcating spaces among oppressed black people in the Americas. This alternative practice of mapping is seen variously throughout the text: Sixo's many nightly journeys guided by the stars, the plan to leave Sweet Home when the corn stalks were high, and Paul D following the cherry blossoms North from Georgia to freedom.[5] The prominent cartographic historian J.B. Harley has long noted the power-implications of cartographic practices, arguing that the very production of maps is an assertion of power and is embedded in a specific system of knowledge (286). These alternative maps, ostensibly ignoring the Cartesian coordinate system of imperial map-making practices, route social action and agency through a subversive spatial matrix that can only be interpreted by those who have been implicated in a subversive identity. These mapmaking processes, rather than disrupting the time-space continuum, as is often the case with the Cartesian methodology, demonstrate an acute understanding of the appropriation of the natural world into images and signs that reflect both an assertion of power and the subversion of the naturalizing power of maps produced largely by white men.

But while Sethe's "heart started beating the minute she crossed the Ohio River" (147), her crossing signifies more than one individual's identity; rather, her individual encounter stands proxy for the experiences of countless other enslaved Africans bent on achieving self-actualization through a contestation of boundaries. Only hours before Sethe crossed the river and moments after giving birth, the narrator steps away from the immediate scene of mother-child-white woman and describes the physical texture of their surrounding in what can only be taken as a grand metaphor for the potential of existing within a border space:

> Spores of bluefern growing in the hollows along the riverbank float toward the water in silver-blue lines hard to see unless you are in or near them, lying right at the river's edge when the sunshots are low and drained. Often they are mistook for insects—but they are seeds in which the whole generation sleeps confident of a future. And for a moment it is easy to believe each one has one—will become all what is contained in the spore: will live out its days as planned. This moment of certainty lasts no longer than that; longer, perhaps, than the spore itself.
>
> (84)

Sethe, even while existing in a space that is embroiled in contestation and danger, is able to rest—find peace, even. It is by existing in a liminal space where certainty is not guaranteed yet hope exists for future generations that Sethe and others before her develop a national black sense of place and belonging. However, Sethe's identity is in no way fully realized in this act of crossing and engagement with a hybrid space—for the earlier trauma of her physical and psychic abuse at the hands of schoolteacher never fully escapes her. Nevertheless, her life outside Sweet Home is marked by engagement with other contested spaces that continue to reflect on her racial identity and sense of self—namely 124 Bluestone and The Clearing.

If Sethe's act of crossing the Ohio River works within a national perspective on a black sense of place, then her subsequent movement into 124 Bluestone and the various spaces associated with the surrounding community offers a more localized portrait of black spaces. It should be noted, though, that these local spaces are always and at once subsumed within this national backdrop: the contestation of the local and of the home was being enacted all across the borders between slavery and freedom. These spaces share the common ground of confronting and living within white violence even under the guise of legal freedom and, as noted previously, even in a seemingly safe environment, the national is oft to invade: one only has to look at the tenets of the Fugitive Slave Act and schoolteacher's willingness to transgress the boundary between slavery and freedom to realize that a black sense of place and home was constantly in danger. The safe confines of community and individual identity were perched precariously on laws that bypassed both cartographic and social boundaries. Thus, when Sethe leaves the riverside and moves into 124 Bluestone, she is not moving *out* of the border zone; rather, she moves further *in*. That borderland expands from its most central site of contestation, the Ohio River, to the outworking of a more fully realized black community.

That 124 Bluestone still represents a borderland is most prescient within a capitalistic framework: it is possible to forget that Sethe and Baby Suggs never own 124 Bluestone and only exist there as tenants. The Bodwins only seem to act as bookends to any narrative that involves the house and are relatively forgotten until the culminating scene on the front porch. But this framework is important, as it continues to reinforce the borderland space that is 124 Bluestone. If both space and race are defined by inequality and difference, and dominant interest groups continually regulate and define spatial construction, then the importance of the home's ownership should remain at the forefront of any critique of the process of identity formation. It is within this capitalistic, contractual confine that the novel's primary living space defines itself as an ulterior, organic space of human development and interaction. In " 'Black and 'Cause I'm Black I'm Blue': transverse racial geographies in Toni Morrison's *The Bluest Eye*," McKittrick notes, in reference to another border space in Morrison's *oeuvre*, that "consumerism, uneven development, thwarted opportunities and (in)consistent possibilities all demonstrate how the black community . . . moves through, against, and within a capitalistic framework" (130). This space in *The Bluest Eye* mirrors the development of the home space in *Beloved*. For example, the novel begins with a portrait of 124 Bluestone, but the house "didn't have a number then, because Cincinnati didn't stretch that far" (1). The house only stood as an emblem of the Bodwins' "goodwill" toward Baby Suggs and did not yet have enough value to be assigned a postal code. But the house's eventual address, 124, developed alongside its occupants and is as much a demarcation of Sethe's family unit and the missing third child as a numerical marker for a physical place. The house's naming and outward identity comes only after being inhabited by Baby Suggs and Sethe, only then is it a socially defined, associatively thick space.

The move from the global to the local and, more specifically, these lived-in spaces, provides a glimpse of the lived experiences of black identity within the border. Part of the contractual agreement between Baby Suggs and the Bodwins was that "she was clean" (145) and that cleanliness would reflect itself in the maintenance of the house—a house that was bereft of color upon her arrival (1). The transformation from a whitewashed, stark home bereft of identity is perhaps most explicitly seen as Sethe remembers Baby Suggs on her deathbed. Baby Suggs was "starved for color" in 124—an odd signifier of someone's identity. But taken within the context of racialized space, it seems all too fitting. Sethe notes that

> there wasn't any [color] except for two orange squares in a quilt that made the absence shout. The walls of the room were slate-colored, the floor earth-brown, the wooden dresser the color of itself, the curtains white, and the dominating feature, the quilt over an iron cot, was made up of scraps of blue serge, black, brown and gray wool.
>
> (38)

Upon this act of re-memory (which, as noted previously, is the narrative of the oppressed in space), Sethe becomes "as color conscious as a hen" and purposely fills the house with bright and vibrant colors—the space of 124 Bluestone, contesting the white-washed vision of the Bodwins, takes on the colors and hues of its inhabitants.

124 Bluestone also acts as a primary space for contesting communal identity, and we see this in the lived experience of multiple individuals in *Beloved*. Sethe, Beloved, Paul D, and Baby Suggs all experience a strong bond to that place even without outright ownership. But 124 Bluestone acts as more than an isolated space for individuals to create an identity; rather, the home is created through an amalgamation of multiple identities and serves as a "way station" for the entire community (249). Critics have long noted[6] this communal aspect of the home and its implications on identity formation. However, what is noteworthy is the way in which the community becomes fractured over the contestation of this home only to come together at the end. Within the border zone, contestation does not just occur between opposing forces; rather, this contestation is scaled down to encapsulate even like-identities as representatives of those living within this border.

124 Bluestone is a significant place for identify formation, but it is not the oppositional referent to Sweet Home Plantation, the place that most haunts Baby Suggs and Sethe. Sethe warns Denver of the dangers of remembering certain places that stand outside of the time-space continuum and in doing so, begins to point to a third space of cultural enunciation, the Clearing:

> Places, places are still there. If a house burns down, its gone, but the place—the picture of it—stays, and not just in my rememory, but out there, in the world . . . its when you bump into a rememory that belongs to somebody else. Where I was before I came here, that place is real. It's never going away. Even if the whole farm—every tree and grass blade of it dies. The picture is still there and what's more, if you go there—you who never was there—if you go there and stand in the place where it was, it will happen again; it will be there for you, waiting for you.
>
> (36)

Sethe's memory is explicitly imbricated with Sweet Home—the place that "wasn't sweet and sure wasn't home" (14). Sethe's concern for Denver, that some places never disappear and wield a real and present threat of trauma, demonstrates the historical, relational weight of space in identity formation. But just as Sweet Home seems to possess an identity of its own, Sethe and all those associated with 124—and most notably Baby Suggs—discover an alternative to Sweet Home plantation in the Clearing. Sweet Home and the Clearing represent spaces that transcend dimensionality—they cannot be destroyed or forgotten by the simple act of leaving or the progression of linear time. They exist as real places as well as symbolic retreats and prisons of the mind. But the Clearing is an essential place for identity formation within the border, as it also provides a psychic clearing where individuals can reimagine and re-create themselves.

Locating the Clearing

My analysis of the Clearing will follow a simple assertion and rejoin itself to the spaces and places of *Song of Solomon*: the Clearing from *Beloved* and Solomon's Leap, the space into which Milkman jumps at the end of *Song of Solomon*, are representative equals. Both places are highly dangerous—physically, socially, and spiritually—and both places offer moments of unrequited freedom and possibility. They are both imbued with voices in song, and both share borders made of human bodies (spectral and real). They both exist as real, physical locales—places that are tangible and accessible for those that know their coordinates. But both of these very real places are situated within physical grasp of transcendental places that defy temporal flow, seemingly separated only by a thin veil:[7] Milkman is within leaping distance from the rock perch and Sethe, also on a rock perch, is physically grasped by Baby Suggs from beyond death, even leaving bruises on her throat. They are at first found and experienced by large groups (a hunting party and the black community of Cincinnati), before a trio of three characters later return and, to some degree, reenact previous events. These spaces seem to be unique to the border zone and represent the social and economic possibility afforded within. In their uniqueness, these spaces actively decolonize colonial bodies by divorcing, for example, the relationship between body and property, or by drawing out the rhythms of call-and-response against the starkness of print newspapers that define and stratify identity. They ultimately become spaces where black individuals— and communities—reconstruct and critique the sociopolitical and geographic boundaries of the border space in all its evocations. This is the space where the collective experience of all external flows that converge in a boundary space are brought, sorted, and even potentially replaced.

There are two planes on which we might consider these spaces: the physical place and the experience of that place. The real, physical and material locale of the Clearing is significant in that it immediately decolonizes property ownership. Even as a site of potential identity formation, 124 Bluestone is still owned by white people, operates under the associative legal provisions, and holds Sethe and Denver captive under that external, systemic framework. This is not the case with the Clearing. The Clearing is described as "a wide-open place cut deep in the woods nobody knew for what at the end of a path known only to deer and whoever cleared the land in the first place" (51). The Clearing is excluded from processes of commerce and property ownership, and the very inaccessibility of the Clearing mirrors the larger, topographical barriers surrounding the greater border zone. A ring of trees surrounds the Clearing, with a large, flat rock in the center. This rock is the place where Baby Suggs "bowed her head and prayed silently" while "the people waited among the trees" (51) before stepping out one by one and forming a circle around her. The visual is not insignificant: it is a boundary, but one formed by black bodies that have temporarily replaced the legislative, social, and economic borders of the Mason-Dixon line.

This boundary of bodies, encircled by a mute and cloaking ring of trees, enacts what Ingrid Reneau calls the formation of a kinship structure through the West African ritual of Ringshout. Reneau's analysis of the Clearing is tied to her larger claims about creating an intellectual life and space in academia. But her analysis is also prescient in that it draws out the connections between community and spatial configurations. The Clearing is where Reneau suggests Baby Suggs calls the community to remember themselves through the "polyrhythmic expression of their b/ Body (where b indicates the individual body and B the collective body)" (322). In this rhythmic call and response, the individual shouts with herself as she shouts simultaneously with the b/Body, achieving a cathartic release, rearticulating words of empowerment, and envisioning limitless possibilities. Reneau ties this geographic, spiritual, and political space together, arguing that the Clearing "allows for transcendence of the disabling effects of cultural and political domination . . . resulting from the enslavement, colonization, neo-colonization, imperialism and their attenuating fixtures of capitalism, materialism, and consumerism" (323). But the Ringshout does more than marry the geographic, spiritual, and political together in a way that allows for transcendence. Reneau argues that this ritual articulates a philosophical system of balance and reciprocity between an array of dichotomies: "the individual and collective, the old and new world; the sacred and the secular, the oral and the written, the intellectual and the spiritual; the living, the dead and the unborn" (325). This system of balance and reciprocity, as it juggles these contradictions and dichotomies of the border space, "dismantles apparent divisions and boundaries between varying dimensions of our historical, intellectual and psychic existence" (325). In other words, the Clearing also constitutes a "clearing" in the psyche—not an erasure, but an open space in which to conceive of the course of history through the b/Body politic, or diaspora bodies of all kind as they exist outside of and separate from white, Western, colonizing, and enslaving ideologies. The boundaries of the trees and their silence and the boundaries of the bodies and their call-and-response become the borders and boundaries that separate the "here" and "yonder" of Baby Suggs' sermon. It is a space where each individual calls out a new line or division between the immediate self and the "other" self of history that was defined by whiteness and enforced by legal and social boundaries—this new drawing of the line is reciprocated by the response of the community. In a sense, it is an oral cartography of a space where Western science and cartography has been unable to map, as it could only be created and formed in the complete absence of those parameters.

An example of characters redrawing these lines occurs when Sethe, Denver, and Beloved revisit the Clearing, years after Baby Suggs' death, and reenact the Ringshout. Before this visit with her two daughters, Sethe expresses a desire "to be there now. At the least to listen to the spaces that the long-ago singing had left behind" (89). Sethe found this longing to be forceful enough to take her daughters back to the Clearing, leading her to "Baby's old preaching rock" where she "remembered the smell of leaves simmering in the sun, thunderous feet and the shouts that ripped pods off the limbs of the chestnuts." As she sat on the stone, "Denver and Beloved [were] watching her from the trees," just as the community used to watch Baby Suggs before emerging one-by-one in song (56). Sethe longs for Baby Suggs, and soon feels her "caressing fingers" on her neck, fingers that become increasingly forceful in the amount of pressure applied. Textually, this uptick in force occurs when Sethe begins to remember Paul D and Halle, travelling to that specific mental space in her rememory. These "new pictures and old rememories" subsequently began to "break her heart." While the narrator does not go into great detail about these particular rememories, they are articulated in poignantly spatial terms: this rememory is "the empty space of not knowing about Halle—a space sometimes colored with righteous resentment," and the "empty place of no definite news" (56). With these traumatizing memories now in her psyche, the fingers "moved slowly around toward her windpipe" in a grip that would not let her breathe (57). Much like their predecessors who, upon hearing Baby Suggs' calls would emerge from the trees, Denver and Beloved leave the ring of trees and rush toward Sethe, shouting. The two approach Sethe and become the embodied vision of Baby Suggs, who calls to the community to take their hands and

> Touch others with them, pat them together, stroke them on your face 'cause they don't love that either. You got to love it, you! And no, they ain't in love with your mouth . . . So love your neck; put a hand on it, grace it, stroke it and hold it up.

As the three women reenact the Ringshout, the pressure on Sethe's neck is released and she is able to breathe again. Immediately, Beloved "reached out her hand and touched the splotches" on her neck, and her "fingers were heavenly. Under them and breathing evenly again, the anguish rolled down. The peace Sethe had come there to find crept into her" (57). Within the Clearing, enacting the Ringshout, Sethe rediscovers a psychic clearing. This psychic clearing is so profound that, after leaving,

> Sethe was bothered, not because of the kiss, but because, just before it, when she was feeling so fine letting Beloved massage away the pain, the fingers she was loving and the ones that had soothed her before they strangled her had reminded her of something *that now slipped her mind.*
>
> (58, emphasis added)

Of course, the memory she can no longer remember was of Paul D and Halle, the very memory responsible for conjuring and instigating physical pain. The power of the Clearing is so significant that it does not just silence trauma, but converts it into an erotic event, where fingers that choke become "lips that kept on kissing" (58). In a text replete with the act of remembering as a signifier of past experiences with lived-in space, the Clearing offers the only example of a space that mutes past traumatic memories—effectively transforming them into something else entirely.[8] Those that experience the Clearing only seem to remember their previous experiences *within* the Clearing. The Clearing compresses time, even in some cases completely annihilating it. It becomes the space where memory collides with the presence and provides a clear spatial organization for the future.

In a similar fashion, though extrapolated a century (give or take) and with it the redrawing of many boundaries, we find a new Clearing: Solomon's Leap and the rock from which Milkman finally jumps into the air. One consequence of the temporal progression between the novels is that the redrawing of boundaries is done on smaller scales, in ways often veiled under capitalist, populist, or religious expressions or divisions—but no longer as overtly national in scale as the Mason-Dixon line. These nonlinear boundaries are often disorienting, especially for a character that resists geography lessons, like Milkman. But the overall geography of this novel reflects these shifting boundaries that defy spatial configuration and are, in some instances, even paradoxical. For example, as many have noted, there is a bit of geographic irony that Milkman lives on "Not Doctor Street" or the slippages between North Carolina (state) and North Caroline (insurance) and how that might affect travel to Lake Superior. But more paradoxically, it seems, are geographic slippages from the narrator. Consider this oddity, barely off the first page of the book:

> Some of the city legislators, whose concern for appropriate names and the maintenance of the city's landmarks was the principal part of their political life . . . they had notices posted in the stores, barbershops, and restaurants in that part of the city saying that the avenue running northerly and southerly from Shore Road fronting the lake to the junction of routes 6 and 2 *leading to Pennsylvania*, and also running parallel to and between Rutherford Avenue and Broadway.
>
> (4, emphasis added)

Is it not considerably odd that a public notice to the residents of a medium-sized city in Michigan would include a clause reminding the readers that the road was also leading them to Pennsylvania? It strikes me as even stranger that a road running north to south in Michigan would have any directional association with the state of Pennsylvania, far to the east, as opposed to Ohio, Indiana, or Wisconsin, its real southerly neighbors. And considering the intimation that Lake Superior is just to the north, then this fictional town might even be located in the Upper Peninsula of Michigan, meaning this Michigan city legislator is reminding residents of a non-neighboring state at least several hundred miles away. It could just be a quirky city legislator, but I think it is more likely that these geographic slippages belong to the narrator, and they are indicative of the psychic pull of a border zone, one that does actually carry Milkman first to Pennsylvania, as the road sign forebodes, and later to Virginia.

Milkman spends much of the novel attempting to navigate the non-linear borders he encounters, which eventually leads him South to Shalimar, Virginia. Critics have spilled much ink over Milkman, Guitar, and Pilate's last moments at Solomon's Leap, as such moments in literature rightly call for. I think, along with others, that the ending presents such openness that few, if any, of these claims are mutually exclusive. In conclusion, I'd like to make a few simple linkages back to the scene in the Clearing with Beloved, Denver, and Sethe. Immediately after Pilate is shot, she laughs; like Sethe, her pain is taken away. After she dies, and after Milkman sings, he begins the Ringshout ritual, standing on the rock and surrounded by the expanse of Solomon's Leap. He is answered first by the echo of the hills, second by the echo of the rocks, and third by an unnamed source. This unnamed source, which echoes "life" again and again, is perhaps first contact "across the veil" that exists simultaneously in the Clearing, pointing to a similar transcendence experienced by Sethe. The ending beckons readers to continue imagining Milkman's flight. We witness his takeoff, his transcendence. What next? In the novel, it is just the open space of the remainder of the page itself, where readers continue that imaginative flight. That open space is representative of the clearing of the psyche. It is at that moment, and only at that moment, that Milkman *knows* something with a level of certainty, a certainty that is powerfully indicated by his leap into the clearing before him and the emptiness of the unwritten page. Milkman, to borrow Morrison's imagery from *Playing in the Dark*, leaps out of the fishbowl, the invisible container of white spatial constructs.

Notes

1. In short, borders exclude, boundaries contain. Borders represent that which is meant to hold off, boundaries that which hold in. The boundary is the outer limit for one moving out from a center, a border the first line of contact with the center for one desiring to move within. They are not mutually exclusive, but they aren't always interchangeable.
2. A "palimpsest," in its most literal definition, refers to marks on a page that have been erased, but whose original meaning can still be determined despite this erasure. Spatially, this term refers to the continual, historical layering and obfuscation of objects in space where one can (literally and figuratively) see the remnants of previous objects. As objects in space (buildings, roads, homes, ports) are destroyed and rebuilt, the visible and historical remnants of each previous object becomes archived in the collective memory and consciousness of those who encounter it.
3. See the 1848 Daguerreotype of Cincinnati taken by Charles Fontayne and William Porter. The Daguerreotype was photographed from a high knoll on the Kentucky border, looking across the river into Cincinnati, offering a similar view to that which would have been shared by Sethe and Denver as they stood atop the pine ridge.
4. This stairway, constructed by the abolitionist John Rankin, led to his home, which served as a temporary haven for fugitive slaves.
5. Sethe's scarred back also acts as a rather interesting alternative map, though the significance of which is beyond the scope of this essay.
6. The following articles all bring attention to the communal nature of 124 Bluestone, albeit from different perspectives and theoretical fields: Dara Byrne's " 'Yonder they do not love your flesh': Community in Toni Morrison's *Beloved*: The Limitations of Citizenship and Property in the American Public Sphere," Nancy Jesser's "Violence, Home, and Community in Toni Morrison's *Beloved*," Andrew Hock Soon Ng's "Toni Morrison's Beloved: Space, Architecture, and Trauma," and J. Miller's "Boundaries in Beloved." Doreen Fowler's *Drawing the Line: The Father Reimagined in Faulkner, Wright, O'Conner, and Morrison* also explores the relationship between community and individual identity, though not explicitly through the context of the home as space.
7. Perhaps the same "veiled over and shut away" border created by the arrival of the infant ghost at 124, which ostensibly separated Sethe and Denver from the rest of the community.
8. This is significant for several reasons. For example, in Andrew Ng's excellent analysis of space, architecture, and trauma in *Beloved*, he surmises that "the house is the key to Sethe's healing" (231). Ng, drawing on Deleuze, argues that the house reflects the *"pli"* (fold), or a site that liberates through entrapment, where the subject situated within the *pli* "encounters immobility and violence, but also finds redemption and freedom." I argue that this is only a partially true assessment. 124 Bluestone is significant as a lived-in space that both traps

and transforms, but it does not offer the psychic clearing—the open and clean mental space—obtained inside the Clearing, which becomes a necessary component of Sethe's reimagined self.

Works Cited

Byrne, Dara. " 'Yonder they do not Love your Flesh': Community in Toni Morrison's *Beloved:* The Limitations of Citizenship and Property in the American Public Sphere." *Canadian Review of American Studies.* Vol. 29, No. 2, pp. 25–59. 1999.

Delaney, David. "The Space that Race Makes." *The Professional Geographer.* Vol. 54, 2002.

Fontayne, Charles and William Porter. *Cincinnati Panorama.* Cincinnati Public Library Digital Reserves.

Foucault, Michel. *Of Other Spaces.* Trans. Jean Khalfa. London: Routledge. Spring, 1986.

Fowler, Doreen. *Drawing the Line: The Father Reimagined in Faulkner, Wright, O'Connor, and Morrison.* Charlottesville: U of Virginia P. 2013.

Harley, J. B. "Deconstructing the Map." *Cartographica.* Vol. 26, No. 2, pp. 1–20. Spring, 1989.

Jesser, Nancy. "Violence, Home, and Community in Toni Morrison's *Beloved.*" *African American Review.* Vol. 33, No. 2, pp. 325–45. 2009.

Massey, Doreen. *Spatial Divisions of Labour: Social Structures and the Geography of Production.* London: Macmillan. 1984.

———. *Space, Place and Gender.* Minneapolis: U of Minnesota P. 1994.

McKittrick, Katherine. "Black and Cause I'm Black I'm Blue: Transverse Racial Geographies in Toni Morrison's *The Bluest Eye.*" *Gender, Place and Culture.* Vol. 7, No. 2, pp. 125–42. 2000.

——— "On Plantations, Prisons, and a Black Sense of Place." *Social and Cultural Geography.* Vol. 12, No. 8, 2011.

Miller, J. Hillis. "Boundaries in *Beloved.*" *symplokē.* Lincoln: U of Nebraska P. Vol. 15, No. 1–2, pp. 24–39. 2007.

Morrison, Toni. *Beloved.* New York: Penguin Group. 1988.

———. *Unspeakable Things Unspoken: The Afro-American Present in American Literature.* Ann Arbor: U of Michigan P, 1989.

———. *Song of Solomon.* New York: Random House. 2004.

Neely, Brooke and Michelle Samura. "Social Geographies of Race: Connecting Race and Space." *Ethnic and Racial Studies.* Vol. 32, No. 11, pp. 1933–52. 2011.

Ng, Andrew. "Toni Morrison's *Beloved*: Space, Architecture, Trauma." *Symplokē.* Lincoln: U of Nebraska P. Vol. 19, No. 1–2, pp. 231–45. 2011.

Price, Patricia. "At the Crossroads: Critical Race Theory and Critical Geographies of Race." *Progressive Human Geography.* Vol. 34, No. 147, 2010.

Reneau, Ingrid. "Dancing the 'Clearing' in Academia." *The Western Journal of Black Studies.* Vol. 28, No. 1, Spring 2004.

Smith, George. *Ohio-Kentucky Cincinnati Quadrangle.* U.S. Geological Survey. 1899.

Soja, Edward. *Postmodern Geographies.* London: Verso. 1989.

18 Remapping the Present
Dave Eggers's Spatial Virtuality and the Condition of Literature

Nathan Frank

Circles are classic tropes for imagining sovereignty: they literally circumscribe ins and outs, inclusions and exclusions, heres and theres. They diagram political worlds in spatial terms. They map power through their indications of that which is present or absent, contained or excluded. But maps of "that which is present" have a tendency to temporalize into maps of "the present," even for certain "political cartographers" who are considered central to the spatial turn in literary and cultural studies.[1] Consider Michel Foucault's introduction to *Discipline and Punish*, in which he is "only" interested in diagramming power relations of "the past" if it "means writing a history of the present" (31), or Lauren Berlant's motivation in *Cruel Optimism* to explore political inclusions and exclusions via a "stretched-out present moment" if it helps to apprehend "affect in the present," or if it means better understanding "the activity of world-making, which may be hooked on futures, or not." (12–14). Foucault and Berlant are two very influential mappers of power who make plenty of spatial turns elsewhere but who just as often situate political reality as presents lodged between pasts and futures, shifting from that which is spatially *here* to that which is temporally *now*. Similarly, Foucault and his interlocutors—Berlant but others, too—tend to read such presents as actualities, and therefore to read the problems of and solutions to such presents as temporal virtualities, by which I mean (and I think they usually do, too) that the alternatives to their historical presents are suspended in time, embedded in the memory of the past or sequestered in the hope of the future.

Given the staying power of the circle in diagramming power relations (more on this in later paragraphs) and the mutual investment of circles and historical presents in mapping and interrogating political realities, highlighting problems, and posing solutions, I propose a spatial virtuality predicated on a turn back from the temporal present to that which is spatially present, or from present to presence, as a way of conceiving of alternatives and world-making that matches the spatiality of circles, and as a way of putting the mutually invested aspects of virtuality together on a single axis. For this to occur, what is needed is a definition of spatial virtuality that also holds up and works as a theory. As I am interested in interactions between textual and material worlds, I seek ways that contemporary theory might dovetail with literature to map that dynamic. My argument, then, is two-fold. First, I define a spatial virtuality that realigns with the spatial turn in literary and cultural studies as that which is present without being local. The utility of this definition is that it enhances our circular maps of power by allowing us to think through what it means to be in or out, contained or excluded, even if/when physical location seems at odds with one of these designations.

The second part of my argument is that spatial virtuality as a conceptual enhancement can double as a resistance to these difficult-to-map conditions of sovereignty when it lends itself to what I am calling a "condition of literature," which is a condition in which literary texts refer to the conditions they create instead of referring to the conditions that create them. These conditions that are textually referred to or privileged by a work of literature determine the direction of a virtual projection. When the "direction of the projection" goes the other way—that is, when a textual build-up of information refers to and therefore perpetuates the difficult-to-map conditions of sovereignty at the expense of any material conditions that a text could otherwise invoke—then a spatial virtuality thwarts a condition of literature and fuels the very sovereignty that literature attempts to map. Remapping the present by aligning virtuality with the spatial turn, then, means extending the spatial turn to a material(ist) turn, and implicating literature in this endeavor.[2]

To appreciate the movement from temporal to spatial virtuality, it is worth tracing the various virtualities already volunteered, as well as how and why they developed, after which I can elaborate my spatial adjustment. As to what it *is* that is present without being local, I offer Judith Anderson's notion of "intertext" as the virtuality that is either the presence of outside worlds inside a circle or else the presence of inside worlds outside a circle (but this is still overly abstract). Anderson's intertext is a connector of inside and outside worlds in much the same way that, as will be shown, temporal virtuality connects pasts and futures to the present. Once the intertext shifts from time to space, it proves instrumental in mediating interactions between the circles of material worlds and textual worlds, giving (more concrete) shape to that which lies between the circumscriptions of actual political landscapes and alternative topographies, and measuring the distance between the spheres of reality and possibility. In the best case scenario, a condition of literature develops, and a virtual intertext inserts itself into, or extricates itself from, these other worlds, and it therefore asserts itself as an alternative to, or within, those worlds.

Finally, I use a literary perspective to highlight the potential of a spatial virtuality as a world connector. If using a literary method to explore the possibilities for "a condition of literature" sounds redundant, I should clarify that while literature certainly makes up textual worlds, not all textual worlds are necessarily literary, or made up of literature. Under the (inter)textual umbrella, literature finds shelter, but so do other worlds of discourse. The point of intertext is to see how everything under the umbrella transforms everything else under the same umbrella, and even, in some cases, things beyond the umbrella. To this end, my selected texts are literary, or so I argue. They are Dave Eggers's antepenultimate and penultimate novels, *A Hologram for the King* (2012) and *The Circle* (2013). In them, I find both creative and destructive obsessions with intertextual connectivity; that is to say, Eggers intuits spatial virtuality as a new way that subjects deal with material situations, and his fictions explore whether such virtuality is a symptom of, or a solution to, contemporary circumscriptions of sovereignty. Through my readings of Eggers, I find a subjectivized remapping of that which is present—to such a degree that the efficacy of spatial virtuality in making present the non-local, though it lends credence to my redefinition, can also be troubling. If the best-case scenario is the development of a condition of literature, the worst-case scenario is an ever-compounding virtuality under layers of information that put material worlds further out of reach, and so I cite my lyrical epigraph in concluding that some connections are not worth making.

The Appeal of Presence

I carefully worded my introduction so that "actual" and "actuality" are pitted against what I have called temporal virtuality. The temptation to substitute "real" for "actual" and "reality" for "actuality" provides a good point of departure for thinking through what is meant by the virtual. The virtual is a scandal of meaning, often conjuring a vortex of things that it is *not*, or of things that it *is* albeit without being something *else*: the virtual is neither real nor actual, or it is possible without being real, or it is real without being material, or it is actual even though it is not present, or (as I argue) it is present without being local. Virtuality has been theorized as unrealized potential or a not-yet-arrived future, as a solution or an alternative, as a danger or a threat, as a latent vital force, a consciousness, or even as a spirit or a soul. The virtual can indicate differences in both degree and kind—something that is virtual is *almost* complete or *practically* enough, whereas something that is virtually *x* is of a different *kind* than what is actually or really *y*. Though John Wood makes an etymological connection between the virtual and the virtuous (4), there is a strong tendency to privilege reality over virtuality on a hierarchy of meaning and experience, as my epigraph by Adam Levin exhibits. It is a trend that I admit to participating in, as becomes clear in my conclusion. Sometimes "virtual reality" assumes its own subfield under a more scientific rubric and there it becomes abbreviated as VR, and in this case the virtual is associated with the artificial, in the same vein as artificial intelligence (AI), or else with simulations—which can be the simulations of consciousness or of the conditions in which virtual and/or actual and/or real consciousness operate(s). Though some theorists are careful to distinguish VR from virtuality, many use them synonymously. As a rhetorical sobriquet for colloquial use more recently, the virtual has come to stand simply for that which is digitized—it is the stuff of cyberspace. If Gilles Deleuze's observation that "we have ceaselessly invoked the virtual" carried weight in 1968, it has only intensified in the decades since (208). Given the proliferation of interest and meanings that virtuality has garnered since the arrival of the Internet, pinning down the development of the concept helps to clarify not only what is (or what can be) meant by virtuality, but also what is at stake and therefore why its (re)definition matters.

The pitting of "virtual" against "actual" (as opposed to "real") stems from Deleuze's reading of Henri Bergson, and the formulation of virtuality as "being *something* without being something *else*" stems from Deleuze's citation of Marcel Proust, for whom "the virtual is real without being actual, ideal without being abstract" (to which Deleuze adds: "symbolic without being fictional"), both of which lead to Deleuze's somewhat slippery and circular postulate that "*the virtual is fully real in so far as it is virtual*" (208, emphasis in original). Taylor Hammer's unpacking of these readings (of Bergson and Proust) by Deleuze helps to clarify that the difference between "real" and "actual" has to do with their relationships with "possibility" and "virtuality," respectively: "if our terminology is consistent," he explains, "we must say that virtualities are actualized and possibilities are realized," and that "actualization and realization are two very different processes" (60).

So what is the difference between the processes of actualization and realization? It is the same as the difference between the virtual and the possible, which is that the possible realizes (in part) through its resemblance to the real, whereas actuality bears no resemblance to the virtual (Hammer, 60–61). One way to appreciate this difference is through temporality—to think of "the actualization of a virtual past," wherein the *actual* is in the present, versus "the realization of a possible future," wherein the *real* is also in the present.[3] However, as these formulations show, virtuality and possibility find themselves on opposite ends of the temporal divide, separated by a gulf of real and actual presents. For Deleuze, virtuality is lodged in memory, in the past, and "the appeal of the present" lies in its ability to access these past memories or recollections so that "they no longer have the ineffectiveness, the impassivity that characterizes them as pure recollections; they become recollection images, capable of being 'recalled,'" as Proust suggests by his title, *In Remembrance of Things Past*.[4]

Another "actualization" that Deleuze reads into Bergson's philosophy is that of the *élan vital*, which in turn leads to a consideration of "the actualization of 'a life,'"—both of which follow the same Deleuzian principle of *differentiation* that allows actualization of a virtual past (Hammer, 63–64). Namely, the actuality in each of these cases—that is, the virtual thing-of-the-past that actualizes into something else in the present—bears no resemblance to the virtuality from which it springs. Most commentators explain that this aspect of differentiation is important to Deleuze because of the creative potential, causality, and agency that it implies. Indeed, Hammer, along with Michael Hardt and Antonio Negri, points to this as one of Deleuze's reasons for preferring to think in terms of actualization over realization. Hardt and Negri go in a different direction, however, annotating their own definition of virtuality in *Empire* with the following:

> Our conception of virtuality and its relationship to reality is somewhat different from the one Deleuze derives from Bergson, which distinguishes between the passage from the virtual to the actual and that from the possible to the real. Bergson's primary concern in this distinction and in his affirmation of the virtual-actual couple over the possible-real is to emphasize the creative force of being and highlight that being is not merely the reduction of numerous possible worlds to a single real world based on resemblance, but rather that being is always an act of creation and unforeseen novelty. . . . We certainly recognize the need to insist on the creative powers of virtuality, but this Bergsonian discourse is insufficient for us insofar as we also need to insist on the reality of the being created, its ontological weight, and the institutions that structure the world, creating necessity out of contingency.
>
> (468)

But if Hardt and Negri express their preference for thinking in terms of the realization (instead of *actualization*) of possibilities, then, following Bergson and Deleuze (and Hammer's helpful rehearsal), it should come as no surprise that their virtualities are *future*-oriented. Possibility dwells in the future. But before diving headlong into the futuristic, kairotic, and utopian inflections that are so characteristic of Hardt and Negri's work and that give them *their* appeal, there is another aspect of *Empire* that speaks once again to the appeal of presence that I want to sketch, and that is its role, in some ways, as an interlocutor of Foucault's late work.

Foucault's notions of biopower and governmentality, which he began to explore in the later part of his career, have been picked up in a variety of divergent and interesting ways by contemporary theorists. Some have attempted to rearticulate models of sovereignty (e.g., Agamben) while others have attempted to rethink the implications of such power relations and ethical modes of negotiating these interpreted power arrangements (e.g., Bersani and Phillips). Some theorists, such as Hardt and Negri, have

ambitiously attempted both: Empire is the name they give to their interpretation of a contemporary biopolitical sovereignty, and their chapter
called "Virtualities" combines the "ontological weight" that they are sensitive to, and which they cite as their reason for following a virtual path
linking reality to the future instead of a virtual path linking actuality
to the past, with an "ethico-political" discourse designed to "calculate
passions and interests" (353). It is here that many strands of scholarship
converge on a foundation of Foucault. We have seen Foucault's interest in the present, which is how he opens *Discipline and Punish* and
which inspires the likes of Lauren Berlant to take up a similar methodological vocabulary. Foucault's *History of Sexuality* trilogy introduces
his landmark biopower but it also sets him on a new foray into ethics.
But there is also something scattered throughout these later works that
seems to verge either on futurity or spatiality, depending on how such
things as "utopia" and "distance" are read, synthesized, and resolved.
For example, *Discipline and Punish* ends on (what *might* be called) a
futuristic note in its allusion to "the distant roar of battle" (308). If we
read this "distance" against "the present" that begins this volume as a
spatial metaphor for time, then Foucault's battle is one that happens not
in some far-away place, as "distance" spatially and literally indicates, but
in the future: the battle that will take place later. Similarly, the utopia that
he defines to pave the way for his neologistic heterotopia is an entirely
spatial concept, and he means it as such: utopia is a place with no location (23–24). But the overt spatiality of utopia has not kept so-called
utopian tracts, such as Hardt and Negri's *Empire*, from being read as
future-oriented manifestos more so than *spatial* manifestos, laden with
emphasis on the future possibilities for present realities, as Hardt and
Negri are quick to embrace.

This convergence of space with the future is not necessarily surprising. After all, it takes time to get somewhere. What I think is surprising,
or at least unexpected, is that Foucault's interlocutors are responding
to difficult-to-define conditions of power relations with just-as-difficult-
to-define ontologies, ethics, and politics. Hardt and Negri collapse the
ontological and ethico-political "weights" of this response and call it
virtuality, while others, such as N. Katherine Hayles, are calling virtuality *itself* a condition (more on this later), so that, following Hayles,
one result of taking Foucault's biopolitical cue is to respond to the subjectivizing conditions of sovereignty with the ontological, ethical, and
political conditions of virtuality—that is, responding to conditions with
conditions, a very contingent exercise; and we will recall that "creating
necessity out of contingency" is something that Hardt and Negri "need
to insist on." Moreover, we have seen how these conditions of virtual
response seem to have shifted from actuality to reality in the wake of
Foucault. In terms of Bergson and Deleuze's virtuality, this shift gives
the appearance of a shift from the past to the future, though it might

actually be a shift from time to space altogether—from virtual or possible things converging on the present to arrive at actuality or reality from the opposite ends of the past and the future, respectively, to a preoccupation with spatial presence, in which virtual or possible things converge on *presence* to arrive at information or materiality, also from the opposite ends of dislocation. But instead of a virtual past and a possible future, with actualities and realities hanging out in the present, a spatial model of virtuality means that we have virtually dislocated heres and possible theres, with information and material bodies filling some textual or linguistic gap known as presence. Deleuze's "appeal of the present" thus becomes a post-Foucaultian "appeal of presence," as virtuality becomes the spatial response to biopolitical conditions of sovereignty.

Returning to Hardt and Negri's "Virtualities" in *Empire*, we should not be surprised to find an overwhelmingly spatial description of the virtual condition that links up with futurity: "We are situated precisely at that hinge of infinite finitude that links together the virtual and the possible, engaged in the passage from desire to a coming future (*This ontological relation operates first of all on space)*" (361, emphasis added). Here we are given, quite explicitly, the "hinge" to swing straight from the future into space. It is a movement that resonates. Brian Massumi defines the virtual "as that which is maximally abstract yet real, whose reality is that of potential," and potential, he says, "is the space of play—or would be, were it a space. It is the *modification* of a space" (58, 75). Daniel Downes is one of those careful theorists who distinguishes virtual reality from virtuality and describes the latter as "a person's incorporation of, or adaptation to, a new technologically mediated situation" (72), which is not necessarily temporal or spatial by itself but it does allow for either, and further, it shares an affinity with Marshall McLuhan's "electronic tribalism," which invests subjects with "a new ability feel *present* across vast distances. Presence in this context concerns the assumption of an *optimum range* for the self beyond which it fragments, dissolves, and disappears" (71, emphasis in original). McLuhan's own flirtations with virtuality are remarkable not only for preceding the work done by those post-Deleuze who take the futuristic turn in virtuality, but for preceding much of the technology and vocabulary that triggered that turn in the first place. It is one thing for Downes to follow Bachelard's seminal "poetics of space" with his own "poetics of cyberspace" in 2005, but quite another for McLuhan to discuss, in the late 1960s (just after Bachelard's *The Poetics of Space* and amid the spatial turn happening more broadly in critical circles but apart from virtual theory), the implications of technological media in which his "typographical man takes readily to film just because, like books, it offers an inward world of fantasy and dream" (391). McLuhan, punning on the difference between the "Reel World" of movies and the real world, sets up the virtuality of art as an avatar nearly half a century before the release of James Cameron's *Avatar* (2009), and he does so with a heightened proprioceptive attention to how the body moves in both space and time as well as with a working concept of art, broadly, as an "inward world."[5]

Before exploring the inward world of art, however, a final definition of virtuality is in order that grounds my spatial adjustment toward *presence* in my own ethico-political preference for materiality over information, since materiality, as we are about to see, aligns with a presence-absence coupling, in contradistinction to the pattern-randomness coupling that aligns with information. The definition comes from N. Katherine Hayles, for whom "virtuality is the condition millions of people now inhabit" (182). I alluded to this condition earlier to make the point that the condition of virtuality is a response to the condition of Empire as a power structure, but the precise nature of the condition is what matters here: "*Virtuality is the cultural perception that material objects are interpenetrated by information patterns*" (182, emphasis in original). Hayles clarifies that the condition is a cultural perception, and this cultural perception, she continues, is the result of "a historically specific construction that emerged in the wake of World War II" that posits "*information as the site of mastery and control over the material world*" (184–85, emphasis in original). To illustrate this point, Hayles close-reads the Human Genome Project as a narrative that somehow manages to conceive of DNA "as the originary informational pattern that produces the body, even though logically the gene is contained within the body, not the other way around."[6] The appeal of the narrative is that "if human beings are essentially informational patterns" (186), then they are free of material and therefore of physical, political, real-world limitations, and a virtual existence creates immortality: "the great dream and promise of information is that it can free from the material constraints that govern the mortal world. If we become the information we have constructed, we too can soar free, immortal like the gods" (188).

In addition, Hayles explains that information relies on a pattern/randomness dialectic as opposed to the presence/absence dialectic that aligns with materiality (if I was careful to pit "virtual" against "actual" in my introduction, I was also careful to mention a circle's concern with presence and absence), and she finds that she self-consciously wants to transgress the narrative in which information wins on the grounds that "the efficacy of information depends on a highly articulated material base" (185), that "the perceived primacy of information over materiality obscures the importance of the very infrastructures that make information valuable" (186), and that "information must *always* be instantiated in a medium" (189, emphasis in original). In a lively piece, then, Hayles-the-posthumanist goes to bat for materiality, which leads her to fight for spatiality, which leads her to fight for what she claims to be at stake for literary theory:

> When information is privileged over materiality, the pattern/randomness dialectic associated with information is perceived as dominant over the presence/absence dialectic associated with materiality. The condition of virtuality implies, then, a widespread perception that presence/absence is being displaced and preempted by pattern/randomness.

As this displacement suggests, the impact of virtuality on literary theory and practice will be far-reaching and profound. At present, virtuality is largely *terra incognito* for the literary establishment. In *City of Bits*, William Mitchell has written insightfully about how technologies of information are forcing a reconceptualization of literary theory and practice. Part of what is at stake for me in this analysis is to show that materiality, far from being left behind, interacts at every point with the new forms that literature is becoming as it moves into virtuality (190).

Hayles's concomitant defense of spatiality is elided in this passage, but it is logically nestled between her defense of materiality and her understanding of how the new, virtual condition of literature relies on materiality—an insight corroborated (in an unrelated project) by Elizabeth Grosz, who complicates and nuances the relations between spatiality and materiality. For Grosz, it is precisely that mind and body *cannot* be separated—the *opposite* of Cartesian dualism—that leads her to connect spatiality to materiality in much the same way that she connects virtuality to reality (81). For Grosz as for Hayles, the inseparability of mind and body extends to the inseparability of all the other related false dichotomies (this "relation between the virtual and the real prefigures and is entwined with a whole series of other oppositional terms—among them, mind and body, culture and nature, origin and copy," 81), including and especially the inseparability of some sort of informationalized and therefore abstracted presence from a material presence. Since it is precisely the virtual object's ability to enact "real" effects and to engage our "real" senses that affords it virtual status, and since the putative abstractness or disembodiedness of an object still relies on some material medium if we are ever to experience those real senses, then virtuality as a concept of informationalized materiality is shaky at best. Grosz's suggestion is to reconceive of the virtual as, essentially, "the strangeness of writing, of inscription" (77), which is "just as rife with potential"—just as open to the future—"as cyberspace itself"; as a "(temporal) displacement, not simply deferral but endless openness" that "poses no threat to the real because it is a mode of production and enhancement of the real: an augmentation, a supplementation, and a transformation of the real by and through its negotiation with virtuality" (89–90).

However they may differ tonally about what virtuality has to offer, Hayles and Grosz are united to the extent that they distrust the dominant cultural narrative espousing a purely informational interface bereft of materiality. Just as Hayles reads the narrative of DNA as culture's constructed triumph of information over materiality, for example, she also analyzes the popular computer game *Myst* and its treatment of books. In her analysis, Hayles says that *Myst* gives books a "fetishistic quality" that "is consistent with their representation as [material] anachronisms" (192). According to the computer game, books are subject to the condition of virtuality, and so, as material objects, they become products interpenetrated by informational patterns as their material presences (appear to) wane.

No wonder that Hayles heads toward a vision of "spatiality and virtual writing"—it is her attempt to cope with a condition, as she defines it, just as the condition of virtuality copes with the condition of subjectivizing power. But to continue responding to conditions with conditionality only compounds the condition of virtuality with ever-increasing layers of information and virtualities end up housing virtualities. I once had a "virtual desktop" installed on my office computer, which meant that I could click an icon from my "actual desktop" and be taken "behind the screen" to another so-called "desktop." Presumably, *that* desktop could have had a hyperlink to another virtual desktop, too. By Hayles' definition of virtuality, a book is shot through with information to the point that it becomes secondary to the pattern-over-randomness dialectic, which means that computer-game books are subject to the condition of virtuality in the same way that my virtual desktops are perceived as virtually housed in non-physical locations—or in the way that they are present without being local. By reprioritizing materiality over information, however—that is, by privileging a presence-over-absence dialectic—the information patterns of computer-game books would be re-infused with materiality, and the "virtuality of books" would acquire a new, inverted sense. Books (of any kind) could now be subject to what I suggest we call a condition of literature: a book's virtuality now refers to its own "inward world" *that it creates*, instead of only and always referring to the fact that it resides in the "inward world" of something else *that created it*,[7] which preserves the agency that Bergson and Deleuze would have wanted for it and which builds on Grosz's wonderful "strangeness of writing" in a way that spatializes her openness to the future. Hence the appeal of presence.

I have argued for *presence* as the basis for a spatial virtuality, and not for an obliteration of virtuality, because even a materially driven presence might, following Grosz, be just as virtual as it is real or actual (especially if the presence in question is called into being through writing or inscription), or, because there is still the question of interaction and mediation between that which is present and that which is not. A spatial virtuality is something that is present without being local. This will appeal to anyone, like Bruno Latour, attempting to "reassemble the social," since it implies a way of "localizing the global," "redistributing the local," and "connecting sites" (2005).

What if a condition of literature means that language and texts are the presence around which information and material bodies congregate? Then languages and texts would act as intermediaries, which is exactly what languages and texts do. In addition, the virtuality of that which is present without being local would be animated by a positive content, meaning that, as a condition, virtuality need not retreat into further conditions but that it could engage in relationships. If a spatially virtual site is to be a nexus for conditions and relationships, languages, and texts, then Judith Anderson has already constructed the "allegorical intertext" as precisely this thing that can "operate virtually" as a nonlocal presence. She even compares it to the Internet, so that it resonates both virtually and spatially:

> The title of this volume, *Reading the Allegorical Intertext: Chaucer, Spenser, Shakespeare, Milton,* plays on "surfing the Internet." I conceive the intertext, like the Internet, as a state, or place, of potential, one that can variously be narrowed or expanded, minimized or enlarged. More exactly, the intertext is a convenient term for a relationship or a series of relationships with a single text or multiple texts that enrich and reorient the signification and reception of the text in question. The intertext can be imagined on a continuum between deliberate imitation and intentional allusion, on the one hand, and on the other, an intertextuality in which the unlimited agency of the signifier *operates virtually* without regard for context, whether sentential and textually specific or broadly cultural, societal, and historical. While authorial agency and linguistic free play are opposing binaries in the abstract, in practice they coexist interestingly, elusively, and indefinitely. The same applies to the coexistence of individual agency with cultural and societal determinism.
>
> Necessarily, as a condition of potentiality and relationship, the intertext, like any good fiction, is conceptually and functionally unstable.
>
> (1–2, emphasis added)

What I am doing here is metatheoretical, metacritical. I am accepting Anderson's invitation to surf the intertext. However, instead of entering at one of the recommended portals called Chaucer, Spenser, Shakespeare, or Milton, I am wading into Anderson's own textual waters and I am making it my intertextual wave. Moreover, I am holding Anderson to her own claim that *her* "authorial agency" and *my* "linguistic free play" indeed "coexist interestingly, elusively, and indefinitely." By way of example, I will co-opt her use of the word "virtually" to suit my purposes. Although I am nearly certain, based on her use of the word elsewhere in the book and within its context here (which she says we can disregard), that she intends for this word to be taken more loosely than my co-option of it, I have taken literally and technically the notion that intertextuality operates virtually. The virtuality—that is, "the condition of potentiality and relationship"—that Anderson builds into her theory works instantly: I have just used it to connect her textual world to my material world.

And Michael Taussig wonders whether, "with disembodiment," does "presence expand?" And then he answers, yes, that "language is like that too" (3). Taussig's insight (though it erroneously tethers language to disembodiment) together with Anderson's intertext (that corrects Taussig's error while affirming his insight regarding expanded presence) provides a new perspective on the "inward worlds" of art that McLuhan gestures toward, and transitioning now into literary worlds we can see how inward worlds made up of language carry the potential to expand their presences into materiality, but also that they can shrink into themselves and pad themselves with information, depending on whether they are virtual in reference to what they create, or to what creates them. Hayles offers a reading of George Gamow's *Mr. Tomkins Inside Himself* (1968), a story in which,

> on a visit to his doctor, Mr. Tomkins is sitting in the waiting room when he hears a sucking sound and feels a strange sensation of constriction. Somehow he is drawn into a hypodermic needle and then injected inside his own body.
>
> (184)

Hayles sees this as a reenactment of information's victory over materiality, an illogical narrative parallel to the story of DNA that turns the world inside out. She then turns to Hans Moravec's *Mind Children* (1990), which entertains the possibilities of downloading consciousness onto a computer:

> As "you" are transferred into a computer, the trashed body is left behind, an empty husk. Once "you" are comfortably inside your shiny new body, "you" effectively become immortal. For when that body wears out or becomes obsolete, "you" can simply transfer your consciousness to a new model.
>
> (186)

Hayles's readings are consistent with her definition of virtuality as a condition of being created by information, which strips text of its agency.

This is why she goes to bat for literature via spatiality via materiality. Others are more optimistic, perhaps intuiting a condition of literature that reverses this tendency of virtuality to shrink inside itself, and to use textual language to expand its presence instead. Leo Bersani, for example, offers a reading of Henry James's *A Beast in the Jungle* (1903) in which "the rare dignity" of "a life lived as pure virtuality" might provide a model for anonymous interactions within our current circle of Empire so long as one doesn't "speak of it as if it were an affective and moral failure" (24). Bradley Smith finds that Richard Powers "destroys the boundary between the material world and the virtual world" in his 2001 novel, *Plowing the Dark*, since "in a virtual reality there can be the perception of reality without the presence of things-in-themselves" (100). Smith is still operating on a temporal virtuality (of the futuristic, real-possible variety) to think that virtual reality displaces presence, but that is only because he equates presence and locality; his insight that virtuality can destroy the boundaries between worlds gets even more mileage when we separate presence and locality in a spatial virtuality, as Dave Eggers does. Reading Eggers, the question becomes not whether the presence of language expands, but indeed, what are the limits, if any, of the intertext's presence?

A *Hologram* and a *Circle*: Eggers's Spatial Virtualities

In Eggers's *A Hologram for the King*, an American salesman, Alan Clay, travels to Saudi Arabia to pitch his company's hologram projection technology to King Abdullah. Alan's company, Reliant, is an American-based conglomerate, "the largest IT supplier in the world," and Alan needs this deal to go through to pay down his debts, fund his daughter's college tuition, and to reestablish himself as a functional and respectable member of society (20). Alan is therefore extremely reliant on Reliant, but upon his arrival in Saudi Arabia, things do not go according to plan. He and his Reliant staffers stay in a hotel a good distance from the King Abdullah Economic City, KAEC (the Saudi answer to Dubai); when they arrive on-site at KAEC, they are housed in a tent without air conditioning and spotty Wi-Fi, which they will need to have working optimally in order to project their hologram. The crew spends days driving to and from KAEC, sweltering in the tent, waiting for the king. Virtuality beckons as one kind of connectivity is leveraged for another kind of connectivity and layers of privileged information begin to mount.

But the idea for spatial virtuality is based on the hologram itself, and the process that brings it to fruition. If temporal virtuality hinges on the processes of actualization and realization, then spatial virtuality depends on a process of present-ation, or "presencing,"[8] the process of making something present, which in turn depends on the material substrate that Hayles insists upon. Back at KAEC, Alan Clay and his team struggle with material conditions. "For a holographic presentation, they needed a hard line, and if not that, a massive signal, nothing faint or poached" (57). The word "signal" here is "crucial," as Hayles explains:

> In information theoretic terms, no message is ever sent. What is sent is a signal. The distinction information theory posits between signal and message is crucial. A message has an information content specified by a probability function that has no dimensions, no materiality, and no necessary connection with meaning. It is a pattern, not a presence. Only when the message is encoded in a signal for transmission through a medium—for example, when ink is printed on paper or electrical pulses are sent racing along telegraph wires—does it assume material form.
>
> (187)

A "massive signal," then, for massive "presence," which is precisely what Reliant's holographic presentation is intended to be. By the time the material infrastructure is in place to rehearse the presentation, the result is "astonishment":

> One of their colleagues in London appeared to be walking around the stage in their Red Sea tent, could react to live questions, could interact with Rachel or Cayley on the stage. It was the kind of technology that only Reliant had, only Reliant could deliver for a price. Making the prototype in the U.S. had been catastrophically expensive, but they'd found a supplier in Korea who could build the lenses into their specs, at about a fifth of the cost in America, even cheaper if they shopped it out to a Chinese factory. Reliant would make a robust profit on any unit, but more than that, the telepresence technology was part of an overall juggernaut of baseline telecom abilities, the ability to wire an entire city, and on the higher end, this kind of astonishment. Alan was utterly confident that the presentation, when Abdullah arrived, would seal the deal quickly.
>
> (199)

Astonishing, indeed. The colleague who appeared to be walking on the stage achieves a spatial virtuality through his or her non-local presence. This colleague, projecting holographically in a tent by the Red Sea, is able to interact in and with the material reality of KAEC from London. Eggers's effect, like Richard Powers's virtuality, "destroys the boundary between the material world and the virtual world." The hologram, having "localized the global" and having "redistributed the local" appears to succeed in "connecting" Latour's "sites." And with the insertion of a cosmopolitan English presence into a traditional Arabian kingdom, and with the dispersal of audio and video feeds back to London, it is perhaps not too strong to state that a "reassemblage of the social" occurs via spatial virtuality, if by "the social" we mean (still following Latour) "that which is associated" (Latour, 5). Reliant's tele*presence* technology connects and associates two spatially distinct worlds, but it does so without locality. The hologram does not effect a change in proximity but in presence.

Of course there is a material situation in London allowing this to occur. There is also a material situation in Saudi Arabia allowing this to occur. And there is a material situation mediating these two sites and contributing to and cooperating with the material infrastructure set up by Alan's team inside the tent, just as the global outsourcing of the hologram's contracts and manufacturing also participate in a material situation. Eggers describes a condition of neoliberal capitalist flows as the condition to which the hologram, in turn as a condition in its own right, responds. This is how the existence of London's materialist situation does nothing to vitiate its virtual presence in Saudi Arabia. The location of London is involved, yes, but the cultural perception is that its informational presence preempts or displaces its material reality—according to Hayles' definition, it is precisely the informatic trappings that give the hologram its virtuality. And despite her complaint that this is tantamount to locating London inside itself in the same way that a gene located inside a body is credited with the materialization of that body, the response nevertheless supports the narrative. The material body that is a colleague in London is outstripped by information in another location; in this particular location, KAEC, information wins and materiality loses because the conditions of virtuality adhere to the conditions that create it. The hologram is a commodified piece of technology that supports the conditions that brought it into existence. It will probably, if things go Reliant's way, even become responsible for increased sales of itself, if it ends up in the right boardrooms, conference halls, and convention centers where executives can use the technology to close deals selling the technology.

But this spatial virtuality is virtual in another sense, too. Just as the virtuality of books is for Hayles the result of their being trapped under layers of information inside a computer game, an *actual* and *real* book is still virtual in that sense that McLuhan, Norton, Grosz, and Moslund identify. Art and inscription create presence. A hologram cannot help responding to a neoliberal condition if that's the situation it finds itself in, just as a book cannot decide who writes it. But the hologram, like the book, *is* a virtuality, after all, and it *does* simulate presence. No, "simulate" is the wrong word, since it evokes the origin-copy dichotomy that Grosz challenges. Rather, holograms and books as virtualities *create presence* in the way that Moslund and the geocritical school insist: they *presence*, as a verb. The worlds that get created and connected need not be mutually reinforcing of the conditions that bring them together, just as a book need not be an autobiography. At one extreme, the hologram perpetuates the conditions that make it. At another extreme, the hologram can be used as a tool in its own destruction.[9] We don't want the hologram sucked through a needle and shot inside itself, like Mr. Tompkins, but neither do we want it subsumed by that which it might oppose, either. But *between* these two extremes, where virtuality is most at home,[10] is an intertext, a condition of potentiality and relationship. Who is to say which worlds the hologram connects? Why not textual worlds? In the right hands, the hologram could project exhibits, performances, protests, dialogues, films, and even *materially real* books, as much as it could project heads of state, dignitaries, corporate executives, celebrities, and sales pitches. If the hologram is truly used for communication more than it stands in as a symbol of Haraway's Informatics of Domination, then various worlds of discourse and text and language all have access to each other. The inward worlds of art can interact, and the intertext hums with engaged surfers. The hologram thus carries in it the appeal of virtual presence.

Determining which version of virtuality Eggers's hologram represents—the hopeful, supplementary, intertextual model, or one of the extremes as articulated by Grosz—seems to depend on what relationships, in Eggers's textual world, can accomplish, or else on the degree to which technology is seen as helpful in facilitating these relationships. In the first instance, we are told very early on that "relationships no longer mattered, Alan knew this. They did not matter in America, they did not matter much of anywhere, but here, among the royals, he hoped that friendship had meaning" (20). This is a deflating condition of the world to which a virtuality predicated on a condition of relationships might not respond well. But in the second instance, it is hinted that the connecting of worlds might simply be an undertaking that does not ask much of technology—certainly not "catastrophically expensive" technology. Toward the end of the novel, Alan has a conversation with a medical doctor, Zahra, who removes a lipoma from the back of his neck. He also happens to be falling in love with her. As he is a middle-aged American salesman, and she is a slightly younger woman of Lebanese-Arab-Swiss-Greek-Dutch heritage practicing medicine in Saudi Arabia, Alan is curious about the conditions of potentiality and relationship that bring them together. He is, in short, curious about their intertext:

- What do you think our kids would make of this? he asked.
- How do you mean? You and me? Because we represent some kind of culture clash?
- I guess so.
- Please. We're separated by the thinnest filament.
- Well, that's the way I think.
- That's the way it is. She looked at him sternly. I won't let us play those games. It's so tiresome. Leave that to the undergraduates.

(292)

This "thinnest filament" is still an acknowledgment of a world divider, but perhaps Zahra's larger point is that a common language and some proximity is technology enough to remove this filament and to bridge the gap with the meaningful presence of something that is not local. The possible conclusions seem to include that (1) a spatial virtuality that *simulates* presence (instead of *creating* presence) is not necessary when you've got proximity, (2) that a spatial virtuality that *simulates* presence (instead of *creating* presence) is ineffective when relationships don't matter, or (3) that a spatial virtuality that *does create* presence is not given the chance to show what it is capable of in a setting where relationships *do* matter. In *A Hologram for the King*, Eggers sets up this last option as an as-yet unconducted experiment, though the first two options may form hypotheses. Eggers saves the conduction of his experiment for *The Circle*.

Richard Norton tells us that, without virtuality, the world would collapse (500). The line is delivered tongue-in-cheek—Norton's writing is delightfully witty—but the point, having to do with completion, is serious in light of how Eggers's experiment in *The Circle* plays out, how the intertextual conditions of potentiality and relationships unfold, how presence (or absence) obtains. What is at stake in the relationship between a spatial virtuality and completion has everything to do with remapping the present, since the purpose of shifting to presence is to determine a virtual space in relation to the circles of sovereignty—the open or closed, broken or whole, single or plural, separate or overlapping circles that do or do not contain or exclude a presence.

If there is any doubt as to the ubiquity of circles in mapping conceptions of sovereignty, look no further than Jacques Rancière's *Dissensus*, which, as I understand it, is another Foucault interlocution as well as a redrawing of Agamben's iron-clad circle in *Homo Sacer*, and Hardt and Negri's circle with no edge from *Empire* to *Commonwealth*. Rancière's work conceives of a politics for "those who simply fall outside of the happy circle of state and right" (11) (or of "fact and law," [102]), a way to escape the "vicious circle of a theory" that identifies "the subject of the Rights of Man with the subject deprived of rights" (71), a way to assist Derrida in breaking "the circle of the self" (52), and a way to erase the consensual "circle of 'infinite injustice'" (103). It is nothing short of a way to redraw "the very circle of 'political philosophy' itself" (40).

How does Eggers's circle fit? What sort presence map does *The Circle* provide? How does the desire to collapse the weight of ontological along with ethico-political concerns into the dimensions of the circles that we imagine to map presences of power operate within the experiment that Eggers conducts? I think it confirms that another experiment is needed. If what was missing in *A Hologram for the King* was an acknowledgement that relationships matter, we will see that what is missing in *The Circle* is an intertext. In this "inward world," there are emphasized and prioritized relationships, but they are all internal—they comprise an insular text that either refuses to or simply cannot move between textual presences. The singular world of *The Circle* responds only to the mapping of the present *as* a circle and nothing else. Conditions stack up and virtualities locate themselves within their own casings. In some ways, fiction writers are every bit the theorists as are Foucault's interlocutors who envision new modes of relationship in order to cope with or respond to certain power structures. If Bersani detects a virtual "intimacy" in James' *The Beast in the Jungle*, for example, perhaps Eggers also imagines new ways for people to "connect," equally virtual. But, if so, then Eggers also imagines the nightmare of using virtuality to compound its conditions and create more of itself, so that *The Circle* is drawn into its own inward world much like Mr. Tomkins ends up inside his own body.

Mae Holland is an employee of The Circle, which is somewhat reminiscent of *Hologram*'s Reliant but much more heavily invested in social media formats. The Circle presents itself with "its name and logo—a circle surrounding a knitted grid, with a small 'c' in the center" (2). This visual metaphor cannot be more literal: by the end of the novel, this totalizing and totalitarian company envisions "completing the circle," modifying the logo so that it goes from the small 'c' to a circular 'o': "Completion is the end. We're closing the circle around everyone—it's a totalitarian nightmare" (481). It is a map of power with very clearly defined boundaries.

From gaining employment at this prestigious company to finding herself warned in this dialogue about the consequences of completing The Circle, Mae is encouraged to get connected. She learns to participate through nine screens of social media on her desk at once. (Presumably each of those screens can house virtual desktops within virtual desktops within virtual desktops.) Mae watches people communicate with advanced telecommunications technologies even when they have direct proximity to those with whom they share information. She sees people watching the projection of a figure who stands several feet away from them. Her response time to emails and text messages approaches instantaneous. In short, Mae undergoes a steady transformation in which she negotiates a dialectic of "knowing" and "not knowing"—eventually, "knowing" (like information) triumphs, and Mae attributes the broken feeling inside her, described throughout as a black tearing of her inner fabric, to a condition of "not knowing." But this is a gradual process. There are times before the nightmare is complete in which Mae is convinced that there might be such a thing as *too much* information, that not every facet of a personal life needs to be shared publically, and that the material presence of those with whom she might relate matter as much or more than the information-sharing itself that makes such a hyper relational environment possible. The tearing inside her morphs from a condition of knowing too much (information overload) to never being able to know enough (information addiction).

To be sure, material presence within The Circle is given consideration before it is dismissed in favor of pure information. Just as there is
no denying the material conditions that contribute to the projection of
a hologram, there is no escaping that The Circle must store its information cloud in physical, water-cooled, underground tanks. The Circle must
keep its employees fit and sane. It must expand its circumference by buy-
ing up the surrounding properties and converting them to its campus. But
each of these material considerations is
    deprioritized according to an information narrative that renders The
Circle's material infrastructure invisible and irrelevant.
    In a telling passage before Mae has been completely won over by the
"need to know," two of her supervisors, Denise and Josiah, confront her
about her lack of participation in the company's social media. Denise
and Josiah learn that Mae has been dealing with her father's MS without
"reaching out to any Circlers during this crisis." They want to know
why, and Mae explains:

> "I wasn't very present."
> Denise raised a finger. "Ah, *present*. That is a wonderful word. I'm
> glad you used it. Do you consider yourself usually present?"
> "I try to be."
> Josiah smiled and tapped a flurry into his tablet.
> "But the opposite of present would be what?" Denise asked.
> "Absent."
> "Yes. Absent. Let's put a pin in that thought, too."
>
> (182, emphasis in original)

If Mae puts a pin in that thought, it falls out. She progresses through the
ranks of The Circle (indeed, through her "PartiRank") with increasing
commitment to the company's vision of complete transparency based on
the unfettered flows of information, and her physical presence steadily
diminishes while her informational presence increases. Mae succeeds in
being present without being local. And it is her very reliance on The
Circle's hyperconnectivity that destroys "the condition of potentiality
and relationship" that should otherwise be obtained between her and her
parents, and between her and her ex-boyfriend, Mercer. In other words,
information overload vitiates Mae's intertextual relations and confines
her to the terms and conditions—that is, the insular textual world—of
The Circle. Finally, Mae eventually gains so much informational, social-
media presence through The Circle that her material presence suffers to
the extent that it becomes foreign and unintelligible, and she no longer
understands the needs of others' for privacy outside of The Circle. Mae
no longer comprehends the shape of a circle as a map of power, and therefore has lost the ability to understand that she has been fully integrated
into the self-perpetuating designs and conditions of an all-subsuming

structure of sovereignty, and that her virtuality can therefore refer to nothing apart from the conditions of this very structure.

In The Circle, the drive to completion is a drive to perfection, and perfection is "based on complete information." Sitting in Bailey's office (Bailey is one of the Three Wise Men who controls The Circle), Mae is given the full explanation. Secrets (and therefore privacy) have never helped anyone, Bailey explains, and incomplete information is like a broken mirror that distorts our "view of ourselves" and therefore distorts our relationships. By the end, Mae is convinced that the tear inside her can be cured by complete information:

> She knew what the tear was and how to sew it closed. The tear was not knowing. Not knowing who would love her and for how long. The tear was the madness of not knowing. . . . It was not knowing that was the seed of madness, loneliness, suspicion, fear. But there were ways to solve all this. Clarity had made her knowable to the world, and had made her better, had brought her close, she hoped, to perfection. Now the world would follow. Full transparency would bring full access, and there would be no more not-knowing. Mae smiled, thinking how simple it all was, how pure. Bailey shared her smile.
>
> (287, 465)

Without virtuality, the world would collapse. Norton knows what Mae Holland does not: that virtuality should be a creative force to support and connect worlds. Such a force can be found in art. Art can be compared to a mirror. Norton knows that the reflection in a mirror is not a fully accurate representation of reality—he says that it is dangerous because it lies, but that it also gives us what we want, and so we use it for its ability to *respond* to reality without confusing it with reality (505). A mirror responds to and reflects real conditions, but it also creates and conditions its own reality. Mirrors, then, use reality to create their own worlds, their own realities, and to move between worlds. Grosz uses a mirror analogy, too, in describing a Lacanian basis for understanding virtualities that both invert and supplement external worlds—a view that "both affirms and undermines the reliance of the real on the space of virtuality, showing the necessity and impossibility of their separation":

> The mirror surface creates a virtual field that reflects the real, duplicating its spatiality and the object's visual characteristics. Gilles Deleuze later identifies a reciprocal interaction between the virtual and the real, an undecided reversibility, as if the image could take the place of the object and force the object behind the constraints of the mirror's plane. Each makes a certain imperceptible contribution to

the other, not adding any particular feature or quality but a depth of potential, a richer resonance.

(80)

Mae, on the other hand, believes that complete information is the piecing together of a broken mirror, as Bailey tells her, and that the mirror will allow us to know the truth:

> "If we look into a broken mirror, a mirror that's cracked or missing parts, what do we get?"
> Now it made sense to Mae. Any assessment, judgment, or picture utilizing incomplete information would always be wrong. "We get a distorted and broken reflection," she said.
> "Right," Bailey said. "And if the mirror is whole?"
> "We see everything."
> "A mirror is truthful, correct?"
> "Of course, it's a mirror. It's reality."
>
> (181–82)

In other words, Mae cannot appreciate Grosz's "richer resonance" precisely because virtuality's "contributions" are "imperceptible." She mistakes a mirror's virtual field for reality, which is to say that, for her, virtuality refers only to the conditions that create it and cannot meaningfully engage with broader conditions of potentiality and relationship. For Mae, the virtuality of The Circle is a virtuality devoid of intertext. Completion of The Circle—the Oircle, I suppose—is therefore the condition of virtuality that Hayles describes, and not an intertextual condition of literature. It is the result of a narrative that prioritizes information at the expense of material presence. A spatial virtuality can counter this tendency, but only if there is an intertext to plug into. A mirror may project a non-local presence similar to a hologram, but only if and when there is something outside of itself to form the conditions of potentiality and relationship. Facing mirrors, on the other hand, invert these conditions entirely. They nest virtualities inside each other so that there is no escape from the unending reflections of their own internal information, which, after a while, may cease to be information at all, and degenerate from pattern to randomness. Without an intertext, we run the risk of being caught up in our own unintelligible oircle, subject to unmappable conditions of sovereignty.

Conclusion: The Direction of the Virtual Projection

To clarify, I do not argue that Eggers's novels are subject to Hayles' condition of virtuality; rather, they are metavirtual insofar as they are virtualities depicting virtualities that project in a particular direction. Taking a cue from Robert T. Tally Jr., who takes *his* cue in discussing "The Spaces of Literature" from Thomas Pynchon's 1966 novel *The Crying of Lot 49*, I want to close by considering the nature of literature's virtual capacity to project worlds. After all, it is Pynchon's Oedipa Maas who asks, "*Shall I project a world?*" and Tally who comments that "'projecting a world' seems an entirely appropriate phrase for describing the role of literature, and a great many literary works have undoubtedly functioned as imaginary maps, diagrams, constellations, and the like" (42). Even so, a number of tensions continue to inflect and even strain my intonations of a spatial virtuality culminating, hopefully, in a condition of literature. Time and space are twin pranksters of theory, forever sliding past and into each other, disguising each other and masquerading as the other. Information and materiality mimic the pranks of time and space. There is an ever-shifting hierarchy in which privilege is assigned and reassigned to a steady rotation of actualities, realities, and virtualities. Virtuality itself eludes definition, and when definition can be agreed upon, it still remains unclear as to whether virtuality is "good" or "bad," both, or neither. In short, the tension between Grosz's "unabashed apologists of cybertechnologies" and her "nostalgic Luddites yearning for days gone by," who, by turns, detect in virtuality "a powerful force of liberation" or a "a form of ever-encroaching fascistic control," remains an unresolved and perplexing dilemma.

I don't pretend that my spatial redefinition of virtuality does much to alleviate these tensions, but I do claim it might enhance the way we think about how literature maps and negotiates power, or at the very least, how it can provoke new thinking. I can use Grosz's seminal insights, for example, to push back against her assertion that virtuality *never* threatens reality— a move which at once reveals my sympathies for material realities as well as my more extreme readings of virtual conditions. But if I have a tendency to gravitate toward the poles, it is based on an "inter(con)textual" belief that literature qua virtuality creates its own internal realities rather than merely representing some external reality—that, to appreciate Benny Liew's "postmodern sensibilities," as he calls them, literature can enact a "blurring" of "texts and contexts" (25–30). And to blur texts and contexts returns us not only to intertext, but also to Moslund's notion of "presencing," which explicates that literature projects and connects worlds and that those projections and connections—at least according to the geocritical lens that he advocates—flow in a particular direction:

> it is not so much the work that is uprooted from its locality and distributed to the nearness of a distant reader as much as it is the distant reader who stretches toward the place or the nearness of the work. It is not a matter of experiencing a location inside our "present here," to paraphrase Heidegger, but to let our thinking, our embodied thinking, "get through, persist through, the distance to

that location," to the nearness of the place from where the work "begins its presencing."[11]

Moslund has just described for us the direction of the virtual projection, and he has clarified that a spatial virtuality that remaps and renegotiates the present is a force of liberation *not* when an outside world is brought into a given circle of sovereignty, but when subjects within that circle are transported via a self-referential literature to an outside, to a beyond—to a *non-local* presence. The object of resistance is always to move *outside* those circles that Rancière so carefully tracks from antiquity to postmodernity, not to break *into* Empire from beyond its grasp. Perhaps this is why Grosz feels no threat: hers is an "architecture from the *outside*," never from within. Grosz teaches us, then, that containment is more threatening than exclusion; exclusion at least allows for Rancière's dissensus in a way that containment does not.

Moslund's clarification works in reverse, too. Just as a literature can extricate a reader from a circle, from a sovereign space to a location beyond, so can a literature that "presences" outer locales within a circle project the subjectivities from an outer world of freedom onto an inner screen of domination—it can re-subject itself to a local power arrangement. And when this happens, it is still virtuality: there is still the presence of the something that is not local, which is how we know that virtuality can be a threat. Nobody has a monopoly on virtuality (although that is a scary prospect, too, as Eggers makes clear) in the sense that if virtuality is an "augmentation" of reality, following Grosz, it may be a grim and threatening reality indeed that augments. After all, reality *itself* can be and often is threatening. A bad reality, like a bad virtuality, threatens itself.

But it is not that information is bad and that materiality is good; it is that information, like language and texts, is generally misread as immaterial. It is that information, like virtuality, has come to stand for the disembodied abstraction of knowable stuff when it is in fact a process of *inform*ing or shaping the very materiality that it appears to supersede or transgress. Digitally, information is confused for the binary codes of 1s and 0s that the opening and closing of actual-and-material gates produce, the impressions of writing, and cutting of not-random patterns onto microchips. Messages are taken for signals, and vice versa. Unfortunately, language and texts are similarly confused. Because they are so mobile, and transportable via minds, they are taken as knowable-but-immaterial codes in the same fashion as binary 1s and 0s when in fact they are incursions into material worlds. I asked earlier: What if a condition of literature means that language and texts are the presence around which information and material bodies congregate? Such a question presupposes a linguistic physicality that is technologically sufficient to project and connect worlds, to (re)map and (re)negotiate present realities.

I am ready to commit to a condition of literature that is at once virtual, but also: possible, real, actual, physical, material, symbolic, fictional, ideal, and present—but not abstract and certainly not local. *Shall I project a world?* It depends. It depends on the condition of the literature—which world and into which location? It depends on the direction of the projection. And it pays to remember that *some connections are not worth making.*

Notes

1. See Tally, 11–20. Tally opens his section on "The Spatial Turn" with a quotation from Michel Foucault's "Of Other Spaces" (1986), and he puts Foucault in the company of Jean-François Lyotard, Jacques Derrida, and Gilles Deleuze as well as David Harvey, Ed Soja, J. B. Harley, and Fredric Jameson as a cohort of theorists for whom spatiality makes gains over temporality in its usefulness in analyzing and explaining postmodernity.

2. By "extending the spatial turn to a material(ist) turn," I may appear to run the risk of ascribing to a decidedly Cartesian view of space. As Tally explains, "Descartes maintains a notion of Euclidean space in which space cannot be separated from the bodies *in* space. Following the Aristotelian definition, the term *body* here refers to anything with mass and dimensionality, and for Descartes all bodies have a fundamental characteristic, spatial extension, so that what we think of *as* space is really just this extension of bodies" (Tally, 27). Similarly, my desire to "implicate literature in this endeavor" might be seen as a willingness to engage in Edward Soja's theory of thirdspace, which, building on Henri Lefebvre's trialectics and Foucault's heterotopia, is a way to synthesize "subjectivity and objectivity, the abstract and the concrete, the real and the imagined, the knowable and the unimaginable, the repetitive and the differential, structure and agency, mind and body, consciousness and the unconscious, the disciplined and the transdisciplinary, everyday life and unending history" (Soja, *Thirdspace* 57). As to this first appearance of conflating spatiality and materiality, I turn to Elizabeth Grosz later in this piece for complication and nuance; as to the second appearance of engaging with Soja, among others, it is true, and I confess that while this chapter only tangentially flirts with thirdspace and trialectics, I imagine them as compatible with this paper and, further, I suggest that separate, explicitly intertextual treatments of thirdspace are worthwhile, as Russell West-Pavlov also seems to intuit in *Space in Theory: Kristeva, Foucault, Deleuze* (2009), though West-Pavlov is only flirting, too, with the intersection between Foucault's "positivity" and Kristeva's "intertextuality" (130).

3. Hammer, 61. Hammer uses the phrase "The Actualization of the Virtual Past," and he discusses the futurity of possibility without using the phrase "the realization of a possible future"—but I mimic the formulation and invoke the phrase in order to illustrate the temporal distance between virtuality and possibility.

4. Deleuze, *Bergsonism* 63, qtd. in Hammer, 62. The more common translation for Proust's work is *In Search of Lost Time*, but since I am reading Deleuze reading Proust, I defer to his French reading of the French novelist; either way, both versions of Proust's title testifies to the point Deleuze makes, to "the appeal of the present."

5. See Zingrone, 43–48, and Norton, 499–505. Both Zingrone and Norton conclude, in their ways, that art is always virtual.

6. Hayles, 183. Hayles cites Richard Doyle, *On Beyond Living: Rhetorical Transformations in the Life Sciences* (1997) to substantiate this point.

7. There are many angles from which to come at this—many theoretical enterprises (postmodernists and feminists leading the charge) that suggest that texts create reality rather than reflect or represent it, but there is one interesting for its intersection with spatiality studies by way of "world literature." Maurizio Ascari, discussing "The dialectics between words and reality" in *Literature of the Global Age: A Critical Study of Transcultural Narratives* (2011), identifies a "self-referential" "condition" of literature with an "emphasis on the distance between author and reader" (30–31). Ascari's discussion includes Thomas Pynchon's *The Crying of Lot 49*, which I pick up on in my conclusion because of Robert T. Tally Jr.'s interest in the same novel for his discussion of the spatiality of literature.

8. See Moslund, 29–43. Moslund, working from Heideggerian foundations, describes "a mode of reading that moves away from the *representation* of place in literature to a direct presencing or sensation of place" (31, emphasis in original), and he defines presencing as the way in which "a work makes *a world present* or how it *produces a presence* in the literal sense of 'production' as a physical 'bringing forth' of something. Presence effects 'exclusively appeal to the senses' the way art, in 'moments of intensity' touches our bodies and brings 'the things of the world close to our skin'" (31–31, emphasis in original). The quoted phrases refer to Hans Ultrecht Gumbrecht's *The Production of Presence: What Meaning Cannot Convey* (18–19).

9. Grosz discusses the two extremes in order to come to her own middle ground: "Unashamed apologists of cybertechnologies and nostalgic Luddites yearning for days gone by see VR as a powerful force of liberation and a form of ever-encroaching fascistic control, respectively" (77). We recall that, for Grosz, virtuality never threatens but only supplements reality. I return to the two extremes and Grosz's non-threatened stance in my own conclusion, in which I argue that the dangers of virtuality or virtuality's liberating qualities depend on which conditions the virtuality projects: those of a mapping literature, or those of the unmappable circles of sovereignty.

10. See Richard Norton, "What Is Virtuality?" (500–01). For Norton, virtuality occupies a place somewhere "between" the standards set by "actual" and "not good enough." Too far to one end or the other, and it ceases to be virtual—too far toward with "actual" standards, and it simply becomes actuality; too far toward with "not good enough" and it fails as virtuality.

11. Moslund, 41. Moslund's quotations are from Heidegger's *Poetry, Language, Thought* (152–56).

Works Cited

Agamben, Giorgio (1998). *Homo Sacer: Sovereign Power and Bare Life.* Trans. Daniel Heller-Roazen. Stanford: Stanford UP.

Anderson, Judith (2008). *Reading the Allegorical Intertext: Chaucer, Spenser, Shakespeare, Milton.* New York: Fordham UP.

Ascari, Maurizio (2011). *Literature of the Global Age: A Critical Study of Transcultural Narratives.* London: McFarland & Company, Inc.

Bachelard, Gaston (1994). *The Poetics of Space.* Boston: Beacon Press.

Berlant, Lauren (2011). *Cruel Optimism.* Durham: Duke UP.

Bersani, Leo and Adam Phillips (2008). *Intimacies.* Chicago: U of Chicago P.

Deleuze, Gilles (1991). *Bergsonism*. Trans. Hugh Tomlinson and Barbara Habberjam. New York: Zone Books.

—— (1994). *Difference & Repetition*. Trans. Paul Patton. New York: Columbia UP.

Downs, Daniel (2005). *Interactive Realism: The Poetics of Cyberspace*. Montreal and Kingston: McGill-Queen's UP.

Doyle, Richard (1997). *On Beyond Living: Rhetorical Transformations in the Life-Sciences*. Stanford: Stanford UP.

Eggers, Dave (2012). *A Hologram for the King*. San Francisco: McSweeney's.

—— (2013). *The Circle*. San Francisco: McSweeney's.

Foucault, Michel (1986). "Of Other Spaces." Trans. Jay Miscoviec. *Diacritcs* 16, 22–27.

—— (1995). *Discipline & Punish: The Birth of the Prison*. New York: Vintage.

Grosz, Elizabeth (2001). *Architecture from the Outside: Essays on Virtual and Real Space*. Cambridge: MIT Press.

Gumbrecht, Hans Ulrecht (2004). *The Production of Presence: What Meaning Cannot Convey*. Stanford: Stanford UP.

Hammer, Taylor (2007). "Difference and Creativity: Virtuality and Actualization in Deleuze's Reading of Bergson." *Philosophy Today* 51.1, 60–68.

Haraway, Donna (2001). "A Manifesto for Cyborgs." In *The Norton Anthology of Theory & Criticism*, 2nd ed. New York: W.W. Norton, 2190–211.

Hardt, Michael and Antonio Negri (2000). *Empire*. Cambridge: Harvard UP.

—— (2009). *Commonwealth*. Cambridge: Harvard UP.

Hayles, N. Katherine (1997). "The Condition of Virtuality." In *Language Machines: Technologies of Literary and Cultural Production*. Eds. Jeffrey Masten, Peter Stallybrass, and Nancy J. Vickers. New York: Routledge.

Heidegger, Martin (2013). *Poetry, Language, Thought*. New York: Harper and Row.

James, Henry (1993). *The Beast in the Jungle*. Mineola, NY: Dover Publications.

Latour, Bruno (2005). *Reassembling the Social: An Introduction to Actor-Network-Theory*. Oxford: Oxford UP.

Lefebvre, Henri (1991). *The Production of Space*. Trans. Donald Nicholson-Smith. Oxford: Wiley-Blackwell Press.

Levin, Adam (2010). *The Instructions*. San Francisco: McSweeney's.

Liew, Tat-siong Benny (1999). *Politics of Parousia: Reading Mark Inter(con)textually*. Boston: Brill.

Massumi, Brian (2002). *Parables for the Virtual: Movement, Affect, Sensation*. Durham: Duke UP.

McLuhan, Marshall (2011). *Understanding Media: The Extensions of Man*, Critical ed. Ed. Terrence Gordon. Berkeley: Gingko Press.

Moravec, Hans (1990). *Mind Children: The Future of Robot and Human Intelligence*. Cambridge: Harvard UP.

Moslund, Sten Pultz (2011). "The Presencing of Place in Literature: Toward an Embodied Topopoetic Mode of Reading." In *Geocritical Explorations: Space, Place, and Mapping in Literary and Cultural Studies*. Ed. Robert T. Tally Jr. New York: Palgrave Macmillan.

Myst © Ubisoft (1994). ASIN: B00000JL60. CD-ROM.

Norton, Richard (1972). "What is Virtuality?" *The Journal of Aesthetics and Art Criticism* 40.4, 499–505.

Powers, Richard (2001). *Plowing the Dark*. London: Picador.

Proust, Marcel (1919). *A la recherché du temps perdu*. Paris: NRF.

Pynchon, Thomas (1966). *The Crying of Lot 49*. New York: Harper and Row.

Rancière, Jacques (2010). *Dissensus: On Politics and Aesthetics*. London: Bloomsbury Press.

Smith, Bradley (2009). "On Reality and Virtuality: A Study of Time-Spaces in *Plowing the Dark*." *Mosaic* 42.3, 95–108.

Soja, Edward W. (1996). *Thirdspace*. Malden, MA: Blackwell Press.

Tally, Robert T., Jr. (2013). *Spatiality*. New York: Routledge.

Taussig, Michael (1997). *The Magic of the State*. New York: Routledge.

U2 (1997). "North and South of the River" on *Staring at the Sun* ©. Polygram Int'l, B0000082X3, Audio CD.

West-Pavlov, Russel (2009). *Space in Theory: Kristeva, Foucault, Deleuze*. New York: Rodopi.

Westphal, Bertrand (2011). *Geocriticism: Real and Fictional Places*. Trans. Robert T. Tally Jr. New York: Palgrave Macmillan.

Wood, John, ed. (1998). *The Virtual Embodied: Practice, Presence, Technology*. New York: Routledge.

Zingrone, Frank (2005). "Virtuality and McLuhan's 'World as Art Form'." In *The Legacy of McLuhan*. Eds. Lance Strate and Edward Wachtel. Cresskill, NJ: Hampton Press.

Part V
Plus Ultra

19 Spatial Literary Studies Versus Literary Geography?

Boundaries and Borders Amidst Interdisciplinary Approaches to Space and Literature

Robert T. Tally Jr.

Although scholars have long paid attention to the relationship between literature and space or place, the development of distinctive scholarly practices related to that work within literary studies or within such spatially oriented sciences as geography are relatively recent. It would be difficult, as well as undesirable, to pinpoint a particular date, but the last few decades of the twentieth century witnessed what has become known as the "spatial turn" in the humanities and social sciences (see, e.g., Warf and Arias), during and after which one may perceive more and more scholarly emphasis being placed on matters of space, place, and mapping, for example. Michel Foucault famously declared ours to be the "epoch of space" in a 1967 lecture, "Des espaces autres" ("Of Other Spaces") that first appeared in print only in 1984, the same year that Fredric Jameson published his epochal essay "Postmodernism, or, the Cultural Logic of Late Capitalism" that introduced to the world his influential concept of cognitive mapping. Among other key figures, these theorists were largely responsible for what Edward Soja, in the subtitle to his *Postmodern Geographies* (1989), referred to as "the reassertion of space in critical social theory," and it seemed that some of the most important work being done in the humanities and social sciences around that time was, in some way or another, tied to spatial criticism, broadly conceived. The geographer Nigel Thrift, in a 2006 article titled simply "Space," affirmed that the "spatial turn in the humanities and social sciences" had occurred roughly within "the last 20 years or so," and he correctly predicted that the relatively recent critical phenomenon will have lasting results on how we think about ourselves and the world.

What I have called *spatial literary studies* has emerged or at least come into some cognizable focus only during this period, along with other areas, methods, or practices associated with what is now sometimes referred to, but also sometimes contested as, the spatial humanities, along with such labels as literary geography, geocriticism, and geopoetics, among others (see, e.g., my Tally, *Topophrenia* 172–79). Given that these terms, and more generally the fields associated with them, are relatively new, there has been little in the way of definitively distinguishing among them; the borders between these "fields" seem quite fluid, and their practitioners often appear to operate in the same domains or, at least, in overlapping territories. Yet it makes sense that, as these critical practices or disciplinary fields develop both internally and in relation to others, practitioners and advocates would begin to draw disciplinary or theoretical boundary lines between their fields and those they see as different. In some cases, this sort of disciplinary border policing is vexed, alienating as it necessarily does those who would appear to be allies, but it may also be the case that such distinctions need to be made in order to avoid confusions that would be unhelpful to all concerned. For my own part, as an editor and as a promoter of the works of others, I have endeavored to be fairly ecumenical in my support of various forms of scholarly activity related to space and literature, even if, in my own research, I have had a narrower or more focused vision of what I am arguing for or against. As such, there seems to be some confusion about spatial literary studies and its relationship to other fields, such as literary geography, and in this essay I would like to address these issues in an attempt to, if not resolve them, then at least think them through more clearly.

To begin with, I am somewhat hesitant to identify *spatial literary studies* as the name of a distinctive disciplinary or subdisciplinary field, but it has in recent years come to signify precisely that for many readers. The occasion for these reflections is the publication of a provocative "Thinking Space" article in the journal *Literary Geographies* by Sheila Hones, "Spatial Literary Studies and Literary Geography" (2018), in which Hones pointedly distinguishes between the two. In Hones's view, the former is an "emerging field" within the humanities, while the latter a more established interdisciplinary subfield of geography with close ties to the social sciences. A co-founder and editor of the journal *Literary Geographies*, as well as the author of *Literary Geographies: Narrative Space in "Let the Great World Spin"* (2014), Hones is a leading authority on and practitioner of literary geography. Hones argues that spatial literary studies and literary geography must be understood as distinct and separate interdisciplinary fields, even if their objects of study, methods, and practitioners may occasionally overlap.

In responding to this argument here, I want to explain my use of the term *spatial literary studies* before examining in greater detail Hones's distinction between spatial literary studies and literary geography. I find that literary geography may not be as stable a category as Hones suggests, before exploring some of the issues arising from the putative interdisciplinarity of these fields, concluding that spatial literary studies may be best imagined as operating strictly within the disciplinary bounds of literature and the humanities, even if those boundaries are themselves subject to constant modification and transgression.

The Origins of Spatial Literary Studies

When I first started using the term *spatial literary studies*, I did not intend it to refer to a particular methodology or approach, but merely as a way of characterizing a wide variety of work in literary studies that paid attention to space, place, mapping, spatial relations, geography, architecture, and so on. Somewhat naively, perhaps, I had thought that the word *spatial* could function as a mere adjective here, but in so doing, I effectively created a category—that is, "Spatial Literary Studies"—that appeared to encompass an array of more-or-less discrete scholarly and critical practices within its rather expansive ambit. This is precisely what Hones criticizes, since it would appear that spatial literary studies is defined in such a way as to engulf what she takes to be the more established field of literary geography, as well as such other methodologies or subfields as geocriticism or geopoetics, without acknowledging the specific characteristics that distinguish spatial literary studies from these others. Even if I wanted to insist that *spatial literary studies* does not refer to a distinct field of its own but simply describes multiple practices and approaches to space, place, and literature, this would not altogether eliminate the confusion over which types of work would appear under this or that categorical label. Besides, the choice may not be mine to make. If I myself can be referred to as "the main proponent of spatial literary studies" (Pegenaute 196) and others have recognized spatial literary studies as an "emerging field" in its own right (Hones, "Spatial" 148), then my own more informal use of the phrase may have little bearing on how it is understood in the wider world. Moreover, there are other important scholars, such as Ying Fang in China, who are already making significant and field-defining contributions to spatial literary studies, which have helped to clarify the distinctions between a range of otherwise apparently similar practices today (see Fang). All of this, in addition to Hones's critique of this terminological and disciplinary conflation, indicates that a clearer articulation of spatial literary studies as a field distinct from literary geography, among others, might be both desirable and productive.

The clearest difference between spatial literary studies and literary geography, one that Hones also identifies, would be that the former maintains itself within the discipline of literature or, more broadly, the humanities, whereas literary geography, as Hones understands it, would be both more interdisciplinary—that is, operating *between* literature and geography—and more closely tied to geography and to the social sciences. While practitioners in each field might engage in interdisciplinary research, those involved with spatial literary studies would remain more closely associated with literature. I am perfectly willing to embrace this distinction, as I will discuss more in the following.

Indeed, my own initial use of the phrase *spatial literary studies* may in fact have arisen as a sort of disciplinary gesture, delimiting the field by inadvertently limiting its interdisciplinarity, without my having consciously intending it at the time. As Hones points out, I did not refer to spatial literary studies by name in *Spatiality* (2013), and the "term seems to have come into use a year or so later, initially as part of the general title for Palgrave Macmillan's series on *Geocriticism and Spatial Literary Studies*" (Hones, "Spatial" 147). Others may have used the term before me, but Hones is correct in connecting my use with the development of this book series. Shortly after my translation of Bertrand Westphal's *Geocriticism: Real and Fictional Spaces* (2011) and my edited collection *Geocritical Explorations: Space, Place, and Mapping in Literary and Cultural Studies* (2011) were published, my editor at Palgrave Macmillan asked if I would be willing to propose a book series on "Geocriticism." Of course, I agreed, but I thought that this term might be too narrowly understood, so I offered "Geocriticism and Spatial Literary Studies" as a more open and welcoming sign. Again, I had not imagined either geocriticism or spatial literary studies to be a discipline or subdiscipline in itself, and my use of the word *spatial* was strictly adjectival, to indicate what sort of literary studies would be published in this series. That the series is part of Palgrave Macmillan's "Literature" list may also be relevant to this discussion, for Hones points out that *The Routledge Handbook of Literature and Space* "was developed and published as a literature title" (147), and the institutional conditions for the possibility of such scholarship ought to be borne in mind. Around the same time, I also organized and edited a special issue of *Reconstruction: Studies in Contemporary Culture* devoted to "Spatial Literary Studies" (2014), which may have further legitimized the understanding of this phrase as a name for a distinctive approach, method, or subfield.

As a literary critic, I consider my own research and teaching to work within the disciplinary parameters of literary studies, even as my research interests may carry me into other disciplinary fields. (Whose don't, after all?) But I suppose I still thought that the "Geocriticism and Spatial Literary Studies" label would be of sufficient breadth to encourage submissions from authors doing a variety of work, whether grounded in literature specifically or more interdisciplinary in nature. As I recall, an art historian friend of mine did question whether I wanted to include the word *literary* in the title of the book series, as she was concerned that it might exclude submissions by scholars in other fields, such as hers. I had considered the phrase "spatiality studies," but I opted to keep *literary* in the name. My reasons for doing so were manifold, but basically, I wanted to promote this sort of work in literary studies itself, acknowledging that it could also involve interdisciplinary research or collaborations, but that literature was ultimately the foundation upon which to build this series. Particularly in an era when literature and the humanities were more broadly coming under increasing attack in the United States and elsewhere, I think I felt that spatial literary studies ought to reflect and promote the value of literature proper and of humanistic research, without having to lean on more widely accepted disciplines such as those in the sciences for its justification. In any event, with few exceptions, the authors and editors whose books have appeared in the "Geocriticism and Spatial Literary Studies" series hail from language and literature departments, rather than from fields associated with the social sciences, and while these books often represent thoroughly interdisciplinary concerns, the focus on literature is evident across all of the titles thus far.

The significance of the word *spatial* is, of course, far broader than that of *geographical*. Spatial criticism may just as easily deal with architecture as geography, not to mention other areas of critical inquiry in which space or spatial relations play important roles. Though my own work has focused especially on what I have called *literary cartography*, and therefore is related to my own sense of a kind of literary geography, spatial literary studies as a field would certainly include rather different sorts of work. For example, volumes in the "Geocriticism and Spatial Literary Studies" series include work on cosmopolitanism (Johansen), women and domestic space (Ng), Virginia Woolf's rooms (Zink), and weird or fantastic spaces (Greve and Zappe). Many others included in the series have engaged more directly with geography as a field and with the work of geographers, but Hones appears to be correct in thinking that spatial literary studies, to the extent that this series or my own writings are representative of that field, should not be confused with literary geography.

If I have appeared to be too carefree in my use of the term *literary geography*, I concede that I have also consistently used the term *geocriticism* in a rather broader way than Westphal and his research team at the Université de Limoges had intended. Westphal had argued for a distinctively geocentric approach, one that began with a particular place and examined the literary and cultural representations of it, and Westphal explicitly contrasted that with the egocentric approach that focused on individual authors and their own representations of a given place which, because it was limited to a single perspective or that of only a few authors, was more likely to include bias or prejudice. However, I have suggested that the word *geocriticism* refer more expansively to criticism that engages with space and spatiality in a variety of ways, including more author-centered studies, such as those examining Dostoevsky's representation of the urban landscape of St. Petersburg in *Crime and Punishment*, Faulkner's depiction of the fictional Yoknapatawpha County in *As I Lay Dying*, or even Tolkien's mapping of Middle-earth in *The Lord of the Rings*. In many respects, my use of the term *geocriticism*, as with my use of *literary geography*, is tied more closely to work in literary studies, and is therefore less interdisciplinary than Westphal's geocritical projects.

My use, or misuse, of the term *literary geography* is related to this broader project within spatial literary studies. The chapter titled "Literary Geography" in *Spatiality* does not at all deal with the disciplinary traditions to which Hones refers in "Spatial Literary Studies and Literary Geography." Rather, literary geography refers to the terrain that is figuratively mapped by the writer's literary cartography. Practically speaking, literary geography is a more spatially oriented version of literary history, and my chapter focuses primarily on literary historians and critics who focus on the spatial or geographical aspects of their subjects. A good example of this is Raymond Williams's *The Country and the City*, which I discuss in *Spatiality* (86–90) and which Neil Alexander has referred to "a seminal text for literary geography." But Alexander also notes that "Williams makes almost no reference at all to relevant studies of rural, urban, and regional geography" (4). In the sense, Williams's "literary geography" remains within the disciplinary parameters of the humanities, and it is thus much more likely to serve as a prototypical work of spatial literary studies than of what Hones defines as literary geography.

Policing the Boundaries

Hones begins "Spatial Literary Studies and Literary Geography" by citing a recent essay published in *Environment and Planning D: Society and Space* by Alan Bradshaw and Stephen Brown. (As disciplinary boundaries are relevant to this discussion, let me point out that Bradshaw is Professor of Marketing in the School of Business and Management at Royal Holloway, and Brown is Professor of Marketing Research at the Ulster University Business School; as far as I know, neither has an academic or professional background in either literature or geography.) In their article, Bradshaw and Brown assert that, terminologically, *literary geography* "goes by a host of semi-synonymous descriptors including 'geocriticism,' 'imaginary geographies,' 'literary cartography,' and 'spatial literary studies,' to say nothing of 'narrative cartography,' '*romans-géographes*' and 'geopoetics'" (332), to which they append the citation "(Peraldo)," without reference to any page number. Before going further, I would note that the book to which they refer, Emmanuelle Peraldo's large edited collection, *Literature and Geography: The Writing of Space Throughout History* (2016) is nearly 500 pages long, with essays by no fewer than 28 different authors, none of whom—not even I, who have an essay in that volume—*ever* say that any of the terms listed by Bradshaw and Brown are in any way synonymous with literary geography. Indeed, the phrase "imaginary geographies" does not appear at all in the volume, and it really ought to go without saying that Marc Brousseau's French term for "geographical novels," *romans-géographes* (1996), cannot conceivably be *synonymous* with "literary geography," anymore than psychological novels could be synonymous with the field of psychology. The statement itself, by Bradshaw and Brown, is an absurdity on its face, and the failure to properly cite its source merely compounds the confusion by attributing such outlandishly unbelievable assertions to Peraldo (and, perhaps, to her contributors as well). It is unfortunate that Hones uses this reference in Bradshaw and Brown's article as a starting point to dispute the idea that "literary geography" and "spatial literary studies" are "semi-synonymous," an assertion no scholars operating in geography or literary studies would be likely to make. However, Hones's citation of this does confirm that, at least among these two writers from disciplines outside of literature or geography, the various terms associated with literary geography are indeed confused.

The remainder of Hones's article focuses on *The Routledge Handbook of Literature and Space* (2017), edited by me. In my Introduction to the volume, I write that

> the variety of critical approaches, theories, methods, or emphases appearing under the banner of *spatial literary studies* (among other labels) indicates not only the diversity and flexibility of the field, but also the potential for confusion. The contributors to *The Routledge Handbook on Literature and Space* themselves may not always agree on these matters, and any strict characterization of what constitutes the definition of spatial literary studies could scarcely be definitive, at least not in a way that all practitioners would readily agree upon. . . . As an editor, I have tried to err on the side of expansiveness and inclusiveness. In my estimation, what is broadly referred to as spatial literary studies—whether it operates under the banners of geocriticism, geopoetics, literary geography, the spatial humanities, or something else along those lines—would cover multiform critical practices that would include almost any approach to the text that focuses attention on space, place, or mapping.

> (3)

Hones takes issue with my apparent subordination of literary geography to spatial literary studies, as I suggest that spatial literary studies may be understood so broadly as to include literary geography, as well as geocriticism and geopoetics, *within* its categorical scope. While I certainly do not and would never suggest that the terms are "semi-synonymous," I do here include literary geography as one among many other kinds of different spatial literary studies. Hones insists that there are crucial generic differences that ought to make one question my facile use of these terms.

The polemical strain of Hones's argument lies in her view that, by putting together a collection of essays in which the work of literary geographers is blended in with that of critics doing quite different sorts of work,

I have essentially elided the differences between spatial literary studies and literary geography, and thus I deny the disciplinary specificity of the latter. Worse, in my overbroad use of the term *spatial literary studies*, I have in a sense colonized literary geography on behalf of spatial literary studies, incorporating literary geography into a field from which it is historically, institutionally, methodologically, and perhaps even philosophically quite distinct. For example, Hones observes that the 32 contributors to *The Routledge Handbook of Literature and Space* include a number of geographers, and she notes that twelve essays were provided by editors or editorial board members of the journal *Literary Geographies*, itself; however, because the essays by these authors are scattered throughout the volume and not, say, grouped into their own section devoted to literary geography, "what they have in common—and what might distinguish them as literary geography rather than spatial literary studies—is not immediately evident" (Hones, "Spatial" 148). Hones neglects to mention that she herself contributed to *The Routledge Handbook of Literature and Space*, and presumably her essay is among those that failed to be identified as being distinctively literary geographical amid the other sorts of approaches on display in that volume. Hence, not only do my introductory remarks place literary geography within the compass of a more comprehensive spatial literary studies, but my decision to distribute the work of those engaged in recognizably literary geographical work across different sections of *The Routledge Handbook* effectively subsumed literary geography within spatial literary studies without further comment.

I take this as a valid criticism, although the divisions within *The Routledge Handbook* were never intended to be based on subdiscipline or methodology. Hones goes on to makes a strong argument for why literary geography and spatial literary studies ought not to be confused, as I discuss in the following section. However, I believe that the definition of literary geography itself is not as stable and straightforward as Hones suggests, as even experts continue to debate the scope of the term's meaning.

What Is Literary Geography?

In fairness, it might be noted that all these terms have been subject to continuously shifting definitions and redefinitions over the years and even recently. For example, Alexander has observed that "there is currently general disagreement over what literary geography means" in his "On Literary Geography," a foundational intervention into this matter which was published as a "Thinking Space" article in the very first issue of *Literary Geographies*. Following this caveat, tellingly, he adds that this "may in fact be a sign of vitality" (Alexander 5), since this latitude with respect to the meaning of the term would allow a great many approaches to be undertaken in the name of literary geography. In that very article, which

Hones also cites, Alexander pointedly states that "literary geography is often carried on under other names: imaginative geography, literary cartography, geocriticism, geopoetics, geohumanities" (5), thus confirming the relationship, if not interchangeability, among these different terms. After mentioning several examples of the diverse forms that such work has taken in recent years, Alexander goes on to assert that

> [m]uch of this research is theoretically eclectic, synthesizing ideas drawn from phenomenology, historical materialism, structuralism and poststructuralism, art history, urbanism, anthropology, and gender theory, as well as geography and literary studies. The plural form of this journal's title, *Literary Geographies*, is intended to accommodate and encourage such diversity.
>
> (5)

Alexander's inaugural gesture is, I believe, intended to leave open the possibilities for a wide variety of approaches to what will be legitimately considered research in the field of literary geography.

Alexander cites the earliest known uses of the term, the 1904 book by William Sharp (who also wrote under the name Fiona Macleod) titled *Literary Geography* and Virginia Woolf's 1905 review-essay also titled "Literary Geography." In both cases, as Alexander puts it, "literary geography means little more than the particular places, landscapes, or regions associated with individual writers, although it can also refer to the various ways in which those geographical entities are reimagined in their texts" (3). Needless to say, Sharp and Woolf were not geographers; rather, they were writing these works strictly in their capacity as literary critics, so one could argue that the earliest, if somewhat limited and tentative, definition of *literary geography* emerged from the field of literary studies, not geography. That is, it is reasonable to assume that professional geographers came to the inquire into literary geography only after literary critics broached the subject.

In an editorial published the first issue of *Literary Geographies*, the founding editors—that is, Alexander and Hones, along with David Cooper, James Kneale, and Juha Ridenpää, all of whom later contributed to *The Routledge Handbook of Literature and Space*, by the way—wrote that

> [t]he new journal is being presented under the plural title *Literary Geographies* in recognition of the many different ways in which the field is and has been defined. It takes the general position that literary geography is essentially a way of reading. In the conventional sense, literary geography can be understood as an approach to literary texts, a geographically-attuned way of reading fiction or poetry or drama. But literary geography can also be understood as a way

of reading in a second sense: not just reading while making connections between geography and literature, but also making connections while reading scholarly work in geography and literary studies, work that may not be defined as literary geography but which nonetheless can be productively read in such a way.

(1–2)

If literary geography be understood as "a way of reading," then surely something like literary studies—an approach whose entire disciplinary bailiwick is defined by reading, analysis, and interpretation, as the geographer Yi-Fu Tuan himself averred (see Tuan 161)—lies at its heart as well.

Nevertheless, Hones insists that literary geography is intrinsically connected to "human geography as an academic discipline" ("Spatial" 146). She makes reference to "a tradition of geographical work with literary texts dating back at least as far as the 1920s," specifically citing the American geographer John Kirtland Wright's 1924 essay, "Geography in Literature," before adding that the "geographical subfield" was "[f]irst termed 'literary geography' in the 1970s" (147). Quoting from Ridanpää's "Geography and Literature" (2013), Hones asserts that literary geography "has been 'following the main epistemological and theoretical turns within the fields of human and cultural geographies' throughout its history" (147). As she concludes, just because human geographers may be interested in working with literature or literary texts, "this is not to say that they are now primarily interested in producing literary criticism" (147). While she acknowledges and insists upon the interdisciplinarity of the research involved, Hones in this article affirms that literary geography is fundamentally situated within the discipline of geography.

Part of Hones's concern with the conflation of spatial literary studies and literary geography seems to partake of a larger intellectual and academic divide between the humanities and social sciences. For example, she notes that "[w]hile literary geography today increasingly incorporates theory and methods developed in literary studies, actively encouraging and valuing the input of literary critics, it nevertheless retains a strong orientation toward geographical and, more generally, social science aims and methods" (148). Spatial literary studies, by contrast, remains part of the humanities, in Hones's view, such that the "appropriation" of literary geography by spatial literary studies "not only disregards a century of human geography historiography, it also strips the interdiscipline of the geographical component of its aims and methods" (148–49). In this sense, whatever else spatial literary studies might be, in Hones's view, it is not tied to geography as a particular discipline nor is it located within the wider purview of the social sciences, as is literary geography.

That said, Hones is also committed to understanding literary geography as a fundamentally interdisciplinary field. Indeed, she asserts that

> the defining characteristic of literary geography . . . is its double interdisciplinarity: the "literary" of literary geography refers both to literary texts and to literary studies, while the "geography" of literary geography refers not only to real and imagined geographies but also to human geography as an academic discipline.
>
> (146)

Hones notes that this "defining characteristic" is also "the feature which most clearly distinguishes it from spatial literary studies" (146), thus suggesting that spatial literary studies is only "singularly" interdisciplinary or, possibly, that it is not interdisciplinary at all. (I shall return to this matter in the following paragraphs.) Underscoring her point, Hones observes that most academic research within the field of literary geography will cite not only literary texts and criticism, but also studies published in social science journals. In fact, she adds that, "in order to sustain its literary/geographical interdisciplinarity, the journal *Literary Geographies* typically sends submissions out for review to one reader from literary studies/the humanities and another from geography/the social sciences" (147). Thus, Hones asserts that literary geography must include social scientific research in addition to any connections it may have to literature and the humanities more widely.

Earlier, in her book *Literary Geographies: Narrative Space in "Let the Great World Spin"* (2014), Hones used the evocative metaphor of the tightrope walker—specially, the famous 1974 wirewalk between the two towers of the then newly built World Trade Center in New York by the French daredevil Philippe Petit—in order to emphasize the interdisciplinary nature of literary geography, which is "performed, as we might say, in the space between the tower of geography, on the one side, and the tower of literature, on the other: two well-established structures, with independent foundations, which afford different views" (4). In this vision, the perils as well as the rewards of interdisciplinary research are highlighted, as literary geography is defined as a balancing act that requires equal participation in distinct disciplines of which one cannot wholly be a part. The literary geographer, in this view, may engage in work that is associated with two disciplines, but this work is also lies outside of both.

The Limits of Interdisciplinarity

Assuming spatial literary studies can now be imagined as its own disciplinary field or subfield, what would its defining characteristics look like? How can we best distinguish its topics, methods, goals, and practices from such other fields as literary geography. If, for example, literary geography is fundamentally a blend of two disciplines, literature and geography, as Hones maintains, then one might prefer to think of spatial literary studies as ultimately situated in the one discipline of literature. This is not to say that those operating within the sphere of spatial literary studies may not also engage in interdisciplinary research, only that the practices would likely be based in literature. To put it another way, they may read the work of geographers, but they will do so *as* literary critics rather than as fellow geographers, which undoubtedly affects they way they would read and use the geographical research.

Hones had asserted in "Literary Geographies, Past and Future" that the interdisciplinary field of literary geography would benefit "not only from present and future collaborations but also from retrospective clarifications, juxtapositions and comparisons," as literary critics and geographers needed to gain a better understanding of each other's discipline-specific terminology, methods, and theories (4). Hones recognizes the distinctive disciplinary limits of the two fields at whose intersection literary geography has emerged, and thus asserts that "a broad understanding of the various pasts meeting up in the field today will enable literary geographers to effect the retrospective construction of a unified historiography as a platform for future interdisciplinary work" (4). Indeed, given Hones's insistence that the "defining characteristic" of literary geography is its "double-interdisciplinarity" ("Spatial" 146), it may be that the best ways to undertake properly literary geographical research will involve either strictly collaborative efforts by teams comprising literary critics and geographers (such as *Narrating Space/Spatializing Narrative* [2016] by the narratologist Marie-Laure Ryan and geographers Kenneth Foote and Maoz Azaryahu) or, perhaps, studies by researchers whose own professional formation combines literature and geography (one thinks of Charles B. Travis's *Abstract Machine: Humanities GIS* [2015], for example, although Travis is a geographer by training, not to mention Hones's own *Literary Geographies* book). But to the extent that a proper literary geography will require these two distinctive fields to come together in a cognizable interdiscipline, it may ultimately mean that literary geography will eventually be recognized as its own disciplinary field, freed from the strictures of literature or geography altogether. Another way of putting it might be to say that only collaborations between researchers whose professional formations lie in different disciplines would be truly interdisciplinary; or else, the aims and methods of a given interdiscipline becomes so rigorously defined in terms of its own practices that it comes to form a new discipline unto itself.

By contrast, spatial literary studies—as Hones understands it, and as I am now willing to assert—maintains itself as part of a single, albeit complex discipline: literature. Scholarly or critical activities within spatial literary studies could consider matters of literature and space without regard to any other disciplinary fields, and they certainly would not need to involve themselves with geography, for example. To the extent that practitioners within its ambit might also take up the works of geographers—or, for that matter, with the work of architects, urbanists, philosophers, historians, sociologists, artists, art historians, musicologists, mathematicians, physicists, astronomers, engineers, and any others who work deals with matters of space or spatiality—they will almost certainly be doing so in support of projects rooted in literary scholarship, literary criticism, literary history, and literary theory. Thus spatial literary studies might encourage transdisciplinary encounters while also staying focused upon those questions or topics associated with literature *per se*, including matters related to the interpretation, criticism, and evaluation of texts.

In this way, spatial literary studies would distinguish itself from the interdisciplinary field of literary geography, as well as from some of these other spatially or geographically oriented approaches to literary or cultural artifacts, precisely by maintaining a firm foothold within the field of literature. I would hope that, as with earlier literary critical texts, such as *The Country and the City* by Williams, literary geographers will still find such disciplinarily specific writings valuable to their own projects, but should these types of work be deemed too humanistic or insufficiently social-scientific, then at least the confusions between spatial literary studies and literary geography will henceforth be dispelled.

Conclusion

In some respects, I think that *spatial literary studies* could still serve as a broad category that could include a number of different scholarly and critical practices involving space and literature, but I understand the desire for clarification when it comes to distinct but related approaches to a given subject. And, no pun intended, I understand how "turf wars" work, although I would hope that researchers in various fields who ought to be allies would not go out of their way to start such wars, even as the impulse to define one's own territorial boundaries may be powerful. Spatial literary studies, understood to be a subfield within literary studies, will undoubtedly continue to find common cause and common ground with literary geography, and I would like to think that literary geography would continue to draw from spatial literary studies. But if the interdiscipline of literary geography must remain separate and distinct from spatial literary studies, then I hope that literary geographers will not be deprived of the insights made available by research in literature and the humanities, lest their balancing act result in a fall. The emergent field of spatial literary studies, by maintaining a firm footing within the established yet dynamic disciplinary bounds of literature, seems likely to develop and inform novel ways of seeing and doing literary criticism and scholarship in the years to come.

Works Cited

Alexander, Neil. "On Literary Geography." *Literary Geographies* 1.1 (2015): 3–6.

Alexander, Neil, Cooper, David, Hones, Sheila, et al. "Editorial." *Literary Geographies* 1.1 (2015): 1–2.

Bradshaw, Alan, and Brown, Stephen. "Up Rising: Rehabilitating J. G. Ballard's High-Rise with R. D. Laing and Lauren Berlant." *Environment and Planning D: Society and Space* 36.2 (2018): 331–49.

Brosseau, Marc. *Des Romans-Géographes*. Paris: L'Harmattan, 1996.

Fang, Ying. "Spatial Literary Studies: Place, Mapping, and Spatiality." *Journal of Aesthetics and Art Review* 19.2 (2019): forthcoming [in Chinese].

Foucault, Michel. "Of Other Spaces." Trans. Jay Miskowiec. *Diacritics* 16 (Spring 1986): 22–27.

Greve, Julius, and Zappe, Florian, eds. *Spaces and Fictions of the Weird and Fantastic: Ecologies, Geographies, Oddities*. New York: Palgrave Macmillan, 2016.

Hones, Sheila. *Literary Geographies: Narrative Space in 'Let the Great World Spin'*. New York: Palgrave Macmillan, 2014.

———. "Literary Geography, Past and Future." *Literary Geographies* 1.2 (2015): 1–5.

———. "Spatial Literary Studies and Literary Geography." *Literary Geographies* 4.2 (2018): 146–49.

Jameson, Fredric. "Postmodernism, or, the Cultural Logic of Late Capitalism." *New Left Review* 146 (July-August 1984): 53–92.

Johansen, Emily. *Cosmopolitanism and Place: Spatial Forms in Contemporary Anglophone Literature*. New York: Palgrave Macmillan, 2014.

Ng, Andrew Hock Soon. *Women and Domestic Space in Contemporary Gothic Narratives: The House as Subject*. New York: Palgrave Macmillan, 2015.

Pegenaute, Luis. "Translation and Cultural Development: Historical Approaches." In Sue-Anne Harding and Ovidi Carbonell Cortés, eds., *The Routledge Handbook of Translation and Culture*. London: Routledge, 2018. 177–206.

Peraldo, Emmanuelle, ed. *Literature and Geography: The Writing of Space Throughout History*. Newcastle-upon-Tyne: Cambridge Scholars, 2016.

Ridanpää, Juri. "Geography and Literature." *Oxford Bibliographies Online* (2013). www.oxfordbibliographies.com/.

Ryan, Marie-Laure, Foote, Kenneth, and Azaryahu, Maoz. *Narrating Space/Spatializing Narrative: Where Narrative Theory and Geography Meet*. Columbus: Ohio State UP, 2016.

Soja, Edward. *Postmodern Geographies: The Reassertion of Space in Critical Social Theory*. London: Verso, 1989.

Tally, Robert T. Jr., ed. *Geocritical Explorations: Space, Place, and Mapping in Literary and Cultural Studies*. New York: Palgrave Macmillan, 2011.

———. *Spatiality*. London: Routledge, 2013.

———. "Introduction: The Reassertion of Space in Literary Studies." In Robert T. Tally Jr., ed., *The Routledge Handbook of Literature and Space*. New York: Routledge, 2017. 1–6.

———. *Topophrenia: Place, Narrative, and the Spatial Imagination*. Bloomington: Indiana UP, 2019.

Thrift, Nigel. "Space." *Theory, Culture, and Society* 23.2–3 (2006): 139–46.

Travis, Charles B. *Abstract Machine: Humanities GIS*. Redlands: Esri Press, 2016.

Tuan, Yi Fu. *Space and Place: The Perspective of Experience*. Minneapolis: U of Minnesota P, 1977.

Warf, Barney, and Arias, Santa, eds., *The Spatial Turn: Interdisciplinary Perspectives*. London: Routledge, 2009.

Westphal, Bertrand. *Geocriticism: Real and Fictional Spaces*. Trans. Robert T. Tally Jr. New York: Palgrave Macmillan, 2011.

Williams, Raymond. *The Country and the City*. Oxford: Oxford UP, 1973.

Woolf, Virginia. "Literary Geography." In Mary Lyon, ed., *Books and Portraits*. New York: Harcourt, Brace, and Jovanovitch, 1977. 158–61.

Wright, John K. "Geography in Literature." *The Geographical Review* 14 (January 1924): 659–60.

Zink, Suzanna. *Virginia Woolf's Rooms and the Spaces of Modernity*. New York: Palgrave Macmillan, 2018.

Notes on Contributors

Sarah Ager is an independent scholar and Academic English tutor at De Montfort International College, Leicester (UK). She previously worked as an English language teacher in Bologna, Italy, for eight years. Her interest in geocriticism was shaped by her experience of exploring new cultural spaces as an Erasmus student at the University of Bologna. From 2011 to 2016, she curated Interfaith Ramadan, a series of inclusive interfaith essays exploring interfaith relationships, plural identities, the empowerment of women and marginalised groups, and LGBTQ advocacy within faith communities. Sarah's work on interfaith has been published in *The Guardian*, as a featured series in ABC Religion and Ethics, as well as in the anthology *Whatever Works: Feminists of Faith Speak* (2015).

Walter Bosse is Assistant Professor of English at Brescia University. He has published articles on Ralph Ellison, Ernest Hemingway, and Charles W. Chesnutt. Most recently, he contributed a chapter on F. Scott Fitzgerald's *The Great Gatsby* and HBO's *The Wire* to the edited collection titled *Popular Modernism and Its Legacies: From Pop Literature to Video Games* (Bloomsbury Academic, 2018). His ongoing research continues to explore the many realms of American modernism in an effort to theorize the formal and ideological impact of modernist culture on twenty-first-century life.

Yann Calbérac is a geographer and professor at University of Reims, Champagne-Ardenne (France). His work deals with the history and epistemology of geography and with social demand for geography.

Ralph Crane is Professor Emeritus of English at the University of Tasmania. With Lisa Fletcher, he is the co-author of *Cave: Nature and Culture* (2015) and *Island Genres, Genre Islands: Conceptualisation and Representation in Popular Fiction* (2017), as well as several articles and book chapters on imperial adventure fiction, illustration and popular fiction in the Victorian Age, and the geohumanities.

Dustin Crowley is Assistant Professor at Rowan University, where he teaches courses in contemporary African literature and literary theory. He is also the co-director of the Environmental Humanities program at Rowan. His book, *Africa's Narrative Geographies: Charting the Intersections of Geocriticism and Postcolonial Studies*, examines how the work of cultural geography can help rethink representations of space, place, nationalism, and urbanity in African literature. Most recently, he has written about space, place, environment, and posthumanism in African science-fiction. He has published articles in *Research in African Literatures*, *Science Fiction Studies*, and *The Cambridge Journal of Postcolonial Literary Inquiry*, among others.

Will Cunningham is Lecturer in English at Clemson University, with a Ph.D. in English literature at the University of Kansas. His interests lie in the intersection of twentieth-century African American and Southern Literature, with a focus in space and place theory. He has previously published articles in *Black Magnolias Literary Journal* and *Southwestern American Literature Journal*.

Michelle Dreiding holds a Ph.D. in English and American literature from the University of Zurich. Her doctoral dissertation, "The Space Between. Toni Morrison's Poetics of Liminality," investigates Morrison's representation of ambivalence as a response to traditional binary subject constitution. Dreiding's research interests include cultural analysis, narratives of trauma, psychoanalytic literary theory, modern and postmodern literature, and film. She is currently writing and teaching in Zurich.

Lisa Fletcher is Professor of English and Head of the School of Humanities at the University of Tasmania. With Ralph Crane, she is the co-author of *Cave: Nature and Culture* (2015) and *Island Genres, Genre Islands: Conceptualisation and Representation in Popular Fiction* (2017), as well as several articles and book chapters on imperial adventure fiction, illustration and popular fiction in the Victorian Age, and the geohumanities.

Rogério de Melo Franco is a Ph.D. student in comparative literature at the University of Washington. He is interested in literary representation of space and the visual arts. His past investigations dealt with European authors from the nineteenth century and their reception in the twentieth century.

Nathan Frank is a Ph.D. student at the University of Virginia, and holds a master of international studies (MIntSt) from the University of Otago in Dunedin, New Zealand, and an MA in literature from the University of Colorado at Boulder.

Beatrice Kohler holds a Master of arts in English literature and film studies from the University of Zurich. Her master thesis treated the subject of "The Cold War Against Ourselves: Alan J. Pakula's 'Paranoia Trilogy.'" Based in Zurich, Switzerland, she is Director of Operations of an international organization specializing in workforce solutions.

Julia Kröger holds a Ph.D. in French literature and culture from the University of Paderborn, Germany. In her thesis on constructions of space in selected preparatory dossiers and novels by Émile Zola, she develops a theory of space in literature based on Henri Lefebvre's threefold dialectic of space, which helps shed new light on naturalism. Her research interests include nineteenth-century French literature and culture, the intersections of literature and science, as well as narrative and spatial theory.

Chris Margrave is Senior Lecturer in English at Texas State University, where he earned his MFA in fiction. He also holds an MA in English literature from Wake Forest University. His scholarly and creative writing has appeared in the *Rio Grande Review*, *Front Porch Journal* (now *Porter House Review*), *Precipitate Journal*, *Southwestern American Literature*, *Texas Books in Review*, and on ESPN's Longhorn Network, where he co-produces the *Longhorn Film Showcase*, a television show featuring short films made by students at The University of Texas at Austin.

Jessica Maucione is Professor of English at Gonzaga University where she also serves as Powers Chair of the Humanities, Interim Director of Native American Studies, and Co-Coordinator of the Underrepresented Minority Post-Doctoral Fellowship Program. Her scholarly publications combine critical race theory with space and place theory applied to popular media and literature. Maucione's publications include articles and book chapters on space and place, critical race theory and pedagogy, Pizzolatto's *True Detective*, the *Rocky* series and Coogler's *Creed*, Silko's *Almanac of the Dead*, Yamashita's *The Tropic of Orange*, Jones's *Lost in the City*, DeLillo's *Cosmopolis*, and Fante's *Ask the Dust*. She has forthcoming articles on Hamid's *Exit West* and Erdrich's *The Future Home of the Living God,* as well as Tintori's *Unto the Daughters: The Legacy of an Honor Killing in a Sicilian American Family* and Grames' *The Seven or Eight Deaths of Stella Fortuna*.

Adam R. McKee is Assistant Professor of English and Chairperson for the Department of English and Digital Media at Elizabeth City State University. He holds a Ph.D. in twentieth-century transnational literature from Florida State University. His research focuses largely on transnational modernism, postmodernism, and urban studies. His work has recently appeared in the *William Carlos Williams Review* and the *Journal of Urban Cultural Studies*.

I. Murat Öner is Assistant Professor at the International Burch University in Sarajevo, Bosnia and Herzegovina. His main research interests are the interdisciplinary field of geocriticism, literary geography and cartography, space theories, and Caryl Phillips. His dissertation, "Transgressive Spatiality in Caryl Phillips's Writing: A Geocritical Study," engages with Phillips's complex spatial discourse. He published articles in special issues of literary journals which particularly address spatiality in literature.

Emmanuelle Peraldo is Professor at the Université Côte d'Azur (France). She specializes in eighteenth-century literature and history of ideas, particularly Daniel Defoe, and her current research focuses on the link between geography and literature in the early modern period. She is the editor of *Literature and Geography: The Writing of Space Throughout History* (2016).

Elizabeth Robertson is Teaching Fellow in the Department of English at Queen Mary University of London. Her research focuses on twentieth- and twenty-first-century literature, drama, and culture. She is currently writing on children and war in Poliakoff's dramas about the Second World War. Other research includes work on combat gnosticism in R. C. Sherriff's play *Journey's End*, using material in the Sherriff archive at Surrey History Centre.

Mariya Shymchyshyn is Professor and Head of the Department of Literary Theory and World Literature at Kyiv National Linguistic University (Ukraine). She is an alumna of the Junior Faculty Development Program (Ames, Iowa State University, 2003–2004) and of the Fulbright Scholar Program (Loyola University Chicago, 2013–2014).

Kate Siklosi lives, writes, and thinks in Toronto. She holds a Ph.D. in English from York University and is currently using her skills and talents to make magical things happen outside the academy. She is the author of three chapbooks of poetry: *po po poems* (above/ground press, 2018), *may day* (no press, 2018), and *coup* (The Blasted Tree, 2018).

Robert T. Tally Jr. is NEH Distinguished Teaching Professor in the Humanities and Professor of English at Texas State University, where he teaches American and world literature. He is the author of *Topophrenia: Place, Narrative, and the Spatial Imagination* (2019), *Fredric Jameson: The Project of Dialectical Criticism* (2014), *Poe and the Subversion of American Literature: Satire, Fantasy, Critique* (2014), *Spatiality* (2013), *Utopia in the Age of Globalization: Space, Representation, and the World System* (2013), *Kurt Vonnegut and the American Novel: A Postmodern Iconography* (2011), and *Melville, Mapping and Globalization: Literary Cartography in the American*

Baroque Writer (2009). The translator of Bertrand Westphal's *Geocriticism: Real and Fictional Spaces* (2011), Tally is also the editor of *Geocritical Explorations: Space, Place, and Mapping in Literary and Cultural Studies* (2011), *Kurt Vonnegut: Critical Insights* (2013), *Literary Cartographies: Spatiality, Representation, and Narrative* (2014), *The Geocritical Legacies of Edward W. Said* (2015), *Ecocriticism and Geocriticism: Overlapping Territories in Environmental and Spatial Literary Studies* (2016; with Christine Battista), *The Routledge Handbook of Literature and Space* (2017), and *Teaching Space, Place, and Literature* (2018). Tally is also the general editor of Palgrave Macmillan's "Geocriticism and Spatial Literary Studies" book series.

Index

Page numbers followed by "n" indicate a note.

338   *Index*